Training for Student Leaders

Joseph L. Murray

Thomas M. Cooley Law School

KENDALL/HUNT PUBLISHING COMPANY
4050 Westmark Drive   Dubuque, Iowa 52002

To the memory of my mother
Mary Margaret Murray
who helped me to appreciate the greatness
that exists in the humblest among us.

Contents

Preface

Democracy is based upon the conviction that there are extraordinary possibilities in ordinary people.

Harry Emerson Fosdick

Throughout its history, a fundamental purpose of American higher education has been to develop future leaders for a democratic society. Implicit in this mission is a recognition of each person's capacity for growth, and a commitment to the realization of this potential, in support of the common welfare. The purpose of this book is to provide college students with the tools necessary to support their ongoing leadership development for the remainder of their college years and into their future beyond graduation.

The book is directed toward both experienced leaders and those who have had little or no exposure to leadership activities. It is written in a conversational tone and presents information in relation to students' immediate frame of reference, the contemporary collegiate campus. In recognition of the value of cocurricular involvement as a means of developing leadership skills, a deliberate effort is made to promote student involvement and to encourage students to apply various principles of leadership to their activities on campus and in their communities.

The chapters are structured to maximize both student learning and motivation. An "advance organizer" provides an overview of the content of each chapter. The various topics are then presented, along with illustrative examples. Much of the information presented is drawn from the literature in a variety of fields, including psychology, sociology, management, education, and philosophy. Each chapter ends with a summary of the material presented and a series of activities.

The activity segment of each chapter is organized with attention to a full range of cognitive processes. The sequence of activities includes the following components:

- **Getting It Straight**: A series of items which measure students' knowledge of the objective content of the text.

- **Both Sides of the Story**: An activity which requires students to discuss conflicting points of view on a specified topic, for purposes of broadening their perspective.

- **Sorting It Out**: An activity which requires that students make judgments about the relative importance of a number of considerations explored in relation to a specified topic.

- **It's Your Call**: A synthesizing activity, requiring actual decision-making and defense of decisions based on the facts and factors involved in a particular case.

The opening chapter explores the value of student leadership, emphasizing the immediate need for leadership on campus and in students' communities as well as the future need for leadership in American society. Although attention is given to the benefits of leadership experience for the individual student, the primary emphasis of the chapter is on the notion of leadership as service.

The second chapter focuses on understanding of self as an initial step toward greater effectiveness as a leader. It provides students with a framework for examining their skills, interests, values, and personal styles.

The third chapter shifts students' attention toward an understanding of others. It emphasizes the importance of dealing effectively with diverse populations, and explores the unique challenges posed to leaders of heterogeneous groups. The concerns of several specific populations are examined. The chapter serves as an introduction to the "diversity movement" in higher education, with attention to the controversy that the movement has generated.

In the fourth chapter, general characteristics of leadership are explored and various theories of leadership which have emerged over the course of history are identified. Students are challenged to ponder the question, "Are leaders born or made?"

The fifth chapter focuses on interpersonal communication. It emphasizes the role of the leader as a facilitator of effective communication within an organization. Specific topics covered in this chapter include: active listening skills, nonverbal communication, assertiveness, and public speaking.

The sixth chapter deals with group dynamics. Its purpose is to enable students to recognize common patterns of behavior as they occur in the life of groups to which students belong. Information is presented on the defining characteristics of groups, typical patterns of group development, and common group member roles and behaviors which can enhance or detract from the group process.

The seventh chapter covers basic skills necessary for working with groups. The specific topics covered in this chapter include: motivation, delegation, running effective meetings, and the overall process of planning and evaluation.

The eighth chapter focuses on ethical issues in leadership. It deals with the influence of the group upon the individual member, and the roles of both the leader and follower in establishing a moral climate within an organization. Six traditional ethical orientations are discussed, along with three contemporary theories of moral development. The chapter also presents specific guidelines for ethical decision-making in groups, along with recommended procedures for developing a code of ethics.

The final chapter provides students with a basis upon which to continue their growth as leaders. It focuses on the establishment of goals, objectives, and action plans. The importance of building support systems is also emphasized. Throughout this chapter, leadership development is presented as an ongoing lifelong process.

Foreword

Developing our leadership skills and knowledge is a lifelong journey. The journey of discovering our leadership gifts and talents is just as important as the contributions we make through our leadership efforts. College is one of the best practice fields for students of leadership to enhance leadership abilities, to learn from mistakes, and to experience the excitement of leadership successes and accomplishments. All students have the potential to assume leadership roles and responsibilities on college campuses and in their communities. There are multiple ways to learn about leadership: through observing role models and other leaders, by taking leadership courses and seminars, from trial-and-error, and by studying historical profiles of leaders.

But why study leadership? Leadership ideas and concepts at face value might seem like common sense, but in practice leadership involves very complex and dynamic processes requiring a wide range of skills and critical thinking abilities. There are thousands of definitions of leadership. The word 'leadership' has different meanings to people from diverse countries and from varying industries and professions. To add to the complex nature of leadership, there is no globally accepted definition of the word.

Leadership is a fluid and elusive concept that is changing in meaning at the same pace as our ever evolving world. Organizations and groups today consist of members and leaders with diverse backgrounds and belief systems. Theories, strategies, and approaches used by leaders ten years ago are, for the most part, considered archaic and ineffective in contemporary organizations. Chaos theory today has replaced leadership theories which attempted to predict behaviors and outcomes in organizations. We no longer think of leaders doing something to or for members. Instead, we think of leaders and members together transforming organizations and collectively learning about leadership from one another. There are many myths and truths of leadership that students of leadership must discover for themselves through practice and formal preparation.

Before we can effectively lead others we should know ourselves well — clarify and affirm our values, know our strengths and areas of growth potential, and know our passions. Growing as a leader requires soul searching and personal reflection. Leaders who are true to themselves and know themselves well probably experience less stress and turmoil in their lives, enabling them to lead healthy lifestyles.

Equally important is the task of understanding others and recognizing and accepting differences in people who interact with us. Leadership is a relational process dependent on interactions among leaders, members, and sometimes outside constituencies. Knowing oneself paves the way for understanding and interacting effectively with diverse others. Author Joe Murray provides many exercises throughout this book for self-exploration and introspection.

Another essential theme of this book is ethical leadership. Our world is hungry for leaders who are committed to doing the right thing and for leaders who are able and willing to walk their talk. Leaders who succumb to such things as greed, misuse of power, or deception often find themselves prematurely forced to end their leadership journeys. The rewards of ethical leadership far outlive the immediate rewards that result from exploitation or the manipulation of people.

Leaders often want to be respected and trusted by others. A critical lesson in leadership is to understand that respect is earned and our actions speak much louder than our words. Good leaders teach others through example. Good leaders hold themselves accountable. And ethical leaders show compassion and care for others around them. Sometimes taking the high road means taking the more difficult or longer path. This often requires leaders to be able to take risks, be courageous, be confident, withstand peer pressure, exercise patience, reflect, and sometimes experience lonely moments in the midst of adverse reaction to unpopular decisions. The theme of ethical leadership is a common thread that runs through most sections of this book.

Students of leadership will find many practical strategies and leadership models in *Training for Student Leaders*. Leadership skills are life skills that can be applied to organizations, careers, personal life, and service to one's community. In the following pages, the author provides opportunities for self-examination and resources for understanding leadership in whichever arena one chooses to exercise her or his leadership gifts and talents.

Nance Lucas
National Clearinghouse for Leadership Programs
University of Maryland at College Park

Acknowledgement

I would like to extend my sincere gratitude to Patricia B. Enos, Assistant to the Vice President for Student Affairs and Services at Michigan State University. Dr. Enos worked closely with me in conceptualizing the basic content and format of this book, and carefully reviewed each chapter before it went to press. Her comments and suggestions at each stage of the book's development have significantly enhanced the overall quality of the finished product.

Introduction

Why Learn about Student Leadership?
Benefits of Student Leadership for the Individual
Benefits of Student Leadership for the Campus
    Community
Benefits of Student Leadership for Society
Choosing a Student Leadership Setting
Summary
Activities

What You Will Learn in This Chapter

This chapter will deal with the following potential benefits of involvement in student leadership activities:

- Benefits to you as an individual
  - Increased likelihood of a satisfying and successful undergraduate experience
  - Group support for the achievement of goals
  - Lasting interpersonal relationships
  - Establishment of a network
  - Interpersonal skills
  - New and diversified interests
- Benefits to your campus community
  - Enriched cultural life
  - Challenging intellectual climate
  - Stronger sense of unity
  - Greater institutional responsiveness to student needs
- Benefits to society
  - Active and concerned citizenry
  - Leadership for the future

This chapter will introduce a theory of student involvement which incorporates the following concepts:

- Physical energy
- Psychological energy
- Quantitative aspects of involvement
- Qualitative aspects of involvement

This chapter will examine the following student leadership opportunities:

- Student government
- Student organizations
- Intramural sports
- Student employment
- Volunteer activities
- Civic involvement

Introduction

It is one of the beautiful compensations of this life that no one can sincerely try to help another without helping himself.
                                                                                    Charles Dudley Warner

Why Learn About Student Leadership?

There are numerous reasons why you may be interested in examining the topic of leadership among students at colleges and universities. Perhaps you already hold a formal leadership position on campus or in your community and wish to increase your effectiveness in your current role. Maybe you would like to participate more in leadership activities but feel you need to develop some basic skills before you can do so. Maybe you have no interest in student leadership, but were unable to get the course that you really wanted and settled for a student leadership course instead.

In any case, I am glad that you have picked up this book. I am confident that you will find its content to be beneficial to you, regardless of your individual background and motivation to study the topic of student leadership. Once you have completed this book, I also suspect that you will have a greater appreciation for the benefits of participation in leadership activities, even if you had no interest in such activities beforehand.

Benefits of Student Leadership for the Individual

Participation in student leadership activities can offer you many immediate benefits, by enhancing the overall quality of your undergraduate experience. In fact, so profound is the influence of participation in certain activities that it may even be a factor in your completion of an undergraduate degree program.

In a long-term study of college dropouts, Alexander Astin (1984), a Professor of Higher Education at UCLA, found that participation in either Greek letter organizations or athletic activities on campus was related to continued enrollment. Students who worked part-time on campus or participated in faculty members' research projects were also less likely to withdraw from school than were other students.

Based upon his own research and that of other scholars, Astin (1984) theorized that the overall growth which occurs as a result of the undergraduate experience is influenced by the student's degree of **involvement** in that experience. Involvement refers to the investment of **energy** in a particular experience.

This energy can be either **physical** or **psychological**. While physical energy manifests itself in actions, psychological energy manifests itself in thoughts and emotions. For example, if you were to engage in a vigorous game of intramural basketball, you would undoubtedly expend a good deal of physical energy in the process. However, if you felt a particular sense of pride in your performance, you might find that the psychological energy that you would invest in the activity would exceed even your physical investment in the game.

According to Astin (1984), involvement has both **quantitative** and **qualitative** dimensions. While the quantitative aspect relates to the amount of time that is devoted to a particular experience, the qualitative aspect relates to the productivity of the time invested. For example, two students attending an Interfraternity Council meeting would probably make similar quantitative investments of energy in the activity. However, if one of the students were to actively contribute to the discussion, while the other barely listened, their qualitative investments of energy in the meeting would hardly be comparable.

According to Astin's theory and related research, it would seem that by becoming more involved in the life of your campus, you would be likely to increase your satisfaction with the overall undergraduate experience. It would also seem that by assuming a more active leadership role in your specific activities you would be likely to benefit more fully from the activities themselves.

An additional benefit of participating in student leadership activities is the ability to work with others whose interests are similar to your own, in order to accomplish common goals which you could not achieve independently. While it is highly unlikely that Jesse Jackson or Jeane Kirkpatrick would be willing to travel across the country to discuss the political issues of the day with you personally, they and other similarly prominent national figures regularly make appearances on college and university campuses to address large audiences composed of individuals who are interested in learning more about their views.

In addition to discovering the practical benefits of working with others who share your interests, you are likely to find that the relationships established through leadership activities can be deeply rewarding on a personal level. Furthermore, the interpersonal relationships established through student leadership activities often last well beyond the undergraduate experience, thus providing a long-term benefit to those participating in such activities.

In addition to the other students with whom you will interact directly during your student leadership experience, you may have an opportunity to establish indirect linkages with a broad **network** of individuals who can be of potential support and assistance to you for many years to come. You may find, for example, that a member of your Greek letter organization is employed by a corporation in which you would like to seek employment three years from now. This individual could probably provide you with some very useful information about the particular employer. In chapter 9, we will deal with the subject of networks in greater depth.

One of the greatest rewards of participating in leadership activities while you are a student is the opportunity to develop skills which will enhance the quality of your life, in each of its many facets. Because we are social beings, the ability to communicate effectively with others and to mobilize a group of individuals toward the achievement of a common goal will be of tremendous value to you, regardless of your specific plans for the future. The challenges which are encountered in student groups are not entirely unlike those which you will later encounter in your work place, in your community, or even in your family. Leadership activities can complement and supplement your formal education, by providing opportunities for you to apply the material that you have learned in the classroom and to further learn from experience, without the risk of costly mistakes which might otherwise accompany future decisions.

In a study of the long-term influences of participation in student leadership activities, Schuh and Laverty (1983) found that a majority of alumni credited their experiences in such activities with contributing significantly to the development of skills in the areas of communication, teamwork, decision making, leadership, assertiveness, planning, organizing, budgeting, and supervision. Research by Bryan, Mann, Nelson, and North (1981) suggested that prospective employers may also recognize the long-term benefits of cocurricular involvement, since the vast majority of those studied indicated that they attached at least some importance to out-of-class activities of job applicants.

In addition to facilitating relationships and the development of various skills, student leadership activities can help you to become a more well-rounded person by enabling you to explore a wide variety of interests. Through your undergraduate leadership activities, you may discover specific areas of interest which you would like to continue to pursue after graduation, in either your personal or professional life.

Benefits of Student Leadership for the Campus Community

In addition to the benefits which your student leadership experience can offer to you personally, you are encouraged to consider the potential contribution that you can make to the campus community through your activities. One of the primary benefits of student leadership is its potential contribution to the overall cultural life of the campus. Because students come from a wide variety of backgrounds, with many different interests, the programs which their organizations sponsor on the campus often reflect this diversity. Consequently, all members of the campus community have an opportunity to become more well-rounded by being introduced to cultural opportunities previously unknown to them. In addition to enabling you to pursue activities in which you already have an interest, participation in student organizations can allow you the opportunity to extend this benefit to others.

For example, suppose you are a devotee of the film, *The Rocky Horror Picture Show*. As unthinkable as the prospect may seem, you could potentially find yourself at a college or university in a remote area, 200 miles from the nearest theatre offering regular midnight showings of the cult classic. By joining together with others of the faith, you could present regular showings on your campus. As a result, you would not only be able to continue enjoying the film yourself, but would also have an opportunity to share it with the uninitiated on your campus.

In addition to introducing the campus community to new cultural opportunities, student sponsored programs can contribute considerably to the intellectual life of the institution by challenging all students to consider multiple perspectives on important social or political issues. Students come to an institution holding widely disparate views on such controversial topics as abortion, affirmative action, gun control, and First Amendment rights. Student organizations which are concerned with such issues typically invite guest speakers who reaffirm their own views. However, because of the diversity of opinion which is found among student groups on most campuses, this type of programming usually results in a "marketplace" of ideas, in which all students are challenged to re-examine their views in light of new information and insights.

Additionally, the programs that are sponsored by student organizations can promote a strong bond between members of the campus community. According to Schmidt and Blaska (1977), "student activities provide a means of uniting the campus and community by enabling friendly contacts and improved relations between students and faculty and encouraging interaction among the variety of peoples: foreign students, minority students, graduates, and undergraduates" (p. 161). They have noted, further, that "student activities create school spirit and improve morale, thus increasing student interest in and service to the college" (p. 161).

One final benefit of student leadership for the campus community is that it enables institutional decision-makers to respond more effectively to the needs of the student body. For example, in negotiating a food service contract for next year, your Director of Residence Life may find that she has three options: (1) reduce services during the school week, (2) eliminate services on weekends, or (3) raise the cost of the board plan. While all of these options may appear to be equally undesirable to her, by conferring with the members of the Residence Hall Council, she may find that students on the campus overwhelmingly favor one alternative over either of the others.

Benefits of Student Leadership for Society

One of the most important benefits of student leadership activities is the part that they play in preparing you to assume a contributing role in society. Our democratic system of government places upon each of us a responsibility to actively contribute to the common welfare. As Honnet and Poulsen (1989) noted, "we are a nation founded upon active citizenship and participation in community life."

Our nation needs individuals who are committed to something bigger than themselves, and who are able to mobilize others to turn a shared vision into reality. We need people who are capable of articulating their own views, but who are also capable of understanding the views of those who are different from them. We need people who are willing to subordinate their own individual interests to the welfare of the community, and are willing to stand by their convictions, even when it is not convenient to do so. In short, we need leaders.

Leadership is a form of service that represents the privilege of living in a democratic nation. The service that you perform on a local level, through your leadership activities, can lay the foundation for future contributions to the overall quality of American life.

Choosing a Student Leadership Setting

There are many ways in which you can exercise leadership as a student, regardless of whether or not you hold a formal leadership position. As you will find in reading this book, many of the traditional functions of leaders are often carried out by those who hold no formal office in an organization. In fact, leaders emerge even in groups where no formal hierarchy exists. For example, a group of friends may choose to rent a house off campus precisely for the purpose of escaping from institutional structures which are perceived to be authoritarian. Nevertheless, it would not be unusual to find that, within the group, a particular individual consistently emerges as a key figure in facilitating decision-making, while another individual plays a stronger role in promoting group cohesion than do other group members.

While leaders can emerge in nearly any group context, several leadership opportunities that are open to college or university students are especially rich in their potential contributions to the personal, communal, and societal benefits mentioned previously. One of the most obvious areas where student leadership opportunities exist is in **student government**. Governing bodies on your campus may include the Student Senate, Residence Hall Council, Interfraternity Council, Women's Panhellenic Association, or National Panhellenic Council. In addition to organizing specific activities and events on campus, these student groups often play a role in the formulation of policies which can have a lasting impact on certain aspects of campus life.

Student organizations also offer numerous opportunities for their members to develop skills in leadership. These groups are typically popular on college and university campuses because they enable students to engage in their favorite activities with others who share their interests. Specific types of organizations often include: fraternities and sororities, academic clubs, religious organizations, student publications, political action groups, and minority student organizations. If the particular organizations on your campus do not appeal to you, you may wish to consider establishing your own student organization. On most campuses, groups with as few as four members can register as student organizations, and consequently qualify for use of various institutional facilities and services.

Many students also enjoy participating in **intramural sports**. On most campuses, intramural team sports include: basketball, softball, volleyball, soccer, football, or bowling. Opportunities exist for both men and women to participate in either single-sex or coed intramural sports. Participating on an intramural team enables you to develop many of the leadership skills which are promoted in intercollegiate athletics, yet the world of intramural sports tends to be a much less competitive environment where having fun is the name of the game.

Student employment, particularly within the student affairs division of your institution, can also offer you many opportunities to exercise leadership. In addition to paid positions, many departments rely heavily upon **student volunteers** to carry out leadership functions on their behalf among the students on campus. Paid or voluntary student leadership positions within the typical student affairs division may include: Resident Assistant, Minority Aide, Orientation Aide, Judicial Board Member, Intramural Referee, Admissions Host, Student Food Service Manager, or Union Programming Assistant.

Thus far, we have dealt primarily with leadership opportunities on campus. However, you can also develop your skills as a leader through **civic involvement**. College and university students often hold positions in municipal government or in various service organizations in the communities where their institutions are located. Institutional officials usually encourage this type of activity, because it tends to strengthen the relationship between the college or university and the surrounding community. A major benefit to the general student body is the representation of students' interests in external decisions that often affect them directly. For students with long-standing ties to the local area, civic involvement can ensure continuation of important relationships throughout the collegiate experience.

Summary

This chapter provided an overview of the potential benefits of student leadership for the individual, for the campus community, and for society. Information was presented on a theory by Alexander Astin, which asserts that the beneficial outcomes of the undergraduate experience can be magnified through student involvement, which entails an investment of physical or psychological energy on the part of the student. Both quantitative and qualitative dimensions of involvement were explored.

Other potential benefits to the individual which were examined included: support for the achievement of goals, relationships with others having similar interests, establishment of a network, skill acquisition, and an opportunity to become a more well-rounded person. Potential benefits to the campus community included: diverse cultural programming, exposure to multiple perspectives on contemporary issues, a stronger sense of campus unity, and greater institutional responsiveness to the needs and interests of students. Potential benefits to society included the development of an active and concerned citizenry and the preparation of future leaders.

The chapter closed with an examination of specific student leadership opportunities. Common contexts for student leadership development which were explored included: student government, student organizations, intramural sports, student employment, volunteer activities, and civic involvement.

===== References =====

Astin, A. W. (1984). Student involvement: A developmental theory for higher education. *Journal of College Student Personnel, 25* (4), 297-308.

Bryan, W. A.; Mann, G. T.; Nelson, R. B.; and North, R. A. (1981). The co-curricular transcript — What do employers think? A national survey. *NASPA Journal, 19* (1), 29-36.

Honnet, E. P., and Poulsen, S. J. (1989). *Principles of Good Practice for Combining Service and Learning.* Racine, WI: Johnson Foundation.

Schmidt, M. R., and Blaska, B. (1977). Student activities. In W. T. Packwood (Ed.), *College Student Personnel Services.* (pp. 153-178). Springfield, IL: Charles C. Thomas.

Schuh, J. H., and Laverty, M. (1983). The perceived long-term influence of holding a significant student leadership position. *Journal of College Student Personnel, 24* (1), 28-32.

Activities

Getting It Straight

After reading the following paragraph, respond to each of the accompanying items by filling in the blanks or choosing from the alternative responses presented.

> Susan dreams of being a great composer some day. She loves to play the piano and practices for about an hour each day, playing mostly original compositions. Although she would like to devote more time to her music, she is unable to do so because she is attending classes full-time and works 20 hours per week. Her job in the dishroom of the college cafeteria, while demanding a good deal of manual work, is not intellectually challenging. At work, Susan prides herself on her ability to function on "automatic pilot," while new piano compositions roll through her mind. Susan's roommate, Brenda, also works on campus, but in a very different capacity. Brenda is employed as a front desk manager at the university's conference center. Her job demands complete attention at all times. However, Brenda is not bothered by this aspect of her position, since her work relates closely to her future career plans. Furthermore, through her work, she has had an opportunity to meet people from many different parts of the country, many of whom are currently employed in her chosen field.

1. Although Susan invests a good deal of _____ energy in her job, her investment of _____ energy is minimal.
2. Although Susan's involvement in her job rivals that in her music where its _____ aspect is concerned, her involvement in her music clearly prevails in its _____ dimension.
3. _____'s job seems to offer more opportunities for the development of a network than does her roommate's position.
4. In comparison to her roommate, _____ seems to invest a great deal of psychological energy in her current employment.
5. Applying Astin's theory of involvement and assuming that Susan and Brenda are satisfied with their jobs on campus, how have their levels of satisfaction with the overall college experience probably been affected by their decision to work on campus?
   a. They are probably more satisfied than they would otherwise be.
   b. They are probably less satisfied than they would otherwise be.
   c. Their satisfaction is probably about the same as it would otherwise be.

Both Sides of the Story

Prepare a defense for both the affirmative and negative positions on the following statements.

1. Most people assume leadership positions primarily for selfish reasons.
2. It is inappropriate for institutionally sponsored programs to include the expression of views which are contrary to the fundamental values of the institution itself.
3. It is inappropriate and exploitative for departments of collegiate institutions to rely on student volunteers to carry out departmental functions.

Sorting It Out

Respond to each of the following questions by taking a position and defending it.

1. Does higher education exist primarily for the benefit of society or the individual?
2. Who is primarily responsible for ensuring that a rich cultural life exists on campus (e.g., students, faculty, staff)?
3. Is experience or formal education a stronger contributor to an individual's effectiveness as a leader?

It's Your Call

Read each of the following scenarios and prepare an essay in response to the questions provided.

1. Using your own campus as a reference point, imagine that you are a new student who is looking for ways to become more involved in campus leadership activities. These activities may include any of the broad categories of involvement opportunities which have been identified in this chapter. You are carrying a heavy course load and are still adjusting to your new surroundings. Consequently, you are limited in the amount of time that you can devote to cocurricular activities. Although you could use some extra spending money, it is not necessary for you to work in order to meet your basic needs.

    a. What are your alternative courses of action, including specific activities and degrees of involvement?
    b. What are the advantages and disadvantages of each course of action?
    c. Which course of action would you follow?
    d. Why have you chosen this course of action?

2. You are the incoming business vice president of the student government association at a small private college. You are responsible for selecting a beverage distributor to install vending machines in the student union for the upcoming year. Classes are not currently in session and the other members of the association are not available for consultation. However, you have been authorized to select a distributor independently. There are two distributors available to you. The first distributor's product, Fizzy Cola, is less expensive than is the second distributor's product, Zesty Cola. Fizzy Cola is also much more popular among the students on your campus, and is the product that you prefer. However, the company has come under a great deal of fire recently because of its exploitative labor practices at its overseas plants. Zesty Cola, on the other hand, has won praise for its efforts to help the disadvantaged in this country through a number of college scholarships for underprivileged high school seniors. On a personal level, you respond more favorably to the people with whom you have dealt at Zesty Cola. In fact, you would like to continue to cultivate a relationship with them in part because it is the type of company where you would be interested in seeking employment upon graduation.

   a. What do you see as your alternative courses of action?
   b. What are the advantages and disadvantages of each course of action for you personally, for your campus community, and for society?
   c. Which course of action would you follow?
   d. Why have you chosen this course of action?
   e. In what ways do you believe that a responsible student government organization should be influenced by the interests of its members, the interests of the campus community, and the interests of society?

Understanding You

Why is Self-Knowledge So Important?
The Johari Window
Self-Disclosure and Feedback
Examining Your Interests
Clarifying Your Values
Assessing Your Skills
Summary
Activities

What You Will Learn in This Chapter

This chapter will introduce the following concepts pertaining to knowledge of self and knowledge of others:

- Johari window
  - Open area
  - Blind area
  - Hidden area
  - Unknown area

- Self-disclosure

- Feedback

In this chapter, you will also learn about the following concepts related to personal style:

- Jungian theory
  - Attitudes
    - Introversion
    - Extraversion
  - Functions
    - Thinking
    - Feeling
    - Sensation
    - Intuition

- Myers-Briggs Type Indicator
  - Introversion vs. extraversion
  - Thinking vs. feeling
  - Sensation vs. intuition
  - Judgment vs. perception

- Kiersey Temperament Sorter

- Personality
  - Temperament
  - Character

This chapter will also present an interest theory developed by John L. Holland, which incorporates the following concepts:

- Personal and environmental types
  - Realistic
  - Investigative
  - Artistic
  - Social
  - Enterprising
  - Conventional

- Personal and environmental patterns

You will also learn about the following concepts related to values:

- Instrumental values

- Terminal values

- Value systems

- Transactive values
  - Transactions
    - Transactional stimulus
    - Transactional response
  - Transactive styles
    - Analytic
    - Catalytic
    - Pragmatic
    - Systemic
    - Harmonic

You will learn about the skills related to the following types of work:

- Work with data

- Work with things

- Work with people
  - Mentoring
  - Negotiating
  - Instructing
  - Supervising
  - Diverting
  - Persuading
  - Speaking-Signaling

- ➤ Serving
- ➤ Taking instructions-Helping

You will learn about the following types of skills which are often promoted through involvement in student organizations:

- ■ Emotional and spiritual development skills

- ■ Intellectual skills

- ■ Vocational skills

- ■ Organizational skills

- ■ Human awareness skills

- ■ Intragroup process skills

- ■ Communication skills

- ■ Personal management skills

Chapter 2

Understanding You

Learn what you are, and be such.

Pindar

Why Is Self-Knowledge So Important?

There are several reasons why it is a good idea for you to begin your study of leadership by developing a better understanding of who you are. First of all, by knowing about your personal style, interests, values, and skills, you will be better able to identify those organizational settings in which you are likely to make a meaningful contribution and to find personal satisfaction. Regardless of your motives for joining an organization, a committee, or a task force, you are more likely to make reasoned judgments with the benefit of increased self-knowledge. For example, if you know that you do not enjoy conflict and tend to avoid it wherever possible, you can anticipate that participation in a group such as the Debate Team will be an unlikely source of fun and relaxation. On the other hand, if you have found that your discomfort with conflict has caused problems for you and you would like to overcome this anxiety, you may decide that participating on the Debate Team would, nevertheless, be very worthwhile.

By familiarizing yourself with your personal style, interests, values, and skills, you are also more likely to recognize those responsibilities which will pose unique challenges to you as a leader, and consequently you will probably be better prepared to meet these demands. For example, if you are the incoming president of your local chapter of Habitat for Humanity and are uncomfortable with the thought of speaking in front of groups, you will probably find that conducting meetings will be one of the more difficult tasks associated with your new role. Recognizing the likelihood of your having difficulty with this task will enable you to prepare in advance of your first meeting, in order to maximize your success.

Evaluating your present level of skill in different areas of leadership will also enable you to establish goals for yourself, and to determine criteria for measuring your progress toward the achievement of these goals. In our most recent example, depending upon your degree of discomfort, your goal may be to conduct a meeting without stammering, without shaking, or without fainting. Once you have specified your goal, you can then chart your progress toward its achievement by measuring the length of time that lapses between instances of the particular behaviors.

One of the most important reasons why the topic of self-knowledge is inextricably linked to leadership is that our relationships with others often have a major impact upon our views of ourselves, which can in turn influence the way that we interact with others in the future. For example, if you believe that you are funny, it is probably because people have communicated this information to you through their laughter. Once this belief has been established, you are more likely to engage in behaviors that will continue to evoke laughter.

Because leadership by its very nature entails interaction with others, the importance of self-knowledge will become particularly evident as you continue to develop as a leader. By being in touch with your personal style, interests, values, and skills, you are likely to function more effectively in your interaction with those in your group or organization. Conversely, as you continue in your leadership activities, your knowledge of yourself is likely to further evolve. Using our example again, it would seem that, in your role as a leader, the way in which you relate to others would probably be affected by your belief that you are funny. If, however, you were to open your first official speech with a joke that fell flat, your confidence in your sense of humor may very well be shaken. On the other hand, you may simply be faced with the challenge of incorporating your new role as a leader into your image of yourself and infusing elements of your personal identity into this new role. In either case, the relationship between leadership and self-knowledge would become increasingly clear to you.

The Johari Window

A concept known as the **Johari Window**, which was developed by Joseph Luft and Harry Ingham (Luft, 1969), provides a particularly effective illustration of the relationship between knowledge of self and knowledge of others. This chart, which is shown on page 21, consists of a square that is divided into four quadrants, each quadrant representing a different area of oneself.

The first quadrant represents information about the individual that is known to him or her and is also known to the person with whom he or she is interacting. For example, if you were to speak with a professor regarding an examination grade with which you were disappointed, it would probably not be very long before your disappointment would be known to both you and her, and would therefore be represented within the first quadrant. We refer to this quadrant as the **open** area.

The second quadrant symbolizes information about the individual that is not known to her or him but is known to others. In our example, your professor may notice that you are interacting with her in a way that creates the appearance that

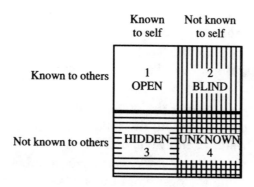

Source: From Luft, Joseph, GROUP PROCESSES, Mayfield Publishing Company, Mountain View, CA. Reprinted by permission.

are angry, while you may believe that you are remaining calm, cool, and collected. Your professor's observation would fall into the category of information represented by the second quadrant. The area that is not known to the self but is known to others is called the **blind** area.

The third quadrant represents information about the individual that is known to her or him, though not known to others. Using our example once again, in addition to feeling disappointed or angry, you may feel worried. If you were to successfully hide these feelings, in order to appear self-confident, the feelings would be represented within the third quadrant. This quadrant is known as the **hidden** area.

The fourth quadrant in the chart symbolizes information about the individual that is known to neither self nor others. In our example, suppose your professor looked very much like someone who hurt you during your childhood. It would not be unusual for you to respond negatively to her, although in all likelihood, neither you nor she would understand the basis for this reaction. This particular element of your personal history, and the nature of its influence upon your interaction with your professor, would therefore be represented within the fourth quadrant. We refer to this quadrant as the **unknown** area.

As one's relationship with another person progresses, the area of the self that is known to both parties becomes larger, while the areas that are invisible to one or both of the interacting parties become smaller. Luft (1969) outlined the following 11 general principles which apply to changes in the Johari Window:

1. A change in any one quadrant will affect all other quadrants.
2. It takes energy to hide, deny, or be blind to behavior which is involved in interaction.
3. Threat tends to decrease awareness; mutual trust tends to increase awareness.

4. Forced awareness (exposure) is undesirable and usually ineffective.

5. Interpersonal learning means a change has taken place so that quadrant 1 is larger, and one or more of the other quadrants has grown smaller.

6. Working with others is facilitated by a large enough area of free activity. It means more of the resources and skills of the persons involved can be applied to the task at hand.

7. The smaller the first quadrant, the poorer the communication.

8. There is universal curiosity about the unknown area, but this is held in check by custom, social training, and diverse fears.

9. Sensitivity means appreciating the covert aspects of behavior, in quadrants 2, 3, and 4, and respecting the desire of others to keep them so.

10. Learning about group processes, as they are being experienced, helps to increase awareness (enlarging quadrant 1) for the group as a whole as well as for individual members.

11. The value systems of a group and its membership may be noted in the way unknowns in life of the group are confronted (p. 14).

Self-Disclosure and Feedback

The process through which we make ourselves known to others is called **self-disclosure**. Johnson (1990) defined self-disclosure as "the act of revealing how you are reacting to the present situation and of giving any information about the past that is relevant to an understanding of your reactions to the present" (p. 30). In our example, you could engage in self-disclosure with your professor by sharing the fact that you are worried. Johnson (1990) cautioned that in order for self-disclosure to contribute to the growth of a relationship, it must be appropriate to the situation. He offered the following guidelines for appropriate self-disclosure:

1. It is not a random or isolated act but, rather, a part of an ongoing relationship.

2. It is reciprocated. Intimate self-disclosure should continue only if it is reciprocated. When people disclose, they expect disclosure in return. When it is apparent that self-disclosure will not be reciprocated, you should limit the amount of disclosure that you make.

3. It concerns what is going on within and between persons in the present.

4. It creates a reasonable chance of improving the relationship.

5. It takes account of the effect it will have upon the other person. Some disclosures may upset or cause considerable distress to the other person. Individual attitudes about disclosure vary considerably, and what you consider appropriate may not be so to everyone else.

6. It speeds up when a crisis develops in the relationship.

7. It moves gradually to a deeper level. Self-disclosures may begin with the information that acquaintances commonly disclose (such as talking about hobbies, sports, school, and current events) and gradually move to more intimate information. Most people become uncomfortable when the level of self-disclosure exceeds their expectations, since receiving self-disclosure can be as threatening as giving it. As a friendship develops, the depth of disclosure increases as well. Intimate or very personal self-disclosure is most appropriate in ongoing close relationships. Disclosures about deep feelings, fears, loves, and concerns are most appropriate in close, well-established relationships (Johnson, 1990, p. 34).

Although self-awareness is a necessary precondition to self-disclosure, the process of self-disclosure can in turn lead to even greater self-awareness. As people share information about themselves, the individuals with whom they interact may respond in ways which will lend further credence to the information shared, or they may respond in ways which will open up new areas of self-knowledge. The information that is shared through the process of response is known as **feedback** (Johnson, 1990). In our example, your professor may respond to the disclosure of your anxiety by commenting on her perception that you are bright but lack the motivation necessary to realize your full potential. By sharing this feedback with you, your professor could contribute to a change in your own level of self-awareness.

Like self-disclosure, feedback must be shared appropriately in order for it to contribute to the growth of the relationship. Johnson (1990) offered the following guidelines for giving effective feedback:

1. Focus your feedback on the person's behavior, not on his [sic] personality.
2. Focus your feedback in descriptions rather than on judgments.
3. Focus your feedback on a specific situation rather than on abstract behavior.
4. Focus your feedback on the "here and now" not on the "there and then."
5. Focus your feedback on sharing your perceptions and feelings rather than on giving advice.
6. Do not force feedback on other people.
7. Do not give people more feedback than they can understand at the time.
8. Focus your feedback on actions that the person can change (p. 38).

By understanding the dynamics of interpersonal relationships and the processes of self-disclosure and feedback, you can take positive action to ensure a healthy exchange of information within your relationships. In so doing, you can contribute to both your own personal growth and that of the people with whom you interact.

Understanding Your Personal Style

Consider the following scenario. You have just met one of your friend's latest romantic interests, and have made mention of the encounter to several other mutual friends. If the scenario plays out in the usual fashion, you will now be bombarded with a whole series of questions. Your friends might ask, for example, whether the new heartthrob is "cool" or "weird" or "gross" or "hot." The reason your friends might ask these questions is that they would like to know more about the individual's **personal style.** In other words, they would like to have a general sense of the type of person with whom your other friend is so taken.

When we first meet or hear about an individual, we are often immediately interested in learning more about his or her personal style, largely because the entire concept of personal style is one that encompasses a number of qualities which permeate all aspects of a person's existence. It is for this very reason that examining your personal style can be an excellent starting point in your own quest for self-knowledge.

One of the most influential figures in the study of personal style was Carl Jung, who developed a system for classifying personality types based on the individual's tendency toward different ways of thinking and relating to the world. This approach to the study of personal style is sometimes called **Jungian theory**, in honor of the man who developed it.

The primary distinction drawn by Jung was between **introverts** and extraverts. He did recognize, however, that people can show signs of both introversion and extraversion, regardless of their principal tendencies (Cartwright, 1979).

The defining characteristic of the extravert is that his or her energy, attention, and interest are directed primarily toward the outer world. Her or his actions are often strongly influenced by environmental factors (Cartwright, 1979). It should come as no surprise that students who are leaders often have a tendency toward extraversion, since their positions generally demand attention toward the outer world and an ability to relate effectively to others in social situations.

In contrast to the extravert, the introvert manifests a "preoccupation with perceptions from within" (Cartwright, 1979, p. 296). Introverts are interested in ideas, and their actions are driven primarily by their subjective responses to the world around them, rather than by the direct influence of environmental factors. Consequently, introverts often react to situations in rather unexpected ways (Cartwright, 1979). Introverts can make important contributions as student leaders, by challenging the "conventional wisdom" of their organizations and by introducing original ideas. Introverts can be influential in bringing about organizational change.

In addition to the two primary attitudes of introversion and extraversion, Jung theorized that individuals can be classified based upon their orientations toward four different functions: **thinking, feeling, sensation,** and **intuition.** As explained by Metzner (1979), "the thinking function is concerned with principles, reason, order, logic, and meaning" (p. 57), while the feeling function "is concerned with values and relationships, with the appreciation of situations, persons, objects, and psychological states" (p. 57). Sensation is defined as "conscious perception of immediately present data, facts, and events" (Metzner, 1979, p. 58), whereas intuition refers to "unconscious perception of possibilities and potentials" (Metzner, 1979, p. 58).

Student leaders whose personal styles are dominated by the thinking function often make a valuable contribution to their organizations by managing tasks which require attention to matters of fact. For example, "thinkers" often make excellent problem-solvers, because of their ability to objectively analyze a situation in order to determine the precise nature of the difficulty. Those whose personal styles are dominated by the feeling function, on the other hand, are often valued for their sensitivity to the emotions of others and their ability to promote harmonious relationships within their organizations.

Student leaders whose personal styles are dominated by sensation often deal effectively with tasks which require the manipulation of data. For example, in the organizations to which you belong, you may have already found that "sensers" often make excellent budgetary managers. On the other hand, you may have also noticed that when the time comes for these same organizations to develop promotional campaigns for organizationally sponsored events, they are more likely to turn to those members whose styles are dominated by intuition, since these individuals more often show a creative streak.

Jung categorized personal styles according to eight basic **types**, resulting from the combination of the primary attitude of the individual with his or her dominant function (Metzner, 1979). Jung's work has inspired several similar models for the study of personal style, and the development of a number of assessment instruments which can be used with individuals.

Perhaps the most notable of these instruments is the *Myers-Briggs Type Indicator*, also known as the MBTI. This particular instrument yields a personality pattern consisting of four letters. The letters represent the individual's preferences on each of the following dimensions: Extraversion (E) vs. Introversion (I); Sensing (S) vs. Intuition (N); Thinking (T) vs. Feeling (F); and **Judgment** (J) vs. **Perception** (P) (Rodgers, 1989).

The first three dimensions relate to those attitudes and functions described previously. The fourth dimension, Judgment vs. Perception, deals with the individual's preferred way of interacting with the outer world. Judging types prefer structured environments with clear expectations. They also tend to be very goal-oriented and feel a strong need to complete tasks. In contrast, perceiving types like to "go with the flow." They prefer unstructured situations and tend not to be particularly concerned about deadlines (Rodgers, 1989).

Both judging and perceiving types can make important contributions to their organizations. Judging types are usually appreciated for their planning and organizational skills. They are generally very attentive to detail. They can usually anticipate possible problems, and plan accordingly. Nevertheless, it is inevitable that the unexpected sometimes occurs, and it is under these circumstances that perceiving types often shine. Their flexibility can enable them to remain calm and to readily abandon an unworkable plan in favor of an alternative course of action which holds more promise.

For example, if your academic club were to plan an awards banquet, it is not likely that a member whose orientation is toward judgment would forget to order plaques for the occasion. However, if one of the plaques were to arrive with an error in the engraving, a group member whose orientation is toward perception would probably feel much more comfortable in improvising than would his judging colleague.

The *Kiersey Temperament Sorter* (Kiersey and Bates, 1978) incorporates the four dimensions employed in the MBTI, but focuses more specifically on the **temperament** of the individual. According to Cartwright (1979) a distinction can be drawn between temperament and **personality**. He noted that "temperament refers to a person's typical moods and emotions, and these are assumed to be related to the physiological functioning of glands and the nervous system" (Cartwright, 1979, p. 28). Personality, however, is a broader term, which incorporates both temperament and **character**. Cartwright (1979) defined character as "the consistency with which a person follows certain rules of life, especially moral and disciplinary rules" (p. 28).

Examining Your Interests

As you plan your leadership activities, it is important that you pay attention to the types of undertakings that interest you. Campus and community involvement can be very enjoyable, provided that you select organizations whose goals and activities are in alignment with your own interests and that you involve yourself primarily in projects that interest you.

A theory proposed by John L. Holland (1985) is particularly useful for examining your interests as they relate to your organizational involvement. Although developed primarily for the purpose of assisting people in planning their careers, the theory applies equally well to decisions concerning a wide variety of other activities. Holland identified six basic interest categories, known as **types**, which can be applied to either individuals or organizations. According to his theory, people are most likely to find success and satisfaction when their own types correspond to those of the organizations to which they belong. The six types identified by Holland are: **Realistic, Investigative, Artistic, Social, Enterprising,** and **Conventional.**

The Realistic person is one who enjoys engaging in physical activities which produce a tangible outcome. According to Holland (1985, p. 19), the Realistic person is likely to be:

Asocial	Materialistic	Self-effacing
Conforming	Natural	Inflexible
Frank	Normal	Thrifty
Genuine	Persistent	Uninsightful
Hard-headed	Practical	Uninvolved

The Investigative person prefers activities of a scientific nature. He or she can often be described as (Holland, 1985, p. 20):

Analytical	Independent	Rational
Cautious	Intellectual	Reserved
Critical	Introspective	Retiring
Complex	Pessimistic	Unassuming
Curious	Precise	Unpopular

The Artistic person enjoys participating in creative activities. Typically, this person can be described as (Holland, 1985, p. 21):

Complicated	Imaginative	Intuitive
Disorderly	Impractical	Nonconforming
Emotional	Impulsive	Original
Expressive	Independent	Sensitive
Idealistic	Introspective	Open

Social individuals enjoy working with and helping other people. They can often be described as (Holland, 1985, p. 21):

Ascendant	Helpful	Responsible
Cooperative	Idealistic	Sociable
Patient	Empathic	Tactful
Friendly	Kind	Understanding
Generous	Persuasive	Warm

Individuals classified as Enterprising enjoy working with others in an effort to persuade or mobilize them toward the accomplishment of some shared goal. They are often described as (Holland, 1985, p. 22):

Acquisitive	Energetic	Flirtatious
Adventurous	Exhibitionistic	Optimistic
Agreeable	Excitement-	Self-confident
Ambitious	seeking	Sociable
Domineering	Extroverted	Talkative

The Conventional person enjoys structured activities that involve the manipulation of data. He or she is likely to be drawn toward clerical work. Individuals classified as conventional can often be described as (Holland. 1985. p. 23):

Careful	Inflexible	Persistent
Conforming	Inhibited	Practical
Conscientious	Methodical	Prudish
Defensive	Obedient	Thrifty
Efficient	Orderly	Unimaginative

Although the individual's primary type refers to that which he or she most closely resembles, in reality, most people bear varying degrees of resemblance to each of the basic types. By ranking these types according to the degree to which a person resembles them, it is possible to obtain a more complex profile, known as a **pattern**. A person's pattern is identified by two or more of the basic labels, presented in sequence and usually abbreviated using the first letter of each. An organization can be similarly described by ranking the prevalence of the individual types among the people who populate the particular environment (Holland, 1985).

Your knowledge of your own interests can influence your choice of organizations in which to participate. For example, if you have primarily a Social orientation, you may choose to join your campus chapter of Circle K, while an Investigative orientation may lead you to join the Pre-med Club instead. Even within a single organization, this type of self-knowledge can help you in determining the specific role that you will assume. If you are an Artistic individual, you would probably relish the thought of appearing in a theatrical production. However, if you are the Realistic type, you would probably prefer to serve on the stage crew instead. While an Enterprising person may be very well suited to the presidency of your student government association, the positions of secretary and treasurer would probably be more appropriate for an individual whose orientation is primarily Conventional.

In addition to helping you to identify organizations and roles in which you are likely to find success and satisfaction, Holland's theory can assist you in determining those organizations and responsibilities which are least suited to your interests. According to the theory, the six basic types vary in their resemblance to one another. For example, Realistic and Investigative types share many common characteristics, while Artistic and Conventional types share little in common with one another. Holland (1985) created a hexagonal model, shown on page 29, which illustrates the relationship between the six types. The shorter the distance between two types, the more similar they are to one another.

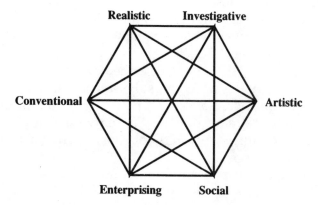

Clarifying Your Values

In addition to your interests, it is important that you be aware of your **values** as you choose your leadership activities. Needless to say, involvement in an organization whose values are contrary to your own would undoubtedly be a distressing activity. Even if you felt indifferently toward the values of a particular organization, it is unlikely that you would feel sufficiently motivated to give of yourself in the way that is so often demanded of student leaders.

According to Rokeach (1973), a value may be defined as "an enduring belief that a specific mode of conduct or end-state of existence is personally or socially preferable to an opposite or converse mode of conduct or end-state of existence" (p. 5). You will note that in order for a belief to be considered a value, it must be "enduring." A craving for something sweet does not constitute an enduring belief that eating Oreo cookies is preferable to eating salads, and therefore, would not fit the definition of a value. However, a belief that based on their nutritional content salads are a better staple in one's diet than are Oreos could reflect an enduring belief in the importance of a healthy balanced diet, which would constitute a value.

A second point that must be emphasized is that values can refer to either "modes of conduct" or "end-states of existence." A mode of conduct is a particular course of action or way of behaving, whereas an end-state of existence is the actual outcome of a particular course of action. Therefore, a value may relate to either a goal or the strategies that are used to achieve that goal. Both the belief that there is a single best way to skin a cat and the belief that skinned cats are more desirable than non-skinned cats constitute values.

Values may be either **instrumental** or **terminal**. Instrumental values are those which relate to modes of conduct, while terminal values are those which relate to end-states of existence (Rokeach, 1973).

Raths, Harmin, and Simon (1978) have described a "process of valuing" (p. 27), which incorporates seven criteria which must be satisfied in order for a particular belief or attitude to be considered a value. The first criterion is that it is chosen freely. If a student were to refrain from cheating only for fear of being subject to disciplinary action, for example, we would not conclude that academic honesty is necessarily a value that he espouses.

The second criterion that must be satisfied in order for a belief or attitude to be considered a value is that it is chosen from alternatives (Raths et al., 1978). If a student were forced to withdraw from school for financial reasons, we would not conclude that she does not value education, since her withdrawal would not represent the choice of one alternative over another.

Values must also be chosen after careful consideration of the consequences of each alternative that does exist (Raths et al., 1978). A student who believes in attending to his physical health, yet decides impulsively to use a "beer bong" once at a party, may realize all too clearly afterward that he has not acted in accordance with his values.

Values can also be recognized, in part, by the fact that they are prized and cherished (Raths et al., 1978). A student may decide to borrow money from his parents in order to pay his tuition. While believing that he has chosen the best course of action available to him, he may still feel badly about asking his parents for financial assistance. Therefore, we would not view his decision as being reflective of a value.

Values are also affirmed by those who hold them. People take pride in their values and are not ashamed to acknowledge choices that are made in accordance with them (Raths et al., 1978). If a student becomes embarrassed and quickly changes the subject when the topic of conversation drifts toward last year's New Year's Eve party, there is a good chance that her behavior on that occasion did not genuinely reflect her values.

While not all of our behavior reflects our values, all of our values do in some way influence our patterns of behavior. According to Raths et al. (1978, p. 27), "nothing can be a value that does not, in fact, give direction to actual living." It would seem that an administrator who speaks of the importance of cultural diversity within a collegiate institution, yet consistently discriminates on the basis of race when hiring his own staff, is one who does not truly value a multicultural organization.

The final criterion which must be satisfied in order for a belief or attitude to be considered a value is that it must influence behavior repeatedly (Raths et al., 1978). During the college years, it is particularly common for traditional aged students to experiment with a variety of activities, many of which they almost immediately regret and never repeat. We would not say that their decisions to engage in such behaviors would be representative of their values.

In addition to individual values, we each possess a **value system**, which Rokeach (1973) defined as "an enduring organization of beliefs concerning preferable modes of conduct or end-states of existence along a continuum of relative importance" (p. 5). Our value systems enable us to make satisfactory choices under circumstances where two or more of our values conflict. For example, if you are like most students, you have probably had the experience of writing a paper the night before it is due. On such occasions, it is often necessary to make a choice between the competing values of timeliness and precision. If timeliness is of more importance to you, it may be necessary for you to convey your thoughts in more general terms, rather than grappling for just the right word. Like individual values, value systems must be enduring. In our example, an arbitrary decision to "blow off" your assignment in order to go out for a drink with your friends would not necessarily be reflective of your value system. On the other hand, if you consistently regard your social life as being more important to you when compared with your academic life, you may systematically choose to go out with your friends rather than completing your assignments in a timely manner.

Although we often think of values as relating to morality, not all values are of a moral nature. As Morrill (1980) noted, "there are, in fact, a large number of different types or spheres of values in addition to those in the moral realm; for example, intellectual, esthetic, political, personal, economic, and social values" (p. 71). He added that "in each of these areas, values characteristically carry demands and press claims, though in nonmoral ways" (Morrill, 1980, p. 71). In our example, your concern for precision in your academic work could be classified as an intellectual value, but it would probably not be considered a moral value. Unless you were deliberately evasive, you could probably communicate in vague generalities without feeling any guilt, though your work would not completely conform to your intellectual values.

While not all values are of a moral nature, certainly ethical considerations in your behavior as a leader are a matter of special concern. In chapter 8, we will examine in greater depth systems of ethical decision-making for leaders. In the meantime, however, we will concern ourselves primarily with those values which are most likely to influence your initial decisions to become involved in leadership activities, regardless of whether or not they relate to issues of morality.

The values which are perhaps most relevant to your involvement in leadership activities are those which guide your interaction with other people in an organizational setting. We call this particular type of value a **transactive value** because of its influence over an individual's **transactions**. A transaction is the basic unit of social interaction. It consists of both a stimulus and a response. A **transactional stimulus** is an initial indication by one person that he or she acknowledges the presence of another person. The second person's communication of his or her reaction to this stimulus constitutes a **transactional response** (Berne, 1964). If you were to pass a stranger while walking across your campus, a simple nod of your head could serve as a transactional stimulus. The other person might then respond by smiling and saying "Good morning," thus completing the transaction.

Raines (1977) developed a classification system for transactive value orientations. The system incorporates five basic **transactive styles**: (1) **analytic**, (2) **catalytic**, (3) **pragmatic**, (4) **systemic**, and (5) **harmonic**.

Those whose transactive values are primarily analytic generally enjoy solving problems through objective analysis of empirical evidence. They are generally comfortable with confrontation and argumentation, and believe that "objective and data-based analysis is the foremost (if not the only) pathway to organizational effectiveness" (Raines, 1977). Comments such as "Let's conduct a survey of the graduating seniors." or "We need to think about the cost/benefit ratio for our organization." can be telltale signs of an individual's analytic style. Individuals with this particular orientation often contribute to their organizations by analyzing the causes of problems and devising strategies for correcting them (Raines, 1977).

The catalytic style manifests itself in a desire to freely examine new ideas and to implement creative solutions to problems. This particular value orientation is based on an assumption that "adapting to change with creative responses is the basis of organization survival in a changing world" (Raines, 1977). The group member whose style is primarily catalytic is likely to make comments such as "There's got to be a better way to do this." or "I've got a great idea!" Catalytic individuals contribute to their organizations by developing initiatives for addressing newly emerging needs, and by promoting interest in innovation among the members of their groups (Raines, 1977).

Individuals who have a pragmatic style are results oriented. They approach tasks efficiently and derive satisfaction from the successful completion of a task. They typically are motivated by tangible rewards, and believe that "tangible and workable results should not be hampered by 'picayune' procedures, 'outmoded' traditions, 'unrealistic' standards and 'fanciful' dreams of other units" (Raines, 1977). Comments such as "Let's be realistic about this." and "Let's just do it." often reveal a pragmatic value orientation. The pragmatist enhances the functioning of his or her organization by "overcoming obstacles which block efficient operation of the organization" and by "devising ways of reducing red tape" (Raines, 1977).

A systemic style is characterized by a preference for order and clearly defined expectations. It is based on a belief that "reliable and consistent outcomes must be the prime target of the work unit" (Raines, 1977) and that "dedication to the task is the key to effective performance" (Raines, 1977). A systemic style manifests itself in comments such as "The residence life staff manual needs to address that issue more clearly." or "Let's contact the national headquarters to find out what the policy is on that." Systemic members benefit their organizations by ensuring that regulations are not applied in an arbitrary manner (Raines, 1977).

Those whose styles are primarily harmonic favor high ideals, respect for tradition, and supportive relationships within their organizations. The harmonic style is grounded in a belief that "strong working relationships bolstered by commitment to high ethical standards are keys to realization of the unit's full potential" (Raines, 1977). Group members whose styles are primarily harmonic may make comments such as "We're all in this together. Let's help each other out." or "We've got to remember that this organization was founded as a service fraternity. Let's not forget what we're about." The harmonic individual contributes to her or his organization by "making certain that the organization lives up to the ideals and commitments of its basic purposes [and] tradition" (Raines, 1977).

Assessing Your Skills

As you plan your leadership activities, you will probably be concerned almost immediately with the skills that you possess, in addition to those which you would like to acquire. If you have been a member of the Business Club for one month, you will probably not be interested in running for president of the organization, since your limited knowledge of the office and the organization would undoubtedly hinder your ability to perform effectively in that role. On the other hand, if you have already served as coordinator of the organization's lecture series for the past year, you may feel that another year in the same position would not provide you with an adequate opportunity to develop additional skills. By arriving at a clear understanding of your current skill level in different areas of leadership, you can establish more reasonable goals and make more sound decisions concerning your organizational involvement.

According to the U. S. Department of Labor's (1977) *Dictionary of Occupational Titles*, work can be classified in three categories, based upon its relationship to **data**, **people,** or **things**. Several specific functions fall under each of the three headings. Each of these functions requires a specific skill or set of skills. Usually, when people begin working, they perform those functions which require relatively simple skills. Over time, they begin to acquire new responsibilities which require increasingly complex skills. The new skills required in a position generally build upon those acquired previously. An individual's work with data generally progresses from "comparing" to "copying," "computing," "compiling," "analyzing," "coordinating," and ultimately "synthesizing" (p. xviii). The progressively complex functions associated with work involving people are: "taking instructions–helping," "serving," "speaking–signaling," "persuading," "diverting," "supervising," "instructing," "negotiating," and "mentoring" (p. xviii). The progression of functions related to things includes: "handling," "feeding–offbearing," "tending," "manipulating," "driving–operating," "operating–controlling," "precision working," and "setting-up" (p. xviii).

In your leadership activities, you will be concerned primarily with those skills required to work effectively with people. A more detailed description of this particular group of skills is presented below:

- **Mentoring**: Dealing with individuals in terms of their total personality in order to advise, counsel, and/or guide them with regard to problems that may be resolved by legal, scientific, clinical, spiritual, and/or other professional principles.

- **Negotiating:** Exchanging ideas, information, and opinions with others to formulate policies and programs and/or arrive jointly at decisions, conclusions, or solutions.

- **Instructing:** Teaching subject matter to others, or teaching others (including animals) through explanation, demonstration, and supervised practice; or making recommendations on the basis of technical disciplines.

- **Supervising**: Determining or interpreting work procedures for a group of workers, assigning specific duties to them, maintaining harmonious relations among them, and promoting efficiency. A variety of responsibilities is involved in this function.

- **Diverting**: Amusing others (Usually accomplished through the medium of stage, screen, television, or radio.).

- **Persuading**: Influencing others in favor of a product, service, or point of view.

- **Speaking-Signaling**: Talking with and/or signaling people to convey or exchange information. Includes giving assignments and/or directions to helpers or assistants.

- **Serving:** Attending to the needs or requests of people or animals or the expressed or implicit wishes of people. Immediate response is involved.

- **Taking instructions-Helping**: Helping applies to "non-learning" helpers. No variety of responsibility is involved in this function (U. S. Department of Labor, 1977, p. 1370).

As you plan your leadership activities, it will be worthwhile for you to identify not only those skill areas in which you are satisfied with your current level of functioning, but perhaps more importantly, those areas in which you would most like to increase your competence. This type of self-assessment will enable you to choose activities which are likely to facilitate development of the skills that you desire.

You will want to pay particularly close attention to those areas of leadership development in which student organizations are often particularly supportive of members' individual growth. Eight such areas of development have been previously identified. The first group of leadership skills, **emotional and spiritual development skills,** includes those which enable you to better understand yourself, to value your own uniqueness, and to arrive at a broad sense of purpose in life. **Intellectual skills** enable you to meet the demands for "brain power" which typically accompany leadership roles. **Vocational skills** enable you to exercise leadership within a satisfying occupation. **Organizational skills** enable you to more effectively manage the resources of your organization to accomplish group goals. **Human awareness skills** enable you to better understand those whose backgrounds and values differ from your own, and to better understand your own relationship to the rest of the world. **Intragroup process skills** enable you to manage the internal dynamics of your group. **Communication skills** enable you to share your thoughts with others more effectively, and to better understand their thoughts as well. Finally, **personal management skills** enable you to maintain a sense of order in your personal life, while fulfilling your obligations to your organization (Murray and Rader, 1990).

Summary

This chapter dealt with the importance of self-knowledge as it relates to goal-setting and decisions concerning organizational involvement. The relationship between knowledge of self and knowledge of others was examined, using a chart known as the Johari Window. The chart is used to classify information about a person, based on whether or not it is known to each of the parties in a relationship. The chart consists of four areas, labeled "open," "blind," "hidden," and "unknown." Two processes contributing to greater openness in relationships, known as self-disclosure and feedback, were examined. Guidelines for each process were presented.

The concept of personal style was introduced and a theory developed by Carl Jung was presented. In his theory, Jung identified eight different "types," which result from the combination of an individual's primary attitude with his or her dominant function. The two basic attitudes identified by Jung were introversion and extraversion. The four functions which he identified were thinking, feeling, sensation, and intuition.

A similar model for the study of personal style, which built upon the work of Jung and served as the basis for an assessment instrument known as the *Myers-Briggs Type Indicator* was also presented in this chapter. The instrument yields a personality pattern which consists of four letters, each of which represents the individual's preference on one of the following dimensions: Extraversion (E) vs. Introversion (I); Sensing (S) vs. Intuition (N); Thinking (T) vs. Feeling (F); and Judgment (J) vs. Perception (P).

This chapter also included information about a similar instrument, known as the *Kiersey Temperament Sorter*, which incorporates the four dimensions used in the *Myers-Briggs*, but applies them specifically to the study of temperament, as opposed to personality. It was noted that personality is a broader concept which encompasses both temperament and character.

The importance of examining your interests was stressed in this chapter. Information was presented on a theory developed by John L. Holland for purposes of classifying both individuals and organizations on the basis of their areas of interest. Holland identified six general categories, known as types. These categories were: Realistic, Investigative, Artistic, Social, Enterprising, and Conventional. It was noted that from these categories it is also possible to obtain a more complete profile, known as a pattern.

In this chapter, the basic characteristics of values were examined. Two types of values, instrumental and terminal, were identified. Seven criteria were presented for use in determining whether or not a belief or attitude constitutes a value. The concept of a value system was presented as a consistent approach to resolving conflicts between individual values.

The concept of a transactive value was presented. It was noted that such values govern human transactions, which consist of a transactional stimulus and a transactional response. Five transactive styles were presented. These included: analytic, catalytic, pragmatic, systemic, and harmonic.

The importance of skills assessment was emphasized in this chapter. It was noted that skills can relate to work with people, with data, or with things. Specific skills were identified within each of these categories, with special attention to the skills associated with people-oriented work. These skills included: mentoring, negotiating, instructing, supervising, diverting, persuading, speaking-signaling, serving, and taking instructions-helping.

Finally, information was presented on eight leadership skill areas in which development is often promoted through involvement in student organizations. These skill areas included: emotional and spiritual development, intellectual, vocational, organizational, human awareness, intragroup process, communication, and personal management.

References

Berne, E. (1964). *Games People Play*. New York: Grove Press.

Cartwright, D. S. (1979). *Theories and Models of Personality*. Dubuque, IA: Wm. C. Brown Company.

Holland, J. L. (1985). *Making Vocational Choices*, Second edition. Englewood Cliffs, NJ: Prentice-Hall.

Johnson, D. W. (1990). *Reaching Out*. Fourth edition. Englewood Cliffs, NJ: Prentice-Hall.

Kiersey, D. and Bates, M. (1978). *Please Understand Me: Character and Temperament Types*, Third edition. Del Mar, CA: Prometheus Nemesis Books.

Luft, J. (1969). *Of Human Interaction*. Palo Alto, CA: National Press.

Metzner, R. (1979). *Know Your Type*. Garden City, NY: Anchor Books.

Morrill, R. L. (1980). *Teaching Values in College*. San Francisco: Jossey-Bass.

Murray, J. L. and Rader, M. S. (1990). *Student Leadership Skills Questionnaire*. Unpublished document.

Raines, M. (1977). *Transactive Values Inventory*. Unpublished document.

Raths, L. E.; Harmin, M.; Simon, S. B. (1978). *Values and Teaching*, Second edition. Columbus: Charles E. Merrill.

Rodgers, R. F. (1989). Student development. In U. Delworth and G. R. Hanson (Eds.), *Student Services: A Handbook for the Profession*, Second edition (pp. 117-164). San Francisco: Jossey-Bass.

Rokeach, M. (1973). *The Nature of Human Values*. New York: Free Press.

U. S. Department of Labor (1977). *Dictionary of Occupational Titles*, Fourth edition. Washington: U. S. Government Printing Office.

Activities

Getting It Straight

After reading the following paragraphs respond to the accompanying items by filling in the blanks or choosing from the alternative responses presented.

> Karen and Gina are roommates who have known each other since high school, but have only recently become friends. This year, both of them applied for Resident Assistant positions. Karen was selected and Gina was not. After both of them were informed of the appointment decisions, Gina congratulated Karen. While acknowledging her disappointment at not being selected herself, she said that she was very happy for Karen. Karen responded by saying that she was also disappointed that Gina had not been selected and that she could not understand the basis for the decision. In reality, Karen was not surprised by the decision at all. While Gina sees herself as a person who is interested in helping others, she is viewed by others as a "busybody," who likes to tell other people how to run their lives. Similarly, Gina was not really pleased that Karen had been selected. In fact, she had hoped that Karen would not be selected. Gina has always felt some resentment over Karen's successes in college, though she does not know why, since Karen has been very supportive toward her throughout their college experience. The actual reason for Gina's feelings of resentment can be traced back to their freshman year in high school, when Karen was elected to the student council, after making false accusations against Gina. At the time, Gina felt hurt, but did not confront Karen. Today, neither of the roommates consciously remembers the incident.

1. Gina's disappointment at not being selected for an R.A. position would be represented in the _____ area of her Johari window because it is _____ to herself and to Karen.

2. Gina's feelings of resentment over Karen's selection for an R.A. position would be represented in the _____ area of Gina's Johari window because they are _____ to herself and _____ to Karen.

3. Gina's domineering tendencies, which formed the basis for her rejection as an R.A. candidate, would be represented in the _____ area of her Johari window because they are _____ to herself and _____ to Karen.

4. Karen's earlier accusations against Gina and the nature of their influence on Gina's feelings toward Karen today would be represented in the _____ area of Gina's Johari window because they are _____ to Gina and _____ to Karen.

5. If Gina were to mention her feelings of resentment to Karen, we would call this type of information-sharing _____.

6. If Karen were to respond to Gina's comments by stating that she has always perceived Gina to be a very competitive person, we would call this type of information-sharing _____.

Ted's most striking characteristic is his intellectualism. He constantly seeks opportunities to engage in logical reasoning. Because his contemplative nature dominates his personality, he has been nicknamed "The Brain." Ted is also frequently described as "quiet" and "shy." Although he is not unfriendly, he prefers to direct his energy and attention inward, rather than toward the outside world. He is preoccupied with ideas and is less interested in interacting directly with other people. He particularly enjoys thinking up new ways of doing things. He is more interested in future possibilities than he is in present realities. Ted insists on maintaining order in his life and control over his environment. He is often described as "neat" and "precise." He believes in having "a place for everything and everything in its place." He also likes to plan his activities in advance and to adhere closely to his plans.

1. Using the classification system developed by Carl Jung, the two terms that would probably best describe Ted's type are _____ and _____ because his primary attitude is _____ and his dominant function is _____.

2. Applying the classification system used in the *Myers-Briggs Type Indicator* and the *Kiersey Temperament Sorter*, Ted's type would probably be identified by the terms, _____, _____, _____, and _____.

3. If we were to describe Ted's typical moods and feelings, in isolation from environmental influences, we would be dealing with his _____. The _____ would be a particularly appropriate assessment instrument for us to use in arriving at our description.

4. If we were to deal instead with Ted's adherence to certain standards of conduct, particularly within the moral realm, we would be concerned with his _____.

5. If our description of Ted were to incorporate the concepts presented in both item 3 and item 4, we would be dealing with something broader, known as his _____.

The Entrepreneurs Club is an organization composed of students who are interested in setting up small businesses while in college. Currently, the organization has 12 members. Four of the group's members, Terra, Kendra, Jeff, and Mike, are business majors who are interested in eventually assuming executive positions in large organizations. They are primarily interested in leadership activities which involve persuading people and mobilizing groups to achieve organizational goals. They have particularly enjoyed operating their t-shirt business, because of the persuasive skills used in generating sales. Jenny, Thad, and Shane are primarily interested in creative expression. They are all art majors and have set up their business mainly for purposes of exposing their original paintings and ceramic works on the art fair circuit. Curt and Mary Jo have established an upholstery business. They enjoy their work because they are primarily interested in working with their hands on projects which have a tangible result. Spencer has made a business out of typing term papers, and has been successful largely because he enjoys working on clearly defined tasks, using the latest office technology. Tanya enjoys scientific activities and has been very successful in her computer software business. As a computer science major, she particularly enjoys developing the software and is less interested in the managerial aspects of her work. Geraldine is an early childhood education major, who enjoys working with people in a helping capacity. She particularly enjoys working with children, and baby-sits regularly. Although she has little interest in business, Geraldine has joined the Entrepreneurs Club mainly because she would like to own a day care center some day and feels she must strengthen her managerial skills.

1. Using the classification system developed by John L. Holland, the single term which would probably be used to describe Terra, Kendra, Jeff, and Mike is _____. Jenny, Thad, and Shane would probably be described as _____. Curt and Mary Jo would probably be described as _____. Spencer's type would probably be identified as _____. The term used to describe Tanya would probably be _____. Geraldine's type would probably be identified as _____.

2. Again using Holland's classification system, the Club's environmental type would probably be identified as _____, and its environmental pattern would probably be identified as _____.

Amy believes that it is important that she secure professional employment in her field upon graduation from college. Toward that end, she believes that it is important that she present a professional appearance in employment interviews. More specifically, she believes that she should wear a conservative business suit. Because she had owned only dresses, Amy decided to buy a suit for her first interview. She began her shopping at the local factory outlet mall, because she does not believe in paying full price for anything. After going through all of the outlet shops, however, she had found only dresses. Afterwards, she went to the upscale shopping mall across the street and found a conservative navy blue suit that fit her perfectly. Unfortunately, it cost almost twice what she had intended to pay. Nevertheless, Amy decided that presenting a professional appearance during her interview was even more important than getting a bargain. Therefore, she decided that she would buy the suit.

1. Amy's belief in the desirability of securing employment in her field constitutes a(n):
   a. instrumental value.
   b. terminal value.
   c. transactive value.
   d. value system.
2. Amy's belief in the importance of buying only discounted items constitutes a(n):
   a. instrumental value.
   b. terminal value.
   c. transactive value.
   d. value system.
3. Amy's desire to secure employment in her field, her belief in the importance of shopping for bargains, and her belief in the importance of presenting a professional appearance during interviews are all elements of her:
   a. instrumental values.
   b. terminal values.
   c. transactive values.
   d. value system.

Michelle was looking at some souvenirs in the campus bookstore when the clerk saw her and asked "May I help you?" Michelle responded, "No, thank you. I'm just waiting for someone."

1. The exchange between Michelle and the salesclerk constituted a _____
   _____.
2. The clerk's question served as a _____.
3. Michelle's answer was a _____.

The members of the Student Admissions Committee all differ from one another in the values influencing their organizational involvement. Heather enjoys dealing with issues in an objective scientific manner. She has made a major contribution to the organization by conducting evaluative research on several of the Committee's projects this year. Rebecca enjoys creative activities, and is constantly looking for new ways of doing things. She introduced a number of new projects this year which have never been done before. Jason has handled a variety of administrative tasks, and has been valued for the "common sense" approach that he has brought to his involvement in the organization. He continuously encourages the other members of the Committee to be mindful of practical considerations. Albert enjoys working on clearly defined tasks. His biggest contribution to the organization this year was his successful completion of a number of projects which are repeated each year. Albert reviewed all of the pertinent records from previous years, patterned his work after that of his predecessors, and did not miss a detail. Andrea joined the Student Admissions Committee because she enjoys interacting with others. Although she has worked on a number of projects over the course of the year, she has been valued by the organization primarily for her ability to resolve conflicts between people and to make them feel good about themselves and one another.

1.   Heather's transactive style is probably _____.
2.   Rebecca's transactive style is probably _____.
3.   Jason's transactive style is probably _____.
4.   Albert's transactive style is probably _____.
5.   Andrea's transactive style is probably _____.

Professor Johnson had a very busy day, which began when she got up early to participate in a local radio broadcast, in which she offered a humorous commentary on contemporary music. Afterwards, she taught a lesson on the components of a well organized essay, in her introductory composition course. When she returned to her office after class, a student came to speak with her about a problem that he was having with his landlord. In addition to providing a listening ear, Professor Johnson offered the student information on several relevant city ordinances. She recommended that he contact a legal services organization in the local community, and gave him the appropriate phone number. Afterwards, Professor Johnson wrote and mailed a letter of recommendation which had been requested by another student who was in the process of applying for admission to graduate school. Professor Johnson then went to a faculty meeting, where she and other members of her department worked to develop a set of recommendations for revising the undergraduate curriculum. After much discussion, Professor Johnson offered a proposal which accommodated the views of all of her colleagues, and consequently won unanimous support from them. After the faculty meeting, Professor Johnson went to another meeting, which was conducted by the Director of Development. At this meeting, Professor Johnson and others who had volunteered to be team leaders for the university's alumni phonathon were given information concerning the procedures to be followed in conducting the phonathon. Professor Johnson listened carefully and took notes. In the evening, Professor Johnson began her work as a team leader by providing general instructions to all of the volunteers who were working on her team. After explaining the procedures to be followed in soliciting contributions from alumni, Professor Johnson gave each volunteer a separate list of phone numbers which were to be called. Finally, Professor Johnson picked up the phone herself and encouraged individual alumni to make contributions to their alma mater.

1.   In her radio broadcast, Professor Johnson engaged in the process of _____.

2.   In her class, she engaged in the process of _____.

3. In her individual meeting with a student, she engaged in _____.

4. By writing a letter in support of a student's graduate school application, Professor Johnson was _____ that student.

5. In her faculty meeting, Professor Johnson showed skill in _____.

6. At the meeting conducted by the Director of Development, Professor Johnson used skills classified as _____.

7. Professor Johnson's actual work as a phonathon team leader required that she engage in the processes of _____, and _____. By making phone calls herself, Professor Johnson also engaged in the process of _____.

Complete the following items by filling in the blank spaces.

1. Skills can relate to work involving _____, _____ _____, or _____.

2. Organizational involvement can promote individual growth in the following eight skill areas:

_____

_____

_____

_____

_____

_____

_____

_____

Both Sides of the Story

Prepare a defense for both the affirmative and negative positions on the following statements.

1. In an intimate relationship, complete openness is always desirable.

2. An individual's personality is shaped primarily by his or her environment.

3. It is generally desirable for members of an organization to be similar to one another in their interests.

Sorting It Out

Respond to the following questions by taking a position and defending it.

1. Applying Jungian theory, which primary attitudes and functions are most likely to characterize an effective leader?

2. When dealing with issues which are not of a moral nature, should leaders' decisions be governed primarily by terminal or instrumental values?
3. When dealing with issues of a moral nature, should leaders' decisions be based primarily on terminal or instrumental values?

It's Your Call

Read each of the following scenarios, and prepare an essay in response to the questions provided.

1. You are a member of an academic club in your major department, and have been encouraged to run for an office. Openings exist for the positions of President, Secretary, Programming Chair, Social Chair, and Publicity Chair.
    a. What types of skills could you acquire or further refine as a result of holding each of these offices?
    b. How might your current skills benefit the organizations if you were elected to each of these offices?
    c. Will you run for an office? If not, why? If so, which office will you seek and why?
2. You have recently joined the Entrepreneurs Club which was described previously. The Club is now in the process of electing a new president and all members are encouraged to vote. The three candidates for the position are Shane, Tanya, and Geraldine. None of the candidates has held the position previously.
    a. Based on your knowledge of the candidates, what strengths do you think each of them would bring to the position?
    b. Which candidate would you choose and why?

Understanding Others

What You Will Learn in This Chapter

This chapter will deal with the following issues pertaining to the "diversity movement" in higher education:

- Demographic changes in the nation, its work force, and its collegiate population.

- Patterns of violence and harassment on college and university campuses.

- The "political correctness" debate.

The chapter will introduce the following concepts and issues related to women's involvement in leadership:

- Women as a nondominant population

- The "glass ceiling"

- Women's socialization
  - Gender
  - Social roles
  - Role conflict
  - Androgyny
  - Bem Sex-Role Inventory

- Attitudes toward women leaders

The chapter will present recommendations for women aspiring to leadership positions and for both men and women who seek to promote leadership opportunities for women on collegiate campuses.

Issues confronting racial and ethnic minorities in leadership will be examined, with attention to the following concepts:

- Ethnicity

- Racial and ethnic groups
  - White (not of Hispanic origin)
  - Black (not of Hispanic origin)
  - Hispanic
  - Asian or Pacific Islander
  - American Indian or Alaskan Native

- Minority groups

- Prejudice
- Discrimination
  - Individual discrimination
  - Organizational discrimination
  - Structural discrimination
  - Reverse discrimination
- Affirmative action
- Racism

Leadership for multinational populations will be examined, and the following concepts will be introduced:

- "Saving face"
- Pan-ethical and utilitarian approaches to problem solving.

Diversity in sexual orientation will be discussed, with attention to the following concepts and issues:

- Homosexuality
  - Homosexual behavior
  - Homosexual attraction or desire
  - Homosexual identity
- Kinsey Scale
- Origins of homosexuality.
- "Homophobia"
- "Heterosexism"
- "Coming out"
- "Outing"

The challenges facing handicapped individuals who aspire to leadership positions will be examined, and the following concepts will be introduced:

- Handicapping conditions
  - Mobility impairments
  - Visual impairments
  - Hearing impairments
  - Learning disability
  - Speech impairments
- "Handicappers"

"Nontraditional students," including commuters, part-time students, and adult learners, will be considered as a nondominant population in higher education. The following concerns of nontraditional students will be examined:

- Mobility issues.
- Multiple life roles
- Integrating support systems
- Developing a sense of belonging
- Communication issues
- Generational differences in interests
- Attitudes of younger students toward adult learners

The following patterns of minority and majority relations will be examined:

- Amalgamation
- Assimilation
- Pluralism

A model of cultural identity development will be presented, which incorporates the following stages for minority and majority populations:

- Stages of majority member identity development:
  - Contact Stage
  - Disintegration Stage
  - Reintegration Stage
  - Pseudo-independence Stage
  - Autonomy Stage
- Stages of minority member identity development:
  - Pre-encounter Stage
  - Encounter Stage
  - Emersion Stage
  - Internalization Stage

A series of recommendations for promoting diversity within individual student organizations will be presented.

Chapter 3

===Understanding Others===

People have one thing in common: they are all different.
Robert Zend

Why Are Issues of Diversity So Important in Leadership?

Leadership involves working with others. It would seem, therefore, that an understanding of other people's points of view would be vital to your success in any leadership role. While the information presented in the last chapter can help you to understand how people differ from one another as individuals, it is also important to understand how members of different populations are sometimes influenced by certain aspects of their experiences.

The composition of our nation's population is changing. Today, racial and ethnic minorities account for one-fourth of our nation's population. If current trends continue, by the year 2000, the Hispanic population will have further increased by 21%, the Asian-American population by 22%, and the African-American population by 12%, while the Caucasian non-Hispanic population is expected to have grown by only 2%. It is expected that in the twenty-first century, today's racial and ethnic minority groups will constitute a new majority (Henry, 1990).

Our nation's work force, once dominated by White men, has also grown increasingly diverse, with increased representation of both women and minorities. According to a recent report in *Nation's Business* (Nelton, 1988), "White males are already in a new minority of their own, representing 45 percent of America's 117.8 million workers in 1986" (p. 14). By the year 2000, this figure is expected to drop to 39% (Nelton, 1988).

In all likelihood, at some time in the future, you will find yourself in an organizational environment that is characterized by a great deal of diversity. If you hope to serve effectively as a leader within this environment, it will be necessary for you to understand organizational behavior as it relates to various characteristics of the individuals involved.

If you are a member of those populations from which organizational leaders have not traditionally been drawn, it will be necessary for you to understand the unique challenges facing you as you aspire to positions of leadership. In addition to learning the rules of the game, you will have a major role to play in redefining those rules, in order to provide greater opportunities for full participation in the organization by individuals from a wide variety of backgrounds.

Even if you are a White man, it will be necessary for you to learn how to work effectively with people who are different from you. One of the key components of leadership is promoting the development of one's followers. In order to accomplish this goal, it will be necessary for you to develop an understanding of any obstacles to their advancement which may exist, and to identify and implement appropriate remedies.

While all of these reasons for studying issues of diversity in leadership are important, there is an even more urgent and equally compelling reason for you to read this chapter. Today, there are few places in the world where the diversity of the human race is reflected more fully than on the campuses of our nation's colleges and universities. According to one expert in the field of higher education, "the diversity of students at all institutions of higher education is increasing in regard to age, race, gender, living arrangements, attendance patterns, nationality of origin, and disabilities" (Jacoby, 1991, p. 281). Today, over half of the college students in the United States are women, and over 80% do not live on campus (Jacoby, 1991). Recent studies have also revealed that approximately 43% of the nation's college students are enrolled on a part-time basis, and about 39% are 25 years of age or older (National Center for Education Statistics, 1989). Racial and ethnic minorities account for approximately 18% of the student population, and international students account for another 3% (Enrollment trends, 1990).

In recent years, campus leaders have also become increasingly aware of the unique concerns of individual student populations which, in the past, were frequently overlooked. While lesbians and gay men have undoubtedly been present on college and university campuses throughout the ages, changing societal attitudes toward homosexuality have resulted in their becoming a stronger political force within the academic world. Since passage of the Rehabilitation Act of 1973, greater attention has also been directed toward the needs of handicapped students in higher education (Sprandel and Schmidt, 1980).

Unfortunately, the growing diversity of our nation's collegiate population and increased awareness of student group concerns have been accompanied by a number of conflicts between segments of individual campus communities, which have sometimes resulted in acts of violence. One of the most widely publicized racial incidents in recent years occurred at the University of Massachusetts at Amherst, following the final game of the 1986 World Series. While the incident began as a shoving match between Red Sox fans and Mets fans, it resulted in a series of random attacks on African-American students by a mob of 3,000 Caucasian students (Wiener, 1989). More recently, groups of lesbians and gay men who were participating in parades at the University of Texas at Austin were bombarded with rocks and beer bottles (Tifft, 1989).

While most of the instances of harassment on campuses across the country have not involved actual physical abuse, they have nonetheless created a distressing environment for individual victims. In one case, swastikas were spray-painted on the Jewish Student Union building at Memphis State University. In another incident, at the University of Chicago, fraudulent classified advertisements were used to identify homosexual students, who were then subjected to exposure against their will (Tifft, 1989). At Dartmouth College, a student publication known as the *Dartmouth Review* regularly launched written attacks on a Black music professor, and on one occasion, members of the *Review* staff confronted him after class, in an apparent effort to provoke him into a fight (Wiener, 1989). Also at Dartmouth, it was found that a Black professor regularly used the term "honky" in his classroom to refer to Caucasians (Williams, 1989).

In addition to cases of harassment against individuals, collegiate institutions have confronted a growing number of incidents in which members of their campus communities have shown insensitivity toward broad segments of the population, within the context of mass communication. In one of the most widely publicized of these cases, derogatory jokes about Blacks were broadcast on the campus radio station of the University of Michigan at Ann Arbor (Wiener, 1989).

As a campus leader, you will have a unique role to play in resolving conflicts within your own institution. In nearly all of the incidents described thus far, in which groups of students took action against other members of their campus communities, the influence of student leadership was present. Undoubtedly some of the students involved in these incidents would not have participated, had they not been persuaded by other students to do so. Student leaders are most assuredly capable of acting as a destructive force on their campuses. However, they are also in an excellent position to bring about positive changes within their campus communities. In order for you to provide the type of leadership necessary to resolve conflicts between various groups at your institution, you will need to develop an understanding of issues concerning diversity.

A Word of Caution

The material presented in this chapter is more controversial than anything else that you will read in this book. In fact, the mere inclusion of this chapter is likely to make some readers bristle. As you are likely to find in discussing this chapter with other students, there are few other topics on which people hold more diverse opinions than on the subject of diversity itself.

In recent years, as institutions of higher education have directed more attention to issues such as racial and gender differences, ideological diversity has likewise become a major issue. Institutional initiatives for increasing diversity and promoting awareness and appreciation of differences have not been met with universal endorsement.

Those who object to current practices in dealing with diversity on college and university campuses often argue that freedom of inquiry and expression have been stifled by an intolerance toward politically conservative views, particularly in matters related to race and gender. It has been argued that faculty and administrators on campuses across the country have attempted to create, through social pressure and coercion, a new political orthodoxy, which has been dubbed "**political correctness**" or "**PC.**" In a recent *Newsweek* cover story on the subject, it was recognized that some "politically correct" views are not even particularly controversial, yet according to the authors, "what is distressing is that at the university, of all places, tolerance has to be imposed, rather than taught, and that 'progress' so often is just the replacement of one repressive orthodoxy by another" (Adler, Starr, Chideya, Wright, Wingert, and Haac, 1990, p. 49).

Some foes of political correctness believe that campus leaders have been superficial in dealing with issues of diversity. According to one author, "notably absent from the demands of the diversity movement is a call for diversity of political opinion" (Bahls, 1991, p. 15). Eugene Meyers, executive director of a conservative organization known as the Federalist Society, has stated that "the politically correct argue in effect that someone who's black but doesn't share the views of the radical left doesn't count as being black" (Bahls, 1991, p.15). According to Mr. Meyers, there appears to be an assumption that all Blacks share a particular way of thinking (Bahls, 1991).

One of the most outspoken critics of higher education's approach to dealing with diversity is an English professor and author named Shelby Steele. Dr. Steele has argued that by calling attention to differences between groups, collegiate institutions have created a new brand of campus politics, which he has termed the "politics of difference." Dr. Steele has described this phenomenon as "a troubling, volatile politics in which each group justifies itself, its sense of worth and its pursuit of power, through difference alone" (Steele, 1989, p. 49). He has argued that "this elevation of difference undermines the communal impulse by making each group foreign and inaccessible to others" (Steele, 1989, p. 53).

Dr. Steele (1989), who is Black, has warned that the politics of difference may ultimately be of particular danger to those who have traditionally been denied power. In a recently published essay on the subject, he stated:

> This politics of difference makes everyone on campus a member of a minority group. It also makes racial tensions inevitable. To highlight one's difference as a source of advantage is also, indirectly, to inspire the enemies of that difference. When blackness (or femaleness) becomes power, then white maleness is also sanctioned as power.

It is certainly true that white maleness has long been an unfair source of power. But the sin of white male power is precisely its use of race and gender as a source of entitlement. When minorities and women use their race, ethnicity, and gender in the same way, they not only commit the same sin but also, indirectly, sanction the very form of power that oppressed them in the first place (Steele, 1989. p. 53).

Clearly in matters concerning race, gender, and other differences between groups, widely divergent opinions exist, even within the groups themselves. The goal of this chapter is certainly not to create new stereotypes, nor is it to instill in you a single "correct" point of view on matters of diversity. Rather, its purpose is to challenge you to examine many different opinions, and to look beyond your own immediate experience in developing your understanding of human nature. I will make every attempt to explore the issues in as evenhanded a manner as possible, and will emphasize immediately that the fundamental differences between people are often found far below the surface.

Women in Leadership

We will begin our discussion by examining issues confronting women who aspire to leadership positions. Though not a numerical minority within our society, women have traditionally been denied access to political and organizational power, and have therefore constituted a **nondominant population**. To this day, within the world of leadership, women remain a minority in the truest sense of the word.

Although women account for approximately half of our nation's electorate, the number of women holding upper level positions in government has continued to lag far behind that of men. As recently as 1992, only three states had female governors (State Yellow Book, 1992) and only two were represented by women in the U.S. Senate (Hermann and Sutherland, 1991).

Thus far, the advancement of women in the corporate world has been similarly disappointing. A team of researchers from the Center for Creative Leadership recently observed that "despite increasing numbers of women in business, women are definitely under-represented in the most powerful management positions — those in the topmost ranks of the largest corporations that account for the bulk of this country's business wealth" (Morrison, White, Van Velsor, and The Center for Creative Leadership, 1987, p. 6).

It has been noted that women in management frequently encounter an invisible barrier to their advancement beyond a particular level within their organizations. This barrier has been dubbed the **"glass ceiling"** (Morrison et al., 1987). Importantly, it has been noted that "the glass ceiling is not simply a barrier for an individual, based on the person's inability to handle a higher level job. Rather, the glass ceiling applies to women who are kept from advancing higher *because they are women*" (Morrison et al., 1987, p. 13).

I emphasize here that the challenges facing women in leadership differ even from those confronting other nondominant populations. This is not to say that many of the obstacles encountered by other such populations are not faced by women as well. However, in addition to these challenges, women often deal with a number of other concerns which are completely unique to their gender.

My use of the word "**gender**," as opposed to "sex," is deliberate. Whereas "sex" refers to a biological classification, determined prior to birth, "gender" encompasses an entire **social role** (Posner, 1992). This distinction is important, as the challenges facing women in leadership appear to relate primarily to their social roles, rather than to any characteristics of their anatomy.

Social roles have been defined as those behaviors which accompany a particular position within a society. These commonly expected behaviors are learned through a process known as **socialization** (Wallace and Wallace, 1985). On your own campus, you have probably noticed that students and faculty members are expected to behave differently from one another. For example, while professors often refer to students by their first names, such informality on the part of a student in addressing a faculty member may be considered inappropriate. The behavioral expectations which accompany your status as a student and someone else's status as a professor constitute two distinctly different roles, which are likely to be reinforced through a variety of subtle and not so subtle rewards and punishments. Each of us plays a number of roles, some of which are confined to very small social units, such as our families, while others may bear upon our interaction with anyone whom we may encounter across the nation.

Gender roles have been defined as "those roles men and women are expected to play according to society's definitions of masculinity and femininity" (Wallace and Wallace, 1985, p. 346). The next time that you are in a bar or at a party, you will probably have an opportunity to observe a number of behaviors which have been incorporated into gender roles which have persisted over the years in our society. For example, you may see men buying drinks for women or initiating conversations with them, but are less likely to see this pattern of behavior reversed. You may see groups of women excusing themselves to use the restroom, whereas men are more likely to do so individually. You will probably also see more men than women playing pool or throwing darts, and will almost definitely see fewer fistfights between women than between men. These patterns of behavior are likely to emerge, at least in part, because of the shared expectations which are placed on men and women in our society.

Of course, the expectations which accompany an individual's status as a man or woman are not the only behavioral demands which are placed upon him or her. Each of the other social positions that a person occupies comes complete with its own set of expected behaviors. These multiple demands will not necessarily cause problems for the individual, provided that the demands are consistent with one another. For example, a student who is majoring in business administration and aspiring to a career in management, may find that a position in student government would complement his academic program very nicely, since the skills which he would develop and apply in his student government activities would be similar to those which he will ultimately need in his work as a manager. In this case, the student would probably have little difficulty both in reconciling his new role (student government officer) with his previously existing role (business administration major) and in adjusting to his future role (manager).

Adjustments are more difficult when successive, or worse yet, simultaneous roles of an individual include behavioral expectations which are not consistent with one another. When an individual occupies two roles simultaneously, and these roles call for different behaviors, **role conflict** is said to exist (Wallace and Wallace, 1985). One example of role conflict may occur when the expectations which other students place upon a Resident Assistant in her role as a friend conflict with the expectations which her employer places upon her in her role as a disciplinarian.

Women in positions of power frequently experience role conflict because the entire concept of power is often seen as inconsistent with the traditional role of women in our society. It has been observed that "since femininity has been associated with such qualities as weakness, passivity, dependence, emotionality, irrationality, subservience, the body and temptation, while masculinity has been associated with potency, action, independence, rationality, domination, the mind, and moral purpose, men who exercise power typically risk no reduction of their manliness in the eyes of others [whereas] (w)omen with power risk being viewed as unwomanly or unfeminine" (Lips and Campbell, 1981, p. 16).

In studying the characteristics of women who had successfully broken through the glass ceiling and those who had failed to do so, the research team from the Center for Creative Leadership found that successful women displayed a rare combination of seemingly contradictory traits. In explaining their findings, the researchers stated:

> The women described to us as success cases and as derailers were put through a number of hoops as they progressed up the corporate ladder. They had to show their toughness and independence and at the same time count on others. It was essential that they contradict the stereotypes that their male executives and coworkers had about women — they had to be seen as different, "better than women" as a group. But they couldn't go too far, to forfeit all traces of femininity, because that would make them too alien to their superiors and colleagues. In essence, their mission was to do what *wasn't* expected of them, while doing enough of what *was* expected of them as women to gain acceptance. The capacity to combine the two consistently, to stay within a narrow band of acceptable behavior, is the real key to success (Morrison et al., 1987, pp. 54-55).

The researchers offered the following recommendations to women seeking to break through the glass ceiling:

1. Take risks, but be consistently outstanding.
2. Be tough, but don't be macho.
3. Be ambitious, but don't expect equal treatment.
4. Take responsibility, but follow others' advice (Morrison et al., 1987, p. 57).

It should be noted that, while women are more likely than men to experience conflicts between their gender and leadership roles, it is sometimes necessary for men to demonstrate traditionally feminine qualities in their leadership activities. As we will discuss in the following chapter, one aspect of leadership is attention to the emotional needs of group members. In this particular area, women have often excelled, because of the nurturing qualities which have been incorporated into the traditional female gender role.

One of the reasons why both men and women have sometimes experienced conflicts between their gender roles and the demands of their leadership positions is that masculinity and femininity have traditionally been viewed as opposite ends of a single continuum. According to this traditional view of masculinity and femininity, an individual's behavior cannot become more feminine without becoming less masculine, and vice versa. An assessment instrument known as the *Bem Sex Role Inventory* (Bem, 1977) provides an alternative model of gender roles which treats masculinity and femininity as two separate dimensions, rather than as opposite ends of a single continuum, thus enabling an individual to be described as both masculine and feminine, a condition known as **androgyny**.

In addition to the differences in behavioral expectations which are placed on men and women in our society, it appears that female leaders are frequently challenged by differences in interpretations of men's and women's behavior. Based on several studies of attitudes toward male and female leaders, it was found that "successful male performance is more often attributed to internal factors related to the person's disposition, such as skill and ability [whereas] (s)uccessful female performance is more often attributed to external factors related to the situation, such as luck or, perhaps, the simplicity of the task" (Adams and Yoder, 1985, p. 49).

As you work with women in an organizational setting, regardless of your own gender, it will be helpful for you to be aware of any biases that you may have, concerning women's ability to serve effectively in leadership positions. This is particularly true if you hold a leadership position yourself, since any prejudices which you may have against women as leaders could interfere with your ability to recognize leadership potential in female members of your organization, and to prepare talented women for future leadership positions.

In addition to recognizing any biases which may prevent the advancement of women in an organization, there are specific actions which can be taken by those in positions of authority or influence, in order to promote women's leadership development. In your organizational involvement on your own campus, you may be in an excellent position to increase women's involvement in leadership activities. Although directed primarily toward those in administrative positions, the following recommendations from two college administrators, one male and one female, are useful for all campus leaders who are seeking to expand female students' leadership opportunities:

1. Exemplify behaviors that are important for effective leadership, including commitment, respect for others, loyalty, courage, moral strength, assistance rather than condemnation during risk taking and failure, preservation of carefully developed relationships, and scrupulous attention to balance in exercising the powers of justice and mercy.

2. Recognize that prejudice and individual failure of self-confidence militate against women's risking leadership roles. Establish a climate and environment that values and rewards risk taking and strong leadership behaviors. This is the responsibility of policy makers and policy implementers from the top down. Once in place, policies must be monitored for effectiveness.

3. Provide structured learning experiences that offer the opportunity to test and reinforce leadership skills, broaden vision, create successes, and make mistakes in a supportive environment. Encourage women to aspire to critical leadership roles, and do so intrusively if necessary.

4. Appoint women to perform visible and substantive roles, particularly in policy making positions.

5. Provide overall an adequate number of female role models who display different, energizing examples of leadership (Bennett and Shayner, 1988, p. 34).

Racial and Ethnic Minorities in Leadership

Much of the literature on human diversity has focused on the concept of **ethnicity**. Bahr, Chadwick, and Stauss (1979) explained this concept as follows:

> The term ethnicity refers to shared culture and background. Shared background includes common ancestry, and the shared culture embraces language, religion, customs, and national or political identification. The essential determinant of ethnic group membership is social identification: If the group defines a person as similar enough to belong to it, and if that person identifies with that group, then he or she belongs to that group, whatever his or her real ancestry may be (p. 4).

The term **race** refers specifically to "a population which shares visible physical characteristics from inbreeding and which thinks of itself or is thought of by outsiders as distinct" (Wallace and Wallace, 1985, p. 309). Not all **ethnic groups** are considered races, since shared backgrounds and cultures can be present even in the absence of distinct physical characteristics.

Citizens of the United States are typically classified according to five primary racial and ethnic groups, though many smaller groups exist within these broad classifications. The five basic categories are:

- **White** (not of Hispanic origin) — a person having origins in any of the original peoples of Europe, North Africa or the Middle East.

- **Black** (not of Hispanic origin) — a person having origins in any of the black racial groups.

- **Hispanic** — a person of Mexican, Puerto Rican, Dominican, Cuban, Central or South American or other Spanish culture or origin, regardless of race.

- **Asian or Pacific Islander** — a person having origins in any of the original peoples of the Far East, Southeast Asia, the Indian subcontinent or the Pacific Islands. This area includes, for example, China, Japan, Korea, the Philippine Islands and Samoa.

- **American Indian or Alaskan Native** — a person having origins in any of the original peoples of North America and who maintains cultural identification through tribal affiliation or community recognition (New York State Department of Civil Service. 1986 p. 41).

We often refer to the nonwhite groups identified above as **minority groups**. There is, of course, a numerical basis for this label, since most Americans are in fact White. However, in defining minority groups, sociologists have typically focused on the concept of dominance, as we have done previously in our discussion of women in leadership. According to the sociologist's definition, "a minority group is one which has less power and influence than the dominant group" (Wallace and Wallace, 1985, p. 310). Within our society, those classified as White are considered the dominant ethnic group, while nonwhite groups are considered nondominant populations.

Members of racial and ethnic minority groups who aspire to positions of leadership often encounter a number of unique obstacles, which ultimately stem from the **prejudice** of others toward them. Prejudice has been defined as "a judgment based on group membership or social status" (Wallace and Wallace, 1985, p. 311). Examples of prejudice may include the assumption that one student is introverted because he is majoring in English or that another student is conceited because she belongs to a sorority. Prejudice can involve either a positive or negative value judgment.

It is important to note that prejudice refers to attitudes, rather than behaviors. For example, a professor may assume that students who major in Communication Arts are more extroverted than are those who major in Philosophy, yet he may treat the two groups of students no differently from each other. In this situation, we would still say that he is prejudiced.

Discrimination, on the other hand, refers to differences in the treatment of individuals, on the basis of group membership or social status (Wallace and Wallace, 1985). In our example, if the professor routinely called on some students because they were Communication Arts majors while ignoring others because they were Philosophy majors, we would say that he had discriminated.

The most commonly recognized type of discrimination is that which is perpetrated by a single person. This type of discrimination is known as **individual discrimination**. If an education professor, encouraged all of his female students to pursue careers in elementary education and encouraged all of his male students to pursue careers in secondary education, without considering the students' individual interests and talents, we would say that he had engaged in individual discrimination. Because his actions would be carried out independently, they would not necessarily reflect the attitudes of his departmental colleagues. Individual discrimination is sometimes deliberate, but often is not (United States Commission on Civil Rights, 1988).

Organizational Discrimination is that which results from established organizational rules, policies, and practices. For example, if a university had historically barred admission of racial or ethnic minorities, current policies granting favored status to the offspring of alumni could result in continued discrimination against minority groups. As in this case, discriminatory organizational policies and practices often have the effect of creating disadvantages for certain racial or ethnic groups, while not outwardly appearing to be discriminatory on the basis of ethnicity (United States Commission on Civil Rights, 1988).

Structural Discrimination refers to interrelationships between various structures within our society, which perpetuate inequality. According to the United States Commission on Civil Rights (1988):

> There is a classic cycle of structural discrimination that reproduces itself. Discrimination in education denies the credentials to get good jobs. Discrimination in employment denies the economic resources to buy good housing. Discrimination in housing confines minorities to school districts providing inferior education, closing the cycle in a classic form (p. 14).

In recent years, you have probably also heard references to **reverse discrimination**, defined as "discrimination against the majority group" (Wallace and Wallace, 1985, p. 339). Most claims of reverse discrimination have been made in relation to **affirmative action** programs, which have been adopted by many institutions in an effort to eliminate organizational and structural discrimination. Affirmative action has been defined as "the policy by which special consideration is given to a member of a group which has suffered discrimination in the past and is therefore considered not as able to compete for the rewards of society, such as education and jobs" (Wallace and Wallace, 1985, p. 340).

Supporters of affirmative action have argued that it is a necessary means of overcoming past barriers to equality. Affirmative action proponents have sometimes drawn analogies, such as the following, in which the current racial situation in our nation is likened to a race in which one runner has been shackled for 200 years while the other has moved freely:

> Suddenly the shackles are removed, but, of course, one runner is still much faster than the other. Removing the shackles doesn't make the two instantly equal in ability to compete. The previously shackled runner has to be given some advantage in order to compete effectively until he gets his legs into condition (Totenberg, 1979, p. 219).

Opponents of affirmative action have argued that preferential treatment on the basis of race cannot be justified, regardless of its specific application. According to one critic, most Americans "oppose preferential treatment as unfair and as a violation of the very principle of equality it is meant to serve" (Short, 1988, p. 48).

It has been further argued that preferential treatment of minorities in the admissions process is at the root of much of the current racial strife on college and university campuses. It has been asserted that "whatever justification may be given for such a practice, it cannot help but build resentment, bitterness, and a sense of unfair play among whites" (Williams, 1989, p. 37), and that "many of the allegedly racist incidents cited are actually protests against preferential treatment of minorities" (Short, 1988, p. 48).

Racism actually refers to "the belief or doctrine that one people must control or act upon another people because of the superior or inferior attributes of the respective groups" (Burkey, 1978, p. 92). Contemporary definitions of racism have generally emphasized the combination of prejudice and power as necessary conditions of racism. On this basis, it has been widely maintained that nondominant populations cannot be racist. According to one author:

> Racism involves the subordination of people of color by white people. While an individual person of color may discriminate against white people or even hate them, his or her behavior or attitude cannot be called "racist." He or she may be considered prejudiced against whites and we may all agree that the person acts unfairly and unjustly, but racism requires something more than anger, hatred, or prejudice; at the very least, it requires prejudice plus power. The history of the world provides us with a long record of white people holding power and using it to maintain that power and privilege over people of color, not the reverse (Rothenberg, 1988, p. 6).

Leadership Within an International Context

Thus far, in our discussion of ethnicity, we have dealt primarily with individuals who are of a single nationality. That is, we have limited our discussion to the major racial and ethnic groups found among United States citizens.

While it is important that we deal with issues of racial and ethnic diversity within our own nation's population, it is also increasingly important that we look beyond our borders to deal with issues of human interaction on a global level. As mentioned previously, growing numbers of international students are enrolling at American colleges and universities. In your leadership activities on your own campus, you have undoubtedly dealt with a number of students who have come to your institution from other countries.

As you look toward your future in leadership, international leadership issues will remain important. Advancements in communication and transportation have increased the extent to which citizens of different nations interact with and depend upon one another on a daily basis.

According to one observer, within the world of business in particular there has emerged a "growing cadre of global managers," such that "today corporate decisions about production and location are driven by the dictates of global competition, not by national allegiance" (Reich, 1991, p. 77). If you are planning a career in a major corporation, it will undoubtedly be necessary for you to deal with citizens of many nations, even within your own organization.

Perhaps the most important reason for developing skills in interacting with people from other lands is the extent to which the citizens of all nations have come to depend upon effective leadership for maintaining world peace. As Dr. Armand Hammer (1980) once observed, "because our peril as a world community of nations has never been greater, our need to achieve international understanding has never been greater" (p. 12).

Often, misunderstandings occur between people from different countries due to a lack of familiarity with the customs and philosophical orientations of various nations. Recently, a research team composed of experts from both North America and China observed that philosophical differences between the cultures of the two regions can have an impact on the manner in which work activities are conducted within these countries. They stressed that the nations of North America tend to be very individualistic in their philosophical orientation, while the Chinese culture is characterized by a collective orientation (Tse, Lee, Vertinsky, and Wehrung, 1988). In the Chinese culture, it is expected that individuals will place the common welfare ahead of their own individual interests and will depend upon one another, while in North America, it is often assumed that individuals will act independently, and will be guided by their own concerns.

The researchers identified several specific ways in which the differences in the prevailing philosophies of the two regions manifest themselves. The first manifestation which they identified was the relative importance which the different nations placed on "**saving face**." "Face" is defined as "the respect, pride, and dignity of an individual as a consequence of his or her position in society" (Tse et al., 1988, p. 83). The people of China, like the Japanese, generally place a higher priority on avoidance of shame than do North Americans (Tse et al., 1988).

The researchers also observed cultural differences in attitudes toward the exchange of favors. They noted that "in Western culture [exchange relationships] are based on principles of balance, clearance, and specific relationships," whereas "in Chinese culture exchanges create long-term moral obligations" (Tse et al., 1988, p. 83).

The third area in which differences were observed was in the significance of consensus and the extent to which subordinates influence decision-making. Chinese leaders tend to be more authoritarian, and their followers more compliant, in comparison to their Western counterparts. In Western cultures, it is considered desirable for subordinates to participate in decision making, and for agreement to be reached in support of a particular course of action. In this respect, the Japanese culture resembles the Western cultures more closely than it resembles that of China (Tse et al., 1988).

The fourth area in which the Chinese culture was found to differ from the West was in its commitment to a **pan-ethical** approach to problem solving, rather than the **utilitarian** approach that is favored in the West. The utilitarian approach to decision making involves a cost-benefit analysis, with the goal being to choose the option which maximizes benefits while minimizing costs. In contrast, the pan-ethical approach places moral ideals and social justice ahead of practical considerations (Tse et al., 1988, p. 83). It should be noted that utilitarianism can itself be used as a system for dealing with ethical matters. We will discuss utilitarian ethics in greater detail in chapter 8.

A recent article in *Business America* dealt with specific social customs as they relate to the conduct of business around the globe. It was noted that "some of the cultural distinctions that U.S. firms most often face include differences in business styles, attitudes towards development of business relationships, attitudes towards punctuality, negotiating styles, gift-giving customs, greetings, significance of gestures, meaning of colors and numbers, and customs regarding titles" (Glover, 1990, p. 3).

Whenever possible, it is best for you to learn more about the particular culture of a person with whom you will be dealing, prior to your first meeting. Your knowledge of the other person's culture will shape the entire course of your interaction with her or him, and will allow you to plan accordingly. If the person is from a culture, such as our own, in which time is regarded as a precious resource, you can plan for a brief meeting in which you will deal strictly with the business at hand. However, if the person is from a culture in which it is considered rude to hurry, you will know to block off a longer period of time for your meeting than would ordinarily be needed, and you will be prepared to make lots of small talk.

You will also want to learn the proper way of greeting and addressing a person before your first meeting. Physical gestures and touch are often used as a form of greeting in many parts of the world, yet the manner in which such greetings are received varies widely across countries. What is considered proper in one culture may create discomfort or offense in another. The level of formality that is common in business interaction also varies widely across nations. While in some countries it is considered acceptable to call business associates by their first names upon first meeting them, in other countries business associates are addressed by titles even after an ongoing working relationship has been established (Glover, 1990).

It is also a good idea to learn more about the other nation's customs concerning gift-giving. Cultures differ dramatically from one another in this area. In some countries it is considered insulting to present a gift in a business relationship, while in other countries the failure to do so is regarded as an insult (Glover, 1990).

Of course, you will not always have an opportunity to prepare in advance of your interaction with people from other countries. Furthermore, much of your involvement with multinational populations will take place on American soil, with the general customs of our society prevailing. Nevertheless, by being aware of differences between cultures and learning more about the customs of other nations on an ongoing basis, you can reduce the likelihood that you will one day find yourself in an uncomfortable situation.

Diversity and Sexual Orientation

One of the most complex and controversial aspects of the "diversity movement" in higher education is its growing emphasis on the concerns of lesbians and gay men. Unlike women and racial or ethnic minorities, homosexual students are not identified (or identifiable, for that matter) on the basis of their outward appearance. Instead, they constitute a segment of the population that is defined in social, psychological, and behavioral terms. Three different aspects of **homosexuality** have been identified: (1) homosexual behavior, defined as "sexual activity with another person of the same anatomical sex" (Geer, Heiman, and Leitenberg, 1984, p. 268); (2) homosexual attraction or desire, defined as "erotic and emotional interest in members of the same sex" (Geer et al., 1984, p. 268); and (3) homosexual identity, defined as "a person's self-acknowledged preference for sexual partners of the same sex" (Geer et al., 1984, p. 268).

According to one estimate, 3 to 4% of all men and 1 to 2% of all women in the United States are exclusively homosexual in their orientation. It should be noted, however, that individuals vary widely in the exclusivity of their preferences for sexual partners of one sex or the other. It has been observed that bisexuals actually constitute a larger segment of the population than do homosexuals (Geer et al., 1984).

One of the most extensive studies of male sexual behavior was conducted during the 1940's by a team of researchers led by Dr. Alfred C. Kinsey. Based on their findings, Dr. Kinsey and his associates developed a rating scale for classifying an individual's sexual orientation. The "**Kinsey Scale**," as it has come to be known, ranges from a rating of 0 for those who are exclusively heterosexual to a rating of 6 for those who are exclusively homosexual (Kinsey, Pomeroy, and Martin, 1948).

There is much that needs to be learned about the origins of homosexuality, despite the fact that a good deal of research has already been done on the subject. Some of the studies which have been conducted have led researchers to believe that social factors are the primary determinants of one's sexual orientation, while other studies have pointed toward genetic causes.

One of the most frequently examined social factors which may account for the development of a homosexual orientation is the dynamics of the individual's family during early childhood. According to one psychologist, currently working with gay men who are dissatisfied with their sexual orientation, "research has shown repeatedly that a poor relationship with a distant, aloof father and an overpossessive, domineering mother could cause homosexuality in males" (Gelman, Foote, Barrett, and Talbot, 1992, p. 53). Other social factors which have been commonly cited as influential in the development of a homosexual orientation include early sexual experience and difficulty in conforming to the demands of childhood sex-role stereotypes (Geer et al., 1984).

In contrast to much of the earlier research, two highly publicized studies which were conducted recently have lent support to the belief that homosexuality is biologically based. In one of these studies, it was found that gay men differed significantly from heterosexual men in the physical structure of their brains (LeVay, 1991). In the second study, which dealt with the sexual orientation of gay men's brothers, it was found that 52% of identical twin brothers were also gay, as were 22% of fraternal twin brothers, and 11% of adoptive brothers (Holden, 1992). The findings of this study suggest that similarities in sexual orientation tend to be stronger when genetic relationships are stronger, and weaker when genetic relationships are weaker or nonexistent.

While much of the debate surrounding the origins of homosexuality has focused on questions of "nature vs. nurture," a number of scientists believe that a combination of factors enters into the development of one's sexual orientation. According to one university professor who has specialized in both psychology and biology:

> It is still all too common to see early experience, social learning, or choice pitted against biology, but these are false dichotomies. This is because the brain has been shown or is assumed to be the underlying mechanism in these processes. Several

decades of empirical work have shown that the brain is a product of early experience, social environment, and genetic instructions. So, it manifests the workings of both nurture and nature (Schoenfeld, 1991, p. 630).

Because one's sexual orientation is seen by many as the product of her or his environment, and therefore subject to change, intolerance toward lesbians and gay men is common even among those who are not necessarily prejudiced against other nondominant populations. The behavioral aspect of homosexuality also appears to be a factor in the particularly strong negative feelings toward homosexuals which many Americans harbor.

Much of the opposition to homosexual behavior appears to be based on religious beliefs. Those who condemn such behavior often cite Biblical passages, such as Leviticus 20, which reads in part, "if a man lies with a man as with a woman, both of them have committed an abomination." Others who object to homosexual behavior offer arguments stemming more generally from the traditional Judeo-Christian prohibition of non-procreative sexual acts (Geer et al., 1984).

Prejudice against lesbians and gay men has also been frequently attributed to fear and misconceptions. Dr. George Weinberg (1972) advanced the view that such biases represent an irrational fear when he coined the term "**homophobia**," in reference to "the revulsion toward homosexuals and often the desire to inflict punishment as retribution" (p. 133).

Another popular term, "**heterosexism**," refers to "oppression of those of sexual orientations other than heterosexual" (Von Altendorf and Von Altendorf, 1991, p. 132). It has been noted that "this can be inadvertent, by not acknowledging the existence of those with different sexual preferences" (Adler et al., 1990, p. 54). While homophobia may simply involve prejudice against lesbians and gay men, heterosexism involves actual discrimination against them.

Because of the discrimination that lesbians and gay men experience in our society, many homosexuals choose not to publicly disclose their sexual orientation. Those who do so risk rejection from their families and friends. Nevertheless, many lesbians and gay men find that living in secrecy can create a great deal of psychological stress and loneliness. Believing that the benefits of living openly outweigh any risks involved, a growing number of homosexuals have chosen to "**come out**," meaning that they have publicly acknowledged their homosexual orientation (Geer et al., 1984).

It should be noted that even lesbians and gay men who are "out" may remain quite selective in choosing those individuals with whom they will share information about their sexual orientation. For example, a student living in a residence hall may choose to live openly as a gay man within the campus setting, while not disclosing his sexual orientation to his parents. It has been noted that "the decision regarding how open to be about one's sexual preference — whether to tell no one in the heterosexual community, to tell just one or two people, or to be completely open about it — is often a difficult one" (Geer et al., 1984, p. 286).

This decision is particularly difficult for lesbians and gay men in positions of leadership, because by openly acknowledging their homosexuality, they risk a loss of support from their followers. In fact, an individual could potentially lose his or her leadership position by making such a disclosure. It is not surprising, therefore, that many homosexuals in public life choose to maintain a great deal of privacy concerning their sexuality.

In recent years, many gay rights activists have become frustrated with the invisibility of lesbians and gay men in public life, maintaining that visibility is the key to greater societal acceptance. As Randy Shilts (1990), a prominent author who has written extensively on gay issues, explained recently:

> Because the vast majority of lesbians and gay men do not acknowledge their sexuality, a certain lie has been allowed to pervade society. This lie maintains that homosexuals are some fringe group colonizing Greenwich Village, San Francisco and West Hollywood, and that gays truly do not play a major role in American life. . . .
> If the truth about homosexuals were to emerge and Americans were to realize gays are among this country's most respectable citizens, antigay prejudice would rapidly evaporate (p. 166).

The frustration of those seeking to promote greater acceptance of homosexuality has given rise to a practice known as "**outing**," which involves publicly disclosing another person's homosexuality (Shilts, 1990). According to a recent *Newsweek* report on the subject, gay rights activists who engage in this practice maintain that bringing prominent homosexuals into the open will "swell the ranks of role models for young gays and help lift the curse of secrecy from homosexual life" (Gelman, Denworth, and Joseph, 1990, p. 66). However, this practice has not been universally endorsed, even among gay rights activists. One activist recently characterized outing as a form of "philosophical rape," saying "If we don't want policemen coming into our bedrooms, we have to safeguard other people's privacy too" (Gelman et al., 1990, p. 66).

Conquering Handicaps

The handicapped student who wishes to assume a position of leadership encounters a number of special obstacles, the most obvious of which is the handicapping condition itself. Although each student's disability is unique, five general categories of disabled students have been identified. Descriptions of these categories, according to their characteristic conditions, are as follows:

1. **Mobility impairments** — students who use crutches, canes, wheelchairs, or walk unaided but with difficulty;
2. **Visual impairments** — students who are partially sighted or blind;

3. **Hearing impairments** — students who are hearing impaired or deaf;

4. **Learning disability** — students with average or above average intellectual potential who have mild to severe difficulties in reading, calculating math, listening, writing, or relating socially; and

5. **Speech impairments** — students with articulation problems, esophageal speech, stuttering, or aphasia (Hameister, 1984, p. 67-68).

An additional challenge to handicapped student leaders comes from the attitudes of others toward them. Unlike other nondominant populations, the disabled rarely encounter feelings of hostility. In fact, Americans are generally quite sympathetic toward the handicapped. Nevertheless, popular images of the handicapped are confining because they cast the individual into the role of a "chronic patient," a role that is similar to that of a child. It has been noted that while all adults must occasionally assume the role of a patient, those who are labeled handicapped in our society are placed in "a specially destructive variant of the sick role" (Gliedman, 1979, p. 60), because they are not only viewed as sick but are also seen as being unable to overcome their sickness, and are therefore regarded as "doubly powerless" (Gliedman, 1979, p. 60).

Those whose handicaps are outwardly visible often face unique challenges in their social relationships from the moment of their first meeting with another person. In the process, those with whom they interact are also faced with unique obstacles.

Within our society, standards of propriety dictate that we interact with others in ways that convey an appreciation for the whole person, and that we not fix our attention on any single attribute of an individual (Davis, 1977). For example, if you were talking with a man who was somewhat shorter than average and began to comment at length on his height, he would almost assuredly become annoyed. Even if you were to direct similar attention to a woman's beautiful long hair, she might very well be at least mildly offended by your apparent failure to appreciate the totality of her being, regardless of how much attention she herself might devote to the care of her hair. Recognizing the likely response, most Americans avoid engaging in such behavior.

It has been noted, however, that "when meeting someone with a visible handicap, a number of perceptual and interpretive responses occur which make adherence to this rule tenuous for many" (Davis, 1977, p. 84). The nonhandicapped person often finds it nearly impossible to divert his or her attention away from the handicapping condition, yet in accordance with the unwritten rules that govern social interaction, he or she will usually avoid any direct reference to the condition. His or her discomfort will usually become apparent to the handicapped person, who in turn may not feel free to comment on this apparent uneasiness because of similar social standards governing his or her behavior. Consequently, social interaction between visibly handicapped and nonhandicapped individuals can often become quite strained (Davis, 1977).

Despite the challenges confronting the disabled in our society, it is possible for handicapped students to succeed as campus leaders. One of the key factors in the handicapped individual's success or failure as a leader is her or his own attitude toward the handicapping condition.

It is out of a desire for greater self-determination and a more positive self-image that the term **handicapper** has emerged. As noted in the literature (Gentile and Taylor, 1976):

> Handicapper is a term increasingly used by persons experiencing handicaps to assign to themselves the decision making power as to how their characteristics are to affect their lives. . . . These individuals are fully able and determined to define for themselves the degree to and manner in which their particular characteristics might enhance, direct, or limit their active "pursuit of happiness" (pp. 2-3).

Other Nondominant Campus Populations

In addition to those populations which have occupied nondominant roles within our society in general, several specific segments of the nation's student population have occupied similar roles on their campuses, despite the presence of White, heterosexual, able-bodied, American men within their ranks. We refer to these people as **nontraditional students** because they represent populations which have not been widely served by higher education historically. Specific nontraditional student populations include commuters, part-time students, and adult learners. These categories, of course, are not mutually exclusive. Many adult learners, for example, are enrolled in college on a part-time basis and live off campus.

Nontraditional students often face a variety of barriers which limit their ability to assume leadership roles on their campuses. Several challenges are particularly common in the experience of commuters, many of whom are also adult learners or part-time students. These concerns, as presented in recent literature, include the following:

- **Mobility Issues.** Moving between home, work, and school is demanding in terms of time, energy, and other resources. In order to function effectively, commuters must be extremely efficient in scheduling their time. . . . Busy schedules preclude the luxury of hanging out, meeting people, or taking advantage of other nonclassroom-centered opportunities that exist on campus. . . .

- **Multiple Life Roles.** For most commuters, being a student is only one of several important and demanding roles. In addition to academic pursuits, the student may be holding a job, caring for a child or other relative, and managing household responsibilities. With each additional role, the complexity of the commuter's life increases. Time becomes a commodity to be invested wisely. By necessity, involvements must be streamlined to include only those of greatest importance.

■ **Integrating Support Systems**. The entire support network for a commuting student generally exists outside the campus. Parents, spouses, children, employers, high school friends, coworkers, all may be significant sources of advice, encouragement, and reassurance. In order for them to continue to provide optimal support to the commuter, however, they must be integrated into the student's new world. Unfortunately, upon entering college many commuters experience a dissonance between their new and old worlds that is difficult to overcome. Each semester negotiations with family, employers, and friends are required to establish priorities, time commitments, and responsibilities. At a minimum, these negotiations themselves require time that cannot accordingly be invested on campus. In cases where the significant others are unfamiliar with the campus, its demands, and its opportunities, these negotiations can become even more complicated. Instead of receiving understanding and support for new roles on campus, the commuter may encounter the increased stress of needing to explain and justify them at home and at work.

■ **Developing a Sense of Belonging**. Involvement in campus life is closely related to the student developing a sense of belonging to, or connection with, the institution. For many commuters, multiple roles and commitments limit the amount of time they can invest on campus. Unfortunately, it is often assumed that the amount of time the commuter spends on campus is proportional to his or her desire to be a part of the campus community. Accordingly, commuters are characterized as apathetic and uninterested. All too often, institutions perpetuate a variety of roadblocks that inhibit the student's ability to develop a sense of belonging. The student receives a clear, albeit unintentional, message that the school and its staff are not invested in students who commute. For example, at the most fundamental level, some institutions fail to provide basic facilities such as lounges and lockers — which allow for a sense of ownership, a spot on campus that the commuters can call their own (Wilmes and Quade, 1986, pp. 26-28).

Poor communication concerning campus events appears to pose an additional obstacle to commuter student involvement. It has been noted that "because many commuters are not campus-oriented, . . . traditional media such as campus radio, newspapers, and posters do not appear to be effective vehicles of communication for commuters" (Jacoby and Girrell, 1981, p. 39).

For adult learners, a number of other unique barriers to campus involvement also exist. It has been noted, for example, that activities which are of interest to traditional aged students are not necessarily of interest to adult learners (Shriberg,

1984). In fact, because adult learners cover such a broad age range, many of their concerns are not even necessarily shared with one another (Richter-Antion, 1986).

Negative attitudes on the part of younger students, whether real or imagined, form another potential obstacle to adult learners' participation in leadership activities on campus. A recent survey of adult learners revealed that traditional aged students' attitudes toward them were a matter of common concern to older students (Rawlins, 1979). Another study, which dealt with traditional aged students' attitudes toward adult learners in a variety of situations, revealed that the younger students were generally accepting toward their older student colleagues in nonintimate settings, but were less receptive to social or intimate involvement with them (Peabody and Sedlacek, 1982).

Managing Diversity and Developing a Cultural Identity

As members of different populations attempt to live together in harmony, they will generally adopt one of three patterns of relating to one another. The first pattern, known as **amalgamation,** involves "the blending of two or more groups into a society which reflects the cultural and biological traits of the group" (Wallace and Wallace, 1985, p. 312). The second common pattern, **assimilation**, involves "adoption by the minority group of the majority group culture" (Wallace and Wallace, 1985, p. 312). Finally, there is the pattern known as **pluralism**, in which "various groups actively participate in the same society while retaining distinctive identities" (Wallace and Wallace, 1985, p. 312).

In recent years, pluralism has won growing favor in our society, particularly on college and university campuses. It is widely believed that in order for a truly pluralistic society to develop, each individual member must become aware of cultural differences, and on a personal level, develop a clearly defined **cultural identity**. This identity takes the form of an ongoing awareness of the individual's membership in culturally determined groups.

Drawing upon the previous work of several authors, Drs. W. Terrell Jones and Art Costantino (1988a, 1988b), have developed assessment instruments for gauging the progress of both majority and minority group members in the development of their identities. Both instruments identify stages through which the individual progresses in the development of her or his cultural identity.

The stages identified in association with the development of a **majority member identity** are as follows:

1. **Contact Stage**. At this stage, members of dominant populations begin to recognize members of nondominant populations for the first time. However, they do not see any importance in the differences between culturally defined groups.

2. **Disintegration Stage**. At this stage, the individual begins to recognize the social inequalities that exist between various groups. He or she begins to identify with the dominant group, and consequently may experience feelings of guilt.

3. **Reintegration Stage**. At this stage, the majority group member begins to blame members of nondominant populations for the inequalities that exist within our society. His or her attention is often diverted toward other social problems.

4. **Pseudo-independence Stage**. At this stage, members of dominant groups become more accepting toward minority group members, and develop some interest in examining cultural differences. They begin to associate more with members of nondominant populations, but are drawn primarily toward those minority group members who are seen as least different from them.

5. **Autonomy Stage**. At this final stage, the individual becomes knowledgeable about various culturally defined groups. He or she develops a greater appreciation for both majority and minority populations (Jones and Costantino, 1988a).

The stages identified by Drs. Jones and Costantino (1988b) in their assessment of **minority member identity** development are as follows:

1. **Pre-encounter Stage**. At this stage, the minority group member has limited awareness of differences between groups, and depends upon the majority group for her or his sense of personal worth.

2. **Encounter Stage**. This stage occurs when a significant event in the individual's life prompts openness to the establishment of a new identity. For example, an African-American student, who has never before interacted directly with White people, may be surprised to encounter hostility when she enrolls at a predominantly White college. This experience may lead her to reexamine the significance of racial differences for her personally.

3. **Emersion Stage**. This transitional stage is characterized by an abandonment of the old identity in favor of a new identity. Often, the majority group is viewed negatively while the minority group is idealized. Eventually, both groups are recognized as having both strengths and weaknesses.

4. **Internalization Stage**. At this final stage, the new identity stabilizes and is permanently embraced. The individual begins to again interact with the majority group, and attempts to bring about social change.

Promoting Diversity Within Your Organization

Given the changes which have already been observed in our society, and those which are expected to occur during the years ahead, it would seem advantageous for you to gain experience in working within a diverse student organization. However, if you are currently involved in an organization on your campus, there is a very good chance that most of its members are like you in many ways. Although colleges and universities are now enrolling increasingly diverse student bodies, most student organizations have remained fairly homogeneous. In order for this situation to change, student leaders will need to play an active role in promoting diversity within their groups.

At this point, you are probably thinking to yourself, "But we don't discriminate!" or "It's not our fault that nobody else wants to join our group!" Indeed, you probably do not engage in openly or even deliberately discriminatory practices. If you did, you would almost surely face institutional sanctions. There may even be a grain of truth to the notion that nobody else wants to join your group, but is it necessary for you to accept this condition as a given?

The fact of the matter is that, while formal barriers to diversity in student organizations have generally been eliminated, a number of informal barriers often remain. As a student leader, you can take deliberate measures to eliminate barriers to full participation in your organization, and actually promote diversity within its membership. The following are some questions that you might ask yourself as you go about the business of running your organization:

- *How do you get the word out about your organization's activities? In what publications do you advertise? If you use bulletin boards, where are they located?*
  If you advertise only in minority or majority student publications, it is unlikely that you are drawing full participation from an ethnically diverse population. Similarly, if all of your publicity is concentrated in the residence halls on your campus, there is a very good chance that you are bypassing interested commuters. Try to use a variety of communication channels in publicizing your events. Above all, do not rely exclusively on word-of-mouth advertising. It is guaranteed to kill diversity!

- *Where do you hold your meetings? What are the physical structures and functions of the buildings where meetings are held? Where are they located?*
  The manner in which the buildings are constructed can create barriers which are literally insurmountable for many handicappers. For other populations, the barriers which are created are often psychological, yet they can still have the effect of limiting diversity within an organization. Often commuter students feel excluded if meetings are held in residence halls. If meetings are held off-campus, you will want to pay attention to the extent to which

members of various racial and ethnic groups feel safe and welcome within the particular establishment or neighborhood.

- *When do you hold your meetings?*
  Make sure that you are not excluding interested students because of conflicts with other demands on their time, such as family commitments or religious practices. Try to find times when most students are on campus but not in class. Often, the noon hour works well, especially if you can arrange to meet over lunch. If you must have meetings at night, make sure that escorts are available if needed, since concerns about safety often prevent women from attending meetings after dark.

- *What kind of food do you serve, if any?*
  If you choose to serve food, you will want to make sure that people from different nations will find it palatable. You will also want to make sure that people of different religions will be permitted to eat it. You can generally accomplish both goals by providing a variety of items from which to choose.

- *What activities does your organization sponsor? Do they appeal to students from a variety of backgrounds?*
  When planning a dance, be sure to choose your music carefully, in order to appeal to students from different racial and ethnic groups. Again, variety is the key. Remember also that you can increase the likelihood of married students participating in an activity if they can make it a family event. Try to think of activities which will appeal to a broad age range.

- *What do you talk about in your group? What is your style of communication?*
  Often, students talk with their peers about cultural elements which are not familiar to students from other nations, age groups, or racial and ethnic groups. Avoid the assumption that everyone in your organization is equally conversant on a particular topic. Be prepared to share information with members of your group, and to learn from them as well. Remember also that language can create a cultural or generational barrier, particularly if slang is used excessively or inappropriately. Most people will welcome the opportunity to acquaint themselves with unfamiliar figures of speech, but all too often, the specific manner in which popular expressions are introduced in conversation has an exclusionary effect rather than drawing people closer together.

Summary

This chapter dealt with issues of diversity in leadership. Information was presented on the changing demographics of our nation and student population. The implications of these changes for current student leaders and future national leaders were then explored.

It was noted that Americans' views on issues of diversity vary widely. The issue of "political correctness" was introduced, and readers were encouraged to approach the material in this chapter with critical thought.

Some of the unique challenges facing women in leadership were examined. It was noted that women constitute a nondominant population because they have traditionally been denied access to political and organizational power. It was acknowledged that even today there appears to exist a "glass ceiling" in the hierarchies of many organizations, above which women cannot ordinarily rise.

The concepts of socialization and social roles were introduced. It was noted that women are often socialized into roles which are incompatible with that of a leader, creating a condition known as role conflict for women who assume leadership positions. Several recommendations were made for women aspiring to positions of leadership and for those seeking to promote leadership opportunities for women on their campuses.

The *Bem Sex-Role Inventory* was introduced. The instrument is based on an alternative model of masculinity and femininity, which incorporates the concept of androgyny, the condition of being both masculine and feminine.

The concepts of race and ethnicity were introduced, and the five primary racial and ethnic groups in the United States were identified. Minority groups were defined on the basis of their nondominant positions in our society. The concept of racism was introduced. Distinctions were drawn between the terms prejudice and discrimination, with the former referring to attitudes and the latter referring to behaviors. Several types of discrimination were examined, including individual discrimination, organizational discrimination, structural discrimination, and reverse discrimination. The concept of affirmative action was presented. Both the rationale for affirmative action programs and common objections to their implementation were explored.

Special considerations in dealing with international populations were examined, with attention to differences in the customs and values of various nations. It was noted that eastern and western cultures often differ in the importance that people place on "saving face," and the expectations that they hold concerning the exchange of favors and participation in decision-making. Contrasts were drawn between the pan-ethical and utilitarian orientations toward problem-solving, which prevail in China and North America respectively. It was also more generally noted that nations often differ in their customs concerning punctuality, business styles and relationships, gift giving, greetings, and the use of titles. It was further noted that gestures, colors, and numbers often carry different meanings in various nations.

The chapter also dealt with differences in sexual orientation. Three aspects of homosexuality were presented: (1) homosexual behavior, (2) homosexual attraction or desire, and (3) homosexual identity. It was noted that individuals vary in the extent to which they hold exclusive homosexual or heterosexual preferences. The "Kinsey Scale" was presented as a model for conceptualizing differences in sexual orientation. Various theories on the origins of homosexuality were examined, along with factors contributing to prejudice against lesbians and gay men. The terms "homophobia" and "heterosexism" were introduced in reference to anti-homosexual prejudice and discrimination respectively. The concept of "coming out" was examined, along with its involuntary counterpart "outing."

The unique challenges confronting handicapped students were also examined. Five categories of handicapping conditions were described: (1) mobility impairments, (2) visual impairments, (3) hearing impairments, (4) learning disability, and (5) speech impairments. It was noted that the handicapping condition itself is only one of the challenges facing the disabled student who aspires to a position of leadership. Social and psychological barriers which were examined included the response of the nonhandicapped toward those with visible handicaps and the treatment of the disabled as "chronic patients." The ability of handicapped individuals to conquer obstacles to their success as leaders was emphasized, and the term "handicapper" was introduced to symbolize this power of self-determination.

In this chapter, information was also presented on nondominant populations which are unique to higher education. The term "nontraditional students" was used in reference to those student populations which have not been widely represented on college and university campuses over the course of history. This category includes commuters, adult learners, and part-time students. Four categories of commuter student concerns were presented: (1) mobility issues, (2) multiple life roles, (3) integrating support systems, and (4) developing a sense of belonging. Poor communication was cited as a common barrier to commuter students' involvement in campus activities. Several other barriers to adult learners' involvement were also discussed. These barriers included differences between generations in their interests, and negative attitudes of younger students toward adult learners.

Three patterns of minority and majority relations were presented: (1) amalgamation, which involves a blending of cultures; (2) assimilation, which involves an abandonment of the minority culture; and (3) pluralism, which involves a peaceful coexistence of the minority and majority cultures. The growing popularity of pluralism was acknowledged. The concept of cultural identity was introduced and models of both majority and minority identity development were presented. The model of majority identity development incorporated five stages: (1) Contact, (2) Disintegration, (3) Reintegration, (4) Pseudo-independence, and (5) Autonomy. The model of minority identity development consisted of four stages:

(1) Pre-encounter, (2) Encounter, (3) Emersion, and (4) Internalization. The chapter closed with a series of recommendations for promoting diversity within individual student organizations.

References

Adams, J. and Yoder, J. D. (1985). *Effective Leadership for Women and Men.* Norwood, NJ: Ablex.

Adler, J.; Starr, M.; Chideya, F.; Wright, L.; Wingert, P.; Haac, L. (1990). Taking offense. *Newsweek, 116* (26), 48-54.

Bahls, J. E. (1991). Dissenting opinions. *Student Lawyer, 20* (1), 12-18.

Bahr, H. M.; Chadwick, B. A.; Stauss, J. H. (1979). *American Ethnicity.* Lexington, MA: D. C. Heath.

Bem, S. L (1977) *Bem Sex-Role Inventory.* Stanford, CA: S. L. Bem.

Bennett, S. M. and Shayner, J. A. (1988). The role of senior administrators in women's leadership development. In M. A. D. Sagaria (Ed.), *Empowering Women: Leadership Development Strategies on Campus.* New Directions for Student Services, n. 44.

Burkey, R. M. (1978). *Ethnic & Racial Groups.* Menlo Park, CA: Cummings.

Davis, F. (1977). Deviance disavowal: The management of strained interaction by the visibly handicapped. In J. Stubbins (Ed.), *Social and Psychological Aspects of Disability* (pp. 81-96). Baltimore: University Park Press.

Enrollment trends by race, 1978-88 (1990). *Chronicle of Higher Education, 36* (30), A36.

Geer, J.; Heiman, J.; Leitenberg, H. (1984). *Human Sexuality.* Englewood Cliffs, NJ: Prentice-Hall.

Gelman D.: Denworth, L.: Joseph, N. (1990). 'Outing': An unexpected assault on sexual privacy. *Newsweek, 115* (18), 66.

Gelman, D.; Foote, D.; Barrett, T.; Talbot, M. (1992). Born or bred? *Newsweek, 119* (8), 46-53.

Gentile, E. A. and Taylor, J. K. (1976). *Images, Words & Identity.* Unpublished Manuscript. Michigan State University Office of Handicapper Programs, East Lansing.

Gliedman, J. (1979). The wheelchair rebellion. *Psychology Today, 13* (3), 59-64, 99-101.

Glover, M. K. (1990). Do's & taboos: Cultural aspects of international business. *Business America, 111* (15), 26.

Hameister, B. G. (1984). Orienting disabled students. In M. L. Upcraft (Ed.), *Orienting Students to College* (pp. 6777). New Directions for Student Services, no. 25. San Francisco: Jossey-Bass.

Hammer, A. (1980). Cultural exchanges advance the cause of peace. *American Artist, 44* (453), 12.

Henry, W. A. (1990). Beyond the melting pot. *Time, 115* (15), 28-31.

Hermann, R. L. and Sutherland, L. P. (1991). *Federal Legal Directory,* Spring 1991 Supplement. Washington, DC: Federal Reports.

Holden, C. (1992). Twin study links genes to homosexuality. *Science, 255,* 33.

Jacoby, B. (1991). Today's students: Diverse needs require comprehensive responses. In T. K. Miller and R. B. Winston (Eds.), *Administration and Leadership in Student Affairs* (pp. 281-307). Muncie, IN: Accelerated Development.

Jacoby, B. and Girrell, K. W. (1981). A model for improving services and programs for commuter students. *NASPA Journal, 18* (3), 36-41.

Jones, W. T. and Costantino, A. (1988a). *Target Group Survey Majority Status.* Unpublished assessment instrument.

Jones, W. T. and Costantino, A. (1988b). *Target Group Survey Minority Status.* Unpublished assessment instrument.

Kinsey, A. C.; Pomeroy, W. B.; Martin, C. E. (1948). *Sexual Behavior in the Human Male.* Philadelphia: W. B. Saunders.

LeVay, S. (1991). A difference in hypothalamic structure between heterosexual and homosexual men. *Science, 253,* 1034-1037.

Lips, H. M. and Campbell, L. (1981). Images of power and powerlessness. In H. M. Lips, *Women, Men, & the Psychology of Power* (pp. 3-22). Englewood Cliffs, NJ: Prentice-Hall.

Morrison, A. M.; White, R. P.; Van Velsor, E.; and The Center for Creative Leadership (1987). *Breaking the Glass Ceiling.* Reading, MA: Addison-Wesley.

National Center for Education Statistics (1989). *The Condition of Education,* v. 2. Washington, DC: U.S. Department of Education, Office of Educational Research and Improvement.

Nelton, S. (1988). Meet your new work force. *Nation's Business, 76* (7), 14-17, 20-21.

New York State Department of Civil Service (1986). *Report on the Distribution of Protected Classes in the New York State Agency Work Force 1983-1984-1985.* Albany: New York State Department of Civil Service.

Peabody, S. A. and Sedlacek, W. E. (1982). Attitudes of younger university students toward older students. *Journal of College Student Personnel, 23* (2), 140-143.

Posner, R. A. (1992). *Sex and Reason.* Cambridge, MA: Harvard University Press.

Rawlins, M. E. (1979). Life made easier for the over-thirty undergrads. *Personnel and Guidance Journal, 58* (2), 139-143.

Reich, R. B. (March-April, 1991). Who is them? *Harvard Business Review.* 77-88.

Richter-Antion, D. (1986). Qualitative differences between adult and younger students. *NASPA Journal, 23* (3), 58-62.

Rothenberg, P. S. (Ed.) (1988). *Racism and Sexism.* New York: St. Martin's Press.

Schoenfeld, T. A. (1991). Biology and homosexuality. *Science, 254,* 630.

Shilts, R. (1990). Naming names. *Gentlemen's Quarterly, 60* (8), 160, 165-166.
Short, T. (1988). A "new racism" on campus? *Commentary, 86* (2), 46-50.

Shriberg, A. (1984). A self-audit: Preparing for the adult learner. *NASPA Journal, 21* (4), 24-27.

Sprandel, H. Z. and Schmidt, M. R. (Eds.) (1980). *Serving Handicapped Students.* New Directions for Student Services (No. 10). San Francisco: Jossey-Bass.

State Yellow Book (1992), *4* (1). New York: Monitor Publishing.

Steele, S. (1989). The recoloring of campus life. *Harper's, 278* (1665), 47-55.

Tifft, S. (1989). Bigots in the ivory tower. *Time, 133* (4), 56.

Totenberg, N. (1979). Discriminating to end discrimination. In D.R. Colburn and G.E. Pozzetta (Eds.), *America and the New Ethnicity* (pp. 212-225). Port Washington, NY: Kennikat Press.

Tse, D. K.; Lee, K.; Vertinsky, I.; and Wehrung, D. A. (October, 1988). Does culture matter? A cross-cultural study of executives' choice, decisiveness, and risk adjustment in international marketing. *Journal of Marketing, 52,* 81-95.

United States Commission on Civil Rights (1988). The problem: Discrimination. In P. S. Rothenberg (Ed.), *Racism and Sexism* (pp. 9-19). New York: St. Martin's Press.

Von Altendorf, A. and Von Altendorf, T. (1991). *ISMs: A Compendium of Concepts, Doctrines, Traits, & Beliefs from Ableism to Zygodactylism.* Memphis: Mustang.

Wallace, R. C. and Wallace, W. D. (1985). *Sociology.* Boston: Allyn and Bacon.

Weinberg, G. (1972). *Society and the Healthy Homosexual.* New York: St. Martin's Press.

Wiener, J. (1989). Racial hatred on campus. *The Nation, 248* (8), 260-262, 264.

Williams, W. E. (1989). Race, scholarship, and affirmative action. *National Review, 41* (8), 36-38.

Wilmes, M. B. and Quade, S. L. (1986). Perspectives on programming for commuters: Examples of good practice. *NASPA Journal, 24* (1), 25-35.

Activities

Getting It Straight

Respond to each of the following items by indicating whether the statement is true or false on the line provided.

_____ 1. It is anticipated that nonwhite racial and ethnic groups will constitute a numerical majority of our nation's population in the next century.

_____ 2. Currently, most American workers are White men.

_____ 3. Currently, most students enrolled in colleges and universities are under the age of 25 and live on campus.

_____ 4. Several cases of violence and harassment on college and university campuses have received national attention in recent years.

_____ 5. Prominent members of minority groups appear to be unanimous in their support for the manner in which colleges and universities have attempted to deal with issues of diversity.

_____ 6. Currently, women remain under represented at the highest levels of government and business.

_____ 7. The *Bem Sex-Role Inventory* treats masculinity and femininity as opposite ends of a single continuum.

_____ 8. Prejudice always involves a negative value judgment.

_____ 9. Today, it is almost universally believed that both majority and minority ethnic groups regularly engage in racist behavior.

_____ 10. Various nations of the world often differ from one another in their norms concerning punctuality, gift-giving, negotiation, greetings, use of titles, and the development of business relationships.

_____ 11. The specific meanings attached to almost all gestures, colors, and numbers are universal.

_____ 12. It has been estimated that 3 to 4% of all men and 1 to 2% of all women in the United States are exclusively homosexual in their orientation.

_____ 13. Scientists have not yet resolved the debate over whether homosexuality is primarily a result of "nature" or "nurture."

_____ 14. Prejudice against lesbians and gay men has been universally attributed to religion.

_____ 15. According to the "Kinsey Scale," people can all be divided into two distinct categories, homosexual and heterosexual.

_____ 16. In our society, it is generally expected that an individual not fix his or her attention on any single attribute of another person with whom he or she is interacting.

_____ 17. Interaction between visibly handicapped and nonhandicapped people is often strained because of the nonhandicapped person's difficulty in diverting attention away from the handicapping condition.

_____ 18. One potential obstacle to the advancement of handicapped individuals who aspire to leadership positions is their treatment as "chronic patients."

_____ 19. Nontraditional students often experience conflicting demands on their time and energy because of multiple life roles.

_____ 20. The time required for traveling to and from campus can sometimes pose an obstacle to commuter students' involvement in cocurricular activities.

_____ 21. Commuter students usually have little difficulty in building support systems on their campuses and almost always draw sufficient support from previously existing relationships.

_____ 22. Commuter students often experience difficulty in developing a sense of belonging on their campuses.

_____ 23. Poor communication about campus events can pose an obstacle to commuter students' participation in them.

_____ 24. Adult learners are rarely concerned about younger students' attitudes toward them, and in fact traditional aged students usually enjoy social interaction with older students.

After reading the following scenario, respond to each of the accompanying questions.

Erin and Janet are roommates who are enrolled in two different departments at their university. Erin is majoring in Women's Studies, and Janet is studying Mechanical Engineering. The two roommates often compare their experiences at the university and have found a number of differences between their academic departments.

In Erin's department, the entire faculty is composed of women and it always has been. The department has a female chair and more than 95% of the students enrolled are women.

In Janet's department, women account for less than 20% of the enrollment. There is currently one female faculty member in the department, and she has been engaged as a visiting professor. In the entire history of the department, only two other women have ever served on its faculty, and both of them were denied permanent appointments.

Faculty members in the two departments differ in both their political orientations and their treatment of political issues in their classes. In Janet's department, most members of the faculty are politically conservative, yet political issues are rarely discussed in class. In contrast, the faculty in Erin's department is overwhelmingly liberal, and professors frequently express their political views in class, as they believe political issues are central to any examination of the female experience.

1. Which of the two departments would be a more likely target for accusations of "political correctness?"
2. In which department would women be more likely to encounter a "glass ceiling?"
3. In which department would women be considered a nondominant population?

In the spaces provided, indicate whether each of the following characteristics reflects a person's sex (S) or gender role (G.).

_____ 1. Body shape
_____ 2. Clothing
_____ 3. Voice
_____ 4. Interests
_____ 5. Mannerisms

In the spaces below, list the five primary racial and ethnic groups in the United States.

1. _____
2. _____
3. _____
4. _____
5. _____

Respond to each of the following items by circling the correct response.

1. Which of the following is an example of socialization?
    a. A mother feeds her infant son.
    b. A mother ties a bow in her two-year-old daughter's hair.
    c. A father refuses to allow his thirteen-year-old son to have one of his ears pierced.
    d. All of the above
    e. a and b only
    f. b and c only

2. Which of the following is definitely a description of an androgynous person?
    a. Self-reliant, independent, athletic
    b. Yielding, affectionate, sympathetic
    c. Assertive, loyal, understanding
    d. All of the above
    e. a and b only
    f. a and c only

3. Which of the following is an example of an ethnic group?
    a. Italians
    b. Blonds
    c. Homosexuals
    d. All of the above
    e. a and b only
    f. a and c only

4. Which of the following is an example of a race?
    a. Canadians
    b. Blacks
    c. Handicappers
    d. All of the above
    e. a and b only
    f. b and c only

5. Which of the following is an example of a minority group in the United States?
    a. Caucasians (not of Hispanic origin)
    b. Blacks (not of Hispanic origin)
    c. Hispanics
    d. All of the above
    e. a and b only
    f. b and c only

6. Which of the following is an example of prejudice?
   a. An assumption that Jews are dishonest.
   b. An assumption that Asians are intelligent.
   c. An assumption that Blacks are athletically gifted.
   d. All of the above
   e. a and b only
   f. b and c only

7. Which of the following is an example of discrimination?
   a. The belief that most Irish Americans are alcoholics.
   b. The practice of refusing to rent housing to homosexuals.
   c. The practice of refusing to hire African Americans.
   d. All of the above
   e. a and c only
   f. b and c only

8. Which of the following is an example of reverse discrimination?
   a. A feminist speaker's refusal to entertain questions and comments from male audience members, while providing female audience members with a forum for asking questions and sharing opinions.
   b. A supervisor's assignment of menial tasks to women and placement of men in positions of authority.
   c. A professor's belief that Asian American students are more intelligent than their Caucasian peers.
   d. All of the above
   e. a and b only
   f. a and c only

9. The concept of homosexuality incorporates:
   a. Homosexual behavior
   b. Homosexual attraction or desire
   c. Homosexual identity
   d. All of the above
   e. a and b only
   f. a and c only

Match terms listed on the left with appropriate examples from the right hand column.

_____   1. Individual discrimination.

_____   2. Organizational discrimination.

_____   3. Structural discrimination.

_____   4. Affirmative action.

a. A policy which gives preferential treatment in admission to relatives of current members of an exclusively White club.

b. Over-representation of ethnic minorities at the lowest levels of the socioeconomic scale, which in turn limits opportunities for advancement.

c. An instructor's practice of soliciting comments only from male students.

d. A special admissions program and tutorial services for "at risk" minority students.

In the spaces provided, indicate whether the attitudes and beliefs presented are more characteristic of Chinese (C) or North American (A) cultures.

_____   1. Individuals should be willing to subordinate their personal interests to the welfare of the group.

_____   2. Personal pride is a major consideration in human interaction. The avoidance of shame, or loss of "face," is of great importance.

_____   3. While principles of fairness and balance are important, the exchange of favors does not create any long-term obligation between people.

_____   4. Subordinates should be involved in decision-making and a consensus should be reached.

_____   5. In problem solving, moral ideals must be placed above practical considerations.

Read the following scenarios and respond to the accompanying items by filling in the blank spaces.

A national restaurant chain that has come under attack for its policy of refusing to hire lesbians and gay men recently opened a new eatery adjacent to the college where Renee attends classes. Prior to its opening, Renee was hired to work at the restaurant on a part-time basis.

Although she believes the restaurant's practice of discriminating against homosexuals is fundamentally unjust, Renee sees many benefits in her new position. Believing the overall benefits of her job outweigh her moral objections to the company's hiring policies, Renee has chosen to continue working at the establishment.

Renee's decision has strained her relationship with her sister, Tina, who is a lesbian and a member of an organization that has spearheaded a boycott of the restaurant chain. Tina believes that moral ideals should always outweigh practical considerations in decision-making. On this basis, she has argued that Renee should refuse to work at the restaurant until the company abandons its discriminatory hiring practices.

Renee has experienced a great deal of stress as a result of her decision to continue working at the restaurant. As Tina's sister, she feels particularly compelled to speak out against discrimination on the basis of sexual orientation. However, as a member of the restaurant staff, she also feels obliged to support company policies.

One of Renee's coworkers, Tom, is a highly accomplished student athlete at the college. He is liked and respected by members of the college's faculty, staff, and student body. He has also received a great deal of attention in the local press and is looked upon as a hero by members of the surrounding community.

Tom considers himself homosexual and regularly engages in homosexual activity in his private life. However, in order to avoid losing his job, he has chosen not to reveal his sexual orientation to his supervisor or to his coworkers. Because he values his privacy, Tom has also refused to discuss any aspects of his personal life with newspaper reporters. Consequently, his sexual orientation is not widely known in the community.

Scott is a member of the activist organization to which Tina belongs. In the past, Scott had a very close relationship with Tom, and the two continue to travel in the same social circles. Scott is well aware of Tom's "double life," but has always kept this information private.

In recent months, Scott has grown increasingly frustrated with Tom's refusal to step forward and publicly acknowledge his sexual orientation. Convinced that such a disclosure would lead to greater acceptance of lesbians and gay men in the community, and add strength to the boycott against the restaurant, Scott has threatened to expose Tom's gay lifestyle unless Tom steps forward voluntarily.

1. Renee's approach to decision-making could be classified as _____, while Tina's approach would be considered _____.

2. The competing demands placed on Renee in her roles as Tina's sister and as an employee of the restaurant constitute a form of _____.

3. Most gay rights activists would probably view the restaurant's hiring policy as a form of "_____," and would probably use the term "_____" in reference to the philosophical basis for the policy.

4. Although Tom has adopted a homosexual lifestyle, he has not yet "_____ _____" to his supervisors and coworkers or to the general public.

5.   Scott has threatened Tom with a practice known as "_____."

The students on the first floor of a particular college residence hall experience a variety of disabilities. Cheryl has cerebral palsy and must use a wheelchair. Jason stutters, Beth's vision is limited, Janet is completely blind, and Keith is deaf in his left ear. Although she has above average intelligence, Karen has difficulty in reading. Unlike Karen, Janet, and Jason, who regard themselves as victims and feel enslaved by their disabilities, Cheryl, Beth, and Keith feel complete control over their own destinies.

1.   Cheryl's condition could be classified as a _____
_____.

2.   Jason's condition could be classified as a _____
_____.

3.   Beth's condition could he classified as a _____
_____.

4.   Keith's condition could he classified as a _____
_____.

5.   Karen's condition could be classified as a _____
_____.

6.   Janet's condition could be classified as a _____
_____.

7.   _____, _____, and _____
_____ could be classified as handicappers.

Match the terms in the left hand column with the appropriate examples in the right hand column.

_____   1. Pluralism
_____   2. Amalgamation
_____   3. Assimilation

a. A Mexican American man and an African American woman decide to marry and raise a family. They agree to instill in their children those values which are shared by the Mexican American and African American cultures.

b. Upon entering a predominantly White university, an African American student begins to dress differently, and adopts a hair style similar to that of her Caucasian friends. Although she prefers her former appearance, the student is please that she now "fits in better" in her new surroundings.

c. On an integrated college campus, a group of African American students has registered as a student organization with the goal of preserving African American culture in the cocurricular life of the institution. A group of Hispanic students has followed suit, in an effort to preserve its culture. The two organizations have worked cooperatively with one another on a variety of projects, but neither organization is interested in establishing a formal partnership, preferring instead to maintain two groups with distinct cultural identities.

Read the following paragraphs and respond to the accompanying items by filling in the blank spaces.

Bill, Alan, Andrew, Carl, and Anthony are all able-bodied, heterosexual, Caucasian males, yet they differ from one another in their attitudes toward both their own status as members of a dominant population and the problems confronting minority group members. Similarly, Stephen, Lee, Maria, and Jeanette are members of minority groups who differ from one another in their own cultural identities.

Bill is not particularly concerned about dealing with the problems of nondominant populations. He believes that members of minority groups are to blame for the conditions under which they live.

Although Alan is not particularly interested in dealing with minority issues, his indifference stems primarily from his lack of previous experience in dealing directly with members of minority groups. He is just now beginning to recognize cultural differences between people, but still sees little importance in these differences.

Until recently, Andrew's attitude toward minority group members was similar to Bill's attitude. Within the last year, however, he has become more accepting toward minority group members and more interested in their concerns. Nevertheless, he continues to associate primarily with those minority group members who seem most like him.

Carl has just recently begun to view himself as a member of a dominant population, and to recognize the social inequalities that exist between various groups in our society. Consequently, he has struggled with feelings of guilt.

In the past, Anthony has experienced feelings similar to all of those described thus far. However, today he is both interested in minority concerns and informed about various culturally defined groups. He has a strong appreciation for both majority and minority populations.

Stephen is very much aware of his status as a member of a minority group, and is proud of his membership in this group. He is very interested in minority issues, but feels some hostility toward the majority population.

Lee is also proud to be a member of a particular minority group, and is very interested in minority issues. Unlike Stephen, however, he has begun to overcome his feelings of hostility toward the majority population. He has begun to interact more frequently with majority group members, and to work through established processes to bring about social change.

Maria has very little knowledge of differences between people. She depends very much upon the majority group for her sense of self-worth.

Jeanette is just now beginning to view her minority status as a matter of importance in her life. In the past, she directed very little attention toward those characteristics which differentiate her from others. Recently, however, she enrolled in a sociology course dealing with minority issues. In addition to being intrigued by the subject matter of the course, she was inspired by the instructor who shared Jeanette's cultural background.

1. According to the model of majority member identity development presented in this chapter, Bill is at the _____ stage in the development of his majority member identity.

2. According to the model of majority member identity development presented in this chapter, Alan is at the _____ stage in the development of his majority member identity.

3. According to the model of majority member identity development presented in this chapter, Andrew is at the _____ stage in the development of his majority member identity.

4. According to the model of majority member identity development presented in this chapter, Carl is at the _____ stage in the development of his majority member identity.

5. According to the model of majority member identity development presented in this chapter, Anthony is at the _____ stage in the development of his majority member identity.

6. According to the model of minority member identity development presented in this chapter, Stephen is at the _____ stage in the development of his minority member identity.

7. According to the model of minority member identity development presented in this chapter, Lee is at the _____ stage in the development of his minority member identity.

8. According to the model of minority member identity development presented in this chapter, Maria is at the _____ stage in the development of her minority member identity.

9. According to the model of minority member identity development presented in this chapter, Jeanette is at the _____ stage in the development of her minority member identity.

Number the following stages of majority member identity development according to the sequence in which they occur, with 1 corresponding to the first stage of development and 5 corresponding to the last stage of development.

_____   1. Pseudo-independence stage

_____   2. Disintegration stage

_____   3. Autonomy stage

_____   4. Reintegration stage

_____   5. Contact stage

Number the following stages of minority member identity development according to the sequence in which they occur, with 1 corresponding to the first stage of development and 4 corresponding to the last stage of development.

_____   1. Internalization stage

_____   2. Encounter stage

_____   3. Pre-encounter stage

_____   4. Emersion stage

Both Sides of the Story

Prepare a defense for both the affirmative and negative positions on the following statements.

1. It is inappropriate for a college curriculum to focus on differences between groups of people. Rather, it should focus on what is common to all people.

2. Organizations with past histories of discrimination against certain groups should be required to adopt policies by which special consideration is given to members of these groups.

3. Lesbians and gay men should be given special legal protection similar to that which is given to women and members of racial and ethnic minority groups.

Sorting It Out

Respond to the following questions by taking a position and defending it.

1. On college and university campuses, is it more important that students be free to express their opinions or that they be protected against verbal abuse?
2. In organizational decision-making, should a higher priority be assigned to moral ideals or practical outcomes?
3. Which of the three patterns of majority and minority relations examined in this chapter is most desirable?

It's Your Call

Read each of the following scenarios and prepare an essay in response to the questions provided.

1. You are the lecture series coordinator for the programming board of the student government association at a private liberal arts college. As an institution, the college is committed to promoting an appreciation for cultural diversity. The political climate on campus is overwhelmingly liberal, particularly in matters of civil rights. Several months ago, you invited a prominent political scientist to speak on campus and he tentatively agreed to do so, though no written contract was signed. Recently, the speaker made headlines by publicly endorsing views which were widely regarded as racist. Among the faculty, staff, and students at the college, there has been mounting opposition to his appearance on campus. You have been urged by many to withdraw the invitation.

   a. What do you see as your alternative courses of action?

   b. What are the advantages and disadvantages of each course of action?

   c. Which course of action will you follow?

   d. Why have you chosen this course of action?

2. You find yourself in a situation similar to that described in the previous example. However, in this case, you are attending a private college that is affiliated with a rather conservative church. Most of the students belong to the particular church, and chose the institution largely because of its endorsement of their religious beliefs. The speaker whom you have invited is an ethicist who recently published a controversial article on the subject of homosexuality. The views which he presented were contrary to those espoused by the church with which the college is affiliated, and have since come under attack by many of the students and faculty at the college. Again, you have been urged to withdraw the invitation.

a. What do you see as your alternative courses of action?

b. What are the advantages and disadvantages of each course of action?

c. Which course of action will you follow?

d. Why have you chosen this course of action?

e. Does your course of action differ from the course of action chosen in the previous item? If so, how does it differ and how do you account for this difference?

3.   You are serving as a representative in your institution's student government association, which consists of both an executive council and representatives from all registered student organizations on the campus. The executive council consists of a president, vice-president, secretary, and treasurer. Historically, the executive council has been dominated by White men. Currently, all members of the executive council are White men, with the exception of one White woman who serves as secretary.

You are the voting delegate for an academic club that has been formed in your major department. Although most of the members of the faculty in your department are fairly liberal in their views on issues pertaining to women and minorities, the students in the department are generally more conservative. Approximately 80% of the students enrolled in the department are White men. However, women and ethnic minorities account for approximately half of the membership of the club.

There is currently a proposal before the voting delegates, which would amend the constitution of the student government association. Under this proposal, six new seats on the executive council would be designated for representatives from the Gay/Lesbian Alliance, the Women Students Association, and the four major ethnic minority student organizations on the campus.

Although you are under no obligation to confer with other members of the club or your department before casting your vote, you have solicited the opinions of a number of your constituents. It is your impression that the members of the faculty in your department favor the amendment, while the students in the department generally oppose its adoption. The students in your club appear to be evenly divided in their views on the matter.

a. What do you see as your alternative courses of action?

b. What are the advantages and disadvantages of each course of action?

c. Which course of action will you follow?

d. Why have you chosen this course of action?

Chapter 4

Theories of Leadership

This chapter will present a definition of leadership and will introduce the following related concepts:

- Management

- Formal and informal leadership

The chapter will raise the question, "Are leaders born or made?" Contrasting views on the subject will be presented.

The chapter will present three traditional categories of leadership theories. In the discussion, the following concepts will be introduced:

- Trait theories

- Behavior theories
  - Autocratic, democratic, and laissez-faire leadership
  - Theories X and Y
  - Ohio State leadership studies model
    - Consideration
    - Initiating structure
  - Likert's management systems
    - Exploitative authoritative
    - Benevolent authoritative
    - Consultative
    - Participative group

- Situational theories
  - Fiedler's contingency model
    - Task- and relationship-motivation
    - Situational favorableness
      - Leader-member relations
      - Task structure
      - Position power
    - *Least Preferred Coworker (LPC) Scale*
  - Vroom and Yetton normative model of participative leadership
  - Path-goal theory
    - Expectancy theory
      - Expectancy

- Valence
  - Directive leadership
  - Supportive leadership
  - Participative leadership
  - Achievement-oriented leadership
  - Contingency factors
- ➤ Hersey and Blanchard Situational Leadership model
  - Task and relationship behavior
    - Telling
    - Selling
    - Participating
    - Delegating.
  - Readiness
    - Ability
    - Willingness
  - *Leader Effectiveness and Adaptability Description (LEAD)*

This chapter will present the findings of several recent studies on successful organizations, and researchers' conclusions from these findings. The following topics will be discussed.

- Theory Z
  - ➤ Lifetime employment
  - ➤ Slow evaluation and promotion
  - ➤ Non-specialized career paths
  - ➤ Implicit control mechanisms.
  - ➤ Collective decision making
  - ➤ Collective values and responsibility
  - ➤ Holistic concern for people

- McKinsey 7-S Framework
  - ➤ Structure
  - ➤ Strategy
  - ➤ Staff
  - ➤ Style
  - ➤ Systems
  - ➤ Shared values
  - ➤ Skills

- Peters and Waterman's characteristics of successful organizations
  - Bias for action
  - Close to the customer
  - Autonomy and entrepreneurship
  - Productivity through people
  - Hands-on, value driven
  - Stick to the knitting
  - Simple form, lean staff
  - Simultaneous loose-tight properties
- Transformative leadership
- Bennis and Nanus's "strategies for taking charge."
  - Attention through vision
  - Meaning through communication
  - Trust through positioning
  - Deployment of self through positive self-regard and the "Wallenda factor."

This chapter will include a discussion of Bennis and Nanus's myths of leadership, which include the following:

- Leadership is a rare skill
- Leaders are born, not made
- Leaders are charismatic
- Leadership exists only at the top of an organization
- The leader controls, directs, prods, manipulates

═══Theories of Leadership═══

The theory of our modern technic shows that nothing is as practical as theory.

J. Robert Oppenheimer

Why Study Leadership Theory?

If you are like many undergraduate students, you are probably interested in learning practical skills. This is certainly understandable. When you graduate, you will undoubtedly be required to engage in "real world" activities. Sitting around all day thinking deep thoughts is certainly great work if you can find it, but a quick scan of the classifieds will not provide much encouragement to those contemplating such a career. Even in your personal life, there will be a point at which you will need to move toward action, especially if you hope to provide leadership for others.

Therefore, you may not see the need for studying leadership theory. However, in reality, the gulf between the theoretical and the practical is not nearly as wide as many imagine it to be. In fact, a sound theory is based on observations of "real world" phenomena, and can provide a basis for reasoned behavior.

Consider, for example, one of the oldest and simplest theories of human behavior, which we know as the proverb, "You can attract more flies with honey than you can with vinegar." Grandma was not talking off the top of her head when she observed that by treating people well, we increase the likelihood that they will treat us well in return. This pattern of behavior is so common, in fact, that you might very well have discovered it even had you been left entirely to your own devices. However, having benefitted from the wisdom gained through the previous observations of others, you have probably enjoyed more rewarding interpersonal relationships than you would have otherwise.

The body of leadership theory that now exists represents the collective wisdom of numerous generations of scholars who have studied the successes and failures of leaders in a wide variety of contexts, over the course of several centuries. Why not take advantage of the lessons that others before you have learned the hard way?

Of course, in studying the various theories, you will undoubtedly note some apparent contradictions between them. Furthermore, they will not all be equally consistent with your own experiences. Therefore, it is entirely likely that you will accept some of the theories, in whole or in part, while entirely rejecting others.

It is largely on this basis that you will eventually develop your own personal philosophy of leadership, which will in turn guide your behavior as a leader. Because your decisions will no longer be arbitrary, it is likely that you will become more satisfied with them. Your followers will probably also appreciate the predictability of your actions which will be guided by a coherent philosophy, rather than by momentary whims. Your group will be able to anticipate your response to various circumstances, and will act accordingly.

Defining Leadership

Over the years, leadership has been defined in a number of different ways. It has been noted, however, that nearly all of the definitions of leadership that have emerged over time have treated it as "a group phenomenon involving the interaction between two or more persons," in which "intentional influence is exerted by the leader over followers" (Yukl, 1989, p. 3).

The concept of **management** is related to leadership, and in common practice, the two terms are often used interchangeably. Technically, however, management is a more narrowly defined term. According to the literature (Klein and Ritti, 1984), "leadership is a characteristic of groups and can be studied at the level of individuals and groups apart from considerations of formal structure," whereas "management (or 'managership') is a characteristic of formal structure and must be studied at the structural level, although group considerations are relevant" (p. 78).

In our discussion, we will deal with both **formal** and **informal** leadership. Formal leaders are those who exert influence by virtue of their positions in organizations, while informal leaders are those who are not designated as organizational leaders yet exercise influence over others, primarily as a result of their own personal attributes.

One of the most obvious examples of a formal leader is the president of a student organization. The duties which are assigned to such an individual invariably require that she or he exercise influence over others. In order to fulfill these obligations, therefore, the individual must provide leadership.

Informal leaders are less easily identified, yet they exist in nearly all groups, particularly those groups which are most loosely defined. For example, in small groups of friends, there are no officers and no constitutional powers, yet it seems that certain individuals inevitably emerge as "key players," whose influence over others is undeniable. I am reminded of an anecdote that I once heard about a child who was dubbed the "Queen of Polk Street," because she could singlehandedly bring a game of tag to an immediate halt, simply by declaring that she was no longer interested in playing.

Stories such as this one raise an age-old question: "Are leaders born or made?" This question has intrigued scholars for generations and has provided the basis for much debate, which continues even to this day. Social scientists' interest in the process through which leaders emerge has led to extensive research on the topic, and the formulation of a wide variety of individual leadership theories. In examining these theories, you will note that our understanding of leadership has developed through a long evolutionary process.

Trait Theories

In the earliest studies of leadership, the notion that leaders are born was taken for granted. It was assumed that by identifying the characteristics of great leaders, we could better understand the type of person who could become a leader, and could potentially identify future leaders early in life. Acting on these assumptions, researchers began to focus on the personal traits which were shared by "great men," over the course of history. Interestingly, it has been noted that "despite Joan of Arc, Elizabeth I, and Catherine the Great, great women were ignored" (Stogdill and Bass, 1981, p. 27).

Beginning in the early part of the twentieth century, and continuing into the 1950's, researchers began to identify a number of traits which were believed to be inherently characteristic of effective leaders (Klein and Ritti, 1984). The leadership theories which stemmed from this early research have appropriately been labeled **trait theories.**

Despite their conformity to the conventional wisdom of their day, the trait theories were eventually challenged, in part due to the inconsistency between various researchers' findings on the specific traits which characterized effective leaders. By the early 1980's, it was noted that "after more than seventy years of research only three traits ranked consistently high on most lists: intelligence, initiative, and responsibility" (Klein and Ritti, 1984, p. 401).

An additional criticism of the trait theories relates to their underlying assumption that true leadership is invariably accompanied by social prominence. In the following excerpt from his book, *Leadership*, James MacGregor Burns' (1978) eloquently challenged this assumption:

> By far the most critical bias in the "great man" theory of leadership is neither cultural nor sexual. It is the assumption that "great men" *do* make history, that the causes of real, intended social change can be traced back to the purposes and decisions of the most visible actors on the political stage. . . . Most of us are captive to this general bias, if only as a result of the enormous focus on political celebrities in the mass media. For this reason, and because it is easier to look for heroes and scapegoats than

to probe for complex and obscure causal forces, some assume that the lives of the "greats" carry more clues to the understanding of society, history, and current events than the lives of the great mass of people, of the subleaders and the followers. The truth of this assumption as a general proposition has never been demonstrated (pp. 51-52).

Behavior Theories

A second group of leadership theories, the **behavior theories**, resulted from research focusing on the behavior of leaders rather than on their personal characteristics. By the middle of the twentieth century, this approach to the study of leadership began to grow in popularity, as it became increasingly clear that trait theories would remain essentially a matter of faith. The growing appeal of behavioral approaches to the study of leadership stemmed from the fact that, unlike traits, behaviors could be observed, and consequently lent themselves more readily to scientific examination (Owens, 1981).

Autocratic, Democratic, and Laissez-Faire Leadership.

During the early part of the twentieth century, a number of researchers (Bogardus, 1924; Lewin and Lippitt, 1938) began to draw contrasts between **authoritarian** or **autocratic leadership** and **democratic leadership**. The principal difference between these two styles of leadership can be observed in the extent to which group members are encouraged to play an active role in defining the goals of the group and in establishing policies and procedures for accomplishing these goals. While the authoritarian or autocratic leader attempts to independently make decisions affecting the group, the democratic leader tries instead to facilitate a process whereby group members can arrive at joint decisions.

By the middle of the century, a third category, **laissez-faire leadership**, had been introduced. The laissez-faire leader was described as one who stays removed from the activities of the group, providing followers with little or no direction (Bradford and Lippitt, 1945).

The relatively simple classification scheme described here has remained a popular model for conceptualizing leadership style. The influence of this early work will become evident in our discussion of more recently developed theories as well.

Theories X and Y

Douglas McGregor (1960) examined leadership behavior in relation to underlying assumptions about human nature. He identified two contrasting sets of assumptions which produce distinctly different leadership styles.

The first set of assumptions identified by McGregor (1960) is that embraced by the **Theory X** leader. Those who hold this view maintain that people are inherently lazy and in need of control in the workplace. Adherence to this doctrine produces a leadership style similar to the autocratic style described previously.

In sharp contrast to Theory X, Theory Y holds that people are capable of developing a strong desire to perform well in their work, but that poor working conditions can stifle an individual's potential for motivation. Acting upon these assumptions, Theory Y leaders tend to adopt a leadership style similar to the democratic style described previously.

The Ohio State Leadership Studies Model

A team of researchers at The Ohio State University (Fleishman, Harris, and Burtt, 1955) identified two broad categories of common leadership behaviors. The first category consists of those behaviors which relate to **consideration**. Behaviors in this category demonstrate the leader's concern for group members' interests and welfare. The second category of leadership behaviors includes those which involve **initiating structure**. This type of leadership behavior provides group members with a clearer understanding of the group's goals and the roles which they, as individuals, are expected to play in the accomplishment of these goals.

This model of leadership is different from the other behavioral models described thus far, because the two categories of behavior do not in themselves represent different leadership styles. There is no such thing as a "consideration leader" or an "initiating structure leader." Rather, leaders rate high or low on consideration, and they rate high or low on initiating structure. It is possible for a leader to rate high on both categories or low on both categories. It is also possible for him or her to rate high on one category and low on the other.

Likert's Management Systems

Rensis Likert (1961, 1967), a Professor at The University of Michigan, identified four "**management systems**," which were defined on the basis of a number of factors previously used to distinguish between autocratic and democratic leadership styles. However, rather than drawing a simple dichotomy between the two styles, the four management systems served as a continuum, representing varying levels of group member participation in the management process. The systems were numbered from 1 through 4, with System 1 being the most autocratic and System 4 being the most democratic. The descriptive labels given to Systems 1 through 4 respectively were: (1) **Exploitive authoritative**, (2) **Benevolent authoritative**, (3) **Consultative**, and (4) **Participative group**. The *Profile of Organizational Characteristics* is an assessment instrument which can be used for determining which of these labels most accurately describes an existing organization or the organization that a particular leader is trying to create.

Which Leadership Style Is Most Effective?

The behavior theories described here are quite useful for classifying the styles of individual leaders. As you looked over the descriptions of the various leadership styles, you probably recognized nearly all of them as accurate descriptions of leaders whom you have encountered in your own life. Furthermore, if you were to think back on your own experiences with individual leaders, you would surely be hard pressed to identify one who was not described here in some way.

What the behavior theorists have been less successful in accomplishing is the identification of a single most effective leadership style. As you think back on your own experiences, you will undoubtedly remember effective leaders who differed very much from one another in their styles of leadership.

For example, some of your favorite professors have probably been fairly autocratic in determining the content of their courses as well as their methods of instruction and evaluation. A professor who would enter the classroom and ask "What should we talk about today?," would undoubtedly be met with a response such as "You tell us. You're the teacher." In all probability, he would also earn a reputation for being a bit "flakey" (and undoubtedly with good reason!). On the other hand, if the president of a social organization were to adopt anything but a very democratic leadership style, she might very well encounter hostility in the other members of her group.

Just as the trait theorists failed to identify one set of characteristics that was common to all great leaders, so the behavior theorists failed to identify a single leadership style that was universally effective. These results suggest that neither traits nor behaviors in isolation can guarantee one's success as a leader.

Situational Theories

The third group of leadership theories that we will study, the **situational theories**, is more complex than either the trait or behavior theories. Rather than attempting to identify a single most effective leadership profile, the situational theorists conceded that radically different leadership styles can be equally effective in different organizational contexts. Acting upon this assumption, the situational theorists set out to clarify the nature of circumstantial influences on leadership.

Fiedler's Contingency Model

During the 1960's, Fred Fiedler (1967) introduced a situational theory of leadership, known as the **Contingency Model**. According to this theory, the effectiveness of a leader depends upon her or his leadership style and the "**favorableness**" of the situation. Fiedler (1967) defined favorableness as "the degree to which the situation enables the leader to exert influence over his [sic] group" (p. 13). Three factors contributing to situational favorableness are: (1) **leader-member relations**, defined as the extent to which "the leader is, or feels, accepted and supported by his or her members" (Fiedler, 1974, p. 67); (2) **task structure**, defined as the degree to which "the task is clearcut, programmed and structured as to goals, procedures and measurable progress and success" (Fiedler, 1974, p. 67); and (3) **position power**, defined as the level at which "the leader's position provides power to reward and punish and, thus, to obtain compliance from subordinates" (Fiedler, 1974, pp. 67-68).

According to the contingency model, an individual's primary leadership style can be described as either **relationship-motivated** or **task-motivated**. The relationship-motivated leader is one who "primarily seeks to maintain good interpersonal relationships with coworkers" (Fiedler, 1974, pp. 65-66). In contrast, the task-motivated leader "has as a major goal the accomplishment of some tangible evidence of his or her worth" (Fiedler, 1974, p. 66). He or she "gets satisfaction from the task itself and from knowing that he or she has done well" (Fiedler, 1974, p. 66).

The two types of leaders generally thrive under different circumstances. While relationship-motivated leaders tend to perform most effectively in moderately favorable situations, task-motivated leaders are generally more effective in situations that are either high or low in favorableness (Fiedler, 1974). The diagram below illustrates the relationship between leader effectiveness and the contributing factors of personal style and situational control.

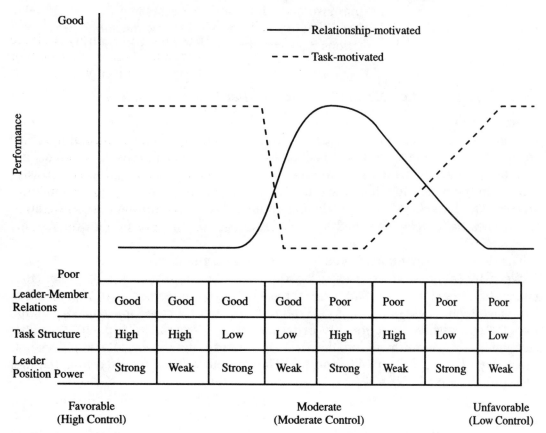

Leader-Member Relations	Good	Good	Good	Good	Poor	Poor	Poor	Poor
Task Structure	High	High	Low	Low	High	High	Low	Low
Leader Position Power	Strong	Weak	Strong	Weak	Strong	Weak	Strong	Weak

| Favorable (High Control) | Moderate (Moderate Control) | Unfavorable (Low Control) |

Reprinted courtesy of the University of Washington School of Business Administration, JOURNAL OF CONTEMPORARY BUSINESS, 3(4), 1974, F.E. Fiedler, "The Contingency Model—New Directions for Leadership Utilization."

The primary assessment instrument used for identifying an individual's leadership style, according to the Contingency Model, is a test known as the *Least Preferred Coworker (LPC) Scale*. The person completing the LPC is asked to describe the person with whom he or she would have the most difficulty working. The coworker can be described either favorably or unfavorably. Based on the person's ratings of his or her coworker, an overall score is obtained, which reveals the orientation of the test-taker. If the person is relationship-motivated, his or her LPC score will be high, because to such a person, no task is so important that it can overshadow the favorable characteristics of another person. In contrast, the task-motivated individual values work so highly that she or he finds it difficult to look favorably upon anyone who interferes with its completion. Consequently, the task-motivated individual obtains a low LPC score. Those who score between the extremes on the LPC are described as "socio-independent" and must identify their personal styles on the basis of information other than their LPC scores (Fiedler and Chemers, 1984).

A series of questionnaires has also been developed for assessing the individual's level of situational control. In addition to a composite score, the questionnaires yield ratings on leader-member relations, task structure, and position power (Fiedler and Chemers, 1984).

The Vroom and Yetton Normative Model of Participative Leadership

Victor Vroom and Philip Yetton (1975) developed a model for decision-making in groups which presents group leaders with five courses of action for dealing with group problems and five courses of action for dealing with individual problems. The various approaches, which are presented in the table on page 107, differ from one another in the extent to which they involve group members in the decision-making process. The letters used in the labeling codes reflect these differences. Individual approaches have been classified as autocratic (A), consultative (C), group (G), or delegative (D).

The Vroom and Yetton model provides a systematic approach for choosing between the alternative courses of action available. The system is based on the assumption that "there are at least three classes of outcomes that bear on the ultimate effectiveness of decisions" (Vroom, 1974, p. 49). These three considerations are: (1) "The quality or rationality of the decision" (Vroom, 1974, p. 49), (2) "The acceptance or commitment on the part of subordinates to execute the decision effectively (Vroom, 1974, p. 49), and (3) "The amount of time required to make the decision" (Vroom, 1974, p. 49).

Table 2.1. Decision Methods for Group and Individual Problems

Group Problems	Individual Problems
AI. You solve the problem or make the decision yourself, using information available to you at the time.	AI. You solve the problem or make the decision by yourself, using information available to you at the time.
AII. You obtain the necessary information from your subordinates, then decide the solution to the problem yourself. You may or may not tell your subordinates what the problem is in getting the information from them. The role played by your subordinates in making the decision is clearly one of providing the necessary information to you, rather than generating or evaluating alternative solutions.	AII. You obtain the necessary information from your subordinate, then decide on the solution to the problem yourself. You may or may not tell the subordinate what the problem is in getting the information from him. His [sic] role in making the decision is clearly one of providing the necessary information to you, rather than generating or evaluating alternative solutions.
CI. You share the problem with the relevant subordinates individually, getting their ideas and suggestions without bringing them together as a group. Then *you* make the decision which may or may not reflect your subordinates' influence.	CI. You share the problem with your subordinate, getting his [sic] ideas and suggestions. Then you make a decision, which may or may not reflect his influence.
CII. You share the problem with your subordinates as a group, obtaining their collective ideas and suggestions. Then you make the decision, which may or may not reflect your subordinates' influence.	GI. You share the problem with your subordinate, and together you analyze the problem and arrive at a mutually agreeable solution.
GII. You share the problem with your subordinates as a group. Together *you generate and evaluate alternatives and attempt to reach agreement (consensus) on a solution.* Your role is much like that of chairman. You do not try to influence the group to adopt "your" solution, and you are willing to accept and implement any solution which has the support of the entire group.	DI. You delegate the problem to your subordinate, providing him [sic] with any relevant information that you possess, but giving him responsibility for solving the problem by himself. You may or may not request him to tell you what solution he has reached.

From: Vroom, V.H. and Yetton, P.W. (1973). *Leadership and Decision-Making* (p. 13). Pittsburgh: University of Pittsburgh Press.

The authors articulated seven rules for decision-making, which balance the factors of quality and acceptance. In some instances, the rules provide several feasible courses of action. In choosing between these options, leaders may consider other factors, including time. The rules have been summarized as follows:

1.   When the decision is important and subordinates possess relevant information lacked by the leader, an autocratic decision (AI, AII) is not appropriate because an important decision would be made without all the relevant, available information.

2.   When decision quality is important and subordinates do not share the leader's concern for task goals, a group decision (GII) is not appropriate because these procedures would give too much influence over an important decision to uncooperative or even hostile persons.

3.   When decision quality is important, the decision problem is unstructured, and the leader does not possess the necessary information and expertise to make a good decision, then the decision should be made by interaction among the people who have the relevant information (GII).

4.   When decision acceptance is important and subordinates are unlikely to accept an autocratic decision, then an autocratic decision (AI, AII) is not appropriate because the decision may not be implemented effectively.

5.   When decision acceptance is important and subordinates are likely to disagree among themselves about the best solution to an important problem, autocratic procedures and individual consultation (AI, AII, CI) are not appropriate because they do not provide the opportunity to resolve differences through discussion and negotiation among subordinates and between subordinates and the leader.

6.   When decision quality is not important but acceptance is critical and unlikely to result from an autocratic decision, the only appropriate procedure is a group decision (GII) because acceptance is maximized without risking quality.

7.   When decision acceptance is important and not likely to result from an autocratic decision, and subordinates share the leader's task objectives, subordinates should be given equal partnership in the decision process (GII), because acceptance is maximized without risking quality (Yukl, 1989, pp. 114-115).

The decision tree presented on page 109 can be used for dealing with group problems. In using the chart, you will begin at the left hand side and will work toward the right. Each time that you encounter a square, you will respond to the question above the chart. Follow the path corresponding to your answers until you arrive at a stopping point, where a particular method of decision-making will be recommended.

Decision Model

Is there a quality requirement such that one solution is likely to be more rational than another?	Do I have sufficient information to make a high quality decision?	Is the problem structured?	Is acceptance of decision by subordinates critical to effective implementation?	Do subordinates share the organizational goals to be obtained in solving this problem?	Is conflict among subordinates likely in preferred solutions?
A	B	C	D	E	F

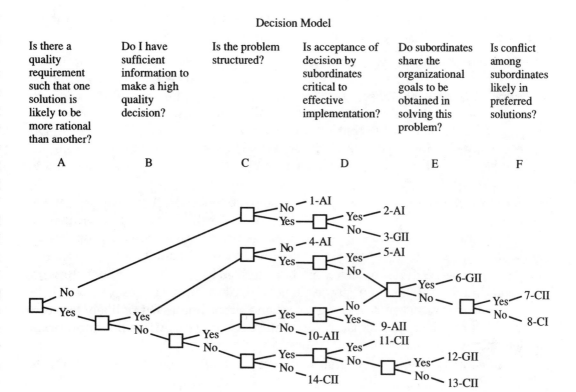

Reprinted courtesy of the University of Washington School of Business Administration, JOURNAL OF CONTEMPORARY BUSINESS, 3(4), 1974, V.H. Vroom, "Decision Making and the Leadership Process."

The Path-Goal Theory

The **path-goal theory** of leadership is based on a theory of motivation, known as **expectancy theory**. According to expectancy theory, a worker's job satisfaction and effort are influenced by two factors, **expectancy** and **valence**. Expectancy refers to the extent to which a worker believes that a particular course of action will lead to certain consequences. Valence refers to the extent to which the anticipated consequences are seen as desirable by the worker. According to the path-goal theory, "the motivational functions of the leader consist of increasing the number and kinds of personal payoffs to subordinates for work-goal attainment and making paths to these payoffs easier to travel by clarifying the paths, reducing road blocks and pitfalls and increasing the opportunities for personal satisfaction enroute" (House and Mitchell, 1974, p. 85).

Four specific kinds of leader behaviors have been examined in relation to these motivational functions. The four kinds of behavior are:

1. **Directive leadership,** which "is characterized by a leader who lets subordinates know what is expected of them, gives specific guidance as to what should be done and how it should be done, makes his or her part in the group understood, schedules work to be done, maintains definite standards of performance and asks that group members follow standard rules and regulations" (House and Mitchell, 1974, p. 83). Directive leadership is similar to the concept of "initiating structure," as presented in the Ohio State Leadership Studies Model.

2. **Supportive leadership,** which "is characterized by a friendly and approachable leader who shows concern for the status, well-being and needs of subordinates" (House and Mitchell, 1974, p. 83). You will notice a parallel between supportive leadership and the Ohio State Model's concept of "consideration."

3. **Participative leadership,** which "is characterized by a leader who consults with subordinates, solicits their suggestions, and takes these suggestions seriously into consideration before making a decision" (House and Mitchell, 1974, p. 83). You will recognize participative leadership as comparable to the "democratic" leadership style described previously.

4. **Achievement-oriented leadership,** which is manifested by a leader who "sets challenging goals, expects subordinates to perform at their highest level, continuously seeks improvement in performance *and* shows a high degree of confidence that the subordinates will assume responsibility, put forth effort and accomplish challenging goals" (House and Mitchell, 1974, p. 83).

The path-goal theory is considered a situational theory, because the influence of the leader's behavior on the attitudes and behaviors of followers depends upon two classes of **contingency factors**. The two categories are: (1) "personal characteristics of subordinates" (House and Mitchell, 1974, p. 85; and (2) "the environmental pressures and demands with which subordinates must cope in order to accomplish the work goals and to satisfy their needs" (House and Mitchell, 1974, p. 85).

It has been found that directive leadership can increase satisfaction among followers, when tasks are ambiguous or when followers have a personal tendency to respond unquestioningly to authority. Those followers whose natural tendency is to challenge authority generally respond negatively to directive leadership, when they are engaged in nonambiguous tasks (House and Mitchell, 1974).

The need for supportive leadership depends in part upon the inherent desirability of a particular task. If the task is not seen as naturally enjoyable, it is necessary that the leader engage more frequently in supportive behavior, in order to increase the satisfaction of the follower (House and Mitchell, 1974).

Participative leadership can have the effect of increasing both satisfaction and motivation when followers see the particular task or decision as a reflection on themselves, or when the demands which it places on them are ambiguous. When tasks are not ambiguous and are not seen as a reflection on the person performing them, followers who have a strong need for independence and self-control will respond favorably to participative leadership, while those who do not feel such a need will respond less favorably (House and Mitchell, 1974).

The need for achievement-oriented leadership is influenced by the ambiguity of the task. When tasks are not clearly defined, achievement-oriented leadership can have the effect of increasing followers' confidence that their efforts will lead to effective performance. When tasks are unambiguous, achievement-oriented leadership appears to have little influence on followers' expectations that improved performance will follow from increased effort (House and Mitchell, 1974).

The Hersey and Blanchard Situational Leadership Model

Paul Hersey and Kenneth Blanchard (1988) have developed a model of **Situational Leadership,** which enables leaders to respond to the varying and changing needs of their followers. According to this model, one's leadership style can be described in terms of two types of leadership behavior: (1) **task behavior** and (2) **relationship behavior.**

The authors defined task behavior as "the extent to which the leader engages in spelling out the duties and responsibilities of an individual or group" (Hersey and Blanchard, 1988, p. 172), adding that "these behaviors include telling people what to do, how to do it, when to do it, where to do it, and who is to do it" (p. 172). By now, this concept should be quite familiar to you, from earlier references to the leadership function of "initiating structure," in the Ohio State Leadership Studies Model.

Hersey and Blanchard (1988) defined "relationship behavior" as "the extent to which the leader engages in two-way or multi-way communication" (p. 172), and noted that "these behaviors include listening, facilitating, and supportive behaviors" (p. 172). Again, comparisons to the Ohio State Leadership Studies Model come to mind, with obvious similarities between the concepts of "relationship behavior" and "consideration."

The Hersey and Blanchard model is also similar to the Ohio State model insofar as the two types of leadership behavior are not seen as representative of two distinct leadership styles. Rather, they are presented as two separate dimensions, which in combination produce four basic leadership styles.

The four styles identified by Hersey and Blanchard (1988) have been described as follows:

Style 1   This leadership style is characterized by above-average amounts of task behavior and below average amounts of relationship behavior.

Style 2	This leadership style is characterized by above-average amounts of both task and relationship behavior.
Style 3	This style is characterized by above-average amounts of relationship behavior and below-average amounts of task behavior.
Style 4	This style is characterized by below-average amounts of both task behavior and relationship behavior (p. 173).

According to the Hersey and Blanchard (1988) model, it is possible for a leader to alter his or her leadership style in response to the demands of current circumstances. In determining the most appropriate leadership style for a particular situation, it is necessary to assess the "**readiness**" of the followers.

Readiness has two major components: (1) **ability**, defined as "the knowledge, experience, and skill that an individual or group brings to a particular task or activity" (Hersey and Blanchard, 1988, p. 175); and (2) **willingness**, defined as "the extent to which an individual or group has the confidence, commitment, and motivation to accomplish a specific task" (Hersey and Blanchard, 1988, p. 175).

Four distinct readiness levels were identified by Hersey and Blanchard (1988), and labeled R1 through R4. The greater the number used to identify the particular level, the greater the group or individual's readiness for the specified task.

According to Hersey and Blanchard (1988), when dealing with R1 followers, those who are both unable and unwilling or insecure, the most appropriate leadership style is Style 1. You will recall that Style 1 is the "High Task and Low Relationship" style. The authors used the word, "**telling**" to describe this leadership style, because the leader tells followers what to do and how to do it.

When working with R2 followers, those who are unable yet willing or confident, Hersey and Blanchard (1988) have recommended Style 2, the "High Task and High Relationship" leadership style. The word that the authors used to describe this leadership style is "**selling**," which they explained "is different from telling in that the leader is not only providing guidance but is also providing the opportunity for dialogue and clarification, in order to help the person 'buy in' psychologically to what the leader wants" (Hersey and Blanchard, 1988, p. 178).

The recommended leadership style for those dealing with followers at level R3 is Style 3. This "High Relationship and Low Task" style is particularly effective for motivating those who are able but unwilling or insecure. Hersey and Blanchard (1988) used the word, "**participating**," to describe this particular leadership style.

Style 4, the "Low Relationship and Low Task" leadership style, is recommended in situations where followers are at the highest level of readiness (R4), meaning that they are both able and willing or confident. "**Delegating**" is the word used to describe this leadership style, because it involves autonomous decision-making on the part of the followers (Hersey and Blanchard, 1988).

The material presented here is summarized in the figure below. The curved line across the chart represents the ways in which a leader must adapt his or her leadership style as followers develop greater readiness.

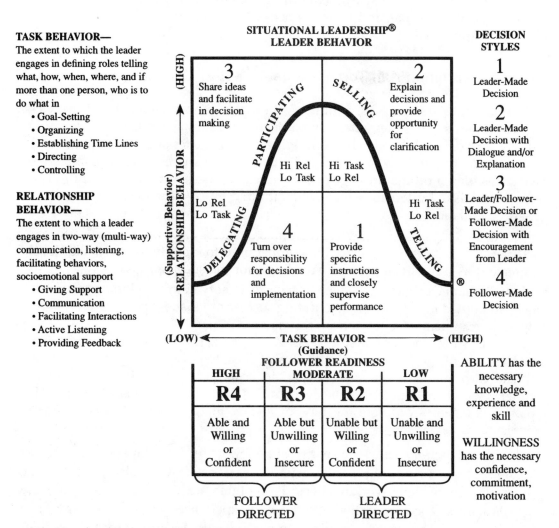

TASK BEHAVIOR—
The extent to which the leader engages in defining roles telling what, how, when, where, and if more than one person, who is to do what in
- Goal-Setting
- Organizing
- Establishing Time Lines
- Directing
- Controlling

RELATIONSHIP BEHAVIOR—
The extent to which a leader engages in two-way (multi-way) communication, listening, facilitating behaviors, socioemotional support
- Giving Support
- Communication
- Facilitating Interactions
- Active Listening
- Providing Feedback

SITUATIONAL LEADERSHIP®
LEADER BEHAVIOR

(HIGH)
(Supportive Behavior)
RELATIONSHIP BEHAVIOR

3
PARTICIPATING
Share ideas and facilitate in decision making
Hi Rel
Lo Task

2
SELLING
Explain decisions and provide opportunity for clarification
Hi Task
Lo Rel

4
DELEGATING
Lo Rel
Lo Task
Turn over responsibility for decisions and implementation

1
TELLING
Hi Task
Lo Rel
Provide specific instructions and closely supervise performance

(LOW) ◄——— **TASK BEHAVIOR** ———► (HIGH)
(Guidance)

DECISION STYLES

1
Leader-Made Decision

2
Leader-Made Decision with Dialogue and/or Explanation

3
Leader/Follower-Made Decision or Follower-Made Decision with Encouragement from Leader

4
Follower-Made Decision

FOLLOWER READINESS

HIGH	MODERATE		LOW
R4	**R3**	**R2**	**R1**
Able and Willing or Confident	Able but Unwilling or Insecure	Unable but Willing or Confident	Unable and Unwilling or Insecure

FOLLOWER DIRECTED   LEADER DIRECTED

ABILITY has the necessary knowledge, experience and skill

WILLINGNESS has the necessary confidence, commitment, motivation

When a Leader Behavior is used appropriately with its corresponding level of readiness, it is termed a High Probability Match. The following are descriptors that can be useful when using Situational Leadership for specific applications:

S1	S2	S3	S4
Telling	Selling	Participating	Delegating
Guiding	Explaining	Encouraging	Observing
Directing	Clarifying	Collaborating	Monitoring
Establishing	Persuading	Committing	Fulfilling

The authors have developed an assessment instrument, known as the *Leader Effectiveness and Adaptability Description (LEAD)* (Hersey and Blanchard, 1973), which is quite useful for those who wish to apply the Situational Leadership model to their own activities. The instrument can be used to identify those styles which are favored by an individual, and to assess her or his ability to adapt appropriately to various circumstances.

Learning From Today's Most Effective Organizations

During the 1970's and 80's, a number of experts on management and the social sciences began to focus their attention on the organizational context of leadership in today's world. Their research dealt with the characteristics of contemporary organizations that have been found to be particularly successful in accomplishing their goals. Based on the findings of their research, these authors have formulated several models of leadership which have captured much attention, even among the general population.

Theory Z

One of the most widely discussed contemporary models of leadership is one put forth by William Ouchi (1981), which he labeled **Theory Z**. In developing this model, Ouchi attempted to explain the astounding success of Japanese corporations, and to help American managers learn from this success.

In contrasting the Japanese "Type Z" organization with the bureaucratic organizations of the West, Ouchi (1981) explained that Type Z organizations "are intimate associations of people engaged in economic activity but tied together through a variety of bonds" (p. 70). He identified the following seven ways in which Japanese companies promote the type of loyalty that ultimately leads to greater organizational effectiveness:

1. *Lifetime employment.* As a matter of policy, many large Japanese companies hire promising young adults with a guarantee of employment for the remainder of their working lives. Promotions are made from within these companies. The corporations do not lure experienced employees away from other firms. This system provides employees with a sense of security in their jobs.

2. *Slow evaluation and promotion.* In many Japanese corporations, workers are not evaluated during the first ten years of their employment, nor are they treated differently from one another with regard to promotions and pay increases during this time. This system discourages new employees from

competing with one another and from engaging in activities which offer short-term benefits, but which have negative long-term consequences.

3. *Non-specialized career paths.* In Japanese companies, job rotation is common. Over the course of their careers, workers often hold a wide variety of positions throughout their organizations. Consequently, each employee develops a broad vision of the organization, and understands the relationship between its subunits.

4. *Implicit control mechanisms.* Whereas American companies often have clearly articulated policies for conducting business, and very specific performance objectives for various organizational units, their Japanese counterparts instill in their employees a broad corporate philosophy that provides direction for individual units. What is expected of Japanese workers is often implied, rather than stated in detail.

5. *Collective decision making.* In Japanese companies, decisions are often made through processes that involve input from those who will be directly affected by the decisions. The goal of such a process is to arrive at a state of consensus. According to Ouchi (1981), consensus has been reached in a group when a single course of action has been chosen and all members of the group can honestly say to one another: (1) "I believe that you understand my point of view" (p. 37); (2) "I believe that I understand your point of view" (p. 37); and (3) "Whether or not I prefer this decision, I will support it, because it was arrived at in an open and fair manner" (p. 37). Collective decision making has been praised for producing creative decisions, which are generally implemented quite effectively.

6. *Collective values and responsibility.* In Japanese companies, individual rewards and incentives are rarely given, because the workers do not see themselves as individually responsible for the success or failure of the group. This recognition of interdependence promotes cooperation between workers.

7. *Wholistic concern for people.* In Japanese companies, the social lives of employees are often integrated with their work lives. This pattern differs from that found in most American companies, where personal and professional concerns are generally kept separate from one another.

The McKinsey 7-S Framework

In a study of successful American companies, Thomas Peters and Robert Waterman, Jr. (1982, p. 9) identified seven factors which demand the attention of organizational leaders. These factors are: (1) "structure," (2) "strategy," (3) "people" (staff), (4) "management style," (5) "systems and procedures," (6) "guiding concepts and shared values (i.e., culture)," and (7) "present and hoped-for corporate strengths or skills." The authors incorporated these seven factors into a model, known as the **McKinsey 7-S Framework**.

In their research, Peters and Waterman (1982) also identified eight common characteristics of successful companies. The authors described these organizational attributes as follows:

1. *A bias for action*, for getting on with it. Even though these companies may be analytical in their approach to decision making, they are not paralyzed by that fact (as so many others seem to be). In many of these companies, the standard operating procedure is "Do it, fix it, try it." . . .

2. *Close to the customer*. These companies learn from the people they serve. . . . Many of the innovative companies got their best product ideas from customers. That comes from listening intently and regularly.

3. *Autonomy and entrepreneurship*. The innovative companies foster many leaders and many innovators throughout the organization. . . . They don't try to hold everyone on so short a rein that he [sic] can't be creative. They encourage practical risk taking, and support good tries. . . .

4. *Productivity through people*. The excellent companies treat the rank and file as the root source of quality and productivity gain. They do not foster we/they labor attitudes or regard capital investment as the fundamental source of efficiency improvement. . . .

5. *Hands-on, value driven*. Thomas Watson, Jr. [of IBM], said that "the basic philosophy of an organization has far more to do with its achievements than do technological or economic resources, organizational structure, innovation, and timing." Watson and [Hewlett Packard's] William Hewlett are legendary for walking the plant floors. . . .

6. *Stick to the knitting*. While there were a few exceptions, the odds for excellent performance seem strongly to favor those companies that stay reasonably close to businesses they know.

7. *Simple form, lean staff*. The underlying structural forms and systems in the excellent companies are elegantly simple. Top-level staffs are lean; it is not uncommon to find a corporate staff of fewer than 100 people running multi-billion-dollar enterprises.

8. *Simultaneous loose-tight properties*. The excellent companies are both centralized and decentralized. For the most part, as we have said, they have pushed autonomy down to the shop floor or product development team. On the other hand, they are fanatic centralists around a few core values they hold dear (pp. 13-15).

Bennis and Nanus's Strategies for Taking Charge

Warren Bennis and Burt Nanus (1985) studied leadership by interviewing a diverse group of leaders drawn from successful organizations in both the commercial and nonprofit sectors. Their study was based on "the belief that leadership is the pivotal force behind successful organizations and that to create vital and viable organizations, leadership is necessary to help organizations develop a new vision of what they can be, then mobilize the organization change toward the new vision" (pp. 2-3). The authors used the term "**transformative leadership**" in reference to the direction provided to an organization by "one who commits people to action, who converts followers into leaders, and who may convert leaders into agents of change" (p. 3).

They also identified four specific "strategies for taking charge." These strategies include the following:

1. *Attention through vision.* Successful leaders are able to craft a clear picture of desired organizational outcomes, which initially captures their own attention, and ultimately that of their followers.

2. *Meaning through communication.* In order for the leader's vision to become real for followers, he or she must be able to communicate it to them, either in words or in images.

3. *Trust through positioning.* The effective functioning of any organization requires trust. According to Bennis and Nanus (1985, p. 43), "trust implies accountability, predictability, reliability." Integrity is a fundamental characteristic of any healthy organization. Bennis and Nanus (1985) have maintained that such integrity can be established by "choosing a direction and staying with it" (p. 48).

4. *The deployment of self through positive self-regard and the Wallenda factor.* Bennis and Nanus (1985) found that interpersonal style was an important factor in successful leadership. While not appearing arrogant or self-centered, nearly all successful leaders demonstrate a favorable attitude toward themselves. This type of attitude can be developed by "recognizing strengths and compensating for weaknesses" (Bennis and Nanus, 1985, p. 58) and through "nurturing of skills with discipline" (Bennis and Nanus, 1985, p. 59). In addition to a positive self-regard, successful leaders often demonstrate an ability to keep their attention focused on success, rather than on failure. Bennis and Nanus (1985) referred to this characteristic as the "Wallenda factor," in honor of the great tightrope aerialist, Karl Wallenda, who demonstrated an extraordinary ability to maintain this type of positive focus.

Born or Made? The Debate Continues

Scholars engaged in the study of leadership remain intrigued by the question of whether leaders are born or made. Bennis and Nanus (1985) touched on this issue in their recent work, when they identified five common "myths" about leadership. The following is a list of those myths, along with the authors' rebuttals:

Myth 1. *Leadership is a rare skill.*

Nothing can be further from the truth. While *great* leaders may be as rare as great runners, great actors, or great painters, everyone has leadership potential, just as everyone has some ability at running, acting, and painting. While there seems to be a dearth of great leaders today, particularly in high political offices, there are literally millions of leadership roles throughout the country and they are all filled, many of them more than adequately.

More important, people may be leaders in one organization and have quite ordinary roles in another. . . .

The truth is that leadership opportunities are plentiful and within the reach of most people.

Myth 2. *Leaders are born, not made.*

Biographies of great leaders sometimes read as if they had entered the world with an extraordinary genetic endowment, that somehow their future leadership role was preordained. Don't believe it. The truth is that major capacities and competencies of leadership can be learned, and we are all educable, at least if the basic desire to learn is there and we do not suffer from serious learning disorders. Furthermore, whatever natural endowments we bring to the role of leadership, they *can* be enhanced; nurture is far more important than nature in determining who becomes a successful leader. . . .

Myth 3. *Leaders are charismatic.*

Some are, most aren't. . . . Our guess is . . . charisma is the result of effective leadership, not the other way around, and that those who are good at it are granted a certain amount of respect and even awe by their followers, which increases the bond of attraction between them.

Myth 4. *Leadership exists only at the top of an organization.*

We may have played into this myth unintentionally by focusing exclusively on top leadership. But it's obviously false. In fact, the larger the organization, the more leadership roles it is likely to have. . . . In fact, nowadays many large corporations are moving in the direction of creating more leadership roles through "intrapreneurship," the creation of small entrepreneurial units within the organization with the freedom and flexibility to operate virtually as small independent businesses. . . . As organizations learn more about this, there will almost certainly be a multiplication of the leadership roles available to employees.

Myth 5.   *The leader controls, directs, prods, manipulates.*

This is perhaps the most damaging myth of all. As we have stressed with monotonous regularity, leadership is not so much the exercise of power itself as the empowerment of others. Leaders are able to translate intentions into reality by aligning the energies of the organization behind an attractive goal (Bennis and Nanus, 1985, pp. 222-225).

Bennis and Nanus (1985) clearly challenged many of the beliefs surrounding leadership that have traditionally prevailed in our society. In contrast, Russell Palmer (1989), an experienced corporate executive and leadership educator, continued to draw upon images of great leaders of the past, in dealing with the question of whether or not leadership can be learned. According to Palmer (1989, p. 101):

Given the many personal attributes that combine to make one person a potential leader and not another — coupled with the peculiar circumstances and opportunities that can enhance leadership and bring it to the fore — it seems only logical to conclude that leadership is too intangible, too mysterious to be learned. After all, academic credentials had nothing to do with how Washington, a man of little formal education, rose to prominence. To assert that leadership can be learned, either in school or out of school, seems to cheapen the very idea of leadership.

Nevertheless, Palmer (1989) did recognize a value in leadership education because of its potential for promoting the development of skills in those who possess a natural talent for leadership. He also observed that "even for people whose leadership potential is modest or non-existent, the study of leadership is still worthwhile" (Palmer, 1989, p. 102), because of the influence that leadership has on the lives of all members of our society.

Summary

This chapter provided an overview of popular theories of leadership. The benefits of studying leadership theory were discussed, with an emphasis on the relationship between theory and practice.

Leadership was defined broadly, to include both formal and informal leadership roles. A contrast was drawn between leadership and the related concept of management, which deals only with formal organizational structures.

Several broad categories of leadership theories were presented, in the sequence in which they became prevalent. The first category is known as the trait theories, because it includes those theories which are built upon the assumption that specific personal characteristics, shared by all "great men," can be identified and used as a basis for recognizing leadership potential in individuals. Over time, it has become evident that strong leaders often differ dramatically from one another in nearly all other respects. Consequently, the trait theories have become less popular.

The second group of theories presented in this chapter is known as the behavior theories, because of their focus on common leadership behaviors. The first general behavioral model of leadership presented here was one that incorporates three styles of leadership behavior: (1) authoritarian or autocratic, (2) democratic, and (3) laissez-faire. It was noted that autocratic leaders tend to be very directive, whereas democratic leaders tend to be more facilitative, involving followers in the process of decision-making. The laissez-faire leadership style was presented as one characterized by a "hands off," nondirective approach.

Douglas McGregor's Theories X and Y were also discussed. It was noted that leaders subscribing to Theory X act on the assumption that people are inherently lazy and need to be coerced and controlled, whereas Theory Y leaders believe that people can develop a natural desire to perform well unless this desire is suppressed by environmental factors. Parallels were drawn between Theories X and Y and the autocratic and democratic leadership styles respectively.

The Ohio State Leadership Studies Model was also discussed in this chapter. This model identified two types of leadership behavior: (1) "consideration," which relates to the personal welfare of followers; and (2) "initiating structure," which involves the establishment of direction and order in the activities of the group. It was noted that the two types of behavior do not represent two separate leadership styles, and that leaders can show strong or weak tendencies toward either type of behavior without affecting their inclination toward the other.

Rensis Likert's four management systems were presented in this chapter. It was noted that the concepts of democratic and autocratic leadership were incorporated into Likert's model, though in the form of a continuum, rather than as a dichotomy. The labels used by Likert to identify the four systems were: (1) Exploitative authoritative, (2) Benevolent authoritative, (3) Consultative, and (4) Participative group.

The third category of leadership theories presented in this chapter is called the situational theories, because these theories are all based on the assumption that the most effective approach to leadership depends upon the specific context in which it is practiced. The first situational theory presented was Fred Fiedler's Contingency Model. This model deals with the relationship between leader effectiveness and the contributing factors of leadership style and the "favorableness" of the situation. Style was presented in terms of relationship vs. task motivation. "Favorableness," as used by Fiedler, referred to the degree to which the leader could control his or her organizational environment. Sources of control identified by Fiedler included: (1) "leader-member relations," (2) "task structure," and (3) "position power."

This chapter also contained information on the "normative model of participative leadership" developed by Victor Vroom and Philip Yetton. The model presents several specific courses of action for dealing with group or individual problems. The different approaches can be broadly categorized as autocratic, consultative, delegative, or group decision-making. The model provides a method of choosing a decision-making style on the basis of the anticipated quality of the decision, the likelihood of its being executed properly, and the time required to arrive at the decision.

The "path-goal" theory of leadership was also discussed in this chapter. This model is based on the "expectancy" theory of motivation, which holds that job satisfaction is influenced by two factors: (1) "expectancy," the perceived likelihood that certain consequences will follow from one's actions; and (2) "valence," the extent to which one values the expected outcomes. According to the path-goal theory, the role of the leader is to maximize both expectancy and valence. This can be accomplished through one or more of four different types of behavior: (1) directive leadership, (2) supportive leadership, (3) participative leadership, and (4) achievement-oriented leadership. The path-goal theory holds that the most effective approach to leadership in a particular situation depends upon the characteristics of the followers and the environmental factors that bear upon the achievement of their work goals and personal satisfaction.

This chapter included information on a model of "Situational Leadership" that was developed by Paul Hersey and Kenneth Blanchard. The model incorporates the concepts of task behavior and relationship behavior. According to Hersey and Blanchard, the proper balance between the two types of behavior depends upon the follower's "readiness" to perform the specified task. The concept of readiness incorporates both ability and willingness. Hersey and Blanchard identified four basic leadership styles. They used the terms "telling," "selling," "participating," and "delegating" to characterize the four different styles.

In addition to the three categories of general leadership theories identified thus far, this chapter included a review of more recent literature on leadership, which has been based largely on research dealing with the characteristics of highly effective contemporary organizations. William Ouchi's research on Japanese companies was cited. Ouchi's work provided the basis for a popular model of corporate leadership, known as "Theory Z." The factors that Ouchi identified as contributing to the success of Japanese corporations included: (1) lifetime employment, (2) slow evaluation and promotion, (3) non-specialized career paths, (4) implicit control mechanisms, (5) collective decision making, (6) collective values and responsibility, and (7) wholistic concern for people.

A similar study of successful American companies, by Peters and Waterman, produced a model known as the "McKinsey 7-S Framework." This model incorporates seven factors which must be considered by organizational leaders. These include: (1) structure, (2) strategy, (3) staff, (4) style, (5) systems, (6) shared values, and (7) skills. Based on their research, Peters and Waterman also identified the following characteristics of successful organizations: (1) "a bias for action," (2) "close to the customer," (3) "autonomy and entrepreneurship," (4) "productivity through people," (5) "hands-on, value driven," (6) "stick to the knitting," (7) "simple form, lean staff," and (8) "simultaneous loose-tight properties."

Similarly, Warren Bennis and Burt Nanus identified four "strategies for taking charge," based on their research involving successful nonprofit and business organizations. The four strategies are: (1) "attention through vision," (2) "meaning through communication, (3) "trust through positioning," and (4) "the deployment of self through positive self-regard and the Wallenda factor." Bennis and Nanus incorporated these strategies into a model of "transformative leadership," which involves the mobilization of others, and preparation of future leaders and change agents.

The chapter closed with a discussion of the ongoing debate over the roles of nature and nurture in the development of leaders. It was noted that Bennis and Nanus touched on this issue, in identifying five common myths about leadership. The five myths are: (1) "Leadership is a rare skill"; (2) "Leaders are born, not made"; (3) "Leaders are charismatic"; (4) "Leadership exists only at the top of an organization"; and (5) "The leader controls, directs, prods, manipulates." A dissenting view from Russell Palmer was also presented. Palmer maintained that a capacity to lead is an innate talent. Nevertheless, he saw a value in leadership education, because of its possible contributions to the development of leadership skills in those who are naturally gifted, and because of the importance of leadership in our society.

References

Bennis, W. and Nanus, B. (1985). *Leaders: The Strategies for Taking Charge.* New York: Harper & Row.

Bogardus, E. S. (1924). *Fundamentals of Social Psychology.* New York: Century.

Bradford, L. P. and Lippitt, R. (1945). Building a democratic work group. *Personnel,* 22 (3), 142-152.

Burns, J. M. (1978). *Leadership.* New York: Harper Colophon.

Fiedler, F. E. (1967). *A Theory of Leadership Effectiveness.* New York: McGraw-Hill.

Fiedler, F. E. (1974). The contingency model — New directions for leadership utilization. *Journal of Contemporary Business, 3* (4), 65-79.

Fleishman, E. A.; Harris, E. F.; Burtt, H. E. (1955). *Leadership and Supervision in Industry.* Columbus: The Ohio State University.

Hersey, P. and Blanchard, K. H. (1973). *Leader Effectiveness and Adaptability Description (LEAD).*

Hersey, P. and Blanchard, K. H. (1988). *Management of Organizational Behavior,* 5th ed. Englewood Cliffs, NJ: Prentice Hall.

House, R. J. and Mitchell, T. R. (1974). Path-goal theory of leadership. *Journal of Contemporary Business, 3* (4), 81-97.

Klein, S. M. and Ritti, R. R. (1984). *Understanding Organizational Behavior,* 2nd ed. Boston: Kent.

Lewin. K. and Lippitt, R. (1938). An experimental approach to the study of autocracy and democracy: A preliminary note. *Sociometry,* 1 (3, 4), 292-300.

McGregor, D. (1960). *The Human Side of Enterprise.* New York: McGraw-Hill.

Ouchi, W. G. (1981). Theory Z. Reading, MA: Addison-Wesley.

Palmer, R. (Fall, 1989). Can leadership be learned? *Business Today,* pp. 100-102.

Peters, T. J. and Waterman, R. H. (1982). *In Search of Excellence.* New York: Harper & Row.

Stogdill, R. M. and Bass, B. M. (1981). *Stogdill's Handbook of Leadership,* Revised and Expanded Edition. New York: The Free Press.

Vroom, V. H. and Yetton, P. W. (1975). *Leadership and Decision Making.* Pittsburgh: University of Pittsburgh Press.

Yukl, G. A. (1989). *Leadership in Organizations,* 2nd ed. Englewood Cliffs, NJ: Prentice-Hall.

Activities

Getting It Straight

Read the following paragraphs and respond to the items presented.

> Jeff, Tyler, Laura, and Erica are members of the Business Club on their campus. Jeff is the President and Laura is the Vice-President. Although Tyler serves in no official capacity, he is a highly influential member of the organization. Other members are often persuaded to adopt his positions on various issues because of his personal charisma. Erica is minimally involved in the Club. She rarely attends meetings, and most of the other members of the organization are not even aware that she is a member.

Based on the information presented here, list all members who have played the following roles in the organization:

1. Leader
2. Manager
3. Formal leader
4. Informal leader

> Professors Ott, Burke, and Smith have each conducted an independent research project on the nature of leadership. Each professor has developed her own leadership theory based on her findings. Professor Ott has observed that effective leaders are those who engage in frequent communication with their followers. Professor Burke has concluded that effective leaders tend to be Caucasian men who are taller than average. Professor Smith has concluded that effective leaders are those who supervise their followers closely until trust has been established, at which time they become less directly involved in overseeing their followers' activities.

1. Which of the professors has developed a trait theory of leadership?
2. Which of the professors has developed a behavior theory of leadership?
3. Which of the professors has developed a situational theory of leadership?

> Dwight, Mark, and Deanna are all student managers at the bookstore on their campus. However, they differ from one another in both their assumptions about human nature and the manner in which they interact with the other students who work at the store.
>
> Dwight assumes that people have an intrinsic desire to perform well in their work, but that their motivation can be reduced under poor working conditions. Dwight strives to motivate his subordinates by taking a personal interest in them, and working with them in making decisions.

Mark assumes that people are inherently lazy and will not perform their duties unless they are coerced. Mark attempts to control his subordinates with threats of punishment. Mark makes all decisions independently. He does not confer with the students who work under his supervision, because he does not trust them to consider the best interests of the organization.

Deanna's leadership style differs from those of Dwight and Mark. She does not interact directly with her subordinates on a regular basis, and allows them complete freedom to make most decisions without any involvement on her part.

1.   Which of the student managers is an autocratic leader?
2.   Which of the student managers is a democratic leader?
3.   Which of the student managers is a laissez-faire leader?
4.   Which of the student managers is a Theory X leader?
5.   Which of the student managers is a Theory Y leader?

Carol and Dawn are both officers of an environmentalist organization on their campus. Although both students enjoy their activities in the organization, their specific sources of satisfaction differ somewhat. Carol enjoys accomplishing the goals of the organization, and seeks tangible evidence of such accomplishment. Dawn enjoys her involvement in the organization because it provides her with an opportunity to interact with others. Recently, members of the organization spent two hours stuffing envelopes, much to the delight of both Carol and Dawn. Carol felt great satisfaction at the end of the meeting, when all of the packets were assembled. Dawn enjoyed the laughing and joking that accompanied the process of stuffing the envelopes.

Applying Fiedler's contingency model, Carol could be described as a _____-motivated leader, whereas Dawn would be described as a _____-motivated leader. Under moderately favorable conditions, we would expect _____ to perform more effectively. However, under extremely favorable or extremely unfavorable conditions, _____ would probably be the more effective leader. Of the two students, _____ _____ would probably score higher on the *Least Preferred Coworker (LPC) Scale*.

Dr. Richards is the Registrar at a college. Recently, she hired four new workers: Mrs. Randall, Mr. Berry, Dr. Stein, and Ms. Collins.

Mrs. Randall is a clerical worker who was recently transferred into Dr. Richards' office from another department in the college. Because of her familiarity with the institution, Mrs. Randall feels completely confident in her ability to perform well in her new job. She is also enthusiastic about working for Dr. Richards and wants to perform well. However, Dr. Richards has found that Mrs. Randall is not aware of some of the unique characteristics of the Registrar's Office that influence the manner in which common tasks are carried out there.

Mr. Berry is a recent high school graduate who is now taking classes at the college. Dr. Richards recently hired him to perform clerical duties in the Registrar's Office on a part-time basis. Mr. Berry has never been employed before, and is completely unfamiliar with the workings of a collegiate registrar's office. Consequently, he also lacks confidence in his ability to perform effectively in his new position.

Dr. Stein was hired to work for a limited time on a special project. He will be developing a new student information system for the college. Dr. Richards hired him because of his expertise in the development of computerized information systems. Dr. Stein has developed similar systems for a number of other colleges. He is completely confident in his ability to carry out his responsibilities in Dr. Richards' office, and he is looking forward to working on the project.

Ms. Collins has been hired as the new Assistant Registrar. She previously held a similar position at another college. Consequently, she has all of the knowledge and skills necessary to perform effectively in her new position. However, because she is still adjusting to her new work environment, she lacks confidence in her ability to succeed.

According to the Hersey and Blanchard situational leadership model, Dr. Richards should adopt a _____ task and _____ relationship style in supervising Mrs. Randall. Dr. Richards should adopt a _____ task and _____ relationship style in supervising Mr. Berry. In supervising Dr. Stein, she should adopt a _____ task and _____ relationship style. Finally, Dr. Richards should supervise Ms. Collins using a _____ task and _____ relationship style.

Identify each of the following as a trait theory (T), a behavior theory (B), or a situational theory (S).

_____   Fiedler's contingency model
_____   Likert's management systems model
_____   Theory X
_____   Theory Y
_____   Hersey and Blanchard situational leadership model
_____   Ohio State leadership studies model
_____   Vroom and Yetton normative model of participative leadership
_____   Path-goal theory

Identify each of the following behaviors as "initiating structure" (I) or "consideration" (C).

_____   Providing followers with a work schedule

_____   Posting a list of instructions for completing a task

_____   Sending flowers to a follower who has lost a close relative

_____   Answering followers' questions about a new policy

_____   Writing a letter of appreciation to a follower who has made an extraordinary contribution to the organization

Identify each of the following behaviors as "directive" (D), "supportive" (S), "participative" (P), or "achievement-oriented" (A) leadership.

_____   Asking a follower if something is bothering him

_____   Providing an experienced follower with new assignments which are not yet familiar to her

_____   Demonstrating to followers the proper technique for accomplishing a particular task

_____   Setting up a "suggestion box" to solicit recommendations from followers

_____   Evaluating the completed work of followers and pointing out ways that they can improve their work in the future

Identify each of the following behaviors as "task behavior" (T) or "relationship behavior" (R).

_____   Taking new members of an organization to lunch, in order to get acquainted with them

_____   Explaining to followers the timeline for completing a project

_____   Setting up a work area

_____   Facilitating a discussion between two followers, in order to resolve a conflict between them

Write the appropriate number for each of the following management systems, according to Likert's model

_____   Participative group

_____   Exploitive authoritative

_____   Benevolent authoritative

_____   Consultative

Place a check mark next to each of the following characteristics that applies to a Type Z organization

_____   Lifetime employment

_____   Early evaluation and rapid promotion

_____ Specialized career paths
_____ Explicit control mechanisms
_____ Collective decision making
_____ Collective values and responsibility
_____ Wholistic concern for people

Place a check mark next to each of the characteristics that Peters and Waterman included in their description of successful organizations.

_____ A bias for action
_____ Close to the customer
_____ Rigid control at all levels
_____ Capital investment as the fundamental source of efficiency improvement
_____ Hands-on, value driven
_____ Stick to the knitting
_____ Simple form, lean staff
_____ Simultaneous loose-tight properties

Place check marks next to all of the following that were presented by Bennis and Nanus as "strategies for taking charge."

_____ Attention through vision
_____ Meaning through communication
_____ Unpredictability
_____ Attention focused on both the possibility of success and the possibility of failure

Place check marks next to all of the following that were presented by Bennis and Nanus as *myths* about leadership.

_____ Leadership is a rare skill
_____ Leaders are made, not born
_____ Leaders are charismatic
_____ Leadership exists throughout an organization
_____ Leaders need not exert control over their followers

List the seven components of the McKinsey 7-S Framework.

1. _____
2. _____
3. _____

4. _____

5. _____

6. _____

7. _____

Complete the following items by circling the letter corresponding to the one best response.

1. According to Fiedler, which of the following contribute(s) to the "favorableness" of a leader's situation?

   a. Feeling accepted and supported by followers

   b. Having a loosely defined group task

   c. Having the power to reward and punish followers

   d. All of the above

   e. a and b only

   f. a and c only

   g. b and c only

2. According to Vroom and Yetton, which of the following bear(s) upon the effectiveness of a decision?

   a. The quality of the decision

   b. The extent to which the decision will be accepted by those who must implement it

   c. The amount of time required to arrive at the decision

   d. All of the above

   e. a and b only

   f. a and c only

   g. b and c only

3. According to Hersey and Blanchard, a follower's readiness to perform a task depends upon:

   a. the extent to which he or she possesses the knowledge and skills necessary to perform the task

   b. the extent to which he or she has the confidence and motivation to perform the task

   c. Both a and b

   d. Neither a nor b

4.   According to Bennis and Nanus, a transformative leader is one who:
a. commits people to action
b. converts followers to leaders
c. may convert leaders into agents of change
d. All of the above
e. a and b only
f. a and c only
g. b and c only

Match each leadership style with the appropriate descriptive term.

_____	1. High task, high relationship	a. Telling
_____	2. High task, low relationship	b. Participating
_____	3. Low task, high relationship	c. Delegating
_____	4. Low task, low relationship	d. Selling

Respond to the following items by indicating whether the statements are true or false.

_____   1. The path-goal theory of leadership is based on the expectancy theory of motivation.

_____   2. Expectancy refers to the extent to which the anticipated consequences of an action are valued by a worker.

_____   3. Valence refers to the extent to which a worker believes that certain consequences will follow from an action.

Both Sides of the Story

Prepare a defense for both the affirmative and negative positions on the following statements.

1.   The ability to lead others is an innate talent that cannot be taught.
2.   The emergence of a body of leadership theory has had very little impact upon the actual practice of leadership in our society.
3.   Trait theories of leadership are of little use to aspiring leaders, because of inconsistencies between the findings of different researchers.

Sorting It Out

Respond to the following questions by taking a position and defending it.

1.   Is it more important for students of leadership to master practical leadership skills or to develop a broad understanding of leadership theories?

2. Is an individual's effectiveness as a leader usually influenced more by external circumstances or by her or his personal characteristics?

3. Is it usually a more serious error for a leader to provide followers with too much or too little control?

It's Your Call

Read each of the following scenarios and prepare an essay in response to the questions provided.

1. You are a manager in the student union game room on your campus. The students whom you supervise vary in the length of time that they have worked there. They also differ in their knowledge of the organizational policies and procedures. Moreover, you have found that some of the student workers have faced unique circumstances in their personal lives that have had an impact on their work. Occasionally, you have made accommodations for individual differences that have resulted in apparent discrepancies in your treatment of different workers. Consequently, individual students who work in the game room have accused you of showing favoritism.

    a. What do you see as your alternative courses of action for the future?

    b. What are the advantages and disadvantages of each course of action?

    c. Which course of action will you follow?

    d. Why have you chosen this course of action?

2. Currently, you are living on a residence hall floor with approximately 20 other students. Although you hold no formal leadership position, you are a very influential member of the group. In fact, the other students on your floor are generally more supportive toward you than toward your Resident Assistant (R.A.). Recently, the R.A. announced his intent to resign with one more semester of service remaining. Because you were previously selected as an alternate R.A., you have been asked to assume the position on your residence hall floor once it becomes open.

    a. What are the advantages and disadvantages of accepting the appointment?

    b. What are the advantages and disadvantages of declining the appointment?

    c. Which course of action will you follow?

    d. Why have you chosen this course of action?

3. You are the President of the student government association on your campus, and are in the process of hiring a new secretary to work in your office. After reviewing all of the applications submitted to you, and interviewing those who appeared to be most qualified, you have narrowed your choices down to two applicants. Both applicants are well qualified in all respects. However, one of

the candidates has demonstrated stronger technical skills, while the other has demonstrated stronger interpersonal skills.

a. What do you see as your alternative courses of action?

b. What are the advantages and disadvantages of each course of action?

c. Which course of action will you choose?

d. Why have you chosen this course of action?

Communication

What You Will Learn in This Chapter

This chapter will introduce you to the following communication concepts:

- The communication process
  - Sender
  - Receiver
  - Messages
    - Content or cognitive component
    - Affective component
  - Channel
  - Encoding
  - Transmission
  - Decoding
  - Response
  - Noise
  - Effective and ineffective communication
  - Win/win communication

- Verbal communication
  - Speaking
  - Listening
    - Passive listening
    - Active listening
      - Minimal verbal responses
      - Open-ended questions
      - Clarification responses
      - Paraphrase
      - Reflection
      - Summarization
    - Leveling
    - Sharpening
    - Assimilation
  - Congruence
  - Empathy
  - Acceptance

- Nonverbal communication
  - Emblems
  - Illustrators
  - Regulators
  - Adaptors
  - Display rules or facial management techniques
    - Intensification
    - Deintensification
    - Neutralization
    - Masking
  - Vocal expression
    - Voice qualities
    - Vocal characteristics
    - Vocal qualifiers
    - Vocal segregates
  - Forms of touch
    - Functional-professional
    - Social-polite
    - Friendship-warmth
    - Love-intimacy
    - Sexual arousal
  - Distance zones
    - Intimate
    - Personal
    - Social
    - Public
  - Body orientation
    - Inclusive
    - Noninclusive
    - Vis-a-vis
    - Parallel
    - Congruent
    - Incongruent
- Communication style
  - Assertiveness
    - Assertive style
    - Nonassertive style
    - Aggressive style

- Passive aggressive style
- DESC script
- ➤ Immediacy
- Public speaking
  - ➤ Purposes of a speech
    - Speeches to inform
    - Speeches to persuade
    - Speeches to entertain
  - ➤ Patterns of discourse
    - Narrative
    - Process
    - Cause-effect
    - Analysis
    - Definition
    - Classification
  - ➤ Methods of delivery
    - Reading from a manuscript
    - Reciting from memory
    - Speaking impromptu
    - Speaking extemporaneously

Communication

Precision of communication is important, more important than ever, in our era of hair-trigger balances, when a false, or misunderstood word may create as much disaster as a sudden thoughtless act.

James Thurber

Why Is Communication Important?

As you attempt to work in groups, you will learn very quickly about the importance of effective communication. Unless members of an organization communicate effectively with one another, they cannot truly work together. While they may work in close proximity to one another, unless ideas and information are shared, their individual efforts will not produce an outcome in which they can all share a sense of ownership and pride.

Perhaps more importantly, unless group members communicate effectively with one another, a great deal of energy will undoubtedly be expended in duplicating the work of others. Consider, for example, the work that must be done when a yearbook staff decides to sell advertising. Direct contact must be made with a number of local business people, and often this is accomplished only after numerous attempts have been made. Unless effective communication is maintained between solicitors, a great deal of energy and time may be devoted to receiving a single answer numerous times. The owner of the local delicatessen, who declined to advertise when first approached, is unlikely to place an advertisement two weeks later, when approached by a different representative. Similarly, the florist who has already placed an advertisement is unlikely to take out additional advertising space, as a result of an additional solicitation.

In addition to reducing the amount of unnecessary work that is carried out within a group, effective communication can enable group members to learn important lessons from one another. For example, consider the work of a new student orientation planning committee. Each year, new students come to campus with a number of fears, anxieties, and special concerns, which may be addressed through the new student orientation program. While entering a college or university for the first time is always a brand new experience for individual students, the challenges that accompany this process have been known to countless other students who have passed through the campus gates before them. Consequently, numerous programming ideas for dealing with these concerns have been implemented over the years, with some of them being more effective than others. You might expect, therefore, that the work of the orientation committee would become easier each year, and that the quality of the program would simultaneously improve. After all, each new committee member would presumably benefit from the insights of more experienced members. Unfortunately, all too often, this type of sharing does not occur. Consequently, each year a sing-along may be planned, even though nobody ever sings. The same print shop may be commissioned to produce the schedule brochures, even though its product is always of substandard quality. The President's welcoming address may be scheduled for a half hour each year, even though he always speaks for at least an hour. Any of these problems could be alleviated through effective communication.

Clearly, effective communication can contribute greatly to both satisfaction and productivity within student or community groups. Regardless of the nature of your own organization or the specific position that you hold, by learning and applying several basic principles of communication, you can play an important role in improving both your own personal effectiveness, and the effectiveness of your group.

An Introduction to the Communication Process

According to Johnson and Johnson (1975), interpersonal communication involves a message that is sent from one person to another, with the sender consciously intending to influence the behavior of the receiver. If you have ever had the misfortune of falling asleep in class, you have probably also had the experience of receiving a strong message from your professor, with the clear intent of promoting alertness in you.

The message that is sent between two people consists of information that is conveyed as a symbol, which may be **verbal** or **nonverbal** (Johnson and Johnson, 1975). Verbal communication is built upon words, while nonverbal communication may include all other forms of communication. In our example, the information that your professor would convey to you would probably include the thought, "I would like for you to stay awake, and pay attention to what I am saying." She may even choose to say these exact words to you, thus conveying this information through the use of a verbal symbol. On the other hand, she may choose to employ a nonverbal symbol, such as a prolonged stare. Either approach could potentially convey the necessary information to you.

In addition to the message itself, effective communication depends upon the availability of a suitable **channel**, which serves as a vehicle for transmitting the message. Common channels of communication include both light and sound waves (Johnson and Johnson, 1975).

A message typically includes a **content** or **cognitive component**, which describes a situation or event, as well as an **affective** component, which expresses the sender's feelings toward the situation or event (Cormier and Cormier, 1979). In our example, the content of your professor's message may include the thought, "You have not been paying attention to what I am saying," while the affective component of her message may include the thought, "I am deeply offended by your behavior." Certainly you can appreciate the importance of understanding both components of her message!

While the content element of a message is generally expressed verbally, the affective component is often expressed nonverbally (Cormier and Cormier, 1979). In our example, your professor may have stated that you had not been paying attention, while maintaining a facial expression that conveyed her displeasure.

Interpersonal communication is a process that includes four basic steps. The first of these steps, **encoding**, occurs when the sender translates his or her ideas, feelings, and intentions into a message suitable for transmission (Johnson and Johnson, 1975). Sometimes, when we have difficulty in communicating, it is because we do not have a sufficient repertoire of symbols for conveying our thoughts. Consider, for example, the first time that you attempted to use a computer. In all probability, you were confronted with sounds and symbols that were entirely new to you, as you attempted to puzzle out your next step. If you sought the assistance of a technician, you might have been embarrassed to find that you simply could not translate your thoughts into a suitable message.

Nowhere does the encoding process become more complex than in the translation of affective information into symbols. Often we experience emotions in complicated patterns which seem to defy description. It is not surprising, therefore, that this portion of a message is often communicated entirely through nonverbal symbols.

The second step in the communication process is called **transmission**. It is during this step that the message is sent to the receiver (Johnson and Johnson, 1975). In our example, after struggling to find suitable terminology to describe your experience with the computer, you might have attempted to send your message to the computer technician, using your own terminology, such as "It went 'blip, blip, blip,'" or "A little round thingie flashed up on the screen."

During the next step in the communication process, known as **decoding**, the receiver interprets the meaning of the message, based on his or her perceptions (Johnson and Johnson, 1975). In our example, the computer technician might have recognized the sound or symbol that you described, based upon his own experience with the computer, which would in turn bring even greater meaning to it.

The final step in the communication process is one which we will call **response**. During this step, the receiver reacts internally to the perceived meaning of the message, and behaves accordingly (Johnson and Johnson, 1975). In our example, if you were fortunate, the computer technician responded with sympathy, and provided you with the information that you needed.

Effective communication takes place when the receiver interprets the message as intended by the sender (Johnson and Johnson, 1975). In contrast, ineffective communication occurs when the receiver's interpretation of the message differs from the sender's original thought. For example, consider the dialogue that occurs between the driver and the navigator, when you and your friends go on a "road trip." At some time during the trip, it would not be unusual for you to approach a fork in the road, at which point, your driver might say "I turn left up here, don't I?" Your navigator might then respond affirmatively by saying "Right!" If the communication process is effective, your driver would then know that he should turn left. If however the communication process is ineffective, he might interpret the navigator's reply as an instruction to turn right, rather than an affirmation of his original intent to turn left.

Barriers to Effective Communication

The communication process can be inhibited by a number of obstacles within the sender, the receiver, or the channel. These interfering factors are called **noise**. Noise within the sender may include her or his frame of reference, attitudes, and prejudices, or the appropriateness of her or his language or other form of expression. Noise within the receiver may include attitudes, beliefs, background, and experiences which influence the decoding process. Noise within the channel may include environmental sounds, patterns of speech, or distracting mannerisms (Johnson and Johnson, 1975).

One common contributer to distortion is the tendency, on the part of receivers, to simplify messages so that the information received conforms to their own interests, tasks, experiences, and frames of reference. This type of distortion can involve three basic psychological processes: **leveling**, **sharpening**, and **assimilation** (Johnson and Johnson, 1975).

Leveling refers to the tendency to reduce the amount of information received, through the elimination of details (Johnson and Johnson, 1975). For example, suppose a university were to implement a new policy for remuneration of Resident Assistants, whereby paychecks would no longer be issued but room and board fees would be waived at registration. Through leveling, the information may be reduced to include only the fact that the institutional policy was being changed, without any attention to the specific ways in which it was being changed.

Sharpening also involves a reduction of the information received. However, when sharpening occurs, certain key elements of a message are made dominant. Often, these selected details are remembered and emphasized, while others are forgotten or ignored (Johnson and Johnson, 1975). In our example, a particularly optimistic student might simply focus on the fact that room and board fees will be waived for R.A.'s, while a more pessimistic student may concentrate only on the fact that R.A.'s will no longer be paid!

Assimilation refers to the receiver's tendency to incorporate information into his or her own frame of reference. Messages are thus interpreted based on the beliefs, attitudes, and experiences of the receiver, rather than on those of the sender (Johnson and Johnson, 1975). In our example, a student who believes that the university administration is distrustful of students may assume that the new policy is designed to ensure that R.A.'s will not mismanage their finances and fall behind on their fee installments. In reality, the policy may simply reflect efforts to streamline the payroll and billing processes.

According to Zuker (1983), fear can also be a barrier to effective communication. Individuals are sometimes reluctant to express their thoughts clearly, because they fear that their ideas will be rejected by others. Fear is a particularly common barrier to effective communication in relationships, such as that of a student and instructor, where a definite power imbalance exists, or in relationships where there is the perception of a power imbalance. Within organizations, those who hold a minority opinion often feel inhibited in expressing their views.

Additionally, **avoidance** of feelings can be a barrier to effective communication (Zuker, 1983). For example, a woman who feels angry toward one of her sorority sisters may deny her feelings, because she believes that it is wrong for a member of a sorority to feel this way. Denial of one's feelings or those of others can result in physical symptoms and indirect expressions which prevent the development and maintenance of satisfactory interpersonal relationships (Zuker, 1983).

Defensive behaviors can interfere with communication as well. These behaviors occur as a response to a perceived psychological threat. While defensive emotions can serve a constructive purpose, by alerting us to possible problems in the communication of others, they can also become destructive if they begin to totally control our responses. Defensiveness can be generated by either the sender or receiver of a message. Some speakers communicate in a tone that is prescriptive, parental, and evaluative, and thus contributes to defensiveness in others. On the other hand, some listeners perceive personal assaults in statements and inquiries that are actually neutral (Zuker, 1983).

Gordon (1970) identified twelve specific types of behavior which, in many situations, can act as roadblocks to effective communication. These behaviors include:

1. Ordering, directing, commanding
2. Warning, admonishing, threatening
3. Exhorting, moralizing, preaching
4. Advising, giving solutions or suggestions
5. Lecturing, teaching, giving logical arguments
6. Judging, criticizing, disagreeing, blaming
7. Praising, agreeing
8. Name-calling, ridiculing, shaming
9. Interpreting, analyzing, diagnosing
10. Reassuring, sympathizing, consoling, supporting
11. Probing, questioning, interrogating
12. Withdrawing, distracting, humoring, diverting (pp. 41-42)

Win/Win Communication

In contrast, Zuker (1983) described a particularly effective type of communication, known as **win/win communication**. This form of communication involves working cooperatively toward a goal that enables two or more parties to achieve their desired outcomes. For example, if a feminist student organization and a minority student organization both wish to use the same facility for guest lectures on a given night, communication between the organizations could result in a solution that would be satisfactory for both student organizations, provided that representatives from both organizations would approach the communication process with a commitment to ensuring that the other organization would achieve its desired outcomes. Members of each organization must also be willing to change their goals, if necessary, to avoid a win/lose situation. If members of both organizations are unyielding in their commitment to inviting specific speakers to a specific facility on a specific night, it is unlikely that win/win communication will occur. If, however, both organizations define the essential purposes of their programs and attempt to reconcile their desired outcomes, a satisfactory solution can probably be achieved by both groups. For example, the organizations might consider pooling their resources, in order to invite a more prominent speaker who would integrate both a minority perspective and a feminist perspective into a presentation on broader issues of social justice.

Zuker (1983) identified several components of successful communication, one of which is known as **congruence**. Congruence refers to authentic communication, where verbal and nonverbal messages are consistent with internal feelings. In our earlier example, the woman who was experiencing feelings of hostility toward her sorority sister would not be acting congruently if she were to smile and talk about the feelings of affection that are shared among all members of a sorority. If she were to scowl at her adversary while speaking of sisterly love, her verbal and nonverbal signals would not even be consistent with each other.

The second component of successful communication identified by Zuker (1983) is known as **empathy.** This term refers to the "capacity and willingness to understand the inner experience of another person" (p. 93). This involves more than simply "putting yourself in someone else's shoes" and thinking about how you would feel. Rather, it involves actually understanding how the other person does feel in response to her or his circumstances.

According to Zuker (1983), successful communication is also characterized by **acceptance**, meaning an "unconditional positive regard" (p. 94) for another person. An accepting person is able to feel favorably toward another person, even if he or she does not personally agree with the beliefs and statements of the other person.

Wycoff (1981) presented four additional principles or "laws" of communication:

1. For every communication action, there will be some internal receiver reaction.
2. One person's thoughts are attracted to another person's thoughts with a force directly proportionate to the similarity of their experience.
3. In order for you to have others see things your way, you must first see things their way.
4. The clarity of your communication is dependent on your willingness to dramatize the important points of your message.

In addition to the general principles presented here, certain specific behaviors on the part of both senders and receivers of messages can promote effective communication. In order to become a facilitator of effective communication within your organization, it is essential that you develop skills in both of these areas.

Sending a Message

As a sender of messages, there are several principles which you can follow, in order to ensure that your thoughts will be correctly understood by the receiver of your message. Johnson and Johnson (1975) offered the following specific guidelines for sending messages to other members of your group:

1. Clearly "own" your messages by using personal pronouns such as I and my.
2. Make your messages complete and specific.
3. Make your verbal and nonverbal messages congruent with each other.
4. Be redundant . . . [Repeat] your messages more than once, using different channels of communication.

5. Ask for feedback concerning the way your messages are being received.

6. Make the message appropriate to the receiver's frame of reference.

7. Describe your feelings by name, action, or figure of speech.

8. Describe other members' behavior without evaluating or interpreting (pp. 114-115).

Receiving a Message

Effective communication can also be facilitated through specific receiver behaviors. According to Abrams (1986), listening can take place with varying degrees of involvement. The lowest level of listening is known as **passive listening.** This type of behavior requires minimal concentration and no feedback. In contrast, **active listening** requires more energy on the part of the listener. It requires that he or she exhibit certain visible behaviors.

These behaviors may include **minimal verbal responses,** such as "I see" and "yes." Such responses indicate that the listener is following what the speaker is saying (Okun, 1976). Similarly, the listener may use nonverbal behaviors to indicate that she or he is truly listening (Cormier and Cormier, 1979). Later in this chapter, the use of nonverbal communication will be explored in greater detail.

Communication can also be facilitated through the use of **open-ended questions.** Unlike closed questions, which can frequently be answered in one or two words (e.g., "yes" or "no"), open-ended questions elicit elaboration. They allow speakers to express themselves, without categories and values imposed on them by listeners (Cormier and Cormier, 1979). For example, if a member of a programming organization were to ask a friend of hers a closed question, such as "Did you enjoy the mime's performance last night?," her friend could easily respond by simply saying "No." This reply would provide only very limited feedback on the program. If, on the other hand, she were to ask an open-ended question, such as "What did you think of the mime's performance last night?," it would be necessary for her friend to provide a more elaborate response. Consider how much more information she would have if her friend were to explain that the show was not bad, but that it was difficult to hear!

Other questions, known as **clarification** responses, enable a listener to check his or her perceptions of a speaker's message. These questions may include such phrases as "Do you mean that . . ." or "Are you saying that . . . ," followed by a rephrasing of the speaker's message as perceived by the listener (Cormier and Cormier, 1979). For example, if the ski club were to plan a fund-raiser in the student union on a particular Sunday, and one member of the organization were to say to another, "I just found out that we can't have our fund-raiser in the union on Sunday," the receiver of the message could seek further clarification by asking a question, such as "Do you mean that we can't use the union?" or "Are you saying that we can't have the fund-raiser at all?" The receiver of the message may find out that the organization cannot use the union on a particular Sunday, but can use the cafeteria on that date, or that the fund raiser can be conducted at the union on the following Sunday. Either of these messages may be quite different from the listener's original interpretation of the statement.

Clear communication of messages can also be promoted through the use of **paraphrase** and **reflection**. Paraphrase refers to a rewording of the content portion of the speaker's message, as understood by the listener. Reflection refers to a rephrasing of the affective element of the speaker's message, as understood by the listener (Cormier and Cormier, 1979). If a friend of yours were to come to you in tears, saying "They cut off my financial aid!" you could paraphrase the content of the message by saying "You've lost your financial aid," or you could reflect the affective portion of the message, conveyed by your friend's tears, by saying "You seem very upset." Remember that the affective component of a message is often at least as important as the content.

Summarization refers to a collection of paraphrases and reflections, which condenses a speaker's message and points out common themes (Cormier and Cormier, 1979). Often, summarization is used to bring closure to a discussion. At some time in your life, you have probably had the experience of being in a meeting where numerous issues were discussed at length. Often, due to time constraints, it is not possible to completely resolve all issues raised in a meeting. The person conducting the meeting can, however, bring some sense of closure by summarizing the key points that were raised, and by confirming any action to be taken on certain matters. An important benefit of summarization is that it reminds participants in a discussion of certain points which might otherwise be forgotten, and provides an opportunity to clarify any misunderstanding which might occur. It also can enable people to understand relationships between issues, which might otherwise seem unrelated.

Nonverbal Communication

Thus far, we have focused primarily on verbal communication, but as I have mentioned, nonverbal symbols can also play an important role in communication, particularly where the affective component of a message is concerned. According to one estimate, in a normal two-person conversation, less than 35% of the social meaning of the situation is conveyed verbally, while more than 65% is expressed nonverbally (McCroskey, Larson, and Knapp, 1971). In fact, a formula has even been devised for determining the proportionate impact of various cues in communicating the feelings of the speaker. According to this formula, 55% of the total message is conveyed by facial expression, 38% is expressed in the speaker's voice, and only 7% is communicated through his or her words (Jandt, 1976). Increasing your understanding of nonverbal communication can contribute greatly to your effectiveness both as a speaker and as a listener.

Richmond, McCroskey, and Payne (1987) drew an important distinction between **nonverbal behavior** and nonverbal communication. While the former refers to any of the behaviors in which we engage that do not involve the use of words, the latter refers only to those nonverbal behaviors which are interpreted as messages by others. Regardless of whether or not the person engaging in a particular behavior intends for it to be interpreted as a message, if it is so interpreted by another person, nonverbal communication has occurred. If it is not interpreted as a message, nonverbal communication has not occurred, again regardless of the sender's intent. The figure below illustrates the distinction between nonverbal behavior and nonverbal communication, according to the thought patterns of both the sender and the receiver.

Receiver

	Interprets Behavior As Message	Does Not Interpret Behavior As Message
Behaves To Send Message	1 Nonverbal Communication	2 Nonverbal Behavior
Behaves With No Intent To Send Message	3 Nonverbal Communication	4 Nonverbal Behavior

Source

Figure 1. Richmond/McCloskey/Payne, NONVERBAL BEHAVIOR IN INTERPERSONAL RELATIONS, ©1987, page 5. Adapted by permission of Prentic-Hall, Inc., Englewood Cliffs, NJ

Richmond et al. (1987) identified several common forms of nonverbal communication. These include: (1) motion and gestures, (2) facial and eye behavior, (3) vocal expression, (4) space, and (5) touch.

Kleinke (1986) identified four basic categories of body language. The first of these, **emblems**, includes those nonverbal acts or gestures which convey a specific meaning, upon which we agree. Examples of emblems include: waving, clapping, nodding of the head, and various gestures which are often employed by angry motorists. **Illustrators** are movements and gestures which emphasize or clarify certain portions of a verbal message. Examples of illustrators include: finger drawings of shapes and figures, pointing, and shrugging of the shoulders. **Regulators** are nonverbal cues which influence the flow of communication. Regulators can indicate a desire to speak, a desire for the other person to speak, or a desire to terminate the discussion. Examples of regulators include: touching the person who is talking, looking toward or away from another person, or looking at one's watch. Finally, **adaptors** are those behaviors which accompany various moods or emotions, in addition to those behaviors which can accompany deception. Examples of adaptors which accompany specific emotions include: smiling and touching in the communication of affection, movement away from others in relation to fear, and muscular tension accompanying anger. Examples of adaptors which accompany deception include: turning away from the receiver of a message, and increased rates of self-manipulation such as scratching and touching oneself.

In exploring the area of facial expression, Richmond et al. (1987) noted that a great deal of research focusing on infants, blind and brain-damaged children, and persons from various countries, has lead many scientists to the conclusion that facial expressions are essentially innate behaviors. Others assert that **primary** facial expressions, those which are linked to the emotions of anger, sadness, fear, disgust, surprise, interest and happiness, initially occur spontaneously. The researchers maintain, however, that as children grow older, they are socialized to observe certain rules which dictate acceptable and unacceptable expressions within a particular culture.

Richmond et al. (1987) described four specific **display rules** or **facial management techniques**, which are used in controlling facial expressions. The four techniques are: (1) **intensification**, (2) **deintensification**, (3) **neutralization**, and (4) **masking**.

Intensification refers to an exaggeration of expressions, in order to meet the expectations of others (Richmond et. al, 1987). An example of intensification may occur at an athletic awards banquet, when an individual is recognized as the most valuable player on the women's basketball team. The winner may have suspected beforehand that she would win the award. She might share the belief that she is indeed the most valuable player on the team. However, if she believes that such an attitude would not be looked upon favorably by her teammates, she may choose to intensify her expression of surprise when her name is announced, in order to meet her teammates' expectations of humility.

In contrast to intensification, deintensification involves the reduction of outward signs of emotion (Richmond et al., 1987). For example, if you were planning to spend the weekend with a friend of yours at another university, and he called you on Thursday to tell you that his grandmother died and that he would not be able to see you, in all probability, you would be understanding and would express your sympathy to him and his family. However, you might also feel disappointed that your plans for the weekend did not materialize. If your friend were to say to you "I'm sorry. I hope you aren't disappointed," you might respond by acknowledging some disappointment, but would probably deintensify your expression of disappointment, in order to avoid upsetting your friend or appearing uncaring.

The third technique, neutralization, involves elimination of all expressions of emotion (Richmond et al., 1987). For example, when you were deciding which college or university to attend, your parents might have told you that it was entirely your decision, and that they would not pressure you to choose a particular institution. Nevertheless, if you began to seriously consider your mother's alma mater, she might well have felt some enthusiasm about the possibility of your following in her footsteps. In this situation, she could use neutralization in order to hide her enthusiasm, and consequently avoid influencing your decision.

The fourth technique, masking, involves hiding the emotion that is actually felt, and creating the appearance of another more acceptable emotional state (Richmond et al., 1987). Each year, during the holiday season, examples of masking abound, as countless people open presents with pleasant looks of surprise on their faces, only to exchange the items the following day for others which are more suited to their tastes.

The voice can communicate information about a person in several ways. Kleinke (1986) identified four specific components of vocal expression, which can serve as a means of nonverbal communication. These include: (1) **voice qualities**, such as resonance and articulation; (2) **vocal characterizers**, such as laughing, crying, and coughing; (3) **vocal qualifiers**, such as intensity and accent; and (4) **vocal segregates**, which include nonword sounds such as "um" and "ah."

Rightly or wrongly, these components of a person's communication can have a major impact on other people's perceptions of that individual's background, personality, and emotional state. Kleinke (1986) offered several recommendations to those who wish to project an image of confidence and credibility. These recommendations include:

1. Use an Expressive Tone
2. Speak Fluently
3. Speak Faster
4. Use Powerful Speech
   a. Avoid the use of hedges, such as "I think," "I guess," "I mean," "sort of," "you know," "OK"
   b. Avoid hesitations, such as pauses and disruptions like "uh," "um," and "well"
   c. Don't be overly polite.
   d. Avoid expressing uncertainty by making statements that sound like questions.

e. Don't overuse intensifiers, such as "very," "really," "for sure"

f. Speak in sentences.

g. Don't overuse big words (pp. 102-104).

In addition to gestures, facial expressions, and voice; posture and positioning of the body can carry powerful messages about an individual's thoughts and feelings. Richmond et al. (1987) identified several characteristics of posture and positioning which can communicate messages. These include the degree of relaxation in one's posture, and one's body orientation in relation to another person. Scheflen (1964) identified contrasting characteristics related to three different aspects of positioning.

The first of these aspects deals with the degree to which positioning is **inclusive** or **noninclusive**. If two people are talking with their backs turned toward a third person, their positions in relation to that person are noninclusive. If, however, they were to hear the person and move apart from one another to allow the person to stand between them, their positioning would become inclusive. The inclusive position invites the person to participate in the discussion, while the noninclusive position does not.

The second aspect of positioning that Scheflen (1964) described is concerned with whether a **vis-a-vis** or **parallel** body orientation is maintained. When the vis-a-vis orientation is maintained, the two participants in a discussion stand or sit across from each other, while the parallel orientation involves standing or sitting next to one another. The vis-a-vis orientation requires that people interact with each other in a way that is **reciprocal**. In other words, they cannot carry out their activities in isolation from each other. In contrast, the parallel orientation is adopted when carrying out activities which do not require that people interact with one another.

The third aspect of positioning identified by Scheflen (1964) deals with the degree of **congruence** or **incongruence** that exists between two people, in the posture and body orientations that they maintain during their interaction. If their posture and body orientations are similar, they are said to be congruent, while differences in posture and body orientation signal incongruence. Congruence would be observed, for example, in interaction between two people who are leaning forward and facing one another. In contrast, incongruence would be observed in a discussion between a person who is leaning forward and a person who is leaning back, or when one participant in a discussion is facing the other person and that person is facing in a different direction. You will recall that previously we used the term congruence to refer to the degree of consistency between the verbal and nonverbal messages sent by an individual and her or his thoughts. Here, we are using the term to refer to the degree of consistency between the nonverbal messages sent by two people.

The distance that is maintained between a sender and a receiver of a message can also be a valuable means of communication. Hall (1966) described four different distance zones, which communicate information about the type of interaction that is taking place between two people. The first of these zones, described as **intimate**

distance, ranges from touching to a distance of 18 inches. We reserve this space for a small group of people who are emotionally close to us, such as lovers, close friends, and immediate family members. The second zone, the **personal distance** zone, ranges from 18 inches to about four feet. This distance is maintained during casual interaction with friends and relatives. The third zone, known as **social distance**, ranges from about four feet to about twelve feet. This is the distance that is typically maintained while we conduct business. The fourth zone, the **public distance** zone, refers to distances of twelve feet and beyond. The outer limit of the public zone is that point at which there is no longer any potential for interaction.

The distance that is maintained between two people is a reflection of both their relationship with each other and the nature of the specific communication. If you were to buy a book from another student on your residence hall floor, you would probably remain in the social distance zone while discussing the cost of the book, even though you may regard the person as a friend. Similarly, if a holiday party were held in the office where you work, you might find that the people in your department would move into the personal distance zone, even though they are primarily business associates.

Closely related to space is the use of touch in interpersonal communication. According to Jandt (1976), our **tactile** sense, the sense of touch, is the first of our senses to develop during infancy. It is largely through this sense that we are first introduced to the world. It is not surprising, therefore, that while the use of touch is highly regulated by societal expectations, it remains a powerful tool for communication.

Richmond et al. (1987) described five different categories of touch which are used in personal interaction. The five categories are: (1) **functional-professional** touch, (2) **social-polite** touch, (3) **friendship-warmth** touch, (4) **love-intimacy** touch, and (5) **sexual arousal** touch.

Functional-professional touch refers to the touching that occurs in a professional relationship as a necessary component of the work activity. This is a highly impersonal form of touch, where the client's body is treated as if it were an object (Richmond et al., 1987). For example, therapists and trainers who work with student athletes must sometimes touch the students' bodies in the course of their work. However, this does not necessarily imply any emotional involvement between the two individuals.

Social-polite touch is used to acknowledge others within a social role. While this form of touch involves treating another as more than simply an object, it implies only limited interpersonal involvement (Richmond et al., 1987). In our culture, the handshake is probably the most common form of social-polite touch.

Friendship-warmth touch communicates a higher level of emotional involvement between two individuals. This form of touch is used to show a special appreciation for the unique characteristics of another person (Richmond et al., 1987).

Love-intimacy touch expresses an even more intense emotional involvement than does friendship-warmth touch. This form of touch is reserved for lovers and spouses. It is an unselfish form of touch that is focused on satisfying the other person's need for closeness (Richmond et al., 1987).

Although love and intimacy are often accompanied by sexual arousal touch, Richmond et al. (1987) drew a distinction between love-intimacy touch and sexual arousal touch. They noted that love-intimacy touch may simply consist of hugging or holding hands, and does not necessarily involve sexual contact. Similarly, they noted that sexual contact can occur between two people with very little emotional involvement. A "one night stand" involving two students who meet in a bar is an example of sexual arousal touch which is not likely to be accompanied by love-intimacy touch.

Athos and Gabarro (1978) added a word of caution regarding interpretation of nonverbal behavior. They pointed out that a particular behavior holds meaning only within a specific context. This behavior cannot be completely understood in the absence of information about the whole person, the situation, and the relationship between the interacting parties.

It is important to also realize that cultural factors play an important role in nonverbal communication. Richmond et al. (1987) described a situation involving a former Vice President of the United States who, while visiting another nation, used our "OK" sign, only to find that the gesture carried an obscene meaning in the country that he was visiting. According to Jandt (1976), the use of space in interpersonal communication is greatly influenced by culture. Hem noted that the distance that is maintained during interpersonal communication in Germany is greater than that which is maintained in the United States, while in Arab countries, people position themselves in closer proximity to one another. Richmond et al. (1987) cited one study focusing on touching behavior of adult couples in coffee shops in four different cities. The study revealed that, within an hour, couples in San Juan, Puerto Rico touched 180 times; couples in Paris, France touched 110 times; those in Gainesville, Florida touched twice; and those in London, England touched once.

Clearly, nonverbal communication has some limitations. Nevertheless, developing an understanding of this unique form of communication can help you to promote greater effectiveness within your organization, provided that you remain attentive to the unique circumstances surrounding each interpersonal encounter.

Assertiveness

In addition to specific communication skills, it is important for members of organizations to pay close attention to their general styles of communication. There are four basic styles of communication, which vary according to the communicator's level of "openness of self" and "respect for others," as illustrated in the figure below.

The four basic styles are: (1) **nonassertive**, (2) **aggressive**, (3) **passive aggressive**, and (4) **assertive** (Zuker, 1983).

	Low Respect	High Respect
High Openness	Aggressive Telling co-workers they must not smoke in the office.	Assertive Telling co-workers you do not like smoke and requesting they not smoke in the office.
Low Openness	Passive Aggressive Acting grumpy and coughing loudly when someone is smoking near you.	Nonassertive Not mentioning your discomfort or wish that people would not smoke in the office.

Figure 2. Behavior matrix[*]

A nonassertive style is characterized by low openness and high respect. Nonassertive individuals do not express their thoughts honestly and directly, and avoid confronting others. For example, if an instructor of a business course were to regularly make sarcastic comments about women in the business world, he would undoubtedly offend a number of students in his class, particularly women. His behavior in this situation would undermine his students' attempts to pursue an education in a non-hostile environment. Under the circumstances, it would be quite appropriate for a student to confront him when sexist comments are made. In this situation, many students would probably behave nonassertively, by sitting silently, rather than confronting his behavior.

The behavior of nonassertive individuals is often based on a belief that their feelings, rights, and ideas are not important (Zuker, 1983). They often believe, further, that it is always wrong to hurt or offend others. They may also have doubts or experience fear and anxiety about making mistakes, appearing incompetent, making others angry, or not being liked (Drury, 1984). In our example, the nonassertive students' behavior may stem from a belief that "the teacher is always right." They may fear that they would be unable to defend their position if

---

[*] Reprinted with permission of the publisher, from MASTERING ASSERTIVENESS SKILLS: POWER AND POSITIVE INFLUENCE AT WORK, ©1983 Elaina Zuker. Published by AMACOM, a division of the American Management Association, All rights reserved.

challenged, or they may fear that they would be penalized in their grades if they were to offend the instructor.

Nonassertive behavior is often followed by feelings of resentment and frustration on the part of those engaging in the behavior. Others may respond with feelings of irritation, impatience, or pity (Zuker, 1983). In our example, a nonassertive student who would not confront the instructor might return to her room and feel like kicking herself, while the instructor may regard her passivity in class as proof that his assumptions are correct.

In contrast to the nonassertive style, the aggressive style is characterized by high openness and low respect. Aggressive individuals express their thoughts clearly and directly, but show little regard for the rights, feelings, and ideas of others (Zuker, 1983). In our example, an aggressive student might respond to the instructor's comments by labeling him a "sexist pig," and possibly even asserting that "all men are pigs." Aggressive behavior is often prompted by feelings of anger, fear, and insecurity, as well as a lack of trust in self and others. Typical responses to aggressive behavior in others include feelings of anxiety, defensiveness, frustration, and anger (Drury, 1984).

A passive aggressive style is characterized by low openness and low respect (Zuker, 1983). This type of behavior combines many of the qualities of both aggressive and nonassertive styles. Passive aggressive individuals do not express their thoughts clearly and directly, and have little regard for the rights, feelings, and ideas of others. In our example, the passive aggressive individual might respond to the instructor's comments by saying nothing, but engaging in a number of irritating behaviors, such as coughing loudly, yawning, dropping pencils, and asking unnecessary questions. Although the disrespectful attitude of the passive aggressive individual manifests itself in very subtle and indirect ways, it nevertheless draws many of the responses elicited by openly aggressive behavior.

An assertive style is characterized by both high openness and high respect. Assertive individuals express their wants, needs, and ideas clearly and directly, without violating the rights of others (Zuker, 1983). Assertiveness is based on the principles of objectivity and a sense of entitlement, as well as feelings of self-esteem and trust in others (Drury, 1984). In our example, an assertive individual would openly challenge the instructor's assumptions concerning the proper role of women in the business world but would not assault the character of the instructor.

Assertiveness is particularly important for student leaders, because of the amount of time that they typically commit to serving the needs of others and the tendency for people to expect progressively more from them. As a student leader, you will regularly be asked to take on additional commitments, and it is important that you not overextend yourself. You have personal needs too. Learning to say "no" is a necessary survival skill.

Although we often think of assertiveness in relation to the expression of negative emotions or communication of unwelcome information, it is also important to consider the ways in which assertiveness can allow you to express a part of yourself that others would undoubtedly be delighted to know. Have you ever had the experience of walking into the student union on your campus and hearing beautiful piano music coming from the lounge, only to find that it immediately ceases when you enter the room? It is an unfortunate fact that many talented performers have never had an audience because of their own fears and insecurities.

Consider also the ways in which assertiveness affects interaction between people on a more personal level. At some time in your life, you have probably known two people who, in both their own judgment and that of their friends, would be "perfect together," a real "cute couple." You might have even been one of these people. In either case, you are probably aware of the sense of frustration that occurs when despite numerous opportunities, both genuine and contrived, the cuties never quite couple.

By behaving assertively, you can give a gift to both yourself and others. Nowhere is this aspect of assertiveness more apparent than in the area of student leadership. Becoming involved in campus or community leadership activities involves some risk. The intramural team that you organize may lose a few games. The concert that you plan may lose money. The local ordinance that you propose may be met with resistance in the community. On the other hand, if you choose to avoid this risk, it is a certainty that you will never win a game, will never sell out a concert, and will never propose a successful piece of legislation. Perhaps more importantly, it is possible that nobody else will either.

Clearly, assertive behavior offers many advantages over other communication styles. Nevertheless, adoption of a more assertive style is often difficult, because it involves a departure from previous patterns of behavior which are deeply ingrained. Development of a more assertive communication style requires deep commitment and a deliberate effort to change.

According to Galassi and Galassi (1977), the first step in this process is assessment of your current level of assertiveness, as measured by your behavior and level of comfort associated with self-affirmation and expression of both positive and negative feelings. Once you have assessed your current style of communication, you can begin to develop greater assertiveness by focusing on specific situations which challenge you to adapt your style.

Galassi and Galassi (1977) recommended that the situation be immediately appraised according to the following three-step process:

1. Determine what you believe the rights and responsibilities are of the various parties in the situation.
2. Determine the probable short-term and long-term consequences of various courses of action.
3. Decide how you will behave in the situation (pp. 31-32).

The next step in learning to communicate more assertively, according to Galassi and Galassi (1977), is to try out new attitudes and behaviors in practice situations. This process involves the following three substeps:

1. Try out your new behavior in [situations provided to you].
2. Write your own situations to practice.
3. Dispute erroneous beliefs and counterproductive attitudes, and replace them with more accurate and productive beliefs (pp. 32-33).

In situations requiring confrontation, a particularly useful tool for practice is a device known as a **DESC script** (Bower and Bower, 1976), which serves as a model for composing assertive statements. Use of this model involves a four-step process.

The first step in the process is to **describe** the particular situation. For example, if your roommate regularly disturbs you by playing his stereo while you are trying to sleep, you might begin your DESC script by saying "Lots of times, when I'm trying to sleep, you play your stereo loudly."

Once you have described the situation, your next step is to **express** your feelings concerning the situation. In our example, you might say "I get really angry and frustrated when you do this."

The third step in the process is to **specify** your legitimate expectations, recognizing the rights of all concerned. In our example, you might say "I'd like for you to use your headphones when you listen to your stereo at night."

The final step in the process is to identify the positive **consequences** which can be expected as a result of compliance with your request or, if necessary, the negative consequences of noncompliance. In our example, you could conclude your DESC script by saying "If you use your headphones, you can listen to your music, I can get a good night's sleep, and we'll probably both be easier to get along with in the morning."

Once you have practiced your new behavior, you will need to evaluate your performance. Galassi and Galassi (1977) developed the following four-step evaluation process:

1. *Determine your anxiety in the situation.*
    Eye contact
    Relaxed posture
    Nervous laughter or joking
    Excessive or unrelated head, hand, and body movements

2. *Evaluate your verbal content*

   Say what you really want to say?

   Comments concise and to the point?

   Comments definitive, specific, and firm?

   No long-winded explanations, excuses, or apologetic behavior. . .

3. *Evaluate how you delivered your message*

   Almost immediately after the person spoke

   No hesitancy or stammering

   Appropriate loudness, tone, and inflection

   No whining, pleading, or sarcasm

4. *Decide whether you were pleased with your performance* (p. 38)

Once you have perfected your assertiveness skills in practice situations, you can begin to implement your new behaviors in everyday life. Galassi and Galassi (1977) recommended the development of a plan for following through on pre-rehearsed interactions, as well as spontaneous responses to naturally occurring interactions. They also recommended the use of a daily log for recording and evaluating both pre-rehearsed and spontaneous interactions. This will enable you to monitor your ongoing progress toward greater assertiveness.

Immediacy

As you focus on the impact that your interpersonal communication style has on your interaction with others in your organization, it is helpful to consider the concept of **immediacy**. Richmond et al. (1987) described the "immediacy principle" as the tendency for people to be drawn toward those whom they like, and with whom they enjoy interacting, and to be drawn away from those whom they do not like or with whom they do not enjoy interacting. The authors arranged a progression of attitudes and behaviors according to the degree to which they are "approach oriented" or "avoidance oriented." The five points along this "immediacy continuum" are characterized by the following attitudes and behaviors: (1) physical violence, (2) verbal hostility, (3) neutrality, (4) immediacy, and (5) intimacy.

As you begin to assume a more active role in providing leadership for your organization, you will undoubtedly find that your effectiveness in mobilizing other group members can be greatly enhanced by applying the immediacy principle. While acknowledging several drawbacks of immediacy, including the tendency on the part of some individuals to mistake immediacy for intimacy and the tendency on the part of some others to become anxious when communication is initiated, Richmond et al. (1987) concluded that the shortcomings of a nonimmediate style are even greater.

The table below presents examples of specific immediate and nonimmediate behaviors, both verbal and nonverbal.

Table 1. Immediacy/Nonimmediacy Behavior Chart

Category	Immediacy Behaviors	Nonimmediacy Behaviors
Verbal Communication	Pronouns like we, us. Talk with others. Statements that infer liking (e.g., I like your dress.) I really like that. You are right.	Use of you, you and I, I. Talk to/at others. Guarded statements of liking. (Your dress is O.K.) That's dumb, That's a stupid idea.
Gesture and Body Movement	Leaning toward another; Open body position; More gestures; more positive affect displays; Relaxed body position; Calm movements; Positive head movements.	Lean away from another; Closed body position; Less gestures; More Negative affect displays. Tense body position; Nervous movements; Negative head movements.
Face and Eye	Eye contact and mutual gaze; Facial expressions that show pleasure; Smile a lot.	Limited eye contact; Avert eye gaze; Facial expressions that show displeasure; Frown a lot.
Voice	Short pauses; Few silences; Positive vocal inflections; Vocal variety; Relaxed tones (calm); Dynamic; Animated; Interested: Friendly vocal cues.	Lengthy pauses/silences; sarcasm; Monotonous; Dull; Irritated tones; Nasal; Harsh sounding; Sneering sounds; Bored; Unfriendly vocal cues.
Space	Move closer to a person; Stand closer to a person. Sit closer; Orient more directly; Lean forward while seated.	Lean away from a person; Sit farther away; Lean away/back while seated; Stand farther away; Indirect body orientation.
Touch	Touch on head, hand, fore-arm, shoulder, back; Pat; Squeeze; friendly handshake; Frequent touch; Stroking; Hugging.	Avoid or withdraw from touch; Clammy/distant handshake; Seldom touches; Slaps; Hitting; Striking another.

Richmond/McCroskey/Payne, NONVERBAL BEHAVIOR IN INTERPERSONAL RELATIONS, ©1987, pp. 199-200. adapted by permission of Prentice-Hall, Inc., Englewood Cliffs, NJ.

Public Speaking

One area of communication that is particularly important for those aspiring to leadership positions is **public speaking**. It is, likewise, an area in which many potential leaders find a great deal of difficulty. It has been estimated that 85% of the general population experiences an uncomfortable level of anxiety when speaking in public. According to some surveys, speaking before a group is the most common fear among Americans, more common even than the fear of death (Motley, 1988).

Nevertheless, several measures can be taken to reduce nervousness and to increase your effectiveness as a public speaker. According to Motley (1988), one approach is to focus on the speech as communication rather than as performance. Anxiety is less common among those who view speech as an opportunity to share ideas and information that are of value to the audience, instead of concentrating on the audience's reactions to them as speakers. Another way to reduce your level of "speech anxiety" is to prepare well before delivering your speech.

As you begin to prepare, one of your first steps will be to analyze your audience, because in order to communicate effectively with its members, it is necessary that you understand their frame of reference. In analyzing the audience, Lucas (1983) recommended that attention be given to demographic information, such as age, gender, religion, ethnic background, and group affiliations. He also recommended that attention be given to audience characteristics that relate to the specific situation, including the size of the group, its members' disposition toward specific topics, their disposition toward you as a speaker, and their disposition toward the occasion.

Once you have analyzed your audience and the occasion, you will be better able to select an appropriate topic. Osborn (1982) recommended a three-step process for selecting a topic. The first step is to generate a list of topics that interest you. Once you have done this, your next step will be to generate a list of topics that are of interest to your audience. Comparing the two lists, you can then identify areas of common interest. These may be specific topics which appear on both lists, or they may be subtopics which fall within the realm of two broader topics. For example, you may have a special interest in social policy issues. If you are giving a speech to a group of students on your campus and are aware of concerns surrounding the issue of racism, you might conclude that you and your audience would share a common interest in the issue of affirmative action.

Once you have selected a general topic (or one has been identified for you, as is often the case), it will be necessary for you to narrow your focus. As Kougl (1988) noted, your audience will not want to hear all that you have to say on a particular topic, and furthermore, you will not be able to share all that you know about the topic. You will be limited by the amount of time that you have available to you, as well as your audience's prior knowledge of the subject. Her recommendation is that, in narrowing down your topic, you remain attentive to the information that you have about your audience. In our example, if you were speaking to a group of minority women, your focus would probably not be the same as it would be if you were speaking to a group of white men. The audience's disposition toward you, as a woman, as a member of a minority group, or as a white man, would also have some bearing on the specific focus of your speech.

In addition to information about the audience it is important that you consider the general purpose of the speech. Samovar and Mills (1983) identified three general purposes of public speaking: (1) to **inform**, (2) to **persuade**, and (3) to **entertain**.

Speeches that inform are intended to increase the audience's knowledge about a particular topic (Samovar and Mills, 1983). In our example, an informational speech might focus on the facts surrounding the history of affirmative action, changes in representation of women and minorities in higher education since the introduction of affirmative action, or specific guidelines for implementing affirmative action programs within organizations.

Speeches that persuade are intended to influence people to think, feel, or act in a particular way that is determined by the speaker (Samovar and Mills, 1983). In our example, a persuasive speech may focus on increasing support for affirmative action programs among white students, or increasing minority students' understanding of the ambivalence that some white students feel where affirmative action programs are concerned.

Speeches that entertain are those which stimulate a pleasurable response in the audience. These speeches may be humorous or dramatic (Samovar and Mills, 1983). In our example, an entertaining speech might satirize the controversy surrounding affirmative action on a particular campus, or it might celebrate the progress made by women and minorities under affirmative action.

Kougl (1988) presented a formula for narrowing the focus of a speech, which she summarized as follows: "Know/think/believe = could use/need to know/like to hear" (p. 37). According to this formula, based on what listeners already know, think, and believe about a topic, it is possible to determine what they could use, need to know, or would like to hear. In our example, if you were delivering your speech to your campus chapter of the NAACP, you would probably be able to assume that the group is fairly knowledgeable about affirmative action and also quite supportive of the policy. In view of these considerations, you might conclude that information about minority student recruitment programs on your campus would be useful to them. They would probably also find the information interesting, and possibly even encouraging.

Once you have identified the specific focus of your speech, you can begin to select information for inclusion in it. In identifying the specific content of your speech, it is generally best to begin with information that is familiar to you. It is recommended that you use information to: (1) prove your points or support your ideas, (2) clarify your points, (3) make certain points memorable, and (4) make your speech more interesting (Fletcher, 1983).

Fletcher (1983) identified eight different types of presentation content. The eight categories are:

1. Examples
2. Quotations
3. Statistics
4. Stories
5. Definitions
6. Comparisons
7. Contrasts
8. Audiovisual aids (p. 46)

Once you have identified the content of your speech, your next step is to organize the material. Your speech should include an **introduction**, a **discussion** segment, and a **conclusion**. The purpose of the introduction is to capture your audience's attention and to provide a preview of the material to be presented. In the discussion segment of your speech, you will present your main points along with any supporting information. The conclusion provides a review of the information presented and leaves the audience with a memorable impression. In planning your speech, it is recommended that you allot 15% of your time for the introduction, 75% for the discussion, and 10% for the conclusion (Fletcher, 1983).

In planning the main body of your speech, it is important that you arrange the material logically. Katula (1987) identified six common methods of organizing information. These **patterns of discourse** are: (1) **narrative**, (2) **process**, (3) **cause-effect**, (4) **analysis**, (5) **definition**, and (6) **classification**.

The narrative pattern arranges information in a simple chronological order (Katula, 1987). This pattern is particularly useful in describing events. In our example, the narrative pattern could be used to trace the university's progress in minority student recruitment, beginning with the inception of the affirmative action program and ending with the current academic year.

The process pattern is used to explain a sequence of interrelated steps or stages in the development of something. It is particularly useful in presenting instructions or explaining how something works (Katula, 1987). In our example, information might be presented on a series of stages in the implementation and expansion of the university's minority recruitment program.

The cause-effect pattern relates outcomes to the factors that gave rise to them. It is particularly useful for organizing arguments on controversial issues, or for explaining how a particular condition has come into being (Katula, 1987). In our example, rates of entering minority enrollment might be presented in relation to the specific recruitment strategies employed by the university, in addition to various external conditions such as shifts in the region's minority population or changes in its economic conditions.

The analysis pattern is used to divide a topic into more specific subtopics. This pattern is particularly useful for dealing with complex topics (Katula, 1987). In our example, an analysis pattern might begin by identifying the university's minority recruitment goals, and subsequently present information on various strategies which have been implemented for achieving each goal.

The definition pattern is used to establish the fundamental nature of something. It is particularly useful when using terms which are widely confused or misunderstood (Katula, 1987). In our example, the definition pattern might be used to establish the meaning of the term, "affirmative action," and to distinguish it from the related term, "equal opportunity."

The classification pattern is used to create groupings according to common attributes. This pattern is widely used, and is particularly helpful for dealing with complex topics involving many different concepts (Katula, 1987). In our example, this pattern might be used to divide the speech into segments focusing on the university's recruitment of students from specific minority classes.

As you prepare for your speech, in addition to selecting and organizing your material, it will be necessary for you to select a **method of delivery**. There are four common approaches for delivering a speech: (1) reading from a **manuscript**, (2) reciting from **memory**, (3) speaking **impromptu**, and (4) speaking **extemporaneously** (Lucas, 1983).

In a manuscript, every word that you are going to say is written down in advance. When the time comes for you to deliver the speech, you read the manuscript verbatim. This approach is used primarily when very precise language is necessary (Lucas, 1983). For example, if you were to deliver a speech on behalf of your supervisor, she would probably ask that you read from a manuscript, to ensure that her own thoughts would not be misunderstood by you, and consequently misrepresented to your audience. A major shortcoming of this method of delivery is that for many speakers, it is difficult to make the words sound natural and convincing when they are being read from a piece of paper.

When done effectively, reciting a speech from memory can make a powerful impression upon an audience. However, this technique requires a great deal of practice, and involves a considerable element of risk, since even a photographic memory can malfunction in times of nervousness. Furthermore, it can be difficult to concentrate on communicating with your audience if you are preoccupied with remembering your next word. For these reasons, public speeches are rarely recited from memory, unless they include only very brief remarks such as introductions (Lucas, 1983).

When giving an impromptu speech, it is necessary to speak "off the top of your head," with no preparation whatsoever (Lucas, 1983). This type of speech is usually given only in response to unexpected questions or requests. For example, if you were on the homecoming committee at your institution, and happened to be at a student government meeting during the preceding week, the student government chair might call on you to say a few words about the weekend's events. Typically, impromptu speeches are brief and pertain to subjects with which the speaker is quite familiar.

When the extemporaneous approach is followed, a speaker refers to notes which include certain key points. However, the precise wording of the speech is determined at the time that it is delivered. This method is quite popular, because it provides the speaker with greater control over the content and wording of the speech than does the impromptu method, but allows for greater spontaneity than does either reading from a manuscript or reciting from memory (Lucas, 1983). In most cases, this is the method of delivery that you will probably choose.

Except in the case of impromptu speaking, it is critical that you practice all public speeches before delivering them. It is through rehearsal that you can begin to develop an accurate image of how your speech will sound, and to make any necessary adjustments.

Osborn (1982) recommended the following seven-step process for rehearsing an extemporaneous speech:

1. Read the entire outline over silently, trying to fix the primary statements in your head.

2. Read the entire outline aloud, looking up from it at appropriate moments to establish eye contact with the imaginary audience.

3. Repeat step 2 several times, trying with each repetition to increase the time spent in eye contact with the audience.

4. Read the outline again silently and slowly, fixing in your mind the orienting material, the initial focus, the final focus, and the subpoints under the primary statement. Do not try to memorize the speech word for word, but do fix the progression of ideas firmly in your mind.

5. Practice the speech aloud, trying not to look at the written outline and reading only quoted material.

6. Check the outline to see what points you may have omitted or placed in improper order.

7. Repeat steps 5 and 6 until you are comfortable delivering the speech (pp. 245-246).

In rehearsing your speech, it is a good idea to tape record one or two practices. If possible, it is recommended that you use a video recorder. Otherwise, an audio recorder should be used. Additionally, it is recommended that you time your speech, but that you not adjust your rate of delivery in order to meet a time assignment (Fletcher, 1983).

As you listen to your speech, pay close attention to your voice. Lucas (1983) recommended paying attention specifically to volume, pitch, and rate of delivery, in addition to pronunciation, articulation, vocal variety, and use of pauses. If you are watching your practice session on videotape, also pay close attention to your nonverbal behavior, including your posture, use of gestures, eye contact, and other facial expressions. When the time comes for you to deliver your speech, if you have prepared properly, you will undoubtedly feel considerably more confident and comfortable than you would otherwise feel. Once you have delivered your speech, be sure to evaluate your performance, so that in the future you can make any necessary changes in your style of speaking. Remember that being able to speak in public is a skill that can be learned only by doing. Consider each successive speech as an opportunity to refine your skills, and you will be amazed at how quickly your ability to speak in public will improve.

Summary

This chapter stressed the importance of effective communication in student and community organizations, and emphasized the role of individual group members as facilitators of effective communication. The basic communication process was reviewed, including four primary steps: (1) encoding, (2) transmission, (3) decoding, and (4) response. The importance of both the content or cognitive component of a message and its affective component was stressed. Effective communication was defined as a process in which the receiver of a message interprets it as intended by the sender.

Several barriers to effective communication, known as noise, were identified. These include factors within the sender, the receiver, and the channel. The tendency on the part of receivers to oversimplify messages was identified as a particularly common form of noise. This type of distortion often involves one of three basic psychological processes: (1) leveling, (2) sharpening, or (3) assimilation.

One particularly effective form of communication, known as win/win communication was identified. This form of communication involves working cooperatively with others, in order to ensure that both parties are able to achieve their desired outcomes.

Elements of successful communication were identified. These factors include: congruence, empathy, and acceptance. Specific skills were identified for both senders and receivers of messages. A distinction was drawn between passive and active listening, and several skills related to active listening were introduced. These include: minimal verbal responses, open-ended questions, clarification responses, paraphrase, reflection, and summarization.

The importance of nonverbal communication was emphasized, and a distinction was drawn between nonverbal behavior and nonverbal communication. Common forms of nonverbal communication were introduced, including the use of gestures and movement, facial expressions, voice, space, and touch.

Four basic categories of body language were identified. These categories, which relate to the nature of the message being sent, include: (1) emblems, (2) illustrators, (3) regulators, and (4) adapters.

The role of socialization in the use of facial expressions was explored. Four specific display rules, or facial management techniques, were identified. The four techniques are: (1) intensification, (2) deintensification, (3) neutralization, and (4) masking.

Several specific components of vocal expression which can serve as a means of nonverbal communication were identified. These include: voice qualities, vocal characterizers, vocal qualifiers, and vocal segregates. Specific recommendations were made for those wishing to project a vocal image of confidence and credibility.

Posture and positioning of the sender and receiver, in relation to each other, was explored as a means of nonverbal communication. Several specific aspects of body orientation were emphasized, including the degree to which the positions adopted by the sender and receiver are inclusive or noninclusive, vis-a-vis or parallel, and congruent or incongruent.

The use of space as a means of nonverbal communication was explored. Four different distance zones were identified. The four zones are: (1) intimate distance, (2) personal distance, (3) social distance, and (4) public distance.

The use of touch as a means of nonverbal communication was also explored. Five categories of touch were identified. They are: (1) functional-professional touch, (2) social-polite touch, (3) friendship-warmth touch, (4) love-intimacy touch, and (5) sexual arousal touch.

Four basic styles of communication were explored in this chapter. These styles relate to the communicator's level of "openness of self" and "respect for others." The four styles are: (1) nonassertive, (2) aggressive, (3) passive aggressive, and (4) assertive. The assertive style was identified as the most effective, and recommendations were made for those attempting to become more assertive. These recommendations included the use of a device known as a DESC script.

In addition to assertiveness, the concept of immediacy was explored as it relates to communication style. While several drawbacks of an immediate style were recognized, immediate behavior was recommended as more desirable than nonimmediate behavior, particularly for those aspiring to leadership positions.

The chapter closed with an overview of the specific area of communication known as public speaking. Recommendations were made for planning and delivering a speech. The importance of understanding the audience was stressed, particularly as it relates to the selection of a specific topic. Three general purposes of public speaking were identified. The three purposes are: (1) to inform, (2) to persuade, and (3) to entertain. The importance of organizing material in a logical manner was emphasized, and six common patterns of discourse were presented. The six patterns are: (1) narrative, (2) process, (3) cause-effect, (4) analysis, (5) definition, and (6) classification. Four methods of delivery were presented. The four methods are:

(1) reading from a manuscript, (2) reciting from memory, (3) speaking impromptu, and (4) speaking extemporaneously. Several recommendations were made for practicing speeches, including the use of recording devices. Finally, the chapter stressed the importance of evaluating a speech after it has been delivered, and learning from this experience.

References

Abrams, K. (1986). *Communication at Work.* Englewood Cliffs, NJ: Prentice-Hall.

Athos, A. G. and Gabarro, J. J. (1978). *Interpersonal Behavior: Communication and Understanding in Relationships.* Englewood Cliffs, NJ: Prentice-Hall.

Bower, S. A. and Bower, G. (1976). *Asserting Yourself.* Reading, MA: Addison-Wesley.

Cormier, W. H. and Cormier, L. S. (1979). *Interviewing Strategies for Helpers.* Monterey, CA: Wadsworth.

Drury, S. (1984). *Assertive Supervision: Building Involved Teamwork.* Champaign, IL: Research Press.

Fletcher, L. (1983). *How to Speak Like a Pro.* New York: Ballantine.

Galassi, M. D. and Galassi, J. (1977). *Assert Yourself! How to Be Your Own Person.* Human Sciences Press.

Gordon, T. (1970). *PET: Parent Effectiveness Training.* David McKay Company, Inc.

Hall, E. (1966). *The Hidden Dimension.* Garden City, NY: Doubleday.

Jandt, F. (1976). *The Process of Interpersonal Communication.* San Francisco: Canfield Press.

Johnson, D. and Johnson, F. (1975). *Joining Together.* Englewood Cliffs, NJ: Prentice-Hall.

Katula, R. (1987). *Principles and Patterns of Public Speaking.* Belmont, CA: Wadsworth.

Kleinke, C. (1986). *Meeting and Understanding People.* New York: W. H. Freeman.

Kougl, K. (1988). *Primer for Public Speaking.* New York: Harper & Row.

Lucas, S. (1983). *The Art of Public Speaking.* New York: Random House.

McCroskey, J.; Larson, C.; Knapp, M. (1971). *An Introduction to Interpersonal Communication.* Englewood Cliffs, NJ: Prentice-Hall.

Motley, M. (1988). Taking the terror out of talk. *Psychology Today, 22,* 46-49.

Okun, B. (1976). *Effective Helping: Interviewing and Counseling Techniques.* North Scituate, MA: Duxbury Press.

Osborn, M. (1982). *Speaking in Public.* Boston: Houghton Mifflin.

Richmond, V.; McCroskey, J.; Payne, S. (1987). *Nonverbal Behavior in Interpersonal Relations.* Englewood Cliffs, NJ: Prentice-Hall.

Samovar, L. and Mills, J. (1983). *Oral Communication.* Dubuque, IA: Wm. C. Brown.

Scheflen, A. (1964). The significance of posture in communication systems. *Psychiatry, 27,* 316-331.

Wycoff, E. (March, 1981). Canons of communication. *Personnel Journal.*

Zuker, E. (1983). *Mastering Assertiveness Skills.* AMACOM.

Activities

Getting It Straight

After reading the following paragraph, complete the accompanying statements by filling in the blanks.

Rob is a disk jockey on his campus radio station. Before going on the air, Rob had an argument with Dianne and said many things that he later regretted. During his program, he decided that he would apologize to Dianne over the air, by playing the song, "I'm Sorry," and dedicating it to her. In the past, Rob had regularly used sarcasm, and the song was one that Dianne always considered rather "syrupy." When she heard it, she assumed that Rob was being sarcastic, and became very angry. She said to her roommate, "Great! Now he's dragging the whole campus into it." Then she picked up his picture and threw it on the floor.

1.   Rob was acting as the _____ of a message when he played the song.

2.   Dianne was acting as the _____ of a message when she heard the song.

3.   Rob began the communication process when he decided to express his thoughts through the use of the song. We call this stage of the process _____.

4.   When he actually played the song, he was engaging in a stage of the communication process known as _____.

5.   When Dianne heard the song and interpreted it, she was engaging in a stage of the communication process called _____.

6.   The airwaves served as a _____ of communication.

7.   Dianne's belief that the song was "syrupy" and her past experience with Rob's sarcasm could be called _____, because of their interference with the communication process.

8.   When Dianne became angry and threw Rob's picture on the floor, she was engaging in a stage of the communication process that is known as _____.

9.   The fact that Rob was involving the rest of the campus in their argument constitutes the _____ or _____ component of Dianne's message to her roommate.

10. Dianne's anger constituted the _____ component of her message to her roommate.

11. When Dianne threw Rob's picture on the floor, she was using a form of _____ communication.

12. When Rob said Dianne's name on the radio, he was using a form of _____ communication.

13. Rob's communication with Dianne was _____ because she did not interpret his message in the way that he had intended for it to be understood.

In the space provided, indicate whether the behavior described in each of the following items is nonassertive (NA), aggressive (AG), passive aggressive (PA), or assertive (AS).

1. _____ Cleaning up after a roommate, rather than confronting her regarding her poor housekeeping.

2. _____ Pretending to lose a roommate's phone messages because of dissatisfaction with her housekeeping.

3. _____ Stating that one is dissatisfied with a roommate's housekeeping and requesting that she clean up after herself.

4. _____ Shouting obscenities at a roommate as an expression of dissatisfaction with her housekeeping.

In the space provided, indicate whether the behavior described in each of the following items is an example of intensification (I), deintensification (D), neutralization (N), or masking (M).

1. _____ Pretending to be disappointed when an appointment with one's supervisor is cancelled, while actually feeling relieved.

2. _____ Pretending to be extremely disappointed when an appointment with one's supervisor is cancelled, while actually feeling only moderately disappointed.

3. _____ Pretending to be only moderately disappointed when an appointment with one's supervisor is cancelled, while actually feeling extremely disappointed.

4. _____ Showing no external signs of emotion when an appointment with one's supervisor is cancelled.

In the space provided, indicate whether the behavior described in each of the following items is an example of functional-professional touch (FP), social-polite touch (SP), friendship-warmth touch (FW), love-intimacy touch (LI), or sexual arousal touch (SA).

1. _____ Jerry sees his friend Bill at a party and pats him on the back.

2. _____ Bill introduces Jerry to his friend, Mike. Jerry and Mike shake hands.
3. _____ Bill and his "significant other," Nancy hold hands.
4. _____ Nancy introduces Mike to her roommate, Angela. Mike and Angela leave together, and wake up the following morning in each other's arms.
5. _____ Jerry wakes up the following morning with a large bump on his forehead. He goes to the student health center, where a doctor examines him. The doctor touches the bump and asks Jerry if it hurts.

In the space provided, indicate whether the behavior exhibited by the R.A. in each of the following items is an example of a minimal verbal response (M), summarization (S), reflection (R), paraphrase (P), an open-ended question (O), or a clarification response (C).

1. _____ **R.A.** How's everything going?

    RESIDENT Fine, except that I just flunked a math test.

2. _____ **R.A.** Do you mean that you got the test back and received a failing grade?

    RESIDENT No. I just took the test, but I know I bombed it.

3. _____ **R.A.** You don't think you'll get a very good grade on the test.

    RESIDENT No, in fact, I'm sure I won't.

4. _____ **R.A.** So things aren't really fine. You're disappointed.

    RESIDENT Of course, I am. I really studied for that test.

5. _____ **R.A.** Mmm hmm.

    RESIDENT I hate getting bad grades, especially when I put in a lot of time studying. Besides, my parents will kill me if I flunk that class. They'll think that all I do is party, and that's not true.

6. _____ **R.A.** So you're concerned about a few things. You don't think you did very well on your test, and are frustrated and disappointed. You like to do well in school, particularly when you put a lot of time into a class. You're also concerned about how your parents will react if you fail a class. You're worried that they might think that you didn't apply yourself.

    RESIDENT That's right.

After reading the following paragraph, complete the accompanying statements by filling in the blanks.

A group of students, Pete, Marla, Cathy, and Kevin, decided to meet each Friday night to play *Dungeons and Dragons*, and decided to reserve a room in the student union on their campus. Pete went to the union manager to reserve the room and was told that he and his friends could not use the space, because they were not a registered student organization. Afterwards, Pete went back to the group and reported that he "ran into some snags" in reserving the room, but gave no further information. Marla then went to speak with the manager, and was also informed of the policy. She then told her friends that they could not use the space, but did not explain that they could use the room if they were registered. Cathy then went to speak with the manager, and was likewise informed of the policy. When she returned to the group, she stated that her experience only confirmed her belief that the university administration did not really care about students, but cared only about making money by renting the rooms out to off-campus groups. Finally, Kevin went to speak with the manager, and was also informed of the policy. Kevin explained to the union manager that he understood the rationale behind the policy, and knew that the manager could not violate it. He pointed out, however, that the group was simply looking for an alternative form of Friday night entertainment that would not involve the use of alcohol. After discussing the matter further, the union manager explained to Kevin that he and the other three students qualified to register as a student organization. He referred Kevin to the student activities office, and even agreed to serve as the group's advisor. The group was then able to use the room.

1. _____ showed sharpening in his/her interpretation of the manager's position on the use of space in the union.

2. _____ showed assimilation in her/his interpretation of the manager's position on the use of space in the union.

3. _____ showed leveling in his/her interpretation of the manager's position on the use of space in the union.

4. _____ demonstrated win/win communication in her/his interaction with the union manager.

In the space provided, indicate whether the pattern of discourse used in each of the following speech outlines is narrative (N), process (P), cause-effect (CE), analysis (A), definition (D), or classification (C).

1. _____   Reasons for alcohol abuse on campus:
   a. Few alternative forms of entertainment
   b. Absence of parental influence
   c. Peer pressure

2. _____ Understanding alcoholism and alcohol abuse on campus:
   a. Alcoholism defined
   b. Alcohol abuse defined

3. _____ The history of alcohol use and abuse on campus:
   a. Prior to 1920.
   b. The 1920's and 1930's
   c. The 1940's and 1950's
   d. The 1960's and 1970's
   e. The 1980's and today.

4. _____ Preventing alcohol abuse on campus through responsible hosting.
   a. Planning your party.
   b. Conducting your party
   c. Seeing that your guests return home safely

5. _____ Nonalcoholic campus entertainment alternatives:
   a. Sports and recreation:
      1. Bowling
      2. Billiards
      3. Roller skating
      4. Table tennis
   b. Fine arts:
      1. Films
      2. Plays
      3. Concerts
      4. Live comedy
      5. Poetry readings
   c. Guest lectures:
      1. Departmentally sponsored lectures
      2. Student sponsored lectures

6. _____ Alcohol abuse on campus:
   a. Historical perspective
   b. Factors contributing to alcohol abuse on campus
   c. Strategies for preventing alcohol abuse on campus:
      1. Institutional policies
      2. Responsible party-planning
      3. Entertainment alternatives

In the space provided, indicate whether each of the following titles describes a speech to inform (I), a speech to persuade (P), or a speech to entertain (E).

1. _____ Cocurricular Involvement Opportunities on Campus
2. _____ Ten Good Reasons to Become Involved in Cocurricular Activities
3. _____ In Recognition of Outstanding Cocurricular Involvement

In the space provided, indicate whether the interaction described in each of the following items would traditionally be carried out at intimate (I), personal (PR), social (S), or public (PB) distance.

1. _____ An applicant for an R.A. position is interviewed by a residence hall director.
2. _____ One student proposes marriage to another student.
3. _____ Two students walk in opposite directions across a large parking lot. They look at each other as they pass, but do not interact verbally.
4. _____ Two roommates share a pizza and talk about the latest developments on their favorite soap opera.

In the space provided, indicate whether the body orientations presented in each of the following items are inclusive (IL), noninclusive (N), vis-a-vis (V), parallel (P), congruent (C), or incongruent (IG).

1. _____ Michael and Jennifer sit across the table from each other in the cafeteria, and talk about a test that they took.
2. _____ Maria leans forward, looks at John, and tells him that she is concerned about something, while John leans back and watches television.
3. _____ Debbie, Carol, and Stuart stand in a circle, during a class break, while Ted stands outside the circle.
4. _____ Todd and Jim sit next to each other in class, and Todd asks to see Jim's notes.
5. _____ Jeff and Larry both lean toward each other while having a discussion about religion.
6. _____ Beth and Lynne are standing close to each other and talking when they notice Laurie approaching. They move apart from each other and turn toward Laurie.

In the space provided, identify each of the behaviors described in the following items as an example of impromptu speech (I), extemporaneous speech (E), reading from a manuscript (MA), reciting from memory (ME), active listening (A), or passive listening (P).

1. _____ The president of a university holds a press conference and reads a statement from the board of trustees.

2. _____ The president refers to some general notes, while commenting on the action taken by the board.

3. _____ A reporter listens to what the president says, but does not respond verbally or nonverbally.

4. _____ The president responds spontaneously to a question from another reporter.

5. _____ The reporter leans forward and looks at the president while the president is speaking. The reporter then asks the president to clarify the response given to the previous question.

6. _____ The president directly quotes the chairman of the board, without referring to any written documentation.

In the space provided, indicate whether the body language described in each of the following items is an example of an emblem (E), illustrator (I), regulator (R.), or adaptor (A).

1. _____ Wendy cries when she hears about her grandmother's death.

2. _____ Frank looks at Jason and points to his watch. Jason, who is on the phone, nods his head and holds up his index finger.

3. _____ Susan spreads her arms apart while describing her sorority's homecoming float.

4. _____ Michelle is in a meeting and another member of her organization is speaking. Michelle holds up her hand, to indicate that she wishes to interject a comment.

In the space provided, indicate whether each of the following items illustrates congruence (C), empathy (E), or acceptance (A).

1. _____ Kimberly and Rachel often disagree about politics and religion, but they are very good friends. Despite their differences, they respect each other completely.

2. _____ Anthony understands the negative feelings that exist between his father and his brother, even though he has always enjoyed a very close relationship with both his father and his brother.

3. _____ Andy is feeling very upset and acknowledges these feelings in a conversation with his roommate.

Complete the following statements by filling in the blanks.

1. The letters in the acronym, DESC, stand for _____, _____, _____, and _____.

2. The _____ principle states that people tend to be drawn toward those whom they like and with whom they enjoy interacting, and tend to be drawn away from those whom they do not like and with whom they do not enjoy interacting.

3. A communication style that is characterized by high openness and low respect is called _____.

4. A communication style that is characterized by low openness and low respect is called _____.

5. A communication style that is characterized by high openness and high respect is called _____.

6. A communication style that is characterized by low openness and high respect is called _____.

7. The ways in which facial expressions are controlled, in order to conform to societal expectations, are known as _____ or _____.

8. Nonverbal _____ refers to all actions that are not verbal in nature, while nonverbal _____ refers only to nonverbal actions that are interpreted as messages.

9. Components of vocal expression include _____, _____, _____, and _____.

Both Sides of the Story

Prepare a defense for both the affirmative and negative positions on the following statements.

1. There are circumstances under which it is appropriate to lie.
2. There are circumstances under which it is appropriate to behave aggressively.
3. There are circumstances under which it is appropriate to behave nonassertively.
4. There are circumstances under which it is appropriate to behave in a passive aggressive manner.

Sorting It Out

Respond to each of the following questions by taking a position and defending it.

1. Is content or delivery more important in a public speech?
2. Is it more important that leaders be able to listen effectively or that they be able to speak effectively?
3. Which type of nonverbal behavior (i.e. gesture and movement, facial expressions, voice, space, touch) is most important in nonverbal communication?
4. Is it more important that leaders be effective in communicating with groups or with individuals?

It's Your Call

Read each of the following scenarios and prepare an essay in response to the questions provided.

1. You are the president of your residence hall council and have become concerned about the interpersonal communication patterns between two of the group's members. The two students have a close relationship, but their communication styles are opposite to each other. One of the individuals has a very aggressive style, while the other has a very nonassertive style. The nonassertive group member seems to be highly dependent upon the aggressive member, despite the fact that the aggressive member is very abusive and domineering, even within their relationship. The dynamics of the relationship have begun to have an impact on the functioning of your group. Several other group members have expressed their concern, and have encouraged you to confront at least one or the other of the two group members.
   a. What do you see as your alternative courses of action?
   b. What do you see as the advantages and disadvantages of each alternative?
   c. Which course of action will you take?
   d. Why have you chosen this course of action?
2. You are a volunteer in the Big Brother/Big Sister program, which was initiated to provide guidance and companionship for troubled youths within your local community. You have been asked to speak about the program to the students enrolled in an introductory sociology course, but have been given a great deal of freedom in planning the details of the speech.
   a. What will you identify as the purpose of your speech?
   b. Why have you chosen this particular purpose?
   c. What specific aspects of the program will you discuss?

d. Why have you chosen to focus on these particular aspects?

e. What method of delivery will you use?

f. Why have you chosen this method of delivery?

g. What pattern of discourse will you use?

h. Why have you chosen this pattern of discourse?

3. You are the president of the international club on your campus, and have recently received complaints from a number of students in the club, regarding your faculty advisor's tendency to touch students while he is talking with them. You have noticed this behavior, and believe that it is due to a difference in culture, since your advisor is from another country. However, the students have told you that they are offended by his behavior. Many of the students regard it as a form of sexual harassment.

    a. What do you see as your alternative courses of action?

    b. What do you see as the advantages and disadvantages of each alternative?

    c. Which course of action will you take?

    d. Why have you chosen this course of action?

4. You are the captain of the rugby club on your campus. Together with your teammates, you have decided to organize a fund raising activity, to help cover the cost of a trip that you will be taking. The project that you have decided to undertake is a St. Patrick's Day happy hour, at which green beer will be sold. The members of the club chose this project because of its fund raising potential and also because of their desire to have a traditional celebration of the holiday. You would like to hold the event in the student union. However, while the university is strongly committed to increasing use of the union by student organizations, a recently adopted policy prohibits consumption of alcoholic beverages in the building. The policy reflects a growing concern within the administration, surrounding the issue of alcohol abuse on campus. You have made an appointment with the manager of the union, and are committed to using win/win communication.

    a. On what points would you be most willing to compromise?

    b. On what points would you be least willing to compromise?

    c. Why have you chosen to set your priorities in this way?

    d. What do you see as your alternative courses of action?

    e. What do you see as the advantages and disadvantages of each alternative?

    f. Which alternative would you most support?

    g. Why would you favor this alternative?

Group Dynamics

What You Will Learn in This Chapter

This chapter will present a definition of groups which incorporates the following characteristics:

- Two or more members
- Interaction between members
- Interdependence
- Sense of belonging
- Mutual influence among members
- Norms
- Roles
- Shared goals
- Rewards for members

Contrasts will be drawn between the group and a related concept, the aggregate.

Motives for joining and remaining in groups will be examined, and the following concepts will be introduced:

- Functions of groups:
  - ➤ Informational function
  - ➤ Interpersonal function
  - ➤ Material function
- Synergy
- Cohesiveness

The following stages of group development will be examined:

- Forming
- Storming
- Norming
- Performing

Three general categories of common group member roles will be presented, along with examples of each:

- Group task roles:
  - Initiator-contributor
  - Information seeker
  - Opinion seeker
  - Information giver
  - Opinion giver
  - Elaborator
  - Coordinator
  - Orienter
  - Evaluator-critic
  - Energizer
  - Procedural technician
  - Recorder

- Group building and maintenance roles:
  - Encourager
  - Harmonizer
  - Compromiser
  - Gate-keeper and expediter
  - Standard setter or ego ideal
  - Group-observer and commentator

- Individual or self-centered roles:
  - Aggressor
  - Blocker
  - Recognition-seeker
  - Self-confessor
  - Playboy
  - Dominator
  - Help-seeker
  - Special interest pleader

Chapter 6

═══Group Dynamics═══════════════

We are all dependent on one another, every soul of us on earth.
George Bernard Shaw

───────────

Why Study Group Dynamics?

The study of group dynamics is important for aspiring leaders because it enables them to understand their followers, not only as individuals but as members of larger social or organizational units. These units invariably have characteristics of their own, which sometimes differ dramatically from those of the individuals who comprise them. In fact, even the individuals in a group often behave differently within the context of that group than they do in other settings.

As a leader, you will often work with your followers as a group. In fact, even when dealing specifically with individual followers, it will be nearly impossible for you to remove yourselves entirely from the influence of the group.

Although each group is unique, certain characteristics and patterns of behavior in groups are nearly universal. By recognizing common group phenomena, as they occur in your own organization, you will be able to anticipate possible problems and can plan accordingly. For example, by observing the behavior of individuals within the group, and applying your knowledge of group dynamics, you will undoubtedly develop a sense of whether or not certain group members could work closely with one another and produce favorable results. This judgement would surely influence decisions that you would make, concerning work assignments.

By developing an understanding of group dynamics, you will also be better prepared to respond to difficulties that might occur within your group. For example, if your group were to fall into an unproductive pattern of behavior, you might use your knowledge of group dynamics to examine the behavior of individual members, and ultimately conclude that the behavior of one group member is the source of the problem. You could then deal individually with that group member.

A strong foundation in group dynamics can also spare you a good deal of anguish, simply by helping you to recognize that which you are powerless to change. For example, at some time in your group experience, you might be faced with interpersonal conflict. This may be quite disturbing to you, yet the basic principles of group dynamics might lead you to conclude that the pattern of behavior is "just a phase," that is necessary to the development of the group. This knowledge may not make the experience any more pleasant, but at least you will not be blaming yourself for it. You will also have some consolation in the fact that, in all likelihood, it will eventually work itself out.

What Constitutes a Group?

Although in common usage, the word "**group**" may be applied to nearly any collection of individuals, social scientists who study group phenomena define the term much more narrowly. While even specialists in group dynamics have yet to settle on a single definition, they are generally in agreement concerning certain basic characteristics of groups.

One of the most obvious of these characteristics is the presence of two or more members within the group. It is certainly possible to identify a human category into which only one person would be classified. For example, at any given time, there can be only one president of your college or university. However, such a category would not constitute a group, for reasons that will become increasingly clear to you as we begin to examine the other characteristics of groups.

While it is necessary that groups have two or more members, this characteristic alone does not make them groups. In order for people to be considered a group, they must interact with one another (Johnson and Johnson, 1991). Obviously, not all collections of individuals could accurately be described as groups, if we apply this standard. For example, if you were to use the local public transit system to commute to your campus, you might encounter the same collection of people at your bus stop each day, without ever communicating with one another. Under the circumstances described, you would not be considered a group.

Another characteristic of groups is that their members are interdependent, meaning that they depend upon one another (Johnson and Johnson, 1991). Using our previous example once again, the people at your bus stop would not automatically become a group simply by your striking up a conversation with them. Although this type of interaction might draw them closer to one another, it would not necessarily lead to interdependence, since the bus would stop at the corner even if only one person were waiting there.

In addition to the characteristics described thus far, members of a group must view themselves as belonging to the group, and they must be viewed by others as belonging to the group (Johnson and Johnson, 1991). In our example, even if you were to form a car pool with the other people at your bus stop, thereby creating interdependence, you would still not necessarily become a group. You might simply regard your arrangement as a matter of convenience, and not develop any feelings of connectedness with one another.

Social scientists specializing in the study of group dynamics have frequently observed that the members of groups exert influence over one another (Johnson.and Johnson, 1991). Of course, one need not be an expert in the field to have observed this particular phenomenon. You have probably already noticed that individuals in your own life often behave differently when they are with different people. Think of how many times you have made comments such as "He's such a jerk when he's with his friends," or "She's so stuck up whenever he's around."

A related characteristic of groups is that their members "share norms concerning matters of common interest and participate in a system of interlocking roles" (Johnson and Johnson, 1991, p. 14). **Norms** have been defined as "the rules or expectations that specify appropriate behavior in the group; the standards by which group members regulate their actions" (Johnson and Johnson, 1991, p. 507). You will recall from our discussion in Chapter 3 that roles are those sets of expectations which are placed upon individuals because of the particular positions that they occupy. Within groups, several specific group member roles commonly emerge. We will discuss these roles in detail, later in this chapter.

In addition to the qualities stated previously, it has been noted that groups are characterized by common goals which are shared by their members (Johnson and Johnson, 1991). On your campus, students who volunteer their time to work on a political campaign may, as individuals, desire to improve their own prospects of holding a public office at some time in the future. However, it is the shared goal of mounting a winning campaign for the present candidate that unites the volunteers as a group.

It has also been noted that members of groups find the group experience rewarding (Johnson and Johnson, 1991). Unless a member finds some satisfaction in the overall experience, it is unlikely that he or she will remain in a group where membership is voluntary.

Social scientists have contrasted genuine groups with other collections of individuals that do not manifest the defining characteristics described here. They use the term, "**aggregate**," in reference to "collections of individuals who do not interact with one another" (Johnson and Johnson, 1991, p. 13). The people at the bus stop, as originally described in our example, would be identified as an aggregate, rather than as a group, because they did not engage in any significant interaction with one another.

Why Do People Join Groups?

We join groups for a number of reasons. It has been noted that groups perform three general functions: (1) an **informational function**, (2) an **interpersonal function**, and (3) a **material function** (Kiesler, 1978). The informational function refers simply to the benefit of other people's opinions, and particularly their reactions to our own behavior. Interacting with others in groups enables us to learn more about ourselves. The interpersonal function of groups refers to the psychological benefits of interacting with others. This process, in itself, can provide us with feelings of security and self-esteem. The material function of groups refers to the power of individual members to enjoy tangible benefits that can be made available to them only by pooling their resources.

In examining the various purposes served by groups, it is helpful to understand a concept known as "**synergy**." This term is used in reference to the total energy available to the group for the accomplishment of its goals (Baird and Weinberg, 1981). The synergy of the group represents the combined energy of the group members. It has been noted, however, that in "synergistic" relationships, the outcome is often "greater than the sum of the individual parts" (Benton and Halloran, 1991, p. 322). In all likelihood, you have seen this phenomenon at work in your own group. Each time that you have had a discussion in which the merits of a particular suggestion were weighed, and improvements were recommended, synergy was at work in your group. Group members working together generally produce a better decision than could be reached with each member developing a proposal independently, because it is usually possible to improve upon even the best individual plan by introducing a different perspective.

It should be noted that the factors which draw people into a group are not always the same factors which lead them to continue their membership in the group. For example, a student might join a service organization that is committed to the elimination of world hunger, simply because his closest friends belong to the group. However, through his participation in the group, he might develop such a strong commitment to the group's goals that he would remain in the organization even if his friends were to no longer participate.

In explaining the longevity of certain groups, and the continued participation of individual members, specialists in group dynamics often use the word, "**cohesiveness**." This term has been defined as:

> All the forces (both positive and negative) that cause individuals to maintain their membership in specific groups. These include attraction to other group members and a close match between individuals' needs and the goals and activities of the group. The attractiveness that a group has for its members and that the members have for one another (Johnson and Johnson, 1991, p. 504).

How Groups Develop

You will recall from our discussion on theories of leadership that two types of group behavior exist: (1) those which relate to the group's task, and (2) those which promote healthy relationships between group members. As you reflect on your own experiences in groups, you will probably realize that it takes time for groups to develop satisfactory patterns, where both types of behavior are concerned. Initially, group members are usually at least somewhat reserved in their interaction with one another. Usually, they are also at least somewhat unsure of the specific demands of their tasks. With time, however, most group members develop a clear sense of what is expected of them and can work productively with one another.

Bruce Tuckman (1965) identified four stages that typically characterize the development of groups, as they become fully functioning units. This "developmental sequence" relates to both the "interpersonal" and "task activity" realms of group behavior.

The first stage in Tuckman's (1965) sequence is one that is characterized by a process which he has labeled "**forming**." At this stage, group members attempt to master their tasks. They also attempt to find out what is expected of them in their relationships with one another. Orientation to both the task and group member relations is accomplished through a process of testing.

In the task activity realm, group members often show dependency during this stage. For example, a group of new Resident Assistants might refer frequently to their staff manuals, in addition to asking frequent questions of their supervisor and one another.

In the interpersonal realm, orientation involves efforts to establish the limits of acceptable behavior, largely through experimentation. Often this process involves a series of progressively greater risks on the part of individual group members. In our example, the Resident Assistants might test the standards of decorum at staff meetings by interjecting slang terms into their speech. If so, they would probably still introduce a few expressions that are considered only slightly vulgar before they would unleash any that are decidedly obscene.

According to Tuckman (1965), the second stage of group development "is characterized by conflict and polarization around interpersonal issues, with concomitant emotional responding in the task sphere" (p. 396). He added that "these behaviors serve as resistance to group influence and task requirements and may be labeled as **storming**" (p. 396). At this stage, the residence hall staff in our example might argue internally over such matters as the R.A. duty schedule, procedures for dealing with disciplinary infractions, or programming requirements. Conflict and resistance might manifest themselves in comments such as "Her floor is noisier than mine," or "Why should I have to take duty on the holiday weekend?"

In the third stage of development, group members become more comfortable and open with one another. Cohesiveness develops within the group. The members of the group overcome their resistance to the task, and develop clearly defined expectations of one another. Tuckman (1965) used the word, "**norming**," in reference to the behavior of groups at this stage.

Again using our residence hall example, we would expect to see some of the conflicts among the R.A.'s resolved at this stage. They might, for example, become more willing to accept undesirable duty nights, with the understanding that such assignments would be distributed evenly among the R.A.'s over the course of the year.

During the final stage of group development, known as the "**performing**" stage, issues related to norms and roles are no longer of central concern. In the words of Tuckman (1965, p. 396), "roles become flexible and functional, and group energy is channeled into the task." In our example, once this stage is reached, the R.A.'s would probably show less concern over such matters as equity in staff assignments, and would focus instead on the quality of life in the residence hall.

The Individual and the Group

In examining behavior patterns which typically emerge in groups, social scientists have identified three different categories of common group member roles. These categories are: (1) **group task roles**, (2) **group building and maintenance roles**, and (3) **individual roles** (Benne and Sheats, 1948[*]).

The group task roles are those which directly facilitate the identification and achievement of group goals. Specific group task roles have been described as follows:

- The *initiator-contributor* suggests or proposes to the group new ideas or a changed way of regarding the group problem or goal. The novelty proposed may take the form of suggestions of a new group goal or a new definition of the problem. It may take the form of a suggested solution or some way of handling a difficulty that the group has encountered. Or it may take the form of a proposed new procedure for the group, a new way of organizing the group for the task ahead.

- The *information seeker* asks for clarification of suggestions made in terms of their factual adequacy, for authoritative information and facts pertinent to the problem being discussed.

---

[*]From "Functional Roles of Group Members" by Kenneth D. Benne and Paul Sheats in JOURNAL OF SOCIAL ISSUES, Vol. 4, No. 2, pp. 41-49. Copyright © by The Society for the Psychological Study of Social Issues. Reprinted by permission.

- The *opinion seeker* asks not primarily for the facts of the case but for a clarification of the values pertinent to what the group is undertaking or of values involved in a suggestion made or in alternative suggestions.

- The *information giver* offers facts or generalizations which are "authoritative" or relates his [sic] own experience pertinently to the group problem.

- The *opinion giver* states his [sic] belief or opinion pertinently to a suggestion made or to alternative suggestions. The emphasis is on his [sic] proposal of what should become the group's view of pertinent values, not primarily upon relevant facts or information.

- The *elaborator* spells out suggestions in terms of examples or developed meanings, offers a rationale for suggestions previously made and tries to deduce how an idea or suggestion would work out if adopted by the group.

- The *coordinator* shows or clarifies the relationships among various ideas and suggestions, tries to pull ideas and suggestions together or tries to coordinate the activities of various members or sub-groups.

- The *orienter* defines the position of the group with respect to its goals by summarizing what has occurred, points to departures from agreed upon directions or goals, or raises questions about the direction which the group discussion is taking.

- The *evaluator-critic* subjects the accomplishment of the group to some standard or set of standards of group-functioning in the context of the group task. Thus, he [sic] may evaluate or question the "practicality," the "logic," the "facts," or the "procedure" of a suggestion or some unit of group discussion.

- The *energizer* prods the group to action or decision, attempts to stimulate or arouse the group to "greater" or "higher quality" activity.

- The *procedural technician* expedites group movement by doing things for the group — performing routine tasks, e.g., distributing materials, or manipulating objects for the group, e.g., rearranging the seating or running the recording machine, etc.

- The *recorder* writes down suggestions, makes a record of group decisions, or writes down the product of discussion. The recorder role is the "group memory" (Benne and Sheats, 1948, pp. 43-44).

The group building and maintenance roles are those which are concerned with promoting healthy relationships between group members. These group member roles are sometimes described as "relationship oriented." Specific roles of this nature have been described as follows:

- The *encourager* praises, agrees with and accepts the contribution of others. He [sic] indicates warmth and solidarity in his [sic] attitude toward other group members, offers commendation and praise and in various ways indicates understanding and acceptance of other points of view, ideas and suggestions.

- The *harmonizer* mediates the differences between other members, attempts to reconcile disagreements, relieves tension in conflict situations through jesting or pouring oil on the troubled waters, etc.

- The *compromiser* operates from within a conflict in which his [sic] idea or position is involved. He [sic] may offer compromise by yielding status, admitting his [sic] error, by disciplining himself [sic] to maintain group harmony, or by "coming half-way" in moving along with the group.

- The *gate-keeper and expediter* attempts to keep communication channels open by encouraging or facilitating the participation of others ("we haven't got the ideas of Mr. X yet," etc.) or by proposing regulation of the flow of communication ("why don't we limit the length of our contributions so that everyone will have a chance to contribute?" etc.)

- The *standard setter* or *ego ideal* expresses standards for the group to attempt to achieve in its functioning or applies standards in evaluating the quality of group processes.

- The *group-observer* and *commentator* keeps records of various aspects of group process and feeds such data with proposed interpretations into the group's evaluation of its own procedures (Benne and Sheats, 1948, pp. 44-45).

Individual roles are those which are intended to support the individual group member's own personal goals, rather than the goals of the group. In fact, the behaviors that characterize these roles often undermine efforts to achieve the goals of the group. Appropriately, these group member roles are also known as **"self-centered roles"** (Baird and Weinberg, 1981, p. 171). They include the following:

- The *aggressor* may work in many ways — deflating the status of others, expressing disapproval of the values, acts or feelings of others, attacking the group or the problem that it is working on, joking aggressively, showing envy toward another's contribution by trying to take credit for it, etc.

- The *blocker* tends to be negativistic and stubbornly resistant, disagreeing and opposing without or beyond "reason" and attempting to maintain or bring back an issue after the group has rejected or by-passed it.

- The *recognition-seeker* works in various ways to call attention to himself [sic], whether through boasting, reporting on personal achievements, acting in unusual ways, struggling to prevent his [sic] being placed in an "inferior" position, etc.

- The *self-confessor* uses the audience opportunity which the group setting provides to express personal, non-group oriented "feeling," "insight," "ideology," etc.

- The *playboy* [sic] makes a display of his [sic] lack of involvement in the group's processes. This may take the form of cynicism, nonchalance, horseplay and other more or less studied forms of "out of field" behavior.

- The *dominator* tries to assert authority or superiority in manipulating the group or certain members of the group. This domination may take the form of flattery, of asserting a superior status or right to attention, giving directions authoritatively, interrupting the contributions of others, etc.

- The *help-seeker* attempts to call forth "sympathy" response from other group members or from the whole group, whether through expressions of insecurity, personal confusion or depreciation of himself [sic] beyond "reason."

- The *special interest pleader* speaks for the "small business man, " the "grass roots" community, the "housewife," "labor," etc., usually cloaking his [sic] own prejudices or biases in the stereotype which best fits his [sic] individual need (Benne and Sheats, 1948, pp. 45-46).

It should be emphasized that both group task roles and group building and maintenance roles are necessary in order for a group to achieve its goals and provide a rewarding experience for its members. Individual roles are destructive insofar as they advance specific group members' agendas at the expense of the shared purposes of the group.

This is not to say that individual needs are not important. One of the reasons why many individuals remain in groups is that their personal needs are fulfilled through their membership. Group leaders can often promote both cohesiveness and group productivity by relating group concerns to those of the individual.

Summary

This chapter provided an introduction to the study of group dynamics. The material in this chapter was presented as a tool for understanding individual groups, and its value to group leaders was emphasized.

A definition of groups was presented. The characteristics identified included: (1) two or more members, (2) interaction between members, (3) interdependence, (4) a sense of belonging, (5) mutual influence among members, (6) norms, (7) roles, (8) shared goals, and (9) group member rewards. A contrast was drawn between groups and aggregates, with the distinction being that members of groups interact with one another while members of aggregates do not.

Reasons for joining groups were examined. It was noted that groups fulfill three basic purposes: (1) the informational function, (2) the interpersonal function, and (3) the material function. The word "synergy" was introduced, in reference to the total energy available for the accomplishment of group goals. The term "cohesiveness" was used to refer to those factors which motivate members of a group to continue their participation in it.

The chapter included a model of group development which applies to both the relationship and task activity realms of group behavior. This "developmental sequence" includes four stages, each characterized by a different type of behavior. The four categories of behavior, respectively, are: (1) forming, (2) storming, (3) norming, and (4) performing.

Information was presented on three categories of common group member roles: (1) group task roles, (2) group building and maintenance roles, and (3) individual or self-centered roles. Examples of specific roles in each category were also presented. Group task roles included: initiator-contributor, information seeker, opinion seeker, information giver, opinion giver, elaborator, coordinator, orienter, evaluator-critic, energizer, procedural technician, and recorder. Group building and maintenance roles included: encourager, harmonizer, compromiser, gate-keeper and expediter, standard setter or ego ideal, and group-observer and commentator. Individual or self-centered roles included: aggressor, blocker, recognition-seeker, self confessor, playboy, dominator, help-seeker, and special interest pleader.

It was noted that both group task roles and group building and maintenance roles serve important purposes in groups. Although it was acknowledged that individual or self-centered roles can hinder the success of groups, it was emphasized that the needs of individual members are a matter of concern to groups.

References

Baird, J. E. and Weinberg, S. B. (1981). *Group Communication*, 2nd ed. Dubuque, IA: Wm. C. Brown.

Benne, K. D. and Sheats, P. (1948). Functional roles of group members. *The Journal of Social Issues, 4* (2), 41-49.

Benton, D. and Halloran, J. (1991). *Applied Human Relations*, 4th ed. Englewood Cliffs, NJ: Prentice Hall.

Johnson, D. W. and Johnson, F. P. (1991). *Joining Together*, 4th ed. Englewood Cliffs, NJ: Prentice Hall.

Kiesler, S. B. (1978). *Interpersonal Processes in Groups and Organizations.* Arlington Heights, IL: AHM Publishing.

Tuckman, B. W. (1965). Developmental sequence in small groups. *Psychological Bulletin, 63* (6), 384-399.

Activities

Getting It Straight

Read the paragraphs below and respond to the items presented.

Four university-owned houses are located along a single block within walking distance of the campus. All of them are currently being used for student housing. The four houses are similar in style, but differ from one another in color, and in the characteristics of their occupants.

The blue house is occupied by a recently married couple. Both partners are students. The two were drawn together by a number of shared interests, along with a feeling of comfort and belonging which they both continue to experience when they are together. The two support each other emotionally, and both contribute to the household financially. The partners have also divided up the various household tasks. It is understood between them that one of the partners will manage their finances and do most of the interior housekeeping, while the other will do all of the yard work and most of the cooking. The partners also have a number of unwritten rules which govern their relationship. For example, they always discuss major decisions with each other, and insist on arriving at a consensus. Also, they take time each night to put their studies aside and talk with each other about the events of the day. Finally, they never go to sleep feeling angry toward each other. The two have found a great deal of personal fulfillment in their marriage. They both agree that they bring out the best in each other, and that together they can accomplish more than they could if they were acting independently. They both look forward to having children some day, and to buying a home of their own.

The white house is the smallest of the four houses. It is currently occupied by one graduate student. His goals are to complete his Ph.D. in English and to write "the great American novel." He enjoys living alone, as it allows him to concentrate on his academic work, and to live in a manner in which he is comfortable.

The pink house is by far the largest on the block. This three-story structure has been divided into six apartments, each of which has its own exterior entrance. Each apartment is occupied by one student. The residents rarely even see one another, much less engage in conversation. Each resident is intensely focused on his or her studies, and is determined to launch a successful career upon graduation. The residents of the building expect very little of one another, except that they be quiet and that they not damage the building. In general, the residents of the building are happy with their living arrangements.

The yellow house is occupied by five members of a religious student organization for men. The organization has clearly established rules which govern its communal life, and each member has been assigned specific responsibilities to the organization. The organization also has a clearly articulated mission of social service, which is supported by all of the members. The five students are all seniors, and all have been members of the organization since their freshman year. The five students were drawn into the organization by their commitment to its stated ideals; a commitment which they continue to share today. Over the years, they have also found a great deal of personal fulfillment in their relationship with one another. Each member of the organization provides emotional support to the other members. Consequently, they all feel a sense of belonging in their home. They have also come to depend upon the advice that they receive from one another. Before making major decisions in their personal lives, the students often ask one another for guidance.

1. List each house which is the home of a group.
2. List each house which is the home of an aggregate.
3. List each house in which the residents have a relationship that is characterized by cohesiveness.
4. The residents of which house are most clearly described as having a synergistic relationship?

List the three main categories of group functions, as described in this chapter:

1. _____
2. _____
3. _____

Number the following stages of group development, according to sequence, with 1 representing the first stage and 4 representing the last stage.

_____   Norming
_____   Performing
_____   Storming
_____   Forming

Label each of the following group member roles as a group task role (T), a group building and maintenance role (B.), or an individual role (I).

_____   Initiator-contributor
_____   Information seeker
_____   Playboy
_____   Standard setter or ego ideal
_____   Dominator
_____   Orienter
_____   Evaluator-critic
_____   Gate-keeper and expediter

_____   Information giver
_____   Opinion giver
_____   Aggressor
_____   Group-observer and commentator
_____   Energizer
_____   Procedural technician
_____   Coordinator
_____   Self-confessor
_____   Harmonizer
_____   Compromiser
_____   Opinion seeker
_____   Blocker
_____   Recognition-seeker
_____   Recorder
_____   Encourager
_____   Elaborator
_____   Help-seeker
_____   Special interest pleader

Respond to the following items by identifying the stage of group development that is described.

1. _____   The members of the Environmental Awareness Committee are hard at work, implementing their plan for protecting the environment and increasing sensitivity to environmental issues on campus. A subcommittee is in the process of distributing leaflets on campus, in support of an environmental protection bill which will be placed before the voters in an upcoming referendum. Another subcommittee is currently negotiating with the administration of the university, in an effort to establish a recycling program on campus. A third subcommittee is in the process of developing a plan for the group's future activities. The group is enjoying a very productive year and morale is high.

2. _____   There is a great deal of turmoil on the Committee. The group recently selected its formal leaders, but the informal leaders have not yet emerged. Several

individuals are now vying for the other group members' attention and support, and are showing resistance toward the officers of the organization.

3. _____   The members of the Committee have now begun to trust one another, and to think of themselves as a group. They have established predictable patterns of relating to one another, and have accepted their own roles within the group. They are in the process of finalizing an action plan, and are enthusiastically looking forward to moving ahead with their activities.

4. _____   The members of the Committee are becoming acquainted with one another. They are fairly cautious in relating to one another, taking some risks but being careful not to offend. They are also attempting to clarify the purpose of the organization.

After reviewing the following dialogue, complete the items presented, according to the instructions provided.

CALVIN	We need to begin our plans for this year's homecoming weekend.
JENNIFER	Well, what do you guys think we should start with?
JANIECE	We should probably start by settling on a theme.
KRISTY	That's a good idea.
JANIECE	I was thinking something like "Celebrating Our Past, Building Our Future."
ASHLEY	That's stupid. It's such a cliche.
KRISTY	Oh, I like it. It was a good suggestion, Janiece.
BEN	How can you say that? Celebrating our past? Come on! This university has a long history of exploiting student athletes, and nothing about that has changed. I couldn't believe that business about the football scholarships. That's what we should be working on. I think we should get the alumni to put pressure on the board of trustees.
CALVIN	Ben, I understand what you're saying, and we have a committee that's working on that, but I really think we need to stay focused on homecoming.
REBECCA	I agree with you, Calvin, but I can also appreciate Ben's concerns about the theme. What if we'd change it to "Embracing Our Past, Building Our Future?"

WENDY	That's good, because it really just implies an acceptance of something that we can't change and a commitment to improving what we can change. I like it.
JENNIFER	Janiece, how do you feel about it?
JANIECE	I'm fine with it. Is it ok with you, Ben?
BEN	I guess, but I just keep thinking about that thing with the scholarships.
REBECCA	I understand how you feel, Ben, but we've got people working on it.
BILL	I just want to clarify where we're at on this homecoming. We've decided that we need to settle on a theme, and at this point it looks like we're leaning toward "Embracing Our Past, Building Our Future." That way, we can keep the basic idea of Janiece's suggestion, but can also address some of Ben's concerns.
WENDY	It will probably also appeal to the alumni.
STEPHEN	Well, they'll be so drunk anything will appeal to them. Remember those two guys last year who T.P.'d the trees outside the union?
GREGORY	Excuse me, Steve. I just want to make sure that we're all clear on some of the details of what we're talking about here. Now the theme will be the actual basis for the events that will be planned, right? So, for instance, as part of "Embracing Our Past," we could have reunion receptions for any of the classes that are at a ten-year mark. For "Building Our Future," we could have the President and Director of Development present an information session on the master plan.
ASHLEY	Oh, not the master plan! I am so sick of hearing about that thing.
WENDY	Well. I'm a little tired of it too, but it would probably be something that the alumni would be interested in.
HEATHER	How many alumni are coming for the weekend?
JAMIE	I checked with the alumni office, and they said that they usually get about 500.
THERESE	We had more than that the year that I was in charge of it. Of course, we were really well organized. I gave everyone a list of alumni to contact, and I made sure I followed up with everyone. If they didn't contact their people, they were out. That's real important. In fact, George, write that down.
MICAH	Contacting people individually might be a good idea. Were you able to determine for sure whether or not that was a factor in people's decisions to come? For example, what proportion of the people who you contacted showed up, in comparison to the rest

	of the alumni? If there was no difference, I don't know that you can conclude that personally contacting them was what brought them here.
THERESE	All I know is that there were a bunch of alumni who came up to me and were telling me what a good job I did on it. They said it was the best one that they'd been to. In fact, a couple of them told me that the last time they came, it was so bad that they weren't going to come to it again, but that after talking with me, they were convinced.
HEATHER	Therese, did people call the alumni or did they just write to them?
THERESE	They called them. I thought that would work best, since it's more personal. I went to so much trouble to get calling cards.
ASHLEY	Therese, would you shut up! Geez, nobody cares!
REBECCA	Oh, I wouldn't say that. I think people are interested in things that worked, but we need to stay focused on ways to use them in this year's program.
KRISTY	That's a good point, Rebecca.
JAMIE	Getting back to Heather's question, some of the people did both. They wrote first, and then they followed up with a phone call.
JENNIFER	What did you think of that? Did it work very well?
JAMIE	Yeah, but the people who did it really wanted to.
JASON	I wasn't comfortable with the phone call part of it, but then I'm really not very good at talking on the phone. If we did it again, I think I'd want someone else to do that part for me.
MICAH	I'm wondering if it will be practical to do it at all. It sounds really time consuming.
HEATHER	Well, how many people did you have working on it?
JAMIE	On the entire project, about ten, but only a couple of us did both phone calls and letters.
THERESE	Well, the letters are no problem, because Andrew can do them on his computer. Jamie, in the next couple of days, stop by the alumni office again and get a list from them. I'll need a copy and so will Andrew. That way, he can get going on the letters, and I'll get everyone else going on the phone calls.
BRENDA	Alice, you've been kind of quiet, and I know you worked on homecoming last year. What did you think of the thing with the phone calls?
ALICE	I don't care. I have been under so much stress lately. The last thing I want to think about is whether we should call or write to the alumni. I have this stupid exam tomorrow, and I'm not ready for it. I hate that class too. It's all a bunch of propaganda.

	If you don't agree with the professor, you get ripped apart. I hate essay exams, anyway. It gives the professor a chance to arbitrarily penalize students. It's just a way for them to exert control over us. That's what it's about, and I resent it.
TOM	In listening to people, it sounds like there's a lot of frustration in the group, and I'm wondering if we might want to rethink the way that we've been conducting our meetings.
BRENDA	Well, people are obviously concerned about the amount of time that we're taking. Maybe if we could put a limit on the amount of time that we spend on a particular topic, we could finish up at a reasonable hour.
ALICE	That would be good. Then I could get to studying for that dumb test.
BRAD	Well, I think we need to make sure that we're balancing our concern about the quality of the program with people's individual needs. I think we need to be mindful of our overall purpose for being here. When all is said and done, we should be able to go back to the statement of our organizational purpose and use that as the criterion for evaluating the success of the entire process.
BILL	Well, I think we've accomplished pretty much tonight. We made some progress on choosing a theme, and I think we're all clearer on how the theme will figure into the actual program. We also talked a little bit about the way we're going to go about contacting alumni.
CALVIN	We've got a lot of work ahead of us, but we're off to a good start, and we can refer back to a lot of the ideas that emerged here. George, did you write down everything that we talked about?
GEORGE	Yeah, and I'll make copies of it available to everyone before our next meeting.
HEATHER	And that will be next Thursday?
JAMIE	It'll be the following Thursday.
HEATHER	Oh, ok. Are we done now?
BRENDA	Just about. I think that Joshua has something he wants to share with us.
JOSHUA	Thanks. Brenda. What I have here is a videotape that I made from last year's homecoming, and I wanted to show it to you, because a lot of times, when you get caught up in all the work, you lose sight of what we all have to look forward to. That's when it gets hard to stay enthusiastic. I figured I'd bring this in

to kind of get you psyched up for it. Andrew, is the VCR all set to go?

ANDREW   Yeah. I'll go hit the lights.

Respond to the following items by identifying a group member who played each role. Some members of the group may have assumed more than one role.

1.   Initiator-contributor
2.   Information seeker
3.   Playboy
4.   Standard setter or ego ideal
5.   Dominator
6.   Orienter
7.   Evaluator-critic
8.   Gate-keeper and expediter
9.   Information giver
10. Opinion giver
11. Aggressor
12. Group-observer and commentator
13. Energizer
14. Procedural technician
15. Coordinator
16. Self-confessor
17. Harmonizer
18. Compromiser
19. Opinion seeker
20. Blocker
21. Recognition-seeker
22. Recorder
23. Encourager
24. Elaborator
25. Help-seeker
26. Special interest pleader

Both Sides of the Story

Prepare a defense for both the affirmative and negative positions on the following statements.

1. Conflict in a group is generally destructive.
2. It is the responsibility of each member to ensure that her or his own needs are being met within a group.
3. The values of an organization can be judged primarily on the basis of its members' behavior.

Sorting It Out

Respond to the following questions by taking a position and defending it.

1. Which is generally stronger, the influence of the individual upon the group or the influence of the group upon the individual?
2. Is it more important for a person to develop an intimate relationship with one person or to build a broad base of personal support in less intimate relationships?
3. Which of the three group functions identified in this chapter is most important?

It's Your Call

Read each of the following scenarios and prepare an essay in response to the questions provided.

1. You are the President of the Alternative Film Society, an organization that regularly sponsors screenings of art films on your campus. The organization is less than one year old and is currently in the "storming" stage of development. You have noticed that two members of the organization have remained highly dependent upon you, while the other five members have become more resistant to your leadership, and have been struggling with one another for control of the group. You have begun to sense growing disappointment and frustration among the two more passive members of the group. They feel their preferences have been disregarded, in matters such as the selection of films. They also believe that other members of the group have successfully imposed their preferences on the entire organization, sometimes through illegitimate means.

   a. What do you see as your alternative courses of action?

   b. What are the advantages and disadvantages of each course of action?

   c. Which course of action will you follow?

   d. Why have you chosen this course of action?

2. You are the Chair of the Student Family Entertainment Council, an organization that is committed to providing students who are parents with opportunities to integrate their academic and family lives. The purpose of the Council is to provide support systems for both the students and their families. The organization regularly sponsors events which are designed to promote interaction between parents and children. Past events have included ice cream socials, roller skating parties, and various holiday celebrations. Until recently, the organization has been highly successful in accomplishing its stated goals.

   However, several months ago, a new member joined the group. This person can best be described as a "special interest pleader." She feels passionately about a number of controversial political issues, and regularly directs the conversation of the group toward these particular topics. Despite her strongly held opinions, she is very even-tempered and a good listener. She is also particularly effective in dissipating tension in groups. Consequently, the members of the group have found the discussions to be both stimulating and enlightening. All of the members of the group appear to have individually benefitted from these discussions.

   Nevertheless, you have noticed that the discussions are preventing the group from accomplishing the purpose for which it was established. The organization has sponsored considerably fewer events, because its meetings have been dominated by political discussions. Moreover, those activities which have been presented have failed to promote interaction between parents and children, because the parents have been engaged in discussions with one another throughout the events. Despite your observations, you have not yet received any complaints from the parents or their children.

   a. What do you see as your alternative courses of action?

   b. What are the advantages and disadvantages of each course of action?

   c. Which course of action will you follow?

   d. Why have you chosen this course of action?

Chapter 7

Working with Groups

What You Will Learn in This Chapter

This chapter will provide an overview of basic principles of motivation. Relevant research and theories will be presented, including the following:

- Hawthorne studies
- Maslow's hierarchy of needs
  - ➤ Physiological needs
  - ➤ Safety needs
  - ➤ Belongingness and love needs
  - ➤ Esteem needs
  - ➤ Need for self-actualization
- Herzberg's motivation-hygiene theory
  - ➤ Satisfiers/Motivators
  - ➤ Dissatisfiers/Maintenance factors/Hygiene factors

Thirty proven motivational strategies will also be presented.

This chapter will introduce the following concepts pertaining to delegation:

- Work assignment
- Authority
  - ➤ Organizational authority
  - ➤ Individual authority
    - Influential authority
    - Intellectual authority
    - Credibility
    - Expert authority
    - Credential authority
    - Prerogative authority
- Responsibility
  - ➤ Ultimate responsibility
  - ➤ Shared responsibility
    - Positive shared responsibility
    - Negative shared responsibility
- Accountability

The chapter will include a discussion of the conditions under which a delegated task can be transformed into a work assignment, and the process through which the transformation occurs.

Reasons for delegating will be discussed. Conditions under which delegation should not occur will also be examined.

Guidelines for choosing a delegate will be presented, followed by a summary of the delegation process.

The purposes and benefits of organizational meetings will be presented, and the following types of meetings will be introduced:

- Information sharing-communication meetings

- Diagnostic or fact finding meetings

- Brainstorming meetings

- Decision-making meetings

- Planning meetings

- Coordination and monitoring meetings

- Ongoing business meetings

The chapter will present specific strategies for conducting effective meetings, including guidelines for action to be taken before, during, and after each meeting.

Guidelines for preparing a meeting agenda will be presented, along with a sample.

A cyclical model for planning and evaluation in student organizations will be described, and the following concepts will be examined:

- Mission
- Goals
  - Societal goals
  - Output goals
  - System goals
  - Product goals
  - Derived goals

- Objectives
  - Regular objectives
  - Problem-solving objectives
  - Innovative objectives

- Measurement
  - Measures of activity
  - Measures of impact

- Action plans
- Resources
  - Money
  - Facilities and equipment
  - Materials, supplies, and services
  - Personnel
- Budgeting
- Effectiveness
- Efficiency
- Evaluation

Working with Groups

When the best leader's work is done, the people say, 'we did it ourselves!'

Lao-Tzu

Why Study the Activities of the Leader?

By now, you should have a fairly clear understanding of how groups function. You should also be familiar with general styles of leadership. In this chapter, we will draw upon your knowledge in both of these areas, by examining the actual "mechanics" of leadership. Although it is important that a leader understand groups and that she or he adopt a clearly defined set of beliefs concerning the essential nature of leadership, the leader's personal philosophy and knowledge base serve no purpose for the group if not to guide her or his actions.

It is also important that the leader attend to the full range of her or his duties to the group, rather than fulfilling certain obligations while ignoring others. All too often, new leaders focus on one or two specific areas of leadership, to the exclusion of all others. There are several reasons why this happens. One reason is that people develop their understanding of leadership roles largely through observations of previous occupants of those roles. If a new leader's predecessor neglected certain areas of responsibility, there is a good chance that the new leader will be similarly neglectful. Furthermore, some new leaders find themselves drawn exclusively toward certain areas of responsibility because of their own inherent interest in these areas. Still others respond to their own insecurities by either avoiding or focusing exclusively on areas of responsibility in which they lack confidence in their own abilities.

The material presented in this chapter will help you to develop greater awareness of the full range of responsibilities that must be assumed by organizational leaders. Specific strategies for fulfilling your duties as a leader will also be examined.

Motivation

Because a leader is one who accomplishes goals through others, rather than by acting independently, it is particularly important that he or she develop skills in motivating others. In many ways, motivation is the essence of leadership. In fact, many of the earliest studies pertaining to leadership focused not on the leader but on the follower, with the assumption being that the key to effective leadership was an understanding of what motivates followers.

The Hawthorne Studies

From 1924 to 1927, the Western Electric Company, in cooperation with a team of researchers from the Harvard Graduate School of Business Administration, conducted a series of experiments at its **Hawthorne Works**, located in the Chicago area. The purpose of the research project was to examine the relationship between the level of lighting in the plant and workers' productivity. In the investigation, certain groups of workers were placed in experimental work conditions, with either brighter or dimmer lighting than would normally be maintained. Although the researchers discovered increases in productivity as conditions changed, there appeared to be little relationship to the specific changes that were made (Roethlisberger and Dickson, 1964).

The lighting experiments were followed by a series of similar experiments, involving changes in a variety of other work conditions, such as scheduling and wage incentives. Workers' recommendations were solicited, and taken into consideration in determining the changes that were made. Additionally, individual workers were interviewed, and allowed to comment on any aspect of their work environment. The experiments continued until 1932, and produced results similar to those observed in the lighting study (Roethlisberger and Dickson, 1964).

The findings of the Hawthorne studies suggested that workers respond favorably to attention from organizational decision makers, and that their productivity increases when they feel their concerns are being taken into consideration. The results of the Hawthorne experiments have had a major impact upon contemporary theories of human motivation. The findings of the studies support the use of what has come to be known as a participative management style (Owens, 1981).

At some time in your life, you have probably experienced the very same phenomenon that was observed in the Hawthorne studies. For example, as you think about the classes that you have most enjoyed, and in which you have achieved your strongest academic performance, you will presumably remember those in which you felt an inherent interest in the subject matter. However, there have probably also been several classes in which you felt little or no initial interest, but became more attentive because the professor called you by name, asked for your opinion, listened to you as you spoke, seemed to be genuinely interested in what you had to say, and allowed you some opportunity to influence the course of the discussion.

As you move forward in your own leadership activities, you will want to bear in mind the motivating effect of attention to individual needs and concerns. By applying the basic principles illustrated in the Hawthorne experiments, you can have a powerful influence on both the satisfaction and productivity of the members of your group.

Maslow's Hierarchy of Needs

One of the most commonly cited theories of motivation is one put forth by Abraham Maslow (1970), which features a "**hierarchy of basic needs.**" Maslow's hierarchy, which is illustrated in Figure 1, consists of five broad categories of needs, which serve as motivating forces for human behavior.

Figure 1

The first category, the "**physiological needs,**" includes the basic elements necessary for health and survival. These needs, which are found even among lower forms of animal life, include such requirements as air, food, water, and sleep (Maslow, 1970).

The second category is known as the "**safety needs.**" This category includes "security; stability; dependency; protection; freedom from fear, from anxiety and chaos; need for structure, order, law, limits; strength in the protector; and so on" (Maslow, 1970, p. 39).

The third category consists of the "**belongingness and love needs.**" This category includes the desire for "affectionate relations with people in general, namely, for a place in [one's] group or family" (Maslow, 1970, p. 43), and avoidance of "loneliness," "ostracism," "rejection," "friendlessness," and "rootlessness" (Maslow, 1970, p. 43).

The fourth category is known as the "**esteem needs.**" Maslow (1970) divided this category into two subcategories. The first of these smaller sets of needs includes "the desire for strength, for achievement, for adequacy, for mastery and competence, for confidence in the face of the world, and for independence and freedom" (Maslow, 1970, p. 45). The second subcategory includes "the desire for reputation or prestige (defining it as respect or esteem from other people), status, fame and glory, dominance, recognition, attention, importance, dignity, or appreciation" (Maslow, 1970, p. 45).

The fifth category, the need for "**self-actualization**," refers to the desire to cultivate one's unique talents to their ultimate potential, and to engage in those activities to which one is best suited. According to Maslow (1970, p. 46), "a musician must make music, an artist must paint, a poet must write, if he [sic] is to ultimately be at peace with himself [sic]."

The five categories of needs are arranged in a hierarchy because, according to Maslow's (1970) theory, those needs which are placed at lower levels must be satisfied in order for higher level needs to emerge as matters of compelling concern to the individual. Satisfaction of the lower level needs will generally serve as the dominant motivating force behind an individual's actions, until those needs are sufficiently met. Once the individual's needs at one level are adequately served, the next higher level of need becomes the primary motivating force behind his or her behavior.

For example, you have probably had the experience of trying to study while you are hungry or tired. Under those circumstances, it would not be unusual for you to find it difficult to concentrate. However, if you were to take a break for a snack or a nap, you would probably return to your studies feeling much more motivated to concentrate. This pattern would be consistent with Maslow's theory, since food and sleep are physiological needs, whereas studying usually relates to esteem needs or the need for self-actualization. If you were continuously deprived of food or sleep, due to your economic conditions or your domestic situation, you might find yourself lacking the motivation to even remain in school, unless you viewed it as a means by which to satisfy these lower level needs.

It is important to note that the dominant needs of an individual are subject to change, and that two or more categories of needs can motivate a person simultaneously, though not necessarily with equal strength. Additionally, Maslow (1970) recognized that, while the order of the hierarchy applies to most people, specific individuals may adopt a slightly different sequence.

As you attempt to motivate members of your organization, be aware of ways that you can link rewards to their dominant needs. For example, if members of the group seem to be preoccupied with their belongingness and love needs, consider offering them more opportunities to work together, rather than independently. Additionally, if an activity is to be inherently motivating at a particular level of the hierarchy, you will need to make sure that all lower needs are satisfied. For example, it is unlikely that group members' desire for belongingness will motivate them to attend a meeting at 7:00 a.m., while their need for sleep calls them in a different direction.

Herzberg's Motivation-Hygiene Theory

Another popular theory of motivation was developed by Frederick Herzberg (1966). This theory is based on the belief that there are two general needs which are common to all people: (1) the "need as an animal to avoid pain" and (2) the "need as a human to grow psychologically" (Herzberg, 1966, p. 71). Accordingly, the theory presents two separate sets of factors which affect satisfaction and motivation in a work situation.

The first set of factors is known as the "**satisfiers**" or "**motivators**." This category includes such factors as achievement, recognition, responsibility, advancement, and various elements of the work itself. These are factors which relate to the human need for psychological growth. Although their absence will not make a person feel "dissatisfied," their presence is necessary if she or he is to feel truly "satisfied." The satisfiers are what distinguishes between a genuinely fulfilling work experience and one that is simply alright. You will notice that the factors in this category relate to the intrinsic characteristics of the person's work (Herzberg, 1966).

In contrast, the "**dissatisfiers**" relate to the environment or context in which the work is carried out. This category, which is also known as the "**maintenance**" or "**hygiene**" factors, includes salary, supervision, interpersonal relations, company policy and administration, and working conditions. These factors relate to the animal need to avoid pain. While they can contribute to a person's "dissatisfaction" with her or his work, they alone cannot make her or him feel fully "satisfied" with the work situation (Herzberg, 1966).

In all likelihood, the difference between the satisfiers and dissatisfiers has been illustrated in experiences from your own working life. For example, if you are like most working people, you have probably said on at least one occasion, "they don't pay me enough for me to have to do that." What this statement implies is that your dissatisfaction could be alleviated if you were paid more generously. However, this is not to say that you could actually enjoy the particular task, no matter what you were paid. The best that you could probably hope for is to find it bearable, though it would still not be genuinely satisfying. In contrast, as you think about the most satisfying moments of your working life, you will probably recall instances in which you felt a sense of accomplishment, recognition, or the simple joy of doing something that you love.

In your leadership activities, it is important that you attend to both motivation and hygiene factors. While providing rewards that are external to your followers' tasks may be sufficient to prevent them from feeling dissatisfied, you must also provide them with intrinsically rewarding work, if you hope to actually satisfy them and motivate them toward excellence.

Motivational Strategies

As a leader, there are specific actions that you can take to motivate your followers. The following recommendations,* drawn from the management literature, are based on a number of studies which were conducted over a period of approximately 25 years. They apply to both paid and unpaid workers.

1. Use appropriate methods of reinforcement.
    - Rewards should always be contingent on performance.
    - Don't give too much reinforcement; too much is almost as bad as none at all.
    - Reinforcement is personal; what reinforces one person may not reinforce another.
    - Dispense reinforcers as soon as possible after the desired performance.
2. Eliminate unnecessary threats and punishments.
3. Make sure that accomplishment is adequately recognized.
4. Provide people with flexibility and choice. Whenever possible, permit employees to make decisions.
5. Provide support when it is needed. And make sure that employees don't hesitate to make use of it.
6. Provide employees with responsibility along with their accountability. Nothing motivates people as much as being given appropriate responsibility. Appropriate responsibility means responsibility that is neither too high nor too low.
7. Encourage employees to set their own goals.
8. Make sure that employees are aware of how their tasks relate to personal and organizational goals.
9. Clarify your expectations and make sure that employees understand them.
10. Provide an appropriate mix of extrinsic rewards and intrinsic satisfaction.
11. Design tasks and environments to be consistent with employee needs. .
12. Individualize your supervision.
13. Provide immediate and relevant feedback that will help employees improve their performance in the future.
14. Recognize and help eliminate barriers to individual achievement.
15. Exhibit confidence in employees.
16. Increase the likelihood that employees will experience accomplishment.

---

17. Exhibit interest in and knowledge of each individual under your supervision.
18. Encourage individuals to participate in making decisions that affect them.
19. Establish a climate of trust and open communication.
20. Minimize the use of statutory powers. Rule of law is sometimes needed, but it does not encourage increased motivation.
21. Help individuals to see the integrity, significance and relevance of their work in terms of organizational output.
22. Listen to and deal effectively with employee complaints. Often task-irrelevant problems can greatly reduce productivity when they are not dealt with.
23. Point out improvements in performance, no matter how small. This is particularly important when employees are beginning work on new tasks.
24. Demonstrate your own motivation through behavior and attitude.
25. Criticize behavior, not people.
26. Make sure that effort pays off in results.
27. Encourage employees to engage in novel and challenging activities.
28. Anxiety is fundamental to motivation, so don't eliminate it completely. Moderate levels of anxiety can increase motivation.
29. Don't believe that "liking" is always correlated with positive performance. A task can be intrinsically boring, while the consequences are highly motivating.
30. Be concerned with short-term and long-term motivation (Spitzer, 1980, pp. 54-56).

Delegation

In addition to motivation, it is important that leaders develop skills in **delegation**. Delegation consists of: (1) a leader's commission of certain of his or her work activities to a follower, who is given full responsibility for making the decisions necessary to see the activities through to their completion; and (2) specification of desired outcomes, while leaving the follower free to decide how the goals are to be accomplished (Steinmetz, 1976).

Delegation vs. Work Assignments

Delegation differs from a **work assignment,** in that the follower's acquisition of the additional responsibility remains outside the scope of his or her job description. Delegative arrangements are generally made by mutual agreement between the leader and the follower. Although the follower may feel a great deal of pressure to comply with the request, he or she is generally not compelled to do so. Furthermore, both parties generally approach the arrangement without any long-term commitments implied. Delegation has been described as a way of experimenting with the follower's potential for growth (Engel, 1983).

Although delegation differs from a work assignment, it is possible for the process of delegation to lead to a long term work assignment. It has been noted that in order for delegation to be transformed into a work assignment, three conditions must be satisfied:

1. The activity reoccurs frequently enough that the supervisor or manager must periodically delegate it.

2. One particular delegate has fulfilled the delegation in a manner that is acceptable — or above average — in the judgment of the delegator. Such successful service may be construed as "passing" a performance test.

3. The delegator determines that a permanent shift of obligations should take place. Up to this point, the delegator's options were retain, rotate among several subordinates, or assign permanently to one person, whose achievement as a delegate had been evaluated and judged effective. The last option is selected (Engel, 1983, p. 21).

It has also been observed that the transition from delegation to work assignment follows a fairly standard pattern.
This process involves three events:

1. An acknowledged transference from the delegator to the subordinate.

2. The subordinate's work assignments are enlarged. New priorities are established or the subordinate may delegate — on a try-out basis — some of his [sic] assignments to lower level employees.

3. The subordinate now no longer functions as a delegate. Role relations with the delegator have been altered (Engel, 1983, p. 21).

Authority

In order to become an effective delegator, it is necessary to understand the basic concept of authority, which has been defined as "whatever influence one possesses, at any instant, that will cause someone else to do what the authoritative individual wants that someone to do, at that time" (Steinmetz, 1976, p. 5). Authority is central to the process of delegation, because a subordinate cannot carry out his or her duties unless he or she has sufficient authority to do so. For example, you could not delegate the task of writing checks on behalf of your organization to a member who is not authorized to do so. It is important to note, however, that authority can take several different forms, and that an individual leader can rely upon several different types of authority simultaneously.

Perhaps the most familiar type of authority is that which is known as **organizational authority**. This particular form of authority has been described as "the conferred legitimate right to carry out the delegation, including the necessary powers to get it accomplished" (Engel, 1983, p. 46). We can think of organizational authority as the "power of position," since it generally stems from the formal structure of the organization. For example, if you are the Chair of the student radio station on your campus, you have undoubtedly found that there are certain activities that you have the authority to carry out, simply by virtue of the fact that you are the Chair.

Other forms of authority are generally more subtle, because they stem from the unique characteristics of the individual, and can exist even in the absence of any formal recognition within the organization. You will recall from our discussion in Chapter 4 that leaders can be found even at the lowest levels of the organizational hierarchy. Forms of authority that are reflective of the individual, rather than the role that she or he occupies, are known as **individual authorities**. There are six types of individual authority: (1) influential, (2) intellectual, (3) credibility, (4) expert, (5) credential, and (6) prerogative (Engel, 1983).

When we speak of **influential authority**, we are referring to "the inclination of others to be emotionally affected by the delegate's personality" (Engel, 1983, p. 46). Over the years, you have probably encountered a number of people who are able to get what they want from others largely because they are well liked. People respond favorably toward them, on an emotional level, often for reasons that are difficult to pinpoint. Think of how often you have heard comments such as "She'll do it if you ask her" or "You ask him. He likes you." The power of influential authority has long weighed heavily in decisions concerning delegation.

Intellectual authority has been defined as "the established ability of the delegate to persuade, through the medium of his [sic] intellect" (Engel, 1983, p. 46). In nearly any organization, there are individuals who are able to rally support for their positions, by offering rationally compelling arguments in their favor. This form of authority has a way of building upon itself. For example, if a member of your organization had developed a reputation for being bright, there is a good chance that her ideas would soon be presumed to have merit until proven otherwise.

Credibility is the perception that an individual is trustworthy. This form of authority is based on honesty and truthfulness. It has been noted that "credibility affects every other personal authority" (Engel, 1983, 41). If you were found to have deceived the members of your organization, for example, it would not be unusual or unreasonable for them to question the genuineness of any of the personal characteristics that might have commanded their respect in the past.

Expert authority can develop when a member of an organization has certain technical expertise that is relevant to the activities of the organization (Engel, 1983). For example, if a member of your organization had extensive experience and education in the areas of accounting and finance, you and the other members of the organization might frequently solicit his opinion on financial matters. You might also ask that he engage in activities requiring expertise in the area, or that he serve as the spokesperson for the organization when communicating about such matters to external constituencies.

Credential authority refers to "the prior acquisition of credentials and testimonials required to gain and maintain acceptance in the organization" (Engel, 1983, p. 46). If you belonged to an academic organization advised by a full Professor with a Ph.D. in a relevant discipline, you would probably put a great deal of stock in her opinions, because of her status as a recognized authority in the field. This would be an example of credential authority.

Prerogative authority is defined as "the highly personal ownership of special delegator privileges permitting the delegate to function in a distinctive manner" (Engel, 1983, p. 46). The individual who holds prerogative authority is one who "is on the inside" or "has connections," such that he or she is uniquely qualified to carry out a particular task. For example, if a particular member of your organization held a work-study position in the Student Activities Office on your campus, and you were planning an activity that required permission from the Director of Student Activities, you might choose the work-study student to act as your spokesperson. Because of his previously established relationship with the Director, he would be in a unique position to effectively communicate the needs of your organization, while also addressing the concerns of the administration.

While organizational authority can be delegated, individual authority generally cannot be. Although it is sometimes possible for a delegator to use her or his own prerogative authority to "pave the way" for a delegate, ultimately the delegate must prove himself or herself to be worthy of continued privilege in any ongoing relationships that are established (Engel, 1983).

Before delegating a particular task to a follower, you will want to consider whether or not the person possesses sufficient individual authority to successfully carry out the task. If individual authority is lacking, you will want to ask yourself whether or not it is possible to delegate sufficient organizational authority to qualify the individual for the particular duty, and whether or not the necessary individual authority can be developed.

Responsibility

Another important consideration in delegation is the concept of **responsibility**, defined as "the obligation to undertake a specific duty or task within the organization" (Steinmetz, 1976, p. 10). It is generally agreed that even after an organizational leader has delegated a particular duty to a subordinate, the leader cannot completely escape responsibility for the consequences. If a follower proves herself to be dishonest, it could be argued that the leader erred in trusting her. If another subordinate lacks the information necessary to carry out his task, it could be similarly asserted that the leader should have provided him with this information.

The term **ultimate responsibility** has been used to convey the idea that leaders must assume some responsibility for the actions of their followers (Engel, 1983).

This is not to say that responsibility cannot be shared with a follower. Two types of **shared responsibility** have been described in the management literature:

1. *Positive shared responsibility.* Here we envision a *partnership* between superior and subordinate. Each understands that he [sic] is working for a common goal and that each party carries his [sic] share of the burden. Success is anticipated. Failure, should it occur, is used to learn how to succeed the next time.

2. *Negative shared responsibility.* This suggests a *division* between the superior and the subordinate. The boss is driven by a concern that he [sic] will have to "take the rap" if his [sic] subordinate fails (Engel, 1983, p. 37).

Related to the concept of responsibility is **accountability**, which involves the assessment of a person's performance in carrying out a particular duty, followed by corrective action if necessary. It has been noted that "many supervisors, managers, and executives fail to make effective delegations because they drop the ball at the point of accountability" (Steinmetz, 1976, p. 11).

Reasons for Delegating

Delegation serves several very important purposes within an organization, particularly as the organization itself becomes larger and more complex. As more workers join the organization and become involved in a wider variety of activities, it becomes increasingly difficult for top level leaders to attend to the full range of organizational functions and to adequately supervise all of the workers (Valentine, 1973). For example, there simply are not enough hours in a day for the President of your college or university to attend to the routine concerns of individual administrators and faculty members, and to make decisions on all matters affecting the delivery of instruction and services to students.

Furthermore, as organizations become more complex, it becomes increasingly necessary to engage the services of individuals with highly specialized knowledge. Often, members of larger organizations are better qualified to perform certain tasks than are their supervisors (Valentine, 1973). Again using your college or university as an example, individual faculty members very clearly qualify as experts in their fields. While the President and Provost are undoubtedly respected scholars in their own right, it would be impossible for them to develop a detailed knowledge of all of the fields in which the institution offers instruction. It is for this reason that deans and departmental chairs are charged with providing leadership for their units of the institution, and why individual faculty members are granted a great deal of autonomy in teaching their own courses.

One last reason why delegation is important is that it allows workers at all levels of an organization to develop new skills (Valentine, 1973). This is not only good for the individual workers, but for the overall organization as well. If a leader does not help his or her followers to develop new skills, the entire organization develops an unhealthy dependence on the leader. Because leaders are mortal beings, the survival of the organization depends upon other members' capacity to function in the leader's absence. If the President of your institution were to suddenly become incapacitated, you might witness a brief period of disarray. However, if he or she has made proper use of delegation in the past, it is unlikely that the activities of the institution would be seriously disrupted for any substantial length of time.

Although your own leadership activities are probably carried out in a small group setting, delegation can still offer you many of the same benefits that it provides to leaders of much larger organizations. It can relieve you of concern for small details, thereby freeing you up to concentrate on the "big picture." It can allow you to benefit from the unique expertise of individual members of your group. It can help the members of your group to develop new skills, and in turn provide you with the peace of mind that comes from knowing that the organization will not fall apart if you are called away.

Knowing When Not to Delegate

It is important to note that there are certain activities which you should not delegate. It is generally agreed that you should maintain direct involvement in most executive functions. These include: establishing goals and objectives: organizing, motivating, and communicating information to the group; integration of the individual into the group and promotion of his or her ongoing development; and evaluation of group outcomes. If you find it necessary to delegate activities which fall into any of the categories identified here, it is advisable to maintain close contact with the delegate, in order to monitor her or his execution of the task. If you find that you are spending your time on numerous tasks which do not fit into any of the categories of executive activity, you probably are not delegating properly. Nonexecutive activities should in fact be delegated, because they have a tendency to draw the leader's attention away from those duties which only she or he can fulfill (Laird and Laird, 1957).

It is generally recommended that the leader not delegate a duplicate of his or her job, but instead identify very specific areas of responsibility which are to be assumed by the delegate. Simply recommending that a follower "help out wherever needed" leaves great potential for him or her to assume either too much or too little authority (Laird and Laird, 1957).

Caution should also be exercised in delegating disciplinary authority. All too often, organizational leaders attempt to escape the unpleasant task of disciplining their followers by delegating that task to "hatchet" people. This approach can create resentment toward the delegator. There is also the potential for abuse on the part of the person to whom disciplinary duties are delegated. A more prudent approach is to create mechanisms for delegates to recommend disciplinary action, while maintaining control over all final decisions in such matters. Remembering, however, that delegates must have sufficient authority to carry out their assigned tasks, it is recommended that leaders help them to develop skills in motivation through nondisciplinary means (Laird and Laird, 1957), and that appropriate disciplinary support be provided when necessary.

In most organizations, leaders must also maintain control over policy making. One of the principal responsibilities of a leader is to make difficult decisions that will have a far reaching impact on the organization, as opposed to routine decisions, in which the preferred course of action is obvious or of little consequence. Although the leader may confer with his or her followers on policy making, the final decision usually belongs to the leader. As you approach policy making in your own organization, you may wish to ask one or more of your followers to assume responsibility for gathering the information needed to make the decision. You might even ask that they recommend a preferred course of action. However, when it comes to actually establishing policy, you will not want to delegate (Laird and Laird, 1957).

Duties that relate to the morale of the overall organization are also the unique domain of the leader. Often followers need to know that what they do makes a difference to the entire organization, and that their efforts are noticed. While a coworker can sometimes provide the "strokes" needed to make a person feel good about his or her work, this type of affirmation has its limitations, because a coworker does not officially represent the organization. Sometimes, there is simply no substitute for a good word from the leader of an organization (Steinmetz, 1976). For example, consider the importance that we attach to the role of a college or university President at a graduation ceremony. Certainly the task of handing a person a diploma and shaking his or her hand is one that could be mastered by the average university professor. However, if the President of your institution chose, for no apparent reason, to delegate to a faculty member the duty of presenting you with your diploma, you would probably feel offended, and rightfully so. You have worked hard for your degree, and the President's action in this case would trivialize your accomplishment.

The leader of an organization must also remain directly involved in resolving conflicts between organizational units under her or his jurisdiction. It is particularly inappropriate to delegate such tasks to a member of the organization who belongs to one of the units involved in the dispute (Steinmetz, 1976). In student organizations, it is not unusual for various committees or organizational officers to find themselves at odds with one another. For example, the Treasurer of your organization and the committee responsible for programming might engage in frequent arguments over money. In all likelihood, they would turn to the leader of the group to resolve the dispute. They would do so, not only because she or he has the authority to solve the problem, but because she or he can approach the issue objectively. The leader can evaluate various alternatives with a focus on what is best for the overall organization, whereas members of individual units sometimes become too narrowly focused on their areas of responsibility.

As you continue in your leadership activities, you will probably receive numerous requests from your supervisor, with the understanding that various tasks can be delegated to your own subordinates. Occasionally, however, you may receive a request from your own supervisor, with the specification that you personally attend to the particular matter. When this happens, the task cannot be delegated (Steinmetz, 1976). If your supervisor specifically asks that you perform a particular task, she or he obviously has a reason for doing so, and you must respect her or his judgement, just as you would expect your followers to personally follow through on requests that you direct toward them as individuals.

Another important consideration in delegation is the matter of confidentiality. In nearly any leadership position, you will deal with certain information that must not become general knowledge if the organization is to function properly. If a particular task requires that a delegate have access to confidential information, you will want to choose your delegate very carefully and impress upon her or him the necessity of maintaining confidentiality. In some instances, you may conclude that due to the confidential nature of the particular work, it simply cannot be delegated (Steinmetz, 1976).

It is generally recommended that you delegate whole projects, rather than parts of projects. If a project is highly complex, it can sometimes be broken down into smaller activities, which can then be assigned to separate delegates. However, it is important that these specific activities be sufficiently independent from one another. Related activities should be grouped together and overseen by a single delegate, since much of the information used to complete related tasks will be the same (Steinmetz, 1976). For example, if you were planning an event and needed both posters and leaflets, it would not make much sense for you to appoint two separate delegates to prepare these materials, since both delegates would then be required to obtain much of the same information from local printers. Such duplication of effort is extremely inefficient.

One final word of caution relates to "pet projects." As a leader, you will undoubtedly become involved in some activities that are not directly related to the purpose of your organization. For example, you might be asked to serve on various committees in your community or in professional associations. Ultimately, you may have work stemming from your involvement in these outside activities, which you would like to delegate to a subordinate in your organization. Before doing so, give careful consideration to whether this use of the subordinate's time contributes to or detracts from the purpose of the organization. In most situations, pet projects cannot legitimately be delegated (Steinmetz, 1976).

Choosing a Delegate

One of the most important decisions made in delegation is the choice of a delegate. Selection of a delegate who has neither the will nor the ability to complete a particular project can doom the project to failure from the outset. Therefore, it is important that you give careful consideration to the type of person that you are seeking for a particular project. There are a number of factors which may enter into your decision.

First of all, in common practice, you should choose your delegate from among your own followers. Other members of the organization almost always have plenty of work to do in response to requests from their supervisors. It is difficult, if not impossible, for additional duties to be assumed without any negative impact on the individual's regular work activities. In general, you should also delegate only to those who report directly to you (Laird and Laird, 1957). In order to delegate to an individual who is uniquely qualified to carry out a particular project, it may occasionally be necessary to "go through" a level of an organization. When the circumstances warrant it, this practice is considered acceptable (Engel, 1983). However, you should always discuss the matter with the individual's immediate supervisor. This is likewise true in those rare cases in which it becomes necessary for you to delegate to an individual outside your organizational unit.

When choosing from among your followers, one of the first questions that you are likely to ask yourself is "Whose turn is it?" While your answer should not be the sole determinant of your ultimate course of action, the question is not entirely without legitimacy. If you were to repeatedly delegate your most desirable projects to a select group of followers while choosing the remaining members of your group to perform all of the more burdensome tasks, morale would undoubtedly suffer. Therefore, matters of equity should be considered in your selection of a delegate (Steinmetz, 1976).

You will also want to consider any special interests that your followers have, as these interests relate to the activities that you are planning to delegate (Hicks, 1988). For example, if a member of your organization had a special interest in computers, you might ask her to set up a data base containing information about the members of your organization. Because of her interest in computers, she would probably find greater satisfaction in this project than would other members of the organization who did not share her fascination with the current technology. Because people are generally more attentive to matters in which they have an inherent interest, there is a good chance that she would also carry out the project more effectively than other group members would.

Competence is another important consideration in choosing a delegate (Hicks, 1988). In our example, if the individual described not only had an interest in computers, but also had extensive experience or formal training in their use, she would probably be an excellent delegate for the activity described. In all likelihood, if you were to assign the project to her, you could feel quite confident that a quality work product would be produced with minimal supervision.

It is important to note, however, that an individual need not have actual experience in completing a task in order to possess the necessary competence. Remember that you are looking for potential. Rather than asking yourself, "Has this person done it?," try asking, "Can this person do it?" Often, by choosing a delegate who has not performed a task previously but has the necessary knowledge to perform the task, it is possible to maintain high morale and increase group members' self-sufficiency. In our example, suppose another member of your group had extensive training in the use of computers but only limited experience. Under such circumstances, you might choose to delegate the project to him rather than to the more experienced member, because the challenge posed to him would probably be both motivational and educational. It is possible to minimize the risk involved in delegating to inexperienced workers by initially delegating tasks on a one-time basis or for a fixed period of time, and later establishing a more permanent arrangement (Laird and Laird, 1957).

Delegation can also be used to help individual group members overcome personal characteristics that undermine their effectiveness in dealing with others (Laird and Laird, 1957). For example, a group member who is rather shy might benefit from the experience of planning "icebreaker" activities for newer group members, because the experience would probably expose him to new ways of meeting people and would also require that he actually talk with people whom he has not met previously.

The Process of Delegation

The delegation process has been summarized in the following eight steps:

1. The superior determines that some objective he [sic] seeks may not be accomplished, or is better accomplished by another.
2. The superior determines the need to shift to another person the obligation for an objective's accomplishment.
3. The superior selects a delegate who will do what the superior cannot or should not do.
4. The superior explains to the delegate the scope of the objective and the nature of the delegate's obligation. Time constraints, if any, are clarified.
5. The superior shifts or loans enough of his [sic] authority to the delegate to achieve the objective. The obligation is accepted by the delegate.
6. The scope of the objective may be narrowed or broadened, with the delegate given wide latitude. Levels of support are understood.
7. The delegate then achieves, fails to achieve, or partially achieves objective.

8. Finally, the superior evaluates the results. He [sic] may or may not withdraw his [sic] loaned authority from the delegate and terminate obligation (Engel, 1983, p. 11).

It must be emphasized that a leader's job does not end once she or he has "handed over" a project to a follower. Remember that ultimate responsibility rests with the leader. In order to ensure the success of a project and to maximize its benefit to the follower, the leader must engage in appropriate follow-up communication.

Establishing an appropriate level of involvement in the project during its execution involves a delicate balance. You will want to allow your delegates sufficient autonomy to enable them to learn from doing, while offering enough guidance for them to feel confident in whatever course of action is chosen. According to one management expert, "the best course is to provide minimal supervision while fostering an open-door policy where the subordinate feels free to seek counsel whenever necessary" (Hicks, 1988, p. 32).

Once a project has been completed, it is extremely important that the outcome be evaluated. The first step in this process is collecting information. Relevant information should be gathered from as many sources as possible.

You will want to gather statistical information. This includes information pertaining to such matters as the cost of the project as well as any profit generated. You will want to keep track of the number of staff hours required for its completion. Whenever you plan an event, you will also want to keep track of the number of people invited and the number who actually attend.

In addition to statistics, you will want to gather subjective information as well. Keep track of any difficulties encountered along the way, or any aspect of the project with which you are not satisfied. If you have planned an event, ask the participants for their reactions. You may even want to develop a brief questionnaire which can be completed upon the conclusion of the event. Also ask your delegate for her or his opinions, and solicit reactions from anyone else involved in carrying out the activity.

Provide your delegate with feedback on her or his performance. Evaluate her or his work based on the standards established previously. Avoid personal attacks or references to previous disappointments. Focus instead on the specific duties related to the delegated project. It is also important to keep an open mind, and allow your delegate to explain her or his point of view. Remember, too, that one of the primary purposes of delegation is to facilitate growth on the part of the subordinate. Acknowledge her or his mistakes, but use them as a basis for learning. If the individual is to remain involved in the particular work activity, you will want to make sure that she or he receives whatever training may be necessary to prevent mistakes from recurring. Finally, it is important that you always remember to recognize progress and to commend workers when a job is done well (Steinmetz, 1976).

Running Effective Meetings

If you are the official leader of a student or community organization, you have probably had occasion to conduct a formal meeting at some time in the past. If not, you may want to consider doing so in the near future. It is extremely difficult for groups to function effectively without meeting regularly. Therefore, it is important that leaders and those who aspire to leadership positions develop skills in conducting meetings, and apply these skills within the context of their own groups.

Types of Meetings

There are seven basic types of meetings, which differ from one another in purpose and often in format as well. The seven types are: (1) "information sharing-communication," (2) "diagnostic or fact finding," (3) "brainstorming," (4) "decision-making," (5) "planning," (6) "coordination and monitoring," and (7) "ongoing business" (Napier and Gershenfeld, 1985, p. 414).

The purpose of **information sharing-communication meetings** is to provide for the exchange of information across various segments of an organization. Such meetings provide an avenue for sharing new information and clarifying misunderstandings between various members of the organization (Napier and Gershenfeld, 1985).

Diagnostic or fact finding meetings exist for purposes of identifying problems, setting priorities, and assessing the current state of affairs. This type of meeting can focus on a particular issue or deal more generally with the condition of the organization (Napier and Gershenfeld, 1985).

Brainstorming meetings provide group members with an opportunity to generate a wide variety of alternative solutions to organizational problems. However, no attempt is made to actually solve problems within the context of the brainstorming meeting. Its purpose is to facilitate the identification of alternatives, which can be evaluated at a later date. It is within the context of **decision-making meetings** that group members actually choose between alternative courses of action (Napier and Gershenfeld, 1985).

The purpose of **planning meetings** is "to establish the means of implementation for decisions made" (Napier and Gershenfeld, 1985, p. 414). Even after a group has decided what should be done, it is necessary to determine how it will be done. It is for this reason that planning meetings are held.

Coordination and monitoring meetings provide leaders with a means of ensuring that activities which have been delegated are progressing in a satisfactory fashion (Napier and Gershenfeld, 1985). The use of coordination and monitoring meetings is one of the most common ways in which delegates are held accountable for their activities.

The **ongoing business meeting** is perhaps the most common type of organizational meeting. This type of meeting provides group members with an opportunity to meet on a regular basis to discuss routine matters which affect the operations of the organization (Napier and Gershenfeld, 1985).

It should be noted that the types of meetings identified here do not constitute mutually exclusive categories. It is possible, for example, to engage in coordination and monitoring functions during an ongoing business meeting or to engage in fact finding and diagnosis during a meeting that was called primarily for purposes of information sharing and communication.

Potential Benefits of Meetings

At times, it may seem inefficient to hold meetings, when equivalent practical outcomes could be achieved through delegation to individuals. Nevertheless, a well run meeting can potentially offer a number of unique benefits to the organization, which it would not otherwise enjoy. These benefits include the following:

1. Meetings give individuals the opportunity to belong or have membership in a number of groups that support the organization. Belonging gives individuals further identity beyond a single job role. This is true at any organizational level but of particular importance when job roles tend to be monotonous or lack variety.

2. Meetings make individuals feel that their ideas are being sought and there is a mutual building from these ideas to new procedures, policies, or programs.

3. Beyond the creation of the ideas, a meeting gives group members the psychological satisfaction of being able to identify with visible outcomes that have value for the organization.

4. People are psychologically committed to ideas that they help generate in meetings, which goes beyond the product itself. Thus, to have a personal point of view forged into a final declaration of a group can be incredibly rewarding.

5. Those involved in meetings have a chance to experience the full cycle of opposition, conflict, and positive resolution. The level of trust in the group may increase and be transferred to the organization because mutually agreed-upon solutions require the sacrificing of personal self-interest or gain. It is the giving up of one's personal vested interest that often increases one's stake in the organization itself.

6.   Accountability within a group is often clearly defined in meetings. A commitment of the group or other individuals to action and the monitoring of areas of responsibility within the group can provide important sources of success, reinforcement, and support necessary in any healthy organization.

7.   The meeting allows the differentiation of roles according to skill and provides a healthy source of status depending on the nature of the role that is taken.

8.   People learn from each other by working together in meetings and enhance their interpersonal or technical skills through the observation of other people's performance.

9.   Meetings help build an overall sense of mutual accomplishment in having succeeded in a mutual goal, having risked certain new ideas or innovations, and having experienced success and overcome failure.

10.   Meetings build personal relationships through the legitimate work process where little time is provided for social niceties. Individuals begin to know each other within the organization on a different and more meaningful level because of shared goals, shared points of view, and the satisfactory resolution of conflict. Put simply, people "get to know each other" by acting together.

11.   Meetings provide the opportunity for fun and social rewards that can occur spontaneously when people work together with common purpose and under some pressure of obligation to each other (Napier and Gershenfeld, 1985, pp. 415-416).

Clearly, there are some very good reasons for holding meetings in an organization. It should be noted, however, that the benefits described here are only *potential* outcomes. Whether or not they are realized depends largely on action taken by the leader before, during, and after the meeting.

Before the Meeting

Once you have established the need for a meeting, one of your first tasks will be to choose a time and date for the meeting. In scheduling your meeting, you will want to make sure that you have allowed sufficient time to discuss any issues that need to be raised. You will also want to make sure that you have chosen a time when people will be interested and will be functioning well. Be careful not to schedule your meeting either too early in the morning or too late at night, or at times when there are major events occurring elsewhere on campus or in the community. It is generally a good idea to have copies of group members' regular schedules, in order to avoid creating conflicts with any of their standing engagements. For ongoing business meetings, it is usually a good idea to have a regularly scheduled meeting time, so that group members will be able to incorporate it into their plans. If this is not possible, it is recommended that you establish a time for each meeting at the close of the previous meeting. This will allow group members to have input in the decision, and thereby increase the likelihood that they will be able to attend.

You will also need to choose a location for your meeting. Obviously it is important that you choose a location that is convenient for your group members. In general, it is also best to choose a neutral location, which will not be seen as the personal domain of any individual or subgroup within the organization. By choosing a neutral location, you can reduce the likelihood that power imbalances will develop within the group. Consequently, you can increase the likelihood that all group members will feel free to participate fully in the meeting. If you must meet in group members' homes, it is usually a good idea for members to take turns serving as the host.

Try to choose locations where there are not a lot of distractions. Avoid locations, such as restaurants and bars, which are overly conducive to socializing. While social activities serve an important purpose by promoting group maintenance, they should be planned as special events, with this specific purpose in mind. At meetings, some socializing is desirable, but it should not become the primary focus of group members' attention.

Once you have selected a time and location for your meeting, you will need to notify the participants. It is recommended that you include only those who are likely to contribute to the meeting or benefit from it. This will help to ensure a high level of participant motivation during the meeting. In addition to the time, date, and location of the meeting, you will want to let participants know the purpose of the meeting and the topics to be discussed. You should also let them know what, if anything, they should bring to the meeting (Napier and Gershenfeld, 1985). Even if you have discussed the meeting with the participants, it is a good idea to send them a written confirmation.

One of the most important tasks that must be performed before each meeting is the preparation of a written agenda. There are several reasons why the agenda is so important. First, it helps the leader and other members of the group to remember everything that needs to be discussed during the meeting, and to remain focused on the business at hand. Additionally, an agenda allows information to be presented in some logical order. Agenda items should be arranged with priority given to those items which are most relevant to the purpose of the meeting. You should also place closely related items in immediate succession, so that group members' attention will not be shifted abruptly. It is a good idea to establish a time allotment for each item on the agenda, in order to ensure that all necessary business will be discussed. The amount of time allowed should be clearly indicated on the agenda, along with the name of the individual responsible for presenting the item (Napier and Gershenfeld, 1985).

There is no single best format for an agenda, but there are several basic categories of information that you will probably want to include. First of all, it is a good idea for you to allow at least a few minutes for opening comments. This will be a time for you to call the meeting to order, to review the purpose of the meeting, and to explain any new procedures which will be followed during the meeting. If the group has met before, you will probably also want to include a reading of the minutes from the previous meeting. This will help members to recall the point at which they left off their discussion, and to ensure that the record is clear and accurate. Following the reading of the minutes, it is usually a good idea to allow time for discussion of unresolved business from the previous meeting, before moving ahead to new business. Meeting agendas typically close with a period allotted for announcements. This can sometimes take the form of a "round table," with time allowed for each group member to share information or raise any concerns that he or she might have, which were not included elsewhere on the agenda. The principal benefit of this arrangement is that it reduces the likelihood of group members interjecting irrelevant comments at other points during the meeting. The format described here is illustrated in the following sample agenda.

AGENDA
Public Interest Law Society General Meeting
March 30th, 3:00 p.m.
Old Main, Room 205

I.	Opening comments (Cassandra, 3 min.)
II.	Reading of minutes from March 16th meeting (Laurence, 2 min.)
III.	Old Business
	A. Presentation on Legal Services (Jack, 10 min.)
	B. NAPIL conference (Bethany, 5 min.)
IV.	New Business
	A. Year-end banquet (Andrew, 15 min.)
	B. Annual awards (Lamar, 10 min.)
	C. Internships in Public Defenders' offices (Cassandra, 5 min.)
V.	Round table (10 min.)

During the Meeting

If you have prepared properly, most of your work will already be done by the time the meeting actually takes place. Nevertheless, even the most well planned meeting can have disappointing results if the leader does not attend to certain responsibilities throughout the entire process.

As indicated previously, one of your first duties at the time of the meeting will be to initiate the discussion. Whether you call the meeting to order by pounding a gavel or simply saying "You guys, we have to get started now," it is important that group members be clearly informed, in some way, that the meeting is about to begin. You will want to keep your comments brief. Explain the purpose of the meeting and any new procedures that will be followed. If you are meeting with a group for the first time, or if there are new members in the group, it is a good idea to spend a few moments on introductions. If it appears that the members of the group feel uncomfortable or inhibited, you may want to spend a few minutes breaking the ice. Otherwise, it is recommended that you forge ahead. If an individual has not been previously appointed to record the minutes of the meeting, it is a good idea to select someone or ask for a volunteer as soon as possible after calling the meeting to order (Brilhart, 1978).

Throughout the remainder of the meeting, you will be responsible for guiding the direction of the discussion. If necessary, remind group members about the purpose of the meeting. If you notice that certain group members are deviating from the agenda, particularly if they are following a hidden agenda of their own, ask them how the topic relates to the stated purpose of the meeting. Keep track of time, and if you notice that the group is dwelling on one particular topic for a long period of time without any apparent resolution, consider tabling the topic, at least momentarily, and moving ahead to the next item on the agenda. Make sure that there is a clear transition from one topic to the next. In closing the discussion on a particular topic, it is a good idea to summarize the points raised in the discussion. At the end of the meeting, it is usually helpful to again summarize the major points that were raised and any decisions concerning future action on the part of the group (Brilhart, 1978).

Throughout the meeting, you will also be responsible for ensuring that all group members have an equal opportunity to participate. Scan the group every few minutes. If it appears that certain group members would like to make comments on a subject but have not yet spoken, ask them if they would like to share their opinions. Try to avoid expressing your own opinions on controversial topics until other group members have shared their points of view. While it is important that you listen attentively to group members, and that you convey your attention nonverbally, try to avoid responding verbally to every comment that is made. Instead, allow group members to respond to one another (Brilhart, 1978).

You may occasionally notice that individual group members are dominating the discussion, in which case, it may be necessary for you to intervene. There are a number of ways in which you can do this, but in general it is best to use the most subtle approach possible. The following are just a few options, drawn from the management literature, which vary greatly in their levels of subtlety:

- When feasible, seat talkative members where you can easily overlook them.

- When you ask a question of the group, let your eyes meet those of members who have spoken infrequently and avoid those of highly vocal members.

- When a compulsive talker has made a point, cut in with, "How do the rest of you feel about that idea?"

- Restate briefly what has been said at length.

- Ask each person to make only one point per speech.

- Have one member keep a count of frequency of participation, then report his [sic] findings to the group.

- In private, ask the frequent talkers to help you get the quiet members to speak more often.

- Point out the problem and ask others to contribute more. For instance, "We have heard a lot from Peter and Marion, but what do the rest of you think about . . .?" (Brilhart, 1978, p. 176).

In addition to ensuring that all group members have an opportunity to participate in the discussion, you will want to make sure that group members are encouraged to think both critically and creatively. Establishing a dynamic organizational climate requires a delicate balance. If group members become overly critical in examining new ideas, individuals may feel reluctant to share any original thoughts. On the other hand, if group members become overly supportive, faulty reasoning may go unchecked, with damaging consequences for the group (Brilhart, 1978).

When conducting a meeting, it is important that you pay close attention to the levels of creative and critical thinking exhibited by the members of the group. If you find that group members are not being sufficiently critical of the ideas presented in the meeting, ask them for evidence to support their claims, and question them on the relevance of the evidence presented, as well as the legitimacy of their sources of information. Ask members to explain the underlying assumptions that form the basis for their value judgments, and ask whether or not these assumptions are shared by the entire group. Sometimes, it is also helpful to solicit opinions from individuals outside the group, or to appoint subgroups within the organization to independently evaluate a proposal before taking action on it. If you find that group members are not exhibiting sufficient creativity, you can encourage them to momentarily suspend judgment of various ideas, by replacing the word, "should," with the word, "might" (e.g., "What might we do?" as opposed to "What should we do?") (Brilhart, 1978).

During the meeting, it is also important that you make efforts to promote understanding between the members of the group. Again, pay close attention to group members' nonverbal behavior. If a particular group member appears to be confused, ask the speaker for clarification. Also be aware that members of discussion groups sometimes use "hot button" words (e.g., "radical," "fascist," "extremist"), which convey strong emotions on the part of the speaker, and often evoke similarly strong emotions in the listener. This type of language often has the effect of distracting group members from the factual information presented and discouraging an open exchange of ideas. You can remedy this situation by quickly detecting biased or emotive language, and rephrasing group members' statements in more neutral terms (Brilhart, 1978).

At some point during the meeting, there is a good chance that you will need to resolve a conflict between group members. It is important that you recognize conflicts within the group and involve the group members in generating solutions. Apply the basic principles of "win-win communication," described in Chapter 5 of this book, and encourage group members to compromise when necessary. Remind group members of the shared purposes which brought them together, and insist that they focus their comments on facts and issues, rather than on personalities. Finally, do not hesitate to make frequent use of humor. It often has the effect of breaking tension within the group and contributing to a more rewarding experience for group members (Brilhart, 1978).

Occasionally, you may want to direct group members' attention toward the actual process of the group. By analyzing the ways in which group members interact with one another during their meetings, it is possible to help individuals develop a deeper understanding of themselves and one another. As group members discover ineffective patterns of behavior, they can work together to promote positive change (Brilhart, 1978).

After the Meeting

Once the meeting is over, you will want to make sure that copies of the minutes are distributed to the members of the group, preferably within two days. If the group arrived at any decisions during the meeting, concerning action to be taken in the future, it is particularly important that these decisions be noted in the minutes. Occasionally, you may want to follow up with certain group members individually, to make sure they have a clear understanding of their responsibilities concerning any of the issues discussed in the meeting, and to see that they do not encounter any major obstacles in following through on these duties. If you find that you are dissatisfied with a decision that was made during the meeting, avoid the temptation to complain about it afterwards to people outside the group, or to wage a campaign for reversal of the decision among individual group members. Instead, place the item on the agenda for the next meeting, and plan to discuss it further as a group (Napier and Gershenfeld, 1985).

After the meeting, it is also a good idea for you to take a few moments to evaluate your own performance in leading the discussion. Ask yourself whether or not you accomplished all that you had hoped to achieve (e.g., Did you cover all of the items on the agenda? Did all of the group members contribute to the discussion?). Occasionally, it is also a good idea to solicit group members' reactions to your meetings. Questionnaires can be useful for drawing out the perceptions of group members. Respondents' candor can usually be increased by allowing them to complete their questionnaires anonymously. Once you have determined specific areas in which your meetings need improvement, try to identify ways in which you might approach future meetings differently.

The Planning and Evaluation Cycle

Figure 2 presents a cyclical model for planning and evaluation in student organizations, which is similar to models used in business (Ackoff, 1970; Binnie, 1970; Humble, 1970; Steiner, 1970), education (California Elementary School

Administrators Association, 1971; California Joint Committee on Educational Goals and Evaluation, 1971; English and Zaharis, 1971; Harpel, 1976; Hartley, 1968; Winstead, 1982), and public administration (Brady, 1973; Quade, 1968; Tarter, 1974). The activities presented in the model are carried out in four separate phases, which are repeated throughout the life of the organization. Each time that the group reenters a phase, the members approach their tasks somewhat differently, as a result of insights gained during the previous cycle, and the placement of new demands upon the group.

A Planning & Evaluation Model for Student Organizations

Phase 1

Establish/Review:
- Mission
- Goals
- Objectives

Phase 2
- Develop action plan
- Allocate organizational resources
- Acquire additional resources if necessary

Phase 3
- Implement action plan
- Monitor activities of the organization

Phase 4
- Evaluate organizational programs and activities
- Reassess needs of constituencies

Phase 1

During the first phase of the process, the leader works with members of the group to establish a shared vision of the organization's future. The first step in this process is to articulate an organizational **mission**. According to the management literature, "an organization's mission statement tells what it is, why it exists, and the unique contribution it can make" (King and Cleland, 1978, p. 47). An organization comes into being because of a perceived need, which the organization is believed to be capable of fulfilling. The organization's mission statement identifies this need, and describes, in very broad terms, the ways in which the organization addresses the particular concern.

For illustrative purposes, let us consider an example. If you were to attend an institution located within an hour's drive of a major metropolitan area, and the institution were to draw a large percentage of its student body from this particular area, it would not be unusual for the institution to emerge as a "suitcase college," with few students remaining on campus during weekends. If you were among those desiring a traditional collegiate experience, complete with a lively weekend social life, you would probably regard other students' behavior as problematic. Given the educational benefits of cocurricular involvement, which were presented in Chapter 1 of this book, you would probably find much support for your position among faculty members and administrators at your institution.

Suppose that you and other concerned students decided to establish a student organization which would promote weekend residency on campus by improving the quality of campus life on weekends. The mission statement of your organization might read:

> The Weekenders Association has been established as a group of students who believe that participation in social activities is an integral element of the collegiate experience. The members of the group believe that the benefits of such activities for all students are enhanced when the overall level of participation is maximized. Therefore, the organization is committed to increasing opportunities for social interaction on campus during weekends, and encouraging weekend residency by improving the quality of life on campus.

It should be noted that an organization's mission statement not only helps members to understand what the group does, but also helps them to understand what it does not do (King and Cleland, 1978). In our example, it is clear that the Weekenders Association is not concerned with recruitment of a national student body. While this might be an effective strategy for increasing weekend residency on campus, it does not fall within the purview of this particular group. The organization's mission statement makes clear its intent to promote weekend residency by altering the quality of life on campus, rather than by altering the composition of the student body.

The clear articulation of an organizational mission is extremely important. It has been noted that failure to discuss the basic mission of an organization ultimately leads to the loss of any existing consensus among members, regarding its purpose. This occurs because the membership of the group changes over time and events in the environment can divert attention away from its original purpose (King and Cleland, 1978).

Once an organization has established its basic mission, it is necessary to develop a statement of **goals**. Goal statements have been described as "long-range, abstract statements describing ideal results" (Harpel, 1976, p. vii). It has been noted that a goal "is general and timeless and is not concerned with a particular achievement within a specified time period" (California Joint Committee, 1971, p. 132). The stated goals of an organization should relate to its mission, but should provide an even clearer sense of direction for the group.

Organizational goals can generally be divided into five categories: (1) "societal goals," (2) "output goals," (3) "system goals," (4) "product goals," and (5) "derived goals" (Perrow, 1970, p. 135). Most organizations establish goals in several of these categories, though not necessarily in all five.

The first category, **societal goals**, consists of those goals which directly address the needs of society (Perrow, 1970). In our example, societal goals of the Weekenders Association would probably relate to the educational benefits of social activities on campus, since education is generally seen as the principal societal contribution of collegiate institutions. One such goal might be "to prepare students who will become actively involved in community organizations after graduation."

The second category, **output goals,** "deals with types of output defined in terms of consumer functions" (Perrow, 1970, p. 135). In our example, an output goal of the Weekenders Association may be "to provide organized weekend entertainment opportunities on campus."

System goals are those which relate to "the state or manner of functioning of the organization, independent of the goods or services it produces or its derived goals" (Perrow, 1970, p. 135). A system goal pertaining to the functioning of the Weekenders Association could be "to establish a computerized bookkeeping system for monitoring the organization's use of its financial resources."

Product goals relate to the characteristics of the services or goods provided by the organization. These characteristics may relate to such matters as quantity, quality, variety, availability, and uniqueness (Perrow, 1970). In our example, a product goal of the Weekenders Association might be "to provide a balanced variety of weekend programs on campus, including films, concerts, dances, and coffeehouses."

Derived goals have been described as relating to "the uses to which the organization puts the power it generates in pursuit of other goals" (Perrow, 1970, pp. 135-136). An organization can exert far more influence over its environment than its members could if they were to act in isolation. Often the power that is derived from the collective action of group members is directed toward matters which do not relate directly to the organization's central purpose. In our example, the Weekenders Association might respond to a particular incident on campus by condemning action taken by other students or by the administration of the university, regardless of whether or not the particular action had any bearing upon the quality of life on campus for weekend residents. Over a period of time, a pattern of involvement in campus politics might emerge, which would reveal the derived goals of the organization. However, in all likelihood, these goals would never be formally stated.

Once an organization has established a set of goals, further clarification is provided through a statement of **objectives**. An objective is defined as "a desired accomplishment that can be verified within a given time and under specifiable conditions which, if attained, advances the system toward a corresponding goal"

(California Joint Committee, pp. 132, 134). Two important characteristics of well conceived objectives are that they: (1) "describe some terminal condition or behavior," and (2) "define some criterion of acceptable performance" (Harpel, 1976, p. ix). In other words, they answer the questions: (1) "How do you know when you get there?" and (2) "How much of what is enough?" (Harpel, 1976, p. ix).

In our example, the Weekenders Association's statement of objectives might specify that "the organization will sponsor at least two weekend social activities, each month during fall term." Unlike the goals presented previously, this objective will provide the group with a very clear basis upon which to measure its success. The group members will know at the end of the term whether or not they have accomplished this objective, simply by counting the number of weekend programs sponsored each month. If they count two events per month, they will know that they have done enough.

The measures which are to be used in determining whether or not objectives have been met can usually be divided into two basic categories: (1) measures of **activity** and (2) measures of **impact** (Harpel, 1976). The first category relates to the specific action to be taken by the group. The objective presented in the previous paragraph includes a measure of activity, since it specifies what the Weekenders Association will do. Measures of impact would instead specify the effect that the activity will have upon its target population. This type of measure can be particularly difficult to establish because a group's desired outcomes will often relate to changes in people's attitudes or levels of knowledge, which are difficult to present in terms of observable behaviors. In formulating measures of impact, you will often find it necessary to think about the ways that a person's internal responses to an organizational activity will manifest themselves externally.

For example, suppose the members of the Weekenders Association were to decide that one of their objectives should relate to students' enjoyment of organizationally sponsored dances. It would be necessary for the group to begin by identifying the ways in which people usually behave when they are enjoying this type of social event. Based upon past experience, the group might conclude that people tend to stay late when they are enjoying a dance and that they tend to leave early when they are bored. The group might specify, therefore, that "a minimum of fifty students will be present during the final hour of each organizationally sponsored dance," or that "no more than 50 students will leave any organizationally sponsored dance during the first hour."

Organizational objectives can be divided into three general categories, on the basis of their relationship to the activities and outcomes of the previous cycle in our planning and evaluation model. The three categories are: (1) "regular objectives," (2) "problem-solving objectives," and (3) "innovative objectives" (Odiorne, 1987, pp. 95-96).

Regular objectives involve "the ordinary, recurring, ongoing, and routine repetitions of what has happened in the past" (Odiorne, 1987, p. 95). Regular objectives reflect satisfaction with certain aspects of the status quo. The purpose of regular objectives is to ensure that the previous accomplishments of the organization will be sustained during the next cycle. In our example, a regular objective of the Weekenders Association might state that "the organization will continue to sponsor at least two weekend social activities per month through the remainder of the academic year."

Problem-solving objectives "state a problem in terms of (a) the present condition and (b) the desired condition," with the objective being "to get from (a) to (b) by a specified time" (Odiorne, 1987, p. 96). A problem-solving objective reflects a desire "to alter something from a specific position or figure to something better" (Odiorne, 1987, p. 96). In our example, the Weekenders Association might establish a problem-solving objective by declaring that "the average weekend occupancy rate in the residence halls for the current academic year will be increased from 75% of the total resident student population to 80% of the same population by April 30th."

Innovative objectives are "objectives that will change things for the better, regardless of how good things may be at present, and even if the present condition does not constitute a problem" (Odiorne, 1987, p. 96). Innovative objectives can lead an organization to undertake completely new activities. In our example, the Weekenders Association might choose to establish an innovative objective by stating that "the organization will implement a weekend lecture series, consisting of at least four separate events, beginning in January and ending in March."

Phase 2

Once an organization has established its mission, goals, and objectives, it must develop an **action plan** for each objective. An action plan is defined as "a plan that is intended to be completed within a definite time period" (Allen, 1982, p. 226). The function of an action plan is to "translate overall, continuing plans into plans that will prompt specific action by individuals" (Allen, 1982, p. 226). Action plans provide group members with a detailed approach for achieving the objectives of the organization. It has been noted that "action plans answer such questions as: Who is going to do it? When is it due? How much will it cost?" (Parson and Culligan, 1985, p. 27).

In developing an action plan, there are five basic steps which must be taken. The five steps are: (1) to identify the tasks that must be completed in order to achieve the stated objective; (2) to determine the sequence in which these tasks must be completed; (3) to determine who will be responsible for completing each task; (4) to specify the resources that will be necessary for completing each task; and (5) to determine how achievement of the objective is to be verified (Herman, 1990).

In order for a student group to arrive at a realistic action plan, its members must have an accurate account of its resources. In planning your group's activities, you will be concerned with four basic categories of resources: (1) money; (2) facilities and equipment; (3) materials, supplies, and services; and (4) personnel (Ackoff, 1970). Before committing your group to a particular course of action, you will need to make sure that you possess or have access to the various resources necessary to support the plan.

If you do not have the resources at your immediate disposal, your first recourse should be to identify potential sources of support outside the organization, and to take steps toward acquiring whatever is needed. If you need additional money, you may be able to acquire funding from the student government association on your campus or an institutional department whose goals are directly supported by a particular activity. You may also want to conduct fund raising activities, or pool your resources with another student group. Joint sponsorship can be an excellent means of accessing both monetary and non-monetary resources.

Realistically, there is a good chance that you will not be able to obtain the resources necessary to support all of the activities that you would like to undertake. It is for this reason that budgeting is also important. The term, **budgeting**, refers to "the allocation of resources to various activities for their accomplishment" (Harpel, 1976, p. xiv). It has been noted that "budgeting implies commitment and a sense of priorities" (Harpel, 1976, p. xiv). In all likelihood, as you begin to allocate resources for various activities, you will be confronted with difficult choices.

In choosing between alternative courses of action, you will need to pay attention to both the effectiveness and the efficiency of the various approaches. **Effectiveness** is "the degree to which performance meshes with goals" (King and Cleland, 1978, p. 11). In contrast, **efficiency** is concerned with maximizing output while minimizing cost, or in simpler terms, "getting the best deal" (King and Cleland, 1978, p. 11). In our example, sponsoring a major rock concert would probably be a highly effective means of enticing students to remain on campus over the weekend, but it would hardly be an efficient use of the Weekenders Association's resources if a similar outcome could be achieved by organizing a euchre tournament.

The final step in developing your action plan will be to decide how the accomplishment of the specified objective is to be measured. If your objective is well conceived, you should already know exactly what information you will need. However, before you can implement your plan, you must also develop a strategy for accessing this information. For example, if your objective were to state that "a minimum of 30 students will attend each organizationally sponsored coffeehouse," you will need to determine how you are to arrive at your count. In this case, you might decide that your figure will be based on the number of people who are seated when the entertainment begins. Remember that you must also decide who will be responsible for doing the counting!

Once you have decided what to include in your action plan, you will need to put it in written form, so that it can be used to guide your activities on an ongoing basis. Table 1 provides an example of a written action plan. Table 2 can be duplicated and used to prepare your own action plans.

Table 1. EXAMPLE OF AN ACTION PLAN

Objective: <u>The organization will implement a weekend lecture series, consisting of at least four separate events, beginning in January and ending in March.</u>

Task	Responsible Party	Completion Date	Resources
1. Conduct survey on general topics	Dale, Yumiko	9/30	Student directory, Computer (30 hours) Photocopies ($10), office supplies ($10), Postage ($30)
2. Select general topics	Megan (chair), Dale, Lori, Evan, Yumiko	10/10	Meeting room with chalkboard (2 hours)
3. Identify possible presenters	Lori	10/20	Student Union Programming
4. Select presenters and alternates	Megan (chair), Dale, Lori, Evan, Yumiko	10/30	Meeting room with chalkboard (2 hours)
5. Schedule program dates	Megan (chair), Dale, Lori, Evan, Yumiko	10/30	Meeting room with chalkboard (1 hour)
6. Obtain commitments and specification of requirements	Megan	11/30	Telephone ($20) Office supplies ($5) Postage ($5) Honorarium allowance ($500)
7. Reserve auditorium	Lori	12/15	
8. Submit A.V. request	Evan	12/30	
9. Post fliers	Yumiko	12/15	$30
10. Place ads in campus newspapers	Dale	12/30	$50
11. Host presenters	Megan	t.b.a.	$200
12. Record attendance figures at the beginning of each lecture	Yumiko	t.b.a.	
13. Evaluate program outcomes	Megan (chair), Dale, Lori, Evan, Yumiko	4/10	Meeting room with chalkboard (2 hours)
14. Write program report	Megan	4/30	Computer (10 hours) Office supplies ($5)

Table 2. ACTION PLAN FORM

Objective:

Task	Responsible Party	Completion Date	Resources

Phase 3

During the third phase of the cycle, you will be concerned with overseeing the implementation of the action plan. The need for strong leadership during this phase cannot be emphasized too strongly. An aerospace program manager once observed that "most programs of action die because people don't adequately plan their work, then *fully* work their plan" (Brown, 1991, p. 19). During the first two phases of the cycle, the leader must focus primarily on planning the group's work. However, upon entering the third phase, the leader must shift his or her attention to the process of working the plan.

During this phase, you will have an opportunity to use nearly all of the general leadership skills presented in this book. However, several specific leadership activities will become particularly important to you.

First of all, you will need to make sure that you are communicating the action plan to those with whom you are working. Remind them continually of the shared vision which has been established. According to one management consultant, "it is far, far better to rip the stapled pages of an action plan apart and post them on a bulletin board than to let them suffocate in a file folder" (Brown, 1991).

It is also important for members of an organization to feel a sense of ownership over the action plan, or at least some small part of it (Brown, 1991). Be sure to recognize the contributions of individual members. To the extent possible, use inclusive words like "us" and "our," and avoid using exclusionary words like "me" and "my."

You should also touch base with the members of your group occasionally, to make sure that they are not experiencing any unanticipated difficulties (Brown, 1991). If necessary, be prepared to make minor adjustments in the group's approach to certain tasks. While it is important that the group conduct its work methodically, it is foolish to continue down a path that is clearly leading in the wrong direction.

Finally, it is important to celebrate the successful achievement of organizational objectives. After all of the hard work that goes into planning and carrying out the activities of an organization, its members deserve a pat on the back. Leaders must attend to organizational morale, if they hope to enjoy future successes. As noted in the management literature, "celebration is a sure-fire way to weld people's attention to an action plan" (Brown, 1991, p. 19).

Phase 4

During the fourth phase of the cycle, you will be concerned with evaluation. The first order of business will be to determine whether or not the objectives of the organization have been achieved, based upon your established criteria. However, you will also need to identify any problems that you might have encountered along the way, and any new insight which you might have gained through the process.

For example, suppose the members of the Weekenders Association were to implement their plan for initiating a lecture series, and successfully achieved their objective of offering four lectures during the specified time period, only to find that no more than ten students attended any of the programs. The members of the organization might conclude that the demand for a lecture series is not sufficient to justify continuation of the program. On the other hand, they might conclude that attendance was low because of poor publicity or the scheduling of the individual events.

In either case, the group would have cause to rethink its objectives. Depending upon the conclusions drawn by the group during the evaluation phase, future statements of objectives may include provisions for increased attendance at organizationally sponsored lectures, or they may not include any reference to a lecture series at all. Once the group has completed the fourth phase of the cycle, its members will be ready to begin the entire process once again, using the knowledge gained from their experience.

Summary

This chapter dealt with the activities of organizational leaders. The need for both a theoretical and practical understanding of leadership was emphasized throughout the chapter.

The importance of motivation was stressed, and an overview of basic principles of motivation was presented. The Western Electric Hawthorne studies of the 1920's were described. It was noted that the principal conclusion drawn from these studies was that attention to the concerns of workers is inherently motivational.

Abraham Maslow's hierarchy of basic needs was also introduced. The five categories of needs identified by Maslow were described. These include: (1) physiological needs, (2) safety needs, (3) belongingness and love needs, (4) esteem needs, and (5) the need for self-actualization. It was noted that the five categories are arranged hierarchically. According to Maslow's theory, people are motivated primarily by their desire to satisfy those unmet needs which are lowest on the hierarchy. Once a particular class of needs is adequately served, the category that is the next lowest on the hierarchy becomes the principal motivating force for the individual.

Frederick Herzberg's motivation-hygiene theory was also examined. According to this theory, workers' satisfaction and motivation can be affected by two separate sets of factors. The first set includes those factors which relate to the inherent characteristics of a person's work. These factors are known as "satisfiers" or "motivators" because they can contribute positively to a person's satisfaction and motivation. The second set of factors, the "dissatisfiers," also known as the "maintenance" or "hygiene" factors, can negatively affect a person's attitude toward his or her work. The dissatisfiers relate to the environment or context in which the person works.

Thirty specific strategies for motivating followers were recommended in this chapter. The recommendations were based on management studies which were conducted over the course of approximately 25 years.

The purposes and benefits of delegation were also explained in this chapter, and contrasts were drawn between delegation and work assignments. The discussion included an examination of the process through which delegated projects are transformed into work assignments and the conditions under which this transformation can occur.

The concept of authority was introduced as a primary consideration in the process of delegation. It was emphasized that leaders must not delegate to subordinates who lack the authority necessary to successfully execute the tasks which are to be delegated. It was noted that two primary types of authority exist: (1) organizational authority and (2) individual authority. Individual authority can be further divided into six smaller categories: (1) influential authority, (2) intellectual authority, (3) credibility, (4) expert authority, (5) credential authority, and (6) prerogative authority. While organizational authority can be delegated, individual authority generally cannot be.

The concept of responsibility was also discussed in this chapter. It was stressed that leaders cannot escape responsibility simply by delegating a task. The term, "ultimate responsibility," was used in reference to the leader's responsibility for the tasks that he or she delegates. It was noted that responsibility can sometimes be shared with subordinates. Both positive and negative forms of shared responsibility were described.

Circumstances under which delegation should not occur were identified. It was noted that executive duties generally should be retained by the leader, as should disciplinary responsibilities. The leader should also assume the primary responsibility for policy making, and for promoting morale within the organization and resolving conflicts between organizational units. It was recommended that leaders not delegate tasks which have been delegated specifically to them by their organizational superiors. Caution was also recommended in delegating "pet projects" and tasks which relate to confidential matters. It was recommended that the leader not delegate a duplicate of his or her job, and that he or she delegate entire projects, rather than isolated tasks, whenever possible.

Guidelines for choosing a delegate were also presented. It was recommended that the chain of command within the organization be respected, and that choices be based on matters of equity, interest, competence, and the need for personal development.

The importance of organizational meetings was discussed in this chapter. Seven types of meetings were identified, and contrasts were drawn between them, based on the organizational purposes which they serve. The seven types of meetings are:

(1) information sharing-communication, (2) diagnostic or fact finding, (3) brainstorming, (4) decision-making, (5) planning, (6) coordination and monitoring, and (7) ongoing business.

The potential benefits of meetings were examined and guidelines were presented for ensuring the realization of these desirable outcomes. Recommendations related to specific actions which must be taken by the leader before, during, and after each meeting.

The importance of the meeting agenda was stressed. Specific agenda components were recommended, and a sample agenda was presented.

The chapter closed with a discussion of the planning and evaluation process in student organizations. A cyclical model, consisting of four phases, was presented. During the first phase of the process, the members of the organization must establish or review the organizational mission, goals, and objectives. Goals can be divided into five categories: (1) societal goals, (2) output goals, (3) system goals, (4) product goals, and (5) derived goals. Unlike goals, objectives must be measurable, in terms of either activity or impact. Objectives can be divided into three categories: (1) regular objectives, (2) problem-solving objectives, and (3) innovative objectives. During the second phase of the cycle, action plans are established for all organizational objectives. Organizational resources must be allocated, with attention to both effectiveness and efficiency. During the third phase of the cycle, the plan must be implemented and the leader must monitor the activities of the organization. During the final phase, the group members must evaluate their programs and activities and reassess the needs of the various populations which are served by the organization.

References

Ackoff, R. L. (1970). *A Concept of Corporate Planning.* New York: Wiley-Interscience.

Allen, L. A. (1982). *Making Managerial Planning More Effective.* New York: McGraw-Hill.

Binnie, J. H. (1970). Analysing and meeting the training needs of management. In J. W. Humble (Ed.), *Management by Objectives in Action* (pp. 236-248). London: McGraw-Hill.

Brady, R. H. (1973). MBO goes to work in the public sector. *Harvard Business Review, 51* (2), 65-74.

Brilhart, J. K. (1978). *Effective Group Discussion.* Dubuque, IA: Wm. C. Brown.

Brown, T. (1991). Keep your action plan alive. *Industry Week, 240* (6), 19.

Burns, F. and Gragg, R. L. (1981). Meeting-evaluation scale. In J. E. Jones and J. W. Pfeiffer (Eds.), *The 1981 Annual Handbook for Group Facilitators,* 10th ed. (p. 89). San Diego: University Associates.

California Elementary School Administrators Association (1971). CESSAA project evaluation. In L. H. Browder, Jr. (Ed.), *Emerging Patterns of Administrative Accountability* (pp. 491-502). Berkeley, CA: McCutchan.

California Joint Committee on Educational Goals and Evaluation (1971). The way to relevance and accountability in education. In L. H. Browder, Jr. (Ed.), *Emerging Patterns of Administrative Accountability* (pp. 127-169). Berkeley, CA: McCutchan.

Engel, H. M. (1983). *How to Delegate: A Guide to Getting Things Done.* Houston: Gulf.

English, F. W. and Zaharis, J. K. (1971). Internal educational performance contracting. In L. H. Browder, Jr. (Ed.), *Emerging Patterns of Administrative Accountability* (pp. 432-440). Berkeley, CA: McCutchan.

Harpel, R. L. (1976). Planning, budgeting, and evaluation in student affairs programs: A manual for administrators. *NASPA Journal, 14* (1), ii-xx

Hartley, H. J. (1968). *Educational Planning-Programming-Budgeting.* Englewood Cliffs, NJ: Prentice-Hall.

Herman, J. J. (1990). Action plans to make your vision a reality. *NASSP Bulletin, 74* (523), 14-17.

Herzberg, F. (1966). *Work and the Nature of Man.* Cleveland: World.

Hicks, N. (1988). Workshop: How to delegate. *Public Relations Journal, 44* (6), 31-32.

Humble, J. W. (1970). Management by objectives — Basic concepts. In J. W. Humble (Ed.), *Management by Objectives in Action* (pp. 3-21). London: McGraw-Hill.

King, W. R. and Cleland, D. I. (1978). *Strategic Planning and Policy.* New York: Van Nostrand Reinhold.

Laird, D. A. and Laird, E. C. (1957) *The Techniques of Delegating.* New York: McGraw-Hill.

Maslow, A. H. (1970). Motivation and Personality, 2nd ed. New York: Harper & Row.

Napier, R. W. and Gershenfeld, M. K. (1985). *Groups: Theory and Experience*, 3rd ed. Boston: Houghton Mifflin.

Odiorne, G. S. (1987). *The Human Side of Management.* Lexington, MA: Lexington.

Owens, J. (November, 1981). A reappraisal of leadership theory and training. *Personnel Administrator*, 75-84, 98-99.

Parson, M. J. and Culligan, M. J. (1985). *Back to Basics: Planning.* New York: Facts on File.

Perrow, C. (1970). *Organizational Analysis: A Sociological View.* Belmont, CA: Wadsworth.

Quade, E. S. (1968). Systems analysis techniques for planning programming-budgeting. In F.J. Lyden and E. G. Miller (Eds.), *Planning Programming Budgeting: A Systems Approach to Management* (pp. 292-312). Chicago: Markham.

Roethlisberger, F. J. and Dickson, W. J. (1964). *Management and the Worker.* New York: Wiley.

Spitzer, D. R. (March, 1980). 30 ways to motivate employees to perform better. *Training*, 54-56.

Steiner, G. A. (1970). Approaches to long-range planning for small businesses. In J.W. Humble (Ed.), *Management by Objectives in Action* (pp. 131-152). London: McGraw-Hill.

Steinmetz, L. L. (1976). *The Art and Skill of Delegation*. Reading, MA: Addison-Wesley.

Tarter, J. L. (1974). *Management by Objectives for Public Administrators*. Washington, DC: National Training and Development Service Press.

Valentine, R. F. (1973). *Initiative and Managerial Power*. New York: AMACOM.

Winstead, P. C. (1982). Planned change in institutions of higher learning. In G. Hipps (Ed.), *New Directions for Institutional Research: Effective Planned Change Strategies*, n. 33. San Francisco: Jossey-Bass.

Activities

Getting It Straight

In the spaces provided, indicate whether the following statements are true (T) or false (F.).

_____ The primary conclusion that researchers at the Western Electric Hawthorne Works drew from their experiments was that factory workers invariably show greater productivity in more brightly lit surroundings.

_____ In Frederick Herzberg's theory of motivation, "satisfiers" are also known as "motivators."

_____ In Frederick Herzberg's theory of motivation, "satisfiers" are also known as "maintenance" factors.

_____ In Frederick Herzberg's theory of motivation, "dissatisfiers" are also known as "hygiene" factors.

In the spaces provided, number the following categories from 1 to 5, according to their placement on Abraham Maslow's hierarchy of needs, with 1 representing the lowest level and 5 representing the highest level.

_____ Belongingness and love needs

_____ Esteem needs

_____ Physiological needs

_____ Need for self-actualization

_____ Safety needs

Read the following scenario and respond to the items presented by filling in the blank spaces.

Five high school seniors recently arrived at decisions concerning their plans for college. They have chosen several different institutions, and differ greatly from one another in the reasons for their choices.

Brad will attend the local community college for two years. Although he would like to go away to a four-year institution, he is concerned about the financial burden that would be placed on his family if he were to do so at this time. His father was recently laid off from his job in a local manufacturing plant, and his mother is currently working two jobs in order to support the family. Brad was attracted to the community college because of its low tuition, and its extensive evening course offerings, which will allow him greater flexibility in seeking part-time employment. He also hopes to save costs on room and board by living at home.

LaTasha will also attend the local community college. However, she has chosen this option primarily because of her desire to maintain ongoing contact with her family and friends. LaTasha has traveled extensively and would feel quite confident in moving to another city. She also possesses sufficient financial resources to do so. However, at this time, she considers her interpersonal relationships the top priority in her life. For this reason, she has chosen to attend college in her local community and to live at home with her family.

Stephanie will attend a private university in her local community. She likewise possesses adequate financial resources to attend a college or university in another city, but has chosen to remain at home with her family. Unlike LaTasha, however, Stephanie feels dependent on her family. She has never been away from home for more than a few days, and is afraid that she would be emotionally unable to cope with the pressure of living on her own. Her insecurity is the primary motivating force behind her decision not to go away to college.

Rob plans to attend a small state university about 200 miles from home. Although the university is not well known outside his state of residence, it offers an excellent teacher preparation program in Music Education. Rob is a talented musician, who has always enjoyed music immensely. He also enjoys working with children. For these reasons, he has chosen to pursue a career as a music teacher at the elementary school level. Although he realizes that he will never become rich and famous as a music teacher, he is confident that he will be happy in his chosen career.

Daryl will attend a prestigious private university in another state, where he will enroll in a pre-law curriculum. He hopes to then attend a similarly prestigious law school and to ultimately pursue a career in law or politics. Daryl has chosen this course of action because of his competitive desire to achieve a position of prominence and high social status.

1. _____ appears to be motivated primarily by the need for self-actualization.

2. _____ appears to be motivated primarily by belongingness and love needs.

3. _____ appears to be motivated primarily by esteem needs.

4. _____ appears to be motivated primarily by physiological needs.

5. _____ appears to be motivated primarily by safety needs.

Applying Frederick Herzberg's theory of motivation, identify each of the following as a satisfier (S) or a dissatisfier (D)

_____	Salary
_____	Insurance benefits
_____	Opportunity to apply one's unique skills
_____	Opportunity to develop new skills
_____	Family leave policy
_____	Social significance of the work
_____	Work schedule
_____	Retirement plan

Place a check mark next to any of the following recommendations that were presented in this chapter.

_____ "Rewards should always be contingent on performance."

_____ "Dispense reinforcers as soon as possible after the desired performance."

_____ "Eliminate unnecessary threats and punishments."

_____ "Make sure that accomplishment is adequately recognized."

_____ "Spare your followers the burden of making important decisions."

_____ "Provide support when it is needed."

_____ "Allow your followers to focus on their own tasks, free from the distraction of larger organizational concerns."

_____ "Provide only rewards that relate to the intrinsic characteristics of the work."

_____ "Treat all followers in the same manner."

_____ "Recognize and help eliminate barriers to individual achievement."

_____ "Exhibit interest in and knowledge of each individual under your supervision."

_____ "Encourage individuals to participate in making decisions that affect them."

_____ "Establish a climate of trust and open communication."

_____ "Make frequent use of statutory powers."

_____ "Help individuals to see the integrity, significance and relevance of their work in terms of organizational output."

_____ "Point out improvements in performance, no matter how small."

_____ "Demonstrate your own motivation through behavior and attitude."

_____   "Criticize behavior, not people."

_____   "Make sure that effort pays off in results."

_____   "Establish uniform procedures for completing tasks, and discourage deviation from these procedures."

_____   "Strive for the elimination of all anxiety within the work group."

_____   "Be concerned with short-term and long-term motivation."

Read the following scenario and respond to the questions presented.

Sharon and Ashley are both members of the Community Arts Council, a local cultural organization. The two students spend about five hours per week at the Council's office, doing volunteer work. Currently, they are involved in very different activities. Sharon has been fulfilling her regular duties of opening the mail and directing it to the proper recipients, stuffing envelopes for the Council's quarterly mailing to its patrons, and updating membership records. Although Ashley ordinarily engages in similar activities, this week she is preparing a special informational mailing pertaining to the organization's upcoming twenty-fifth anniversary celebration. One of the reasons why Ashley has been given responsibility for this activity is that she and her supervisor agreed that it would be a good learning experience for her, since she intends to pursue a career in public relations.

1. Which of the two students is currently involved in a delegated activity?
2. Which of the two students is currently involved in a work assignment?
3. Could the delegated activity be transformed into a work assignment? Explain.

Read the following scenario and respond to the items presented.

Dwight, Stacy, John, Sara, Judy, Paul, and Walter work at the snack bar on their campus. Each of them is able to exert some control over the activities of the group, but the nature of their authority differs.

Dwight is not looked upon favorably by the other members of the group. In his absence, they refer to him as "the dweeb." However, because he is the student manager of the snack bar, they generally comply with his wishes.

Stacy is not well liked, because she tends to be rather temperamental. However, because her father is the Dean of Students at the university, she has been able to effectively communicate the needs of the food service staff to institutional decision makers. As a result, her coworkers have tried to stay on good terms with her.

John is seen as a "nice guy" by the other members of the group. He is easygoing, and has a good sense of humor. Consequently, his coworkers generally try to give him what he wants.

Sara's academic achievement has earned her a four-year scholarship, and has placed her on the Dean's List every term since her initial enrollment at the university. Because she is so bright, Sara is also highly respected by her coworkers. When she makes a recommendation, their usual response is, "If you say so."

Judy is a graduate student who has a bachelor's degree in Food and Nutrition, and is a Registered Dietician. Because of her educational and professional background, her opinion is generally respected by her coworkers.

Paul's opinion is also highly regarded, because of his openness and honesty. He is seen as a person whose word is sincere.

Walter is a valued member of the snack bar staff because of his familiarity with the equipment. He has been working in the snack bar for three years, and there are very few problems that emerge which he has not experienced previously. He does an excellent job of diagnosing the nature of a problem involving the equipment, and making minor repairs if necessary.

A.   In the space provided, write the letter corresponding to the type of authority that each staff member possesses.

_____	1. Dwight	a. organizational authority
_____	2. Stacy	b. influential authority
_____	3. John	c. intellectual authority
_____	4. Sara	d. credibility
_____	5. Judy	e. expert authority
_____	6. Paul	f. credential authority
_____	7. Walter	g. prerogative authority

B.   Circle the names of all members of the group who could be described as possessing individual authority.

Read the following scenario and respond to the items presented.

Two and a half years ago, Alex began a small business, producing and selling a "video yearbook" at his university. From its beginning, the business has been fairly successful. The second year that he was in business, Alex hired Veronica and Fred to work for him. Veronica was given overall responsibility for production, and Fred was placed in charge of distribution. By the end of the second year, two more workers, Dorothy and Troy, were hired to assist Fred with distribution.

In supervising Fred and Veronica, Alex has always worked to establish a partnership. He attempts to build a common vision with them, and to share any burdens involved in making that vision become a reality. He works with them to establish goals pertaining to their own performance, and he meets with each of them individually once a month, in order to evaluate their progress toward the accomplishment of these goals.

In supervising Dorothy and Troy, Fred shares responsibility with them, but he is concerned primarily with ensuring that neither of them will make any mistakes that would reflect badly on him. Although Fred establishes clearly defined goals for Dorothy and Troy, and watches their performance closely, he does not evaluate their work, and provides them with no feedback.

1. _____ has ultimate responsibility for the work of the group.

2. _____ demonstrates positive shared responsibility in supervising his immediate subordinates.

3. _____ demonstrates negative shared responsibility in supervising his immediate subordinates.

4. Does Alex hold Veronica and Fred accountable for the activities that he delegates to them? If not, how might he work with them to establish accountability?

5. Does Fred hold Dorothy and Troy accountable for the activities that he delegates to them? If not, how might he work with them to establish accountability?

Place a check mark next to each of the following items that was cited in this chapter as a reason for delegating.

_____ The inability of one person to remain directly involved in the full range of activities carried out by a complex organization.

_____ The organizational need for specialized knowledge in a variety of areas.

_____ The leader's desire to "unload" unpleasant tasks.

_____ The need for developing skills in workers at all levels of an organization.

Place a check mark next to each of the following items that describes a type of activity that should typically be delegated, according to the recommendations presented in this chapter.

_____ Executive functions

_____ Disciplinary activities

_____ Activities from which the delegate will learn new skills

_____ Policy making

_____ Duties that relate to the morale of the overall organization

_____ Activities in which the delegate has an inherent interest

_____ Activities that require expertise which the leader does not possess

_____ Resolution of conflicts between organizational units

_____ Activities that require unique skills which the delegate possesses

_____ Activities that require access to highly confidential information

_____ Activities that have been delegated specifically to the leader by his or her supervisor

_____ Whole projects (rather than parts of projects)

_____ "Pet projects."

Place a check mark next to each of the following statements that is consistent with the guidelines presented in this chapter.

_____ One should generally choose a delegate from among her or his own followers.

_____ One should never "go through" levels of an organization in choosing a delegate.

_____ When choosing a delegate, matters of equity between group members should be considered.

_____ One should only delegate a task to a subordinate who has successfully completed the task previously.

_____ Delegation can sometimes be used to help group members overcome deficiencies in their interpersonal skills.

_____ Once a task has been delegated, the leader should cease all involvement in overseeing its execution.

_____ Once a project has been completed, it is important that the outcome be evaluated.

_____ It is important to provide a delegate with feedback on his or her performance.

Arrange the following steps in the delegation process sequentially, with 1 representing the first step and 8 representing the last.

_____ "The delegate . . . achieves, fails to achieve, or partially achieves the objective."

_____ "The superior selects a delegate who will do what the superior cannot or should not do."

_____ "The superior evaluates the results. He [sic] may or may not withdraw his [sic] loaned authority from the delegate and terminate obligation."

_____ "The superior explains to the delegate the scope of the objective and the nature of the delegate's obligation. Time constraints, if any, are clarified."

_____ "The superior determines the need to shift to another person the obligation for an objective's accomplishment."

_____ "The superior shifts or loans enough of his [sic] authority to the delegate to achieve the objective. The obligation is accepted by the delegate."

_____ "The superior determines that some objective he [sic] seeks may not be accomplished, or is better accomplished by another."

_____ "The scope of the objective may be narrowed or broadened, with the delegate given wide latitude. Levels of support are understood."

List the seven types of meetings identified in this chapter.
1.
2.
3.
4.
5.
6.
7.

List the five components of the meeting agenda format presented in this chapter.
1.
2.
3.
4.
5.

Indicate whether the following statements are true (T) or false (F.), based on the information and recommendations presented in this chapter.

_____ The seven types of meetings presented in this chapter are mutually exclusive categories.

_____ Meetings should be held only when equivalent practical outcomes cannot be accomplished through delegation.

_____ Meetings should be scheduled for times that are convenient for members of the group.

_____ Group members' homes usually make the best meeting places.

_____ It is not generally recommended that business meetings be held at restaurants or bars.

_____ All members of an organization should be invited to any meetings that are held within that organization.

_____ The individual conducting a meeting is generally responsible for initiating the discussion.

_____ The individual conducting a meeting should help ensure that all participants have an opportunity to contribute to the discussion.

_____ A group should never shift its attention to a new topic of discussion until the issue previously under consideration has been completely resolved.

_____ The individual conducting a meeting should encourage group members to think both critically and creatively.

_____ The leader of a discussion should always respond verbally to any comments that are made by group members.

_____ The leader of a discussion should actively promote understanding between group members.

_____ It is never appropriate for a group leader to discuss the group process itself with members of the group.

_____ The minutes of a meeting should not be distributed to participants until the group's next meeting.

_____ After a meeting, the discussion leader should evaluate his or her performance.

Using the planning and evaluation model presented in this chapter, indicate the phases during which the following activities occur.

_____ The action plan is implemented. The leader monitors the activities of the organization.

_____ The group establishes or reviews its mission, goals, and objectives.

_____ The action plan is developed. Organizational resources are allocated for selected activities. Additional resources are acquired if necessary.

_____ Organizational programs and activities are evaluated. The needs of various constituencies are reassessed.

Identify each of the following as a mission (M), goal (G.), objective (O), or action plan (A).

_____ The organization will obtain an electric typewriter with interchangeable fonts and a correction key, prior to the close of fall term.

_____ The organization exists to provide entertainment to the students, faculty, staff, and local community, and to provide aspiring comedians with an opportunity to perform before live audiences.

_____ To upgrade the organization's office equipment, in order to more efficiently perform routine tasks.

Task	Responsible Party	Completion Date	Resources
1. Obtain product specifications and price quotes from at least 3 vendors	Laurie	10/15	
2. Review information and select typewriter.	Laurie, Jeff, Dave	10/31	
3. Purchase typewriter	Laurie	11/30	$500

Identify the following as societal (So), output (O), system (Sy), product (P), or derived (D) goals. For each item, use all descriptions that apply.

_____ The written goal, "to present live comedy programs on campus on a regular basis."

_____ The written goal, "to present comedy from a variety of genres (e.g., stand-up, improv., etc.)."

_____ The written goal, "to promote interest in comedy among the general public through public access television programming and other outreach activities."

_____ The unwritten goal of opposing censorship as it occurs on campus and in the community.

_____ The written goal, "to maintain up-to-date records on all members of the organization."

In the space provided, indicate whether accomplishment of each of the following objectives is to be determined according to a measure of activity (A) or a measure of impact (I).

_____ "The organization will present at least one comedy program per month, for the duration of fall term."

_____ "Average attendance at organizationally sponsored programs will increase from 35 to 50 by the end of fall term."

In the space provided, identify each of the following as a regular objective (R), a problem-solving objective (P), or an innovative objective (I).

_____ "The organization will initiate a humorous publication, which will be distributed monthly on campus for the duration of fall term."

_____ The organization will continue to present at least one program per month, for the duration of fall term."

_____ "Average attendance at organizationally sponsored programs will increase from 35 to 50 by the end of fall term."

List the four basic categories of resources identified in this chapter.
1.
2.
3.
4.

Read the following scenario and respond to the questions presented.

A student organization is attempting to maximize the number of students on campus who are aware of its organizationally sponsored events. A mass mailing would reach 500 students, at a cost of $150, and would require the work of one group member for a period of six hours. Fliers posted on campus would reach 250 students, at a cost of $10, and would require the work of one group member for a period of three hours.

1. Which form of publicity would be more effective?
2. Which form of publicity would be more efficient?

Both Sides of the Story

Prepare a defense for both the affirmative and negative positions on the following statements.

1. The most important resource in any organization is its people.
2. Most work groups spend too much time in meetings.
3. Most people are incapable of placing the welfare of their groups ahead of their own personal interests.

Sorting It Out

Respond to the following questions by taking a position and defending it.

1. In attempting to maximize satisfaction and motivation in their groups, is it generally more important for organizational leaders to attend to factors classified as satisfiers or to those classified as dissatisfiers?
2. Is it generally more important that leaders of work groups possess sufficient organizational authority or that they possess sufficient individual authority?
3. If given the option, which of the six forms of individual authority would you choose to possess?

It's Your Call

Read each of the following scenarios and prepare an essay in response to the questions provided.

1. You are the president of a student organization on your campus, and have been approached by several other student organization presidents who would like for your group to co-sponsor a full-page advertisement in the student newspaper. The advertisement will feature a statement on a controversial political issue. Although the position taken in the advertisement is not contrary to the mission of your organization, it is not directly related to your group's purpose either. You are personally in agreement with the position taken by the other groups, as are most members of your group. However, a small segment of your membership stands in strong opposition to the position taken in the advertisement. As the official spokesperson for the group, you are responsible for making the final decision on the matter.
    a. What do you see as your alternative courses of action?
    b. What are the advantages and disadvantages of each course of action?
    c. Which course of action will you follow?
    d. Why have you chosen this course of action?

2. You are the president of a student organization on your campus. The group meets only once a month, but you have individual contact with most of the active members of the organization at least once a week. Lately, some of the less active members of the group have expressed a desire to meet more frequently. You have mentioned this idea to some of the members of the group with whom you have more frequent contact, and they have expressed resistance. Some of them have even questioned the necessity of holding monthly meetings. They have argued that individual contact is an efficient way of communicating information to those who have a need for it. They have expressed resentment toward those members who attend the monthly meetings, but do not actively contribute to the work of the group. They have argued that members of the organization have no right to insist on timely information about the activities of the group unless they plan to participate in those activities. As president of the organization, you are free to hold meetings as often as you wish.

   a. What do you see as your alternative courses of action?

   b. What are the advantages and disadvantages of each course of action?

   c. Which course of action will you follow?

   d. Why have you chosen this course of action?

3. You are the manager of the computer lab in one of the residence halls on your campus. Currently, you employ nine students, four of whom have worked in the lab for more than one year. Three weeks from now, you will be leaving town for five days, in order to attend a conference.

   Your supervisor, the Director of Computer Services, has asked that you choose one of the four most experienced members of the computer lab staff to serve as the acting manager in your absence. The four students are Steve, Monique, Carla, and Vincent.

   The most experienced of the four is Steve. He has been working in the lab almost as long as you have. He has previously served as acting manager for as long as two weeks at a time. Monique has also served as acting manager, though never for longer than a week. Both of them have performed satisfactorily in the role, and would be willing to do it again, but they would prefer that you choose someone else. Monique is more open to filling in for you than Steve is, but she has done it the last three times that you were away.

   Neither Carla nor Vincent has ever served as acting manager, even for a few days. Both of them would like to do so, and would probably perform satisfactorily. However, it would be necessary for you to spend some time with them during the next three weeks in order to explain the responsibilities involved. Carla has been working for you slightly longer than Vincent has, and is probably more familiar with the policies and procedures of the computer lab. However, Vincent is probably a bit more enthusiastic about the position of acting manager, since he hopes to open a small software business after graduation, whereas Carla's long-term career goals are not related to the duties of the acting manager in any way.

Your supervisor has not expressed any preference among the four students described here. She has indicated that she will respect your wishes.

a. What do you see as your alternative courses of action?

b. What are the advantages and disadvantages of each course of action?

c. Which course of action will you follow?

d Why have you chosen this course of action?

Chapter 8

Ethics

What You Will Learn in This Chapter

This chapter will include an examination of the need for student leaders to study ethics. The following topics will be discussed:

- Group evil
- Compliance with authority
- Conformity to peer pressure
- Groupthink

The moral influence of the group leader will be examined, with attention to the role of the organization as both a moral agent and a moral environment.

The role of the follower in promoting ethical behavior within a group setting will also be examined. The concept of whistle blowing will be introduced, and the following issues will be discussed:

- Motivation for whistle blowing
- Social pressures against whistle blowing
- Psychological reactions to the whistle blowing experience
- Criteria for determining whether or not whistle blowing is justified

The chapter will include an overview of six traditional ethical orientations:

- Utilitarianism
  - Meaning of consequentialist or teleological ethics
  - Act utilitarianism
  - Rule utilitarianism
  - "Greatest-happiness Principle"
- Kantian ethics
  - Meaning of nonconsequentialist or deontological ethics
  - Good will
  - Sources of motivation
    - Self-interest
    - Direct inclination

- Duty
  - Perfect duty
  - Imperfect duty
  - Duty to self
  - Duty to others
  - Necessary duty
  - Contingent duty
  - ➤ Imperatives
    - Hypothetical imperative
    - Assertorial imperative
    - Categorical imperative

- Natural law
  - ➤ Thomism
    - Theoretical reason
    - Practical reason

- Social contract theory
  - ➤ Commonwealth
  - ➤ Sovereign

- Confucianism
  - ➤ *Tao*
  - ➤ *tê*
  - ➤ *li*
  - ➤ *ren*
  - ➤ *yi*
  - ➤ *xin*
  - ➤ *cheng*
  - ➤ *chün-tzu*

- African traditional ethics
  - ➤ Etiquette
  - ➤ Taboo
  - ➤ Communalism

The chapter will include a discussion of three contemporary theories of moral development:

- Perry's developmental positions
  - ➤ Dualism
  - ➤ Multiplicity
  - ➤ Relativism

- ➤ Commitment in relativism
- ■ Kohlberg's stages of moral development
  - ➤ Preconventional level
  - ➤ Conventional level
  - ➤ Post-conventional, autonomous, or principled level
- ■ Gilligan's female and male voices
  - ➤ Ethic of care
  - ➤ Ethic of justice

This chapter will feature a system for ethical decision-making in groups, which incorporates ten "core values":

- ■ Caring

- ■ Honesty

- ■ Accountability

- ■ Promise keeping

- ■ Pursuit of excellence

- ■ Loyalty

- ■ Fairness

- ■ Respect for others

- ■ Responsible citizenship

- ■ Integrity
  - ➤ Self-integration or centeredness
  - ➤ Principled consistency
  - ➤ Self-candor

Five rules of ethical decision-making, which are based on the ten core values, will be presented.

Four psychological processes involved in ethical decision-making will be presented, along with a ten-step model that incorporates these processes.

Twelve questions will be presented, for purposes of conducting a final check on the morality of organizational decisions.

Codes of ethics will be introduced and the following issues will be discussed:

- Benefits of ethical codes
- Characteristics of effective codes of ethics
- Procedures for establishing ethical codes
  - ➤ Developing codes for large organizations
  - ➤ Developing codes for organizational units

Chapter 8

═══Ethics═══════════════════════════════════

Moral, like physical, cleanliness is not acquired once and for all: it can only be kept and renewed by a habit of constant watchfulness and discipline.

Victoria Ocampo

Why Should Leaders Study Ethics?

As I have mentioned throughout this book, student leaders have the power to act as a force for either positive or negative change on their campuses. Their decisions can affect the lives of many people, often for years to come. If members of your campus community have selected you to serve as a leader, they have placed a great deal of trust in you. They have assumed that you will act in the best interests of all who might be affected by the decisions that you will be making.

Anytime that a leader makes a decision that causes harm to his or her followers, or to external constituencies, a sense of betrayal can develop within the organization. Whether the leader's action was triggered by genuine malice or mere negligence, the demoralizing effect on the organization is a matter of real concern.

It is not enough for you to simply refrain from deliberately engaging in unethical conduct. Unless you make a careful effort to avoid such conduct, there is a good chance that some of your decisions will fall short of your ideals. It is particularly important that you attend to ethical considerations when making decisions within a group context, because of certain unique characteristics of groups, which can sometimes undermine individual efforts to adhere to personal ethical standards. M. Scott Peck (1983) in his best seller, *People of the Lie*, used the term "**group evil**" in reference to the unique propensity toward immoral conduct that can emerge within organizations. Peck attributed this tendency, in part, to the specialization of functions within organizations. By dividing tasks up among individuals, it is possible for a group to increase efficiency in its operations. However, according to Peck, this type of specialization can simultaneously lead to a "fragmentation of conscience" (p. 217), which allows individual members of a group to disclaim moral responsibility for the group's actions or even for their own actions within the group. At some time in your life, you have probably heard comments such as "I just work here," "I'm just following orders," or "I don't make the rules; I just carry them out." This type of comment is often reflective of the phenomenon described by Peck.

Another threat to the moral conduct of groups is the presence of a strong leader whose authority is not questioned by her or his followers. One of the most famous studies dealing with the issue of obedience to authority was one conducted during the early 1960's by Stanley Milgram (1963). Interestingly, this study is remembered today primarily because of the ethically questionable nature of Milgram's experiment, in which subjects were led to believe that they were administering electrical shocks to another participant, under orders from the researcher. Many of the subjects appeared to experience severe emotional distress while administering the simulated shocks; an outcome that, many ethicists would argue, could not be justified even by the advancement of knowledge that would result from it. Nevertheless, Milgram's work did contribute to our knowledge of common responses to authority figures. Despite their apparent discomfort with the process, a majority of the subjects continued to obey orders for the entire duration of the experiment, seemingly administering shocks of increasing voltage, until the maximum level was reached.

The results of further work by Milgram suggest that the influence of authority figures is perhaps matched only by the persuasive power of one's peers. In subsequent experimentation, with actors posing as disobedient subjects, the real subjects were much less inclined to continue administering the shocks than when no peer group influence was present (Milgram, 1965). However, when actors posing as subjects called for increases in voltage, even in the absence of pressure from the experimenter, the actual subjects seemingly administered more powerful shocks than they would have had they relied on their own independent judgment (Milgram, 1964). The experiments revealed that peer pressure can substantially influence ethical decision-making within groups, either positively or negatively.

Irving Janis (1982) explained how certain conditions in the group process can sometimes yield decisions that are ill-advised, in either practical or moral terms. He used the term, "**groupthink**" in reference to "a deterioration of mental efficiency, reality testing, and moral judgment" (p. 9), which occurs in highly cohesive groups, when "members' strivings for unanimity override their motivation to realistically appraise alternative courses of action" (p. 9). Janis (1982) identified the following organizational characteristics which can give rise to patterns of groupthink:

1. An illusion of invulnerability, shared by most or all the members, which creates excessive optimism and encourages taking extreme risks.
2. An unquestioned belief in the group's inherent morality, inclining the members to ignore the ethical or moral consequences of their decisions.

3. Collective efforts to rationalize in order to discount warnings or other information that might lead the members to reconsider their assumptions before they recommit themselves to their past policy decisions.

4. Stereotyped views of enemy leaders as too evil to warrant genuine attempts to negotiate, or as too weak and stupid to counter whatever risky attempts are made to defeat their purposes.

5. Self-censorship of deviations from the apparent group consensus, reflecting each member's inclination to minimize to himself [sic] the importance of his [sic] doubts and counter arguments.

6. A shared illusion of unanimity concerning judgments conforming to the majority view (partly resulting from self-censorship of deviations, augmented by the false assumption that silence means consent).

7. Direct pressure on any member who expresses strong arguments against any of the group's stereotypes, illusions, or commitments, making clear that this type of dissent is contrary to what is expected of all loyal members.

8. The emergence of self-appointed mind-guards — members who protect the group from adverse information that might shatter their shared complacency about the effectiveness and morality of their decisions (pp. 174-175).

According to Janis (1982), groupthink manifests itself in the decision-making process, in several distinct ways. The following are seven specific consequences of groupthink which he identified.

1. Incomplete survey of alternatives
2. Incomplete survey of objectives
3. Failure to examine risks of preferred choice
4. Failure to reappraise initially rejected alternatives
5. Poor information search
6. Selective bias in processing information at hand
7. Failure to work out contingency plans (p. 175).

In examining the moral conduct of group members, acting both individually and collectively, it becomes quite apparent that groups can have a profound influence on an individual's behavior. However, it is important to bear in mind that an individual can also have a powerful impact on the behavior of an entire group, particularly if the individual occupies a position of leadership. By studying ethical issues in leadership, you can protect yourself against the potentially corrupting influence that a group can exert over your own behavior. You can also learn how to encourage other members of your group to adhere to higher ethical standards.

The Role of the Moral Leader

It has been noted that organizational leaders have a unique role to play in overcoming any barriers to ethical decision-making that might exist within their groups. According to a model of moral leadership presented by Hitt (1990), the leader must use his or her influence to establish an organizational climate that promotes ethical conduct, which in turn leads to trust, and ultimately to long-term success. This model implies that honesty is indeed the best policy.

Inherent in this model is a recognition that neither individuals nor their behaviors can be easily classified in two discrete categories, labeled "ethical" and "unethical." It has been argued that a more realistic approach is to conceptualize the moral acceptability of behavior as falling along a continuum, represented numerically as a scale from one to ten (Hitt, 1990). This conceptualization of ethical conduct is illustrated in the figure below.

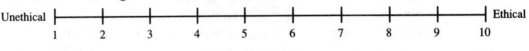

Ethical Conduct Continuum

Within this framework, even the behavior of an individual can vary, depending upon the surrounding circumstances (Hitt, 1990). For example, a student who ordinarily would not plagiarize another student's work might do so, if it were common knowledge that a particular instructor did not read students' papers anyway, and that grades were assigned arbitrarily. In attempting to promote an ethical climate, the leader must work to establish conditions that are conducive to higher levels of ethical conduct among followers (Hitt, 1990).

According to another model of ethical leadership, which was put forth by Goodpaster (1982), the leader of an organization plays a dual role, attempting to promote ethical conduct within two separate categories of transactions. You will recall from our discussion in Chapter 2 that a transaction is the basic unit of social interaction. According to Goodpaster's model, the transactions in which an organization is involved can be classified as either "A-transactions" or "B-transactions." A-transactions are those in which the organization interacts with external entities, whereas B-transactions involve interaction between members of the organization itself. Nearly any organization to which you might belong will invariably become involved in both types of transactions. For example, when a student newspaper sells advertising space to a local business, it engages in an A-transaction. When work assignments are negotiated among the members of the newspaper staff, a B-transaction occurs within the organization.

Both types of transactions have moral implications. However, in A-transactions the organization functions as a "moral agent" (Goodpaster, 1982, p. 5), whereas in B-transactions it functions as a "moral environment" (Goodpaster, 1982, p. 5). It has been noted that "both types of transactions involve issues of policy formulation as well as policy implementation" (Goodpaster, 1982, p. 5).

Because organizational leaders are generally concerned with both the formulation and implementation of policies, they must assume responsibility for promoting ethical behavior on the part of the organization as an entity, while building an organizational environment that encourages individual acts of conscience. It should be noted that a single policy decision can bear upon the organization as both moral agent and moral environment. Again using the example of a student newspaper, if an editor were to regularly censor reporters' contributions in order to advance his own political agenda, both the reporters and the publication's readership would be affected.

In reality, there are very few decisions that are made by group leaders which do not carry some moral implications. It is a leader's duty, both to his or her followers and to those with whom the followers interact collectively, to attend to ethical considerations in all organizational decision-making.

Not for Managers Only

Thus far, our discussion has centered on the ethical responsibilities of those holding official positions of authority within their organizations. It should be noted, however, that in order for a group to overcome common barriers to ethical conduct, each and every member must contribute to the group's collective conscience.

In discussing ways of overcoming the problem of group evil, Peck (1983) observed that "it is in the solitary mind and soul of the individual that the battle between good and evil is waged and ultimately won or lost" (p. 252). He envisioned a world in which young people would learn "that the natural tendency of the individual in a group is to forfeit his or her ethical judgment to the leader, and that this tendency should be resisted" (Peck, 1983, p. 253).

Individual group members must work to maintain their personal integrity, even in the face of pressure to abandon their principles. Additionally, they must share with one another the duty to monitor the behavior of the group as a whole.

There are a number of ways in which conscientious group members can promote ethical conduct within their organizations. Sometimes, a group member's own ethical behavior is sufficient to inspire her or his peers to set high moral standards for themselves. In other instances, it becomes necessary to confront group members who have committed ethical violations or to report violations to the official leaders of the organization. However, occasionally, the concerned group member finds that these leaders are themselves engaged in dubious practices, or are simply indifferent toward the ethical violations that are occurring within the organization. Under such circumstances, a group member may feel compelled to resort to more drastic measures.

One of the most severe actions that a group member can take, in dealing with organizational misconduct, is a practice known as **"whistle blowing."** A whistle blower has been defined in the business literature as "an employee or officer of any institution, profit or nonprofit, private or public, who believes either that he/she has been ordered to perform some act or he/she has obtained knowledge that the institution is engaged in activities which a) are believed to cause unnecessary harm to third parties, b) are in violation of human rights or c) run counter to the defined purpose of the institution and who inform the public of this fact" (Bowie, 1982, p. 142). For our purposes, we will use the term in reference to both paid and unpaid associates within an organization.

It should be noted that whistle blowing is distinct from gossip or tattling, in that the whistle blower is concerned with serious ethical violations, as opposed to minor indiscretions. The whistle blower also differs from the saboteur, since he or she does not engage in any retaliatory activity, but simply exposes corruption within the organization (Bowie, 1982).

The decision to go public with information of wrong-doing within an organization is not to be taken lightly. Loyalty to one's organization is a value that is almost universally acknowledged. Any breach of this loyalty can have a divisive effect on the organization, often with far-reaching negative consequences.

However, it has also been convincingly argued that "one has a duty to be loyal only if the object of loyalty is one that is morally appropriate" (Bowie, 1982, p. 141). Indeed, the expectation that you act in violation of your own moral standards could reasonably be viewed as a betrayal of the trust that you have placed in your leader or in the other members of your group.

There are a number of factors which must be considered in determining whether or not whistle blowing is justified in a particular instance. According to one business ethicist, satisfaction of the following criteria constitutes evidence that whistle blowing is justified.

1. It is done for the appropriate moral motive, namely, as provided in the definition of whistle blowing.

2. The whistle blower, except in special circumstances, has exhausted all internal channels for dissent before informing the public.

3. The whistle blower has made certain that his or her belief that inappropriate actions are ordered or have occurred is based on evidence that would persuade a reasonable person.

4. The whistle blower has acted after a careful analysis of the danger: (a) how serious is the moral violation, (b) how immediate is the moral violation, (c) is the moral violation one that can be specified?

5. The whistle blower's action is commensurate with one's responsibility for avoiding and/or exposing moral violations.
6. It has some chance of success (Bowie, 1982, p. 143).

In addition to the philosophical dilemmas posed in relation to the practice of whistle blowing, members of organizations must concern themselves with a number of practical considerations before actually following through with a public disclosure of wrong-doing. Whistle blowers are often unprepared for the hardship that befalls them and their loved ones, as a result of their decisions. Whistle blowers sometimes lose their jobs, or are harassed in the workplace. Additionally, the dilemmas with which they are faced during the process of exposing corruption can create a great deal of psychological tension (Soeken, 1986).

According to one psychiatric social worker who has worked with a number of whistle blowers, psychological reactions to the process generally follow a pattern consisting of seven stages. These stages have been described as follows.

1. *Discovery.* Anger, shock and a sense of betrayal are common, particularly if the employee has unwittingly assisted the fraud, waste or other corruption. Many prolong the discovery stage by denying it.
2. *Reflection.* During this period, individuals weigh the consequences of silence versus speaking out. For some, the prospect of confronting another, even anonymously, is so threatening that they cannot sleep. Fear is heightened for those who anticipate trouble or for those who lack a sense of direction. Many suffer alone and become obsessed with the problem. Others try to break the tension by acting too quickly, leading to hasty, ineffective actions that cause problems later.
3. *Confrontation.* Once a decision is made, the stress of anticipation is over. Now whistle blowers experience the strain of revealing their charges. If they have acted openly, they may fear retaliation. If they have done it covertly, they worry about being found out.
4. *Retaliation.* This can take many forms, ranging from threats to slander and economic reprisals. Most retaliation is designed to threaten whistle blowers into backing off or to discredit their testimony. Few people are prepared to handle retaliation, particularly if friends and colleagues abandon them when the going gets tough. Many feel like outcasts.
5. *The long haul.* In the months and years between confrontation and resolution, stresses may intensify. . . . Righteous fury can easily tip into obsession, costing whistle blowers whatever friends and supporters they have left. Without professional assistance, and a lot of luck, many whistle blowers never move beyond this stage.

6. *Closure.* Eventually the case is won or lost or the whistle blower stops pursuing it. There is a feeling of relief combined with pain if the outcome is unsatisfactory. For most whistle blowers, a period of mourning is necessary.

7. *Resolution.* Final acceptance may come with closure. Or it may take many years to fully appreciate what has happened, to understand it and to feel healed. Some whistle blowers never reach this stage (Soeken, 1986, p, 46).

Given the suffering that is often endured by whistle blowers and those who are closest to them, you may be wondering why anyone would consider following this course of action. The results of a study involving 21 respondents, all of whom were affected either by their own whistle blowing or by that of their spouses, suggest that individuals who engage in the practice are characterized by a very strong sense of individual responsibility. According to one whistle blower, "the only thing necessary for evil to prevail is for good men [sic] to do nothing" (Glazer and Glazer, 1986, p. 38). The spouse of another whistle blower made a similar observation:

> A corrupt system can happen only if the individuals who make up that system are corrupt. You are either going to be part of the corruption or part of the forces working against it. There isn't a third choice. Someone, someday, has to take a stand; if you don't, maybe no one will. And that is wrong (Glazer and Glazer, 1986, p. 38).

Few of the participants in the study advised against whistle blowing, as a result of their experiences. However, many of them did offer recommendations for minimizing the painful consequences of the decision to expose organizational corruption. Their recommendations included the following:

1. Have the facts and be able to prove them.

2. Act with deliberate thought and care — do not act rashly or in haste.

3. Go through channels unless you are reporting on a supervisor. Then report to his or her boss.

   Don't make the mistake of thinking that someone in authority, if only he or she knew what was going on, would straighten the whole thing out. That can be fatal.

4. Expect the worst: the loss of your job at least.

5. Be prepared to go all the way no matter how far you have to push it.

   Don't tilt at windmills; don't waste your strength and courage fighting a battle you know you will lose. There are more than enough fights around that offer a chance of winning.

6. Know that you will be criticized and humiliated.

7. Do not threaten action unless you mean to follow through. Promise your antagonists action and give it to them, such as by going to the media. They will

only act to remedy the problem when they know you will follow through on your promise.

8. Consult your loved ones — try to get their concurrence and agreement about what you are doing. You will need their support.

   The trials you undergo will either cement together or tear apart your marriage.

9. Do not expect that your life will ever be the same. It will not. You will maintain your self-respect by doing the right thing. You will also suffer losses such as income and possibly health or relationships.

10. Finally, remember that there is nothing on Earth as strong as belief in yourself and your God (Glazer and Glazer, 1986, p. 42).

Defining Ethics

Before pursuing our discussion much further, it is important that we arrive at a common understanding of what is meant by the term, **ethics**. The definition that we will use is drawn from the philosophical literature. According to this definition, the term refers to "a systematic inquiry into the beliefs we have and the judgments we make about what is morally right and wrong and morally good and evil" (Velasquez and Rostankowski, 1985, p. 3). Our decisions concerning specific courses of action — even those with potentially tragic consequences — can be based on a variety of factors, some of which we ourselves may not even be able to explain. However, actions that are driven by emotion, or taken "just for the heck of it," are not reflective of a systematic approach to dealing with questions of good and evil, and therefore, do not signify ethical decision-making. In studying ethics, we concern ourselves with "the rational and critical examination of the reasons, arguments, and theories that can be given to show that one type of behavior is morally right or that another is morally wrong" (Velasquez and Rostankowski, 1985, p. 3).

Traditional Ethical Orientations

Over the ages, philosophers have continuously pondered the nature of goodness, often in hopes of identifying a single pathway to moral purity. Instead, their efforts have resulted in a variety of moral philosophies which are, in many respects, incompatible with one another. There is perhaps no better way for you to begin to appreciate the complexity of ethics than to survey the principal ethical traditions which have emerged over the course of history. With this point in mind, we shall now direct our attention toward six traditional ethical orientations: (1) utilitarianism, (2) Kantian ethics, (3) natural law, (4) social contract theory, (5) Confucianism, and (6) African traditional ethics.

Utilitarianism

As I mentioned in chapter 3 of this book, management decision-making in Western cultures is often characterized by a utilitarian approach, whereby a cost-benefit analysis serves as the basis for subsequent action. In our previous discussion, we dealt with the cost-benefit analysis on a concrete level, focusing only on material goods, without consideration of moral values. On a more abstract level, utilitarianism can itself be used as a basis for ethical decision-making, with moral values being the object of the cost-benefit analysis. When used as a moral philosophy, "**utilitarianism** is the consequential doctrine that asserts we should always act so as to produce the greatest possible ratio of good to evil for everyone concerned" (Barry, 1983, p. 45).

Consider, for example, the role of collegiate administrators in decisions concerning the use of institutional resources. Students, alumni, and other benefactors of a college or university entrust to certain individuals control of various resources, with the understanding that allocations will reflect a concern for the overall mission of the institution. Administrators have an ethical obligation not to betray this trust.

In responding to this duty, however, it is often necessary to make difficult decisions. While there is perhaps no limit to the number of activities that may be undertaken in accordance with the mission of a college or university, the resources needed to support these activities are clearly finite. In determining how best to use the resources that are available, administrators frequently rely on the basic principles of utilitarianism.

Suppose, for instance, that a student union manager must choose between having the piano in the solarium tuned and making MTV available in the television lounge. If the manager is a utilitarian, she will approach her decision by first considering both the positive and negative consequences of each course of action. She will then choose the course of action that is likely to produce as much good and as little harm as possible.

If the manager defines the overall good in purely quantitative terms, her decision will probably hinge on the number of students who would either play the piano or watch music videos. In this case, the whole decision-making process becomes mathematical, with the purpose being to maximize the number of students using the union facilities.

Now suppose the manager also defines the overall good in qualitative terms. In other words, suppose she does not view all student pastimes as being of equal value. Since colleges and universities exist largely for the purpose of cultivating individual talent, the union manager might conclude that it is more central to the institutional mission for a single student to play the piano than for any number of students to watch MTV.

By now, it should be apparent to you that even among utilitarians, individual differences exist. One of the sharpest distinctions that may be drawn between utilitarian ethicists is the contrast between those who subscribe to **act utilitarianism** and those who embrace **rule utilitarianism**. According to act utilitarianism, "the right act is the one that produces the greatest ratio of good to evil for all concerned" (Barry, 1983, p. 46). The union manager in our example could be described as an act utilitarian, because the focus of her attention was on the anticipated consequences of two possible courses of action in a specific situation. Unlike act utilitarians, rule utilitarians favor the adoption of those *rules* which will promote the greatest ratio of good to evil. Among rule utilitarians, "the principle of utility is seen as a guide for deciding what rules we should follow, rather than for deciding what particular actions we should perform" (Velasquez and Rostankowski, 1985, p. 109).

If the union manager in our example were a rule utilitarian, she would approach her dilemma by deciding beforehand upon certain rules which would then dictate her course of action. It is in choosing these rules, rather than in evaluating specific instances of behaviors, that she would be guided by efforts to achieve the greatest net good.

For example, she might consider adopting a rule stipulating that when choices must be made between different types of facilities and services, priority will always be given to those which are used by the greater number of students. In deciding whether or not to adopt this rule, the union manager would compare the probable consequences of always applying the rule against the probable consequences of never applying it.

As in our previous example, the manager's assessment of net good would depend heavily upon the relative emphasis that she would place on quantitative versus qualitative factors. If she were to focus primarily on quantitative considerations, she would probably adopt the rule, since it would always serve the majority of students well. However, if she were to concentrate mainly on qualitative considerations, there is a good chance that she would reject the rule, rather than allow even a minority of students to be denied access to important facilities and services.

The single most influential proponent of utilitarianism was undoubtedly the nineteenth century English philosopher, John Stuart Mill. It was Mill (1963) who introduced the "**Greatest-happiness Principle**," which "holds that actions are right in proportion as they tend to promote happiness, wrong as they tend to produce the reverse of happiness" (p. 249). Mill (1963) defined happiness as "intended pleasure and the absence of pain" (p. 249), and unhappiness as "pain and the privation of pleasure" (p. 249). Mill (1963) used the happiness of all concerned as his criterion for evaluating moral conduct, based on his observation "that pleasure, and freedom from pain, are the only things desirable as ends" (p. 249).

Although Mill recognized that conscientious people value many things, he maintained that anything other than happiness can be valued only insofar as it is believed to contribute to happiness or to detract from unhappiness. Many people value money, for example, but they value it because of what it can be used to accomplish. Mill would undoubtedly contend that people's actual uses of money could invariably be characterized as attempts to promote happiness or to alleviate unhappiness.

Mill (1963) defined "greatest-happiness" in both quantitative and qualitative terms, recognizing that some pleasures should be valued more highly than others. According to Mill (1963, p. 251)), "of two pleasures, if there be one to which all or almost all who have experience of both give a decided preference, irrespective of any feeling of moral obligation to prefer it, that is the more desirable pleasure." Mill (1963) further noted that "it is an unquestionable fact that those who are equally acquainted with and equally capable of appreciating and enjoying both do give a most marked preference to the manner of existence which employs their higher faculties" (p. 251).

Few adults, for example, having experienced the pleasures of both "true love" and "cheap sex," would opt for the latter if given a choice. In all likelihood, the option of a loving relationship would be overwhelmingly favored even by those whose experiences of mature love were sprinkled with large doses of pain. This pattern would be entirely consistent with Mill's observations, since love is a uniquely human emotion that is not experienced by lower forms of animal life. In comparing casual sexual relationships against those which are characterized by love and commitment, we would expect the latter to be favored under the "Greatest-happiness Principle," because of the qualitative differences in the pleasure derived from the two types of relationship.

It should be emphasized that Mill was but one utilitarian, albeit a highly influential one. Individual utilitarians have often wandered far from the specific principles embraced by Mill. They have also differed substantially from one another in the specific criteria which they have used to determine the desirability of various consequences.

What is common to all utilitarians, however, is their reliance on consequences as the basis for determining the morality of a particular course of action. Because of its emphasis on the results of behavior as a basis for moral decision-making, utilitarianism can be classified as a **consequentialist** or **teleological** moral philosophy (Velasquez and Rostankowski, 1985).

Kantian Ethics

Because utilitarianism, in one form or another, is so common in the United States, many American college students make the assumption that attempting to promote "the greatest good for the greatest number" is the only possible approach to ethical decision-making. If this assumption were correct, then all differences in personal moral beliefs would be attributable to differences in criteria for measuring favorable outcomes. It is no wonder, therefore, that individuals who hold this view are sometimes baffled by other people's decisions to pursue courses of action which, by any standard imaginable, could predictably result in less desirable consequences than would the alternative.

Several years ago, as part of a values clarification exercise, undergraduate students in a leadership training class were asked, "Would you be willing to murder an innocent person if it would end hunger in the world?" (Stock, 1987, p. 31). As students shared their responses, the prevailing bias in favor of *act utilitarianism* manifested itself on several levels. First, this bias was reflected in the fact that an overwhelming majority of the students responded affirmatively. Perhaps equally significant, however, was the majority reaction to those who indicated that they would refuse to kill an innocent person, even in the interest of ending world hunger. Many of those who said they would kill the innocent person were astounded to find that *any* of their peers might have said they would not. They wondered how anyone could possibly value the life of one innocent person over the lives of hundreds of thousands of other innocent people.

Indeed, if the dissenters had approached the question from an act utilitarian perspective, their chosen course of action would seem to defy explanation. However, act utilarianism is only one of many different approaches which have traditionally been followed in dealing with moral dilemmas.

We have already seen how *rule utilitarianism* might lead one to adopt a standard that does not produce favorable consequences in a particular case, even though it would produce a favorable overall outcome when applied consistently. Nearly all of us would agree that, under ordinary circumstances, a rule which states that we should not kill an innocent person would produce favorable consequences. It is possible that those students who indicated that they would refuse to kill an innocent person even as a means of ending world hunger were applying this rule, in the interest of producing an overall good that would not be achieved if they were to allow themselves to disregard the rule at will.

There is yet another possibility, however. Suppose the students who indicated that they would allow world hunger to persist, rather than kill an innocent person, had not focused their attention on the consequences of the act at all, but instead concentrated solely on the nature of the act itself. Suddenly, their chosen course of action would make much more sense, since the killing of an innocent person is an act that is almost universally viewed with revulsion. Indeed, even the killing of a non-innocent person, as in the case of capital punishment, is generally regarded as problematic even by those who would see it as morally justified.

We use the words, "**nonconsequential**" and "**deontological**, to describe moral theories which maintain that the goodness of an act is not determined by its consequences. One author summed up the fundamental difference between utilitarianism and nonconsequentialism, when he noted that "utilitarianism focuses on the ends or goals of acts and the most efficient means to those ends, whereas nonconsequential views focus on the means themselves and base a moral determination on features of the means" (Barry, 1983, p. 51). A nonconsequentialist would maintain that an inherently immoral act cannot be justified by its outcome, regardless of how desirable that outcome may be.

One of the most influential deontological ethicists of all time was the eighteenth century German philosopher, Immanuel Kant. In one of his most famous works, *Foundations of the Metaphysics of Morals*, Kant (1785/1985) set forth the basic tenets of a moral philosophy that has since come to be known, in his honor, as **Kantian ethics**.

Kant (1785/1985) opened his treatise with the observation that there is only one human characteristic that can be good without qualification, and that is a "**good will**." He noted that many other characteristics, such as intelligence and courage, can also be good, but that their goodness is conditional. He maintained that unless the individual who possesses these endowments also possesses a good will, the other characteristics which are potentially good can be turned toward evil. In contrast, Kant observed that a good will remains good even in the absence of the capacity to bring about favorable outcomes.

According to Kant (1785/1985), a good will is one that leads an individual to act from "**duty**," as opposed to "**self-interest**" or "**direct inclination**." There are many reasons why a person might do good things, but not all of these reasons would reflect a sense of duty. For example, if a student were to repair his roommate's car, it might be because his roommate agreed to type his term paper in return for the favor or because of his own fascination with auto mechanics. In either case, we would not say that the student had acted from duty. If he had acted in anticipation of his roommate's returning the favor, we would say that he had acted from self-interest. If he had been motivated by his own enjoyment of the act itself, we would say that he had been driven by direct inclination. If, on the other hand, the student were to repair his roommate's car based solely on the belief that it would be "the only decent thing to do," then we would say that he had acted from duty.

According to Kant (1785/1985, p. 79), "duty is the necessity of acting from respect for the [moral] law." He explained, further, that genuine respect for a principle stems from the belief that it should be followed by everyone, even in the absence of any other motivation for doing so. In fact, if a rule is truly universal, it should be followed even if there are factors motivating a person to do otherwise.

Kant (1785/1985) used the term, "**imperative**," in reference to statements of those principles which are imposed upon the will even in the presence of other influences that discourage compliance with them. He identified two kinds of imperative: (1) hypothetical and (2) categorical.

A **hypothetical imperative** is one that should be followed if an individual hopes to attain a particular outcome. For example, suppose your faculty advisor were to tell you that if you want to get into medical school, you should take lots of courses in the natural sciences. You will notice that in this case we have an imperative (i.e., "you should take lots of courses in the natural sciences"), but it applies to you only if you desire a particular outcome (i.e., "if you want to get into medical school").

Had you expressed a desire to pursue graduate studies in anthropology, your advisor probably would have instead recommended that you take lots of courses in the social sciences. In either case, we would be dealing with a hypothetical imperative, because the specific directive that you would follow would be contingent upon your desiring a particular outcome.

It should be noted that all imperatives that presuppose the desire for a particular outcome must be classified as hypothetical, even if the particular outcome is one that all rational people would desire. Consider, for example, that age-old pearl of parental wisdom, "if you want to grow up to be healthy and strong, you must eat your vegetables." No matter how widely accepted this rule may be, we would still classify it as a hypothetical imperative, because its applicability is contingent upon the child's desire for health and strength in adulthood. It is true that few children would want to be sick and weak when they grow up. Nevertheless, the belief that they should eat their vegetables is founded on the assumption that they do in fact wish to be healthy and strong.

According to Kant, even those imperatives which relate to the natural desire for happiness must be classified as hypothetical, because the motive for the particular act stems from the desired end (i.e., happiness), rather than from the inherent worth of the act itself. Kant (1785/1985) used the term, "**assertorial**," to describe "a hypothetical imperative that indicates that it is necessary to perform a certain action as a means to attaining happiness" (pp. 82-83).

Unlike hypothetical imperatives (including those which are assertorial) a **categorical imperative** "commands certain actions directly and not as a means to some end" (Kant, 1785/1985, p. 83). A categorical imperative demands that we act in a certain way because the particular behavior is good in itself, without consideration of any result that might follow from it. Kant (1785/1985) set forth a categorical imperative which places three basic demands upon the individual.

First, Kant's (1785/1985) categorical imperative states that one should not act upon a principle that he or she would not wish to see adopted as a universal law. In other words, before applying a particular principle, we should ask ourselves, "What if everyone did it?"

As Kant (1785/1985) himself observed, there are some principles that simply cannot be incorporated into a universal mode of conduct. Their adoption as universal laws would, in fact, be logically inconceivable. Kant used the example of false promises to illustrate this point. In his attempts to envision a world in which false promises were commonplace, it became immediately clear that under such circumstances the entire notion of a promise would be rendered meaningless. He concluded, therefore, that making false promises simply could not become a universal practice. According to Kant, we have a "**perfect duty**" to act in a certain way if it is logically inconceivable for the alternative mode of conduct to become universal.

Of course, anyone who has ever read a Stephen King novel knows that one can conceive of a world that would be far worse than anything that he or she might be capable of desiring. According to Kant, even if universal application of a principle is conceivable, the principle should be abandoned if one would not desire for it to become a universal law. Under such circumstances, he would say that an **"imperfect duty"** exists.

According to Kant (1785/1985), duties, whether perfect or imperfect, may apply either to oneself or to others. The duty to care for one's own body would be an example of a duty to oneself, whereas the duty to tell the truth would be considered a duty to others.

A second "version" of Kant's (1785/1985) categorical imperative states that you should "so act as to treat humanity, whether in your own person or in that of any other, always also as an end and never merely as a means" (p. 87). What Kant was telling us, in simple terms, is that we should not "use" people. For example, suppose a group of men were to arrange a game in which each of them would bet that his date for the evening would be judged the least attractive by the other men in the group. According to the categorical imperative, this activity would be wrong because it involves the degradation of another person for purposes of personal gain. The men's dates would not be recognized as rational beings, and would instead be made the victims of deception and abuse.

From this second basic principle, Kant (1785/1985) again enumerated specific types of duty, including both those which relate to oneself and those which guide one's behavior toward others. Kant drew a distinction between those duties which are "necessary" (or "strict") and those which are "contingent" (or "meritorious"). A **necessary** duty is one that relates to the basic respect that is appropriately accorded to a rational being. A **contingent** duty involves going "above and beyond" this minimal level of respect, and actually helping people to develop their talents and to achieve their goals.

The third stipulation of Kant's (1785/1985) categorical imperative is that a principle "must be rejected if it is inconsistent with the idea that the will is itself the maker of the universal laws that it follows" (p. 89). It stands to reason that in order for an individual to act from a particular duty, the principle from which this duty stems must be internally imposed upon the will. The individual who responds to an externally imposed principle, which he or she does not embrace as universal, acts not from duty but from self-interest.

Natural Law

Looking once again at students' responses to the question of whether or not to kill an innocent person in order to end world hunger, one outcome was wholly predictable. Despite differences in their ways of dealing with the dilemma, the students were unanimous in recognizing that a dilemma did exist. Students on both sides of the debate expressed concern for both the victims of starvation and the potential murder victim. Both factions also defended their own chosen courses of action based on a reverence for human life. Throughout the discussion, the students challenged one another's beliefs concerning the most appropriate means by which to support human life. However, at no time did anyone question the assumption that human life is to be valued.

Now let us ask ourselves why this assumption was never challenged. To what exactly do we attribute the students' shared belief that human life is to be respected? One possibility is that our nation has held human life in high regard throughout its history, and the severity of our laws concerning homicide has reflected this value. However, another possibility is that human beings, by their very nature, recognize the inherent dignity of all people, and therefore would know that human life should be treated with respect, even in the absence of any written law that might tell them so.

It is the latter assumption that would be supported by nearly all those who subscribe to the body of ethical theory known as **natural law** ethics. Natural law ethicists may differ from one another in the specific details of their moral belief systems. However, by definition, they share three basic beliefs, which have been summarized as follows.

- First, a natural law view of morality holds that there are certain fundamental principles of right and wrong that bind human beings of every nationality

- Second, a natural law view of morality holds that these fundamental principles are based on our human nature: we human beings are made in such a way that we cannot help but value the good these principles protect.

- Third, a natural law theory of morality holds that all human beings are aware of these fundamental moral principles because all normal adults come to know them through the use of their natural reasoning abilities (Velasquez and Rostankowski, 1985, pp. 33-34).

One of the most famous proponents of the natural law view was the thirteenth century Italian theologian, St. Thomas Aquinas, who formulated a specific theory of natural law which has come to be known as **Thomism**, in honor of its originator (Guralnik, 1982). The theory of natural law put forth by Aquinas (1985) was based on his conception of God's plan for the universe. Despite its theological underpinnings, variations on Aquinas's theory could certainly be embraced by others who might recognize a natural order imposed upon the universe yet attribute this order to forces other than God as such (Velasquez and Rostankowski, 1985).

Aquinas (1985) maintained that human beings have a predetermined role to play within the natural order of the universe, but that our natural role is imposed upon us in a manner different from that by which order is imposed upon the rest of the universe. While our individual actions are not directly driven by the laws of nature,

Aquinas maintained that we are endowed with a capacity to reason, which in turn enables us to act in accordance with our proper role in the natural order.

Aquinas (1985) identified two types of reason: (1) theoretical and (2) practical. While drawing distinctions between the two thought processes, Aquinas also recognized certain parallels between them.

Aquinas (1985) described **theoretical reason** as the process through which we arrive at our understanding of the nature of the universe. This process is governed by the rules of logic, which dictate that our conception of reality will be characterized by consistency and order. From the information that is made available to us, these rules lead us to certain inescapable conclusions. For example, if we know that (1) all deontological ethicists embrace the belief that the goodness of an act is not determined by its consequences and (2) John Stuart Mill believed that the morally correct course of action is that which results in the greatest happiness for all concerned, then we cannot help but conclude that John Stuart Mill was not a deontological ethicist.

Practical reason, according to Aquinas (1985), is the process through which we arrive at conclusions concerning the manner in which we should conduct our lives. He maintained that all such conclusions must follow from the assumption that "what is good ought to be pursued in our actions; what is evil ought to be avoided" (Aquinas, 1985, p. 50). He believed, further, that human beings have a natural inclination to accept certain goods as self-evident. These include: (1) preservation of human life, (2) familial relationships, (3) knowledge, and (4) social order.

Aquinas (1985) noted that theoretical and practical reason are similar insofar as both processes lead us to draw specific conclusions from general assumptions. He recognized, however, that whereas there can be only one accurate perception of reality, there can be many equally effective ways to bring about a desired outcome. Therefore, while theoretical reason can lead to only one correct conclusion, practical reason can lead people to many different conclusions, all of which may be equally valid.

For example, suppose there were two cooperative housing units, both of which were populated by students subscribing to Thomism. We would expect theoretical reason to lead students in both houses to accept the scientifically based conclusion that sleep deprivation tends to impair mental functioning. We would further expect that practical reason would lead students in both houses to the conclusion that efforts should be made to ensure that students would not be deprived of sleep. The latter conclusion would be based on: (1) the knowledge that sleep deprivation impairs mental functioning and (2) the Thomistic proposition that knowledge and social order are good and therefore ought to be pursued in action.

Beyond this point, however, we might expect the two groups to move off in different directions, since there are many different approaches which could lead to the desired outcome. The members of one house might conclude that they should establish a "quiet hours" policy, whereby noise must never exceed a specific level between certain designated hours. In contrast, the members of the other group might favor a rule stipulating that residents need not be concerned about the level of noise in the house, provided that nobody complains, but that the level must be reduced immediately upon the first complaint. Although the two rules are different from each other, they are both based on the same desired end, and would probably be equally effective in bringing about that end.

According to Aquinas (1985, p. 45), "a law is something that meets these four conditions: (1) it is an orderly arrangement determined by reason, (2) that is intended to achieve the good of the whole society, (3) that is enacted by the person who is charged with caring for that whole society, and (4) that is promulgated among that society's members." Adherence to these standards results in rules that have genuine legitimacy under Thomism.

Aquinas (1985) maintained that we are always bound by natural law, but are bound by human ordinances only insofar as they are just (and therefore in accordance with natural law). He insisted that a rule is unjust if (1) it is not intended to promote the common good, (2) it is enacted by somebody who does not possess the legitimate authority to do so, or (3) it distributes burdens unfairly.

In our example, suppose the members of the first house were divided into those enrolled exclusively in morning classes and those taking only afternoon classes. Under the circumstances, we might expect the morning students to favor a quiet hours policy that restricts noise at night, but not in the morning. We might also expect that the afternoon students would favor restrictions on noise in the morning, but not at night. If all of the members of the house were to work together, with their goal being to formulate a policy that serves the needs of all residents, they might conclude that the best solution would be to restrict noise during both morning and night. According to the criteria established by Aquinas, we would say that the students had established a just law.

Now suppose instead that the afternoon students called a secret meeting during the morning students' class time, and decided that restrictions would be placed on noise made during the morning hours only. In this case, the resulting rule would not qualify as a just law, under the principles of Thomism. In fact, it would be considered unjust for all three of the reasons cited by Aquinas: (1) it would not be directed toward achieving the common good, but would instead serve only the interests of a small group; (2) it would not be enacted by those who represent the interests of all concerned; and (3) it would place a burden on some members of the group but not on others.

The belief that we must answer to a law higher than those established by human beings places particularly heavy demands upon those who do not hold formal positions of leadership in their organizations. You will recall from our previous discussion that the practice of whistle blowing, along with all of the grief that it often entails, is generally prompted by a strong belief in the responsibility of the individual. The concept of individual responsibility is central to all theories of natural law, since the rules established by a group cannot justify an individual act that violates natural law.

Social Contract Theory

It is difficult to imagine a more sharp contrast than that which exists between natural law ethics and the moral philosophy known as **social contract theory**. Whereas natural law ethicists believe that legitimate "human laws" follow from moral duties which would exist even in their absence, social contract ethicists believe that agreements between people form the basis for moral obligations. The basic assumptions that serve as the foundation for social contract theory have been summarized as follows.

1. There are several morally significant differences between living in an orderly governed society and living in a state of nature.

2. In an orderly governed society, people have generally agreed to adhere to moral norms in their relationships with each other and these moral norms are enforced by society. Consequently, a person in society knows that others will usually behave morally toward himself [sic] and that it is safe for him [sic] to behave morally toward others. In such a lawfully ordered society, it is legitimate to expect people to live up to their moral obligations.

3. The state of nature is the uncivilized state or wild condition of people who have not yet come together to form an orderly society. Because there is nothing to keep people from harming and killing each other in this lawless state of nature, everyone knows that if a person tries to adhere to moral norms others will probably take advantage of him [sic]. Since it is dangerous to put oneself at a disadvantage by acting morally in the state of nature, no one can be expected to act morally. Thus, there is no morality in the state of nature: everyone legitimately can and will do whatever is necessary to preserve his [sic] own life.

4. People move out of the state of nature and into a social state by agreeing to adhere to certain moral norms and to enforce these norms through appropriate sanctions. This agreement is the social contract that holds society together. If this agreement ever breaks down (during a war or a revolution, for example) and people are once again reduced to fighting for their lives with each other, they have returned to the state of nature and can no longer be expected to act morally. In other words, morality makes sense only so long as there is a social contract that forms a basis for orderly human relationships (Velasquez and Rostankowski, 1985, p. 124).

Social contract theory is perhaps most commonly associated with the seventeenth century English philosopher, Thomas Hobbes. In his most famous work, *Leviathan*, Hobbes (1839) shared his vision of the process through which civilizations emerge. According to Hobbes, human beings are relatively equal in their natural endowments. Consequently, it would be impossible for any one individual to develop a sense of security in the state of nature. Human beings recognize, therefore, that agreements which provide for the just treatment of all individuals would be mutually advantageous. However, until people are able to trust one another, it is not in their interest to leave themselves vulnerable to attack. It is for this reason that they agree to invest their power collectively in one person, who is then charged with enforcing the terms of the agreement. Hobbes referred to the group of individuals united in this type of arrangement as a **commonwealth**, and used the term, **sovereign**, to describe the individual in whom authority is invested.

It should be noted that not all social contract ethicists share Hobbes's view that civilization originally came about through a formal agreement long ago. Many believe instead that people, by virtue of their continued participation in society, enter into an implied social contract on an ongoing basis. Still others maintain that morality is not determined by an existing social contract, but rather by the terms that would be incorporated into a just contract between all people, if such a contract were to exist (Velasquez and Rostankowski, 1985).

Confucianism

Thus far, we have dealt exclusively with the work of European philosophers whose thoughts have understandably held great influence in Western nations. It should be noted, however, that many of the questions addressed by the great thinkers of Europe were previously entertained by others, including a Chinese philosopher named Confucius, who was born around the middle of the sixth century B.C. (Waley, 1989).

The teachings of Confucius formed the basis for a school of thought which is known today as **Confucianism**. Over the course of the past 2,500 years, a number of like minded philosophers, many of whom have been influenced by Buddhism and Taoism, have expanded upon the body of work originally set forth by Confucius. In the process, the influence of Confucianism has expanded throughout Eastern Asia. During the years ahead, we might reasonably expect its influence in the West to grow as well. The author of one contemporary work on Confucianism observed recently that "as we try to answer the call of modern times to break out of our limited parochial views of the human condition, we cannot afford to overlook a tradition that has been alive for so long among such a large part of humankind" (Cleary, 1991, p. ix).

In some respects, the basic principles of Confucianism are similar to those embraced by the natural law ethicists of the West. One of the central elements of

Confucianism is a belief that human affairs should be conducted in a manner consistent with a "cosmic order" known as the "*Tao* of Heaven" (Cleary, 1991, p. xi). From the Confucian perspective, "if human conduct departs from the true pattern mandated by Heaven, this invites disaster" (Cleary, 1991, p. xi).

It should be emphasized that the Confucian concept of Heaven is that of a power greater than humanity. This differs from the Western image of Heaven as a desired state in the afterlife. In fact, one of the areas in which Confucianism distinguishes itself most dramatically from many of the religiously based ethical systems of the West is in its emphasis on the "here and now." According to one author:

> First and foremost, Confucianism is a humanistic teaching. It focuses on human life in this world, not on preparing for a life to come, and emphasizes people's relationships with each other, not their dealings with the supernatural. It is concerned with how people should develop their personalities, how to conduct social relations, and how best to order human society (Cleary, 1991, p. x).

Because of its emphasis on human relations, Confucianism provides a particularly appropriate framework for examining ethical issues in leadership. In fact, there are few schools of moral philosophy which give more thorough and direct attention to the topic of leadership than does Confucianism. True leaders, according to the Confucian ideal, build social solidarity and gain the confidence of their followers by satisfying their followers' need for justice (Cleary, 1991). Confucianists use the term, *tê*, to describe the concept of moral authority or virtue. As a foundation for leadership, this form of authority stands in sharp contrast to the power of physical force, known to Confucianists as *li* (Waley, 1989). In the words of one contemporary author, "the Confucian tradition sharply condemns the politics of tyrants, who rule through coercion and trickery, and reserves political legitimacy for true kings, who rule by moral example and adherence to the Tao" (Cleary, 1991, p. xviii).

The Confucian concept of leadership derived from moral authority invites comparisons to St. Thomas Aquinas's teaching concerning the importance of just laws established by individuals possessing the legitimate authority to enact them. Not surprisingly, the significance attached to the individual conscience in the Thomistic tradition is likewise evident in Confucianism. One author observed that "the Confucian tradition places a major emphasis on the full expression of the individual personality and the maintenance of personal integrity in the face of social pressures" (Cleary, 1991, p. xvii), adding that "throughout history, the most celebrated Confucian heroes were those who had the courage to stand up, often at the risk of their lives, and admonish the men in power for their failure to live up to Confucian moral norms (Cleary, 1991, p. xviii).

In addition to social responsibility, self-improvement is an integral element of the Confucian way of life. There are several specific virtues which Confucianists seek to cultivate in themselves. First among these is a quality known *ren*. Sometimes translated as "true humanity," this term refers to "the basic solidarity that allows people to empathize with each other and gives them the innate impulse to do the decent thing" (Cleary, 1991, p. xii). It has been noted that Confucianists embrace a version of the "Golden Rule" that states "What you do not want done to you, do not do to others" (Cleary, 1991, p. xii). You will notice that this particular aspect of Confucianism closely parallels the teachings of Immanuel Kant.

The concept of duty, which is also central to Kantian ethics, is granted similar significance within Confucianism. The term, *yi*, is used to describe a sense of righteousness that leads the individual to act in accordance with the dictates of his or her conscience. One of the most frequently quoted Confucian proverbs states that "to see what your duty is and not do it is cowardice" (Cleary, 1991, p. xii).

Honesty and trust are held in high esteem within the Confucian tradition. Among the virtues which Confucianists seek to cultivate in themselves is *xin*, which involves trustworthiness, honesty to oneself, and strength in one's convictions. A related virtue, which is also valued highly by adherents to Confucianism, is *cheng*. This quality encompasses integrity and genuineness (Cleary, 1991).

Confucianists have often emulated the *chün-tzu*, persons of refinement whose behavior is characterized by moderation. According to one author, "the success of Confucianism, its triumph over 'all the hundred schools' from the second century B.C. onwards, was due in a large measure to the fact that it contrived to endow compromise with an emotional glamour" (Waley, 1989, p. 37).

African Traditional Ethics

Unlike the ethical systems discussed thus far, all of which have their roots in the teachings of prominent historical figures, the system known as **African traditional ethics** evolved from norms adopted by common people within the various nations of Africa. Authors on the subject have often functioned primarily as observers and interpreters rather than as architects of this particular ethical system.

Many casual observers regard African traditional ethics as a religiously based moral code. This is a misconception attributable largely to confusion over the various types of rules which govern the behavior of the African people. Research on the Akan and Yoruban peoples of Africa has revealed three separate categories of rules which guide their behavior. The first category includes those rules which pertain to customary patterns of behavior. Individuals adhere to these patterns simply out of respect for tradition. We refer to these particular norms as the rules of **etiquette**. A second category of rules includes those which prohibit certain behaviors that are believed to invoke the disfavor of various deities. The term, "**taboo**," is used in reference to this particular category of rules. Although the behaviors prohibited by taboo are often destructive from a purely humanistic standpoint, most people uphold these standards primarily for religious reasons. The third category of norms consists of those which are rationally derived from moral values that exist independently from any fear of divine retribution. It is only this much narrower category of behavioral standards that falls within the realm of African traditional ethics (Omoregbe, 1989).

A common concern shared by adherents to African traditional ethics is "goodness of character" (Omoregbe, 1989, p. 89). In striving to achieve this state of goodness, individuals direct their attention toward both the avoidance of vices and the pursuit of virtues (Omoregbe, 1989).

Among the Yoruba, utilitarian considerations weigh heavily in moral decision-making. A great deal of importance is also attached to the Golden Rule (Omoregbe, 1989). We might conclude, therefore, that African traditional ethics is not completely at odds with Confucianism or Kantian ethics either.

The importance that Confucianists attach to social relations is closely paralleled in African traditional ethics. According to one author:

> Africans have traditionally been very conscious of the social dimension of morality. Morality is always seen in the social context. Hence any serious violation of the moral order has a social aspect which involves serious social consequences. The whole society is affected, for every evil act is an anti-social act which has adverse effects on the whole community (Omoregbe, 1989, p. 90).

A central element of African traditional ethics is the concept of **communalism**, which is a shared concern for the welfare of all members of one's group, and an interdependence that exists between individual members. The phrase, "we're all in this together," reflects the basic spirit of communalism. Those who embrace this value freely share both their burdens and their good fortune with other members of their groups (Omoregbe, 1989).

For example, a student whose family subscribes to African traditional ethics might find herself receiving financial assistance from her parents, her siblings, and possibly even her aunts and uncles, over the course of her enrollment in college. However, upon completion of her degree program, if she were to secure lucrative employment, her relatives would undoubtedly expect her to remember the assistance that she received along the way, and to be similarly supportive toward other members of the family who might need her help.

Theories of Moral Development

In contrast to philosophers, who have concerned themselves primarily with the substance of moral behavior, developmental psychologists have focused on the processes through which people arrive at moral decisions during different periods in their lives. Several contemporary figures in the field have proposed theories which characterize moral development as a process through which our reasoning on ethical matters grows increasingly complex, as a result of our incorporating new information and experiences into our frames of reference.

Perry's Developmental Positions

William Perry, Jr. (1970) developed a theory which applies to both intellectual and ethical development. The theory deals specifically with changes that typically occur during the "college years." According to Perry, the developmental process includes four general stages and nine specific "positions."

During the first stage of development identified by Perry (1970), the individual's reasoning is characterized by a quality known as **dualism**. Individuals who are at this stage in their development generally view the world in "black and white" terms. They seek absolute answers concerning matters of right and wrong, and place their trust in established authorities. This stage includes the first two positions in the overall developmental scheme. The basic assumptions that characterize these positions have been summarized as follows.

Position 1   All information is either right or wrong.

Position 2   All information is either right or wrong, and where uncertainty seems to exist, it is really an error committed by a "wrong" authority (Rodgers 1980. D. 31).

As individuals advance beyond the first two positions in Perry's (1970) developmental sequence, they begin to recognize multiple perspectives on various issues, but are unable to critically analyze different opinions. Consequently, they conclude that all opinions are equally valid. Perry used the word, **multiplicity**, in reference to this particular way of dealing with conflicting points of view. Multiplicity is characteristic of the third and fourth positions in Perry's scheme. These positions have been described in terms of the following assumptions.

Position 3   All information is either right or wrong, but uncertainty is acceptable in areas where experts do not know the answers yet. Someday the right answer will be discovered or found.

Position 4   Knowledge is pervasively uncertain. Ideas are of equal value. Opinions are important, but no one has "the answer." . . . A few "right" and "wrong" categories may still exist (Rodgers, 1980, pp. 31-32).

As individuals advance beyond the stage of multiplicity, their reasoning is increasingly characterized by **relativism**, meaning that they are able to recognize that judgments of right and wrong are influenced by the context in which they are made, but that not all judgments are equally valid. This general stage of development includes the fifth and sixth positions in Perry's (1970) model. The following characteristic assumptions have been attributed to individuals in these two developmental positions.

Position 5   Knowledge is contextual. Evidence and non-absolute criteria are available for making contextual judgments of "better" or

	"worse" but not for judgments of absolutely "right" or "wrong."
Position 6	A person's life, especially his/her values, will emerge as commitments are made. Life commitments are foreseen as one applies contextual criteria to identify issues (Rodgers, 1980, p. 32).

During the fourth general stage of development, which is characterized by **"commitment in relativism,"** an individual continues to recognize alternative points of view, and to evaluate them critically but with attention to context. At this stage, however, the individual begins to make personal commitments concerning his or her own values and way of life. The judgments that are made during this stage form the basis for the individual's emerging sense of self, which remains the subject of ongoing reflection. This stage includes the final three positions in Perry's scheme, which have been described as follows.

Position 7	The student makes an initial commitment in some area.
Position 8	The student experiences the implications of commitment, and explores the subjective and stylistic issues of responsibility.
Position 9	The student experiences the affirmation of identity among multiple responsibilities and realizes commitment as an ongoing, unfolding activity through which he [sic] expresses his [sic] life style (Perry, 1970, p. 10).

In dealing with moral issues, we would expect students to differ according to their particular stages of development. This difference would manifest itself in their approaches to moral decision-making, even if their final decisions were very similar.

For example, suppose a student were to arrive at college having always been told that it is wrong to borrow other people's belongings without first asking permission. If she had accepted this rule as absolute without ever questioning it, her ethical standards on the matter of property rights would be considered dualistic. Initially, this pattern would probably cause little difficulty in her life, particularly in her relationship with her roommate.

However, suppose there were to come a time when the student would be ill with a fever, only to find that she did not have any aspirin but that her roommate had an entire bottle. If the roommate were not available to grant her permission to take two of the aspirin, the student would be confronted with a dilemma. Initially, the student might stand firm in her belief that she should not help herself to the aspirin. Eventually, however, she would probably start to question her previous assumptions. She might say to herself, "This is really stupid. I'm sure she wouldn't mind. She's got a whole bottle of them. Besides, I can buy her another bottle later on if she wants me to. Anyway, my health has got to be worth more than a couple of lousy aspirin. . . ."

In all likelihood, the student would conclude that the rule about not borrowing other people's belongings without permission is really not absolute. However, because she would not be accustomed to critically analyzing assumptions concerning right and wrong, she might arrive at the conclusion that property rights are all just a matter of opinion. She might assert that it is completely acceptable to borrow other people's belongings without permission, as long as one feels good about it. At this point, we would say that the student's ethical reasoning had become multiplistic.

If the student were to act upon her multiplistic assumptions and begin to regularly borrow her roommate's belongings without asking permission, her roommate would undoubtedly become annoyed. She might even decide to "fight fire with fire," and soon neither of the roommates would feel any control over her own belongings. In any case, it would probably only be a matter of time before an argument would break out between the two roommates.

Eventually, our heroine would probably be forced to rethink her multiplistic beliefs. In all likelihood, she would continue to maintain that under compelling circumstances, borrowing other people's belongings without permission can be morally justified. However, she would probably also concede that such circumstances are rare. She would draw distinctions between items that are easily replaced and those which have significant monetary or sentimental value. She would also recognize the difference between a presumption of permission that is made in response to an emergency situation and a decision to avoid asking permission simply as a matter of convenience. At this point, we would say that the student's moral reasoning had become relativistic.

Eventually, the student would probably adopt the principle of respect for property rights as part of her personal belief system. She would be able to assume ownership over this particular moral value, by saying, "This is what *I* believe." She would regard herself as a person who has respect for other people's property rights, and would apply this principle to her own decision-making in a manner consistent with other elements of her value system. Once the student would establish a coherent system of moral values and would apply it in her daily living, we would say that she had arrived at the point of commitment in relativism.

Kohlberg's Stages of Moral Development

Lawrence Kohlberg (1971) put forth a theory dealing with changes in moral reasoning which occur over the course of the entire life span. Kohlberg focused on those factors which motivate an individual to behave in a certain way, with special attention to the issue of conformity to societal norms. Kohlberg's scheme includes three general "levels," each of which is further divided into two specific "stages." Kohlberg (1971) presented his model as follows.

I.   **Preconventional level**

At this level the child is responsive to cultural rules and labels of good and bad, right and wrong, but interprets these labels in terms of either the physical or the hedonistic consequences of action (punishment, reward, exchange of favours) or in terms of the physical power of those who enunciate the rules and labels. The level comprises the following two stages:

Stage 1   *Punishment and obedience orientation.* The physical consequences of action determine its goodness or badness regardless of the human meaning or value of those consequences. Avoidance of punishment and unquestioning deference to power are valued in their own right, not in terms of respect for an underlying moral order supported by punishment and authority (the latter being stage 4).

Stage 2   *Instrumental relativist orientation.* Right action consists of that which instrumentally satisfies one's own needs and occasionally the needs of others. Human relations are viewed in terms similar to those of the market place. Elements of fairness, of reciprocity, and equal sharing are present, but they are always interpreted in a physical pragmatic way. Reciprocity is a matter of "you scratch my back and I'll scratch yours," not of loyalty, gratitude, or justice.

II.   **Conventional level**

At this level, maintaining the expectations of the individual's family, group, or nation is perceived as valuable in its own right, regardless of immediate and obvious consequences. The attitude is one not only of *conformity* to personal expectations and social order, but of loyalty to it, of actively *maintaining*, supporting, and justifying the order and of identifying with the persons or group involved in it. This level comprises the following two stages:

Stage 3   *Interpersonal concordance or "good boy — nice girl" orientation.* Good behavior is that which pleases or helps others and is approved by them. There is much conformity to stereotypical images of what is majority or "natural" behaviour. Behaviour is frequently judged by intention: "he means well" becomes important for the first time. One earns approval for being "nice."

Stage 4   *"Law and order" orientation.* There is orientation toward authority, fixed rules, and the maintenance of order. Right behavior consists of doing one's duty, showing respect for authority, and maintaining the given social order for its own sake.

III.   **Post-conventional autonomous, or principled level**

At this level there is a clear effort to define moral values and principles that have validity and application apart from the authority of the groups or persons holding these principles and apart from the individual's own identification with these groups. This level again has two stages:

Stage 5   *Social-contract legalistic orientation.* Generally, this stage has utilitarian overtones. Right action tends to be defined in terms of general individual rights and in terms of standards that have been critically examined and agreed upon by the whole society. There is a clear awareness of the relativism of personal values and opinions and a corresponding emphasis on procedural rules for reaching consensus. Aside from what is constitutionally and democratically agreed upon, the right is a matter of personal "values" and "opinion." The result is an emphasis upon the "legal point of view," but with an emphasis upon the possibility of changing law in terms of rational considerations of social utility, (rather than freezing it in terms of stage-4 "law and order"). Outside the legal realm, free agreement, and contract is the binding element of obligation. This is the "official" morality of the United States government and constitution.

Stage 6   *Universal ethical-principle orientation.* Right is defined by the decision of conscience in accord with self-chosen *ethical principles* appealing to logical comprehensiveness, universality, and consistency. These principles are abstract and ethical (the Golden Rule, the categorical imperative); they are not concrete moral rules like the Ten Commandments. At heart, these are universal principles of justice, of the reciprocity and equality of human rights and of respect for the dignity of human beings as individual persons (pp. 86-88).

If we were to ask a small child for advice on the matter of borrowing other people's belongings without permission, we could reasonably expect a preconventional response. The child might ask us, for example, if we are likely to get caught or if the owner of the property is bigger than we are.

In contrast, a conventional response would convey respect for societal norms. We might, for example, be advised against borrowing other people's belongings without permission, on the grounds that the practice is "rude" or in violation of the rules of "common courtesy."

Those at the post-conventional level of moral development would probably offer us a response that appeals to our sense of justice and fair play. We might be told, for example, that we should respect the property rights of all people, and that we should recognize the universal need for a personal zone of privacy.

Gilligan's Female and Male Voices

Values clarification activities are frequently used in leadership training. In one particularly popular exercise, trainees are asked to read a scenario and to rank five characters according to the moral acceptability of their behavior. The scenario involves a woman who wishes to cross a river, in order to be with her fiance. After exhausting all other options, she meets a man who agrees to transport her across the river by boat in exchange for sexual favors. Unable to reach a decision, she asks a female friend of hers for advice, but the friend refuses to become involved. Finally, the woman agrees to the boatman's request and he transports her across the river. Once there, the woman explains the situation to her fiance, who promptly rejects her. She then speaks with her fiance's closest male friend, hoping that he can intervene. In the process, she and her fiance's friend fall in love and live happily ever after.

When this activity was used in an undergraduate leadership training course a few years ago, an interesting pattern emerged. In comparison to their male classmates, many of the female students were surprisingly harsh in their reaction to the behavior of the woman's friend. In the discussion that followed, an interesting question was raised: Why were these students so offended by this particular character's inaction, when the actions of the other characters were often abusive? The students explained their position by pointing out that friends should be held to a higher standard of conduct than would be applied to mere acquaintances. They maintained that when we enter into close relationships with others, we commit ourselves to assuming a supportive role in their lives. The students insisted that under the circumstances described in the story, it would be wrong for the woman's friend to do nothing.

The reasoning of these students could hardly be considered simplistic. Their responses reflected an awareness of certain subtleties of human interaction which were not acknowledged in the alternative procedure of judging the characters' behavior in isolation from their personalities. However, increased awareness of considerations unique to the relationship is not taken into account when measuring ethical maturity according to Kohlberg's model. In fact, using Kohlberg's scheme, objective application of universal principles is viewed as the end result of the developmental process.

The phenomenon that emerged in the leadership class was not unique. In a number of studies concerning moral development, it was found that women's moral reasoning often did not conform to the model presented by Kohlberg. As a result, women were seen by many researchers as lagging behind men in their ethical maturation.

The developmental psychologist, Carol Gilligan (1982), brought new insight to the discussion of women's moral development. Noting that all of Kohlberg's subjects were men, she maintained that his model could not be used to accurately gauge women's development, if their moral reasoning were in fact qualitatively different from that of men over the course of the entire developmental process. Under such circumstances, to compare men's and women's moral development would be akin to comparing apples and oranges.

Gilligan (1982) undertook her own study, which dealt with women's approaches to moral decisions in both real and hypothetical situations. Her research did in fact reveal a characteristically feminine approach to moral decision-making, which she termed the "**ethic of care**." In her book, *In a Different Voice*, Gilligan (1982) drew comparisons between the ethic of care and the more traditionally masculine ethic of justice, noting that "this conception of morality as concerned with the activity of care centers moral development around the understanding of responsibility and relationships, just as the conception of morality as fairness ties moral development to the understanding of rights and rules" (p. 19). She observed, however, that "in this conception, the moral problem arises from conflicting responsibilities rather than from competing rights and requires for its resolution a mode of thinking that is contextual and narrative rather than formal and abstract" (Gilligan, 1982, p. 19).

When applying the ethic of justice to the dilemma presented in our class activity, there would be no basis for concluding that the woman had a *right* to her friend's time, let alone any advice. According to the ethic of care, however, the woman's friend would have a *responsibility* to provide a listening ear and whatever other forms of support she might have at her disposal. In order to understand this responsibility, it would be necessary to consider the unique characteristics of the relationship that existed between the two women. In contrast, the rules of justice would apply to all human interaction regardless of the relationship between the two parties.

If we were to focus once again on the issue of borrowing other people's belongings without permission, this time applying the ethic of care, we would probably deal less with the question of property rights, and would instead concentrate on the matter of how best to respond to human needs and to promote healthy relationships. We would probably still conclude that asking permission is important, because to do otherwise would probably strain the relationship between the two parties involved and possibly also bring hardship to the rightful owner of the property. However, we might also discover additional duties which would specify a moral response on the part of the owner.

For example, suppose a student were informed of a funeral for a close relative on extremely short notice, and had nothing appropriate to wear. If he were to attend the funeral dressed inappropriately, or simply not attend, his behavior might be interpreted as a sign of disrespect for the deceased and might consequently cause hard feelings in his relationship with the other survivors. Now suppose the man's roommate were to own an appropriate suit that would otherwise remain in his closet throughout the entire time that the man would be at the funeral. Assuming that the two men were on good terms, one who espouses an ethic of care would probably maintain that the owner of the suit *should* allow his roommate to borrow it, even though he may technically have a *right* to refuse.

It should be emphasized that care is not the exclusive domain of women, nor is justice the exclusive domain of men. According to Gilligan's (1982) model, we are all capable of responding to concerns about both care and justice. However, when conflicts emerge between the two ethical systems, most people will show a decided preference for one or the other. Most women prefer the ethic of care, whereas most men prefer the ethic of justice. Hence, when speaking of the internal "voices" that guide our decisions, Gilligan described the "**female voice**" as that which leads us to act in a caring manner and the "**male voice**" as that which leads us to act justly.

Gilligan (1982) attributed the differences between men's and women's preferred modes of moral reasoning to differences in their socialization. Citing previous research, she noted that women are conditioned to see themselves and others as interconnected beings, whereas men's socialization promotes a sense of individualism within them. It is not surprising, therefore, that most men prefer the ethic of justice with its emphasis on objectivity, while most women lean toward the ethic of care with its call for empathy.

Gilligan (1982) did not view either system as superior to the other, but recognized them as different from each other. In most organizations, there is probably something to be said for both systems. Therefore, before committing yourself to a particular course of action, it may be a good idea to seek a second opinion from someone whose perspective might differ from your own.

Guidelines for Ethical Decision-Making

Thus far, we have dealt with ethics in general terms and have drawn primarily upon the philosophical and psychological literature. At this point, let us turn our attention toward the basic principles of ethical decision-making in organizations, as discussed in the management literature. We shall begin our discussion by focusing on commonly held moral values. The following are ten "core values" which generally bear upon the decisions of leaders, as they attempt to respond to problems involving their organizations.

- *Caring* means treating people as ends in themselves, not means to an end. It means having compassion, treating people courteously and with dignity, helping those in need, and avoiding harm to others.

- *Honesty* means being truthful and not deceiving or distorting.

- *Accountability* means accepting the consequences of one's actions and accepting the responsibility for one's decisions and their consequences. This means setting an example for others and avoiding even the appearance of impropriety.

- *Promise keeping* means keeping one's commitments. When promises have been made, they are supported by the fact that the obligation to keep promises is among the most important of generally accepted obligations. To be worthy of trust, promises must be kept and commitments fulfilled.

- *Pursuit of excellence* means striving to be as good as one can be. It means being diligent, industrious, and committed. It means being well informed and well prepared. It is not enough to be content with mediocrity, but it is also not right to win "at any cost." . . . Results are stressed, but so is the manner and the method of achievement.

- *Loyalty* means being faithful and loyal to those with whom one has dealings. . . . Every organization is dependent upon cohesion and demands loyalty from its members. . . . But loyalty is not an unmitigated good. It depends upon to whom and for what purpose the loyalty is given. If loyalty means blind, unquestioning obedience, inevitably the values of the organization clash with broader social and political values.

- *Fairness* means being open-minded, willing to admit error, and not over-reaching or taking undue advantage of another's adversities, and it means avoiding arbitrary or capricious favoritism. It means treating people equally and making decisions based on notions of justice.

- *Integrity* means using independent judgment and avoiding conflicts of interest, restraining from self-aggrandizement, and resisting economic pressure. It means being faithful to one's deepest beliefs, acting on one's conviction, and not adopting an end-justifies-the-means philosophy that ignores principle.

- *Respect for others* means recognizing each person's right to privacy and self-determination and having respect for human dignity. It means being courteous, prompt, and decent, and providing others with information that they need to make informed decisions.

- *Responsible citizenship* means that actions should be in accord with societal values. . . . it is important to obey just laws. If a law is unjust, it should be protested through accepted means. Democratic rights and privileges should be exercised by voting and expressing informed views. When in a position of leadership or authority, one must respect democratic processes of decision making (Guy, 1990, pp. 14-17).

The value of integrity, in particular, has received special attention in the management literature. Integrity has been described as having three components:

1. *Self-integration, or centeredness* — a clear sense of identity and focus for action; the ability to incorporate various activities within an identifiable sense of purpose.
2. *Principled consistency*, entailing the capacity to operate with self-consistency in various roles and settings (for example, at home, at work, at civic occasions, and at societal occasions; with workers, managers, consumers, investors, officials, and so on), based on the same fundamental principles or ways of interacting.
3. *Self-candor* — the absence of self-deception; personal honesty, at least with respect to oneself and generally apparent in relation to others (Adler and Bird, 1988, pp. 247-248).

The ten core values presented previously serve as the foundation for five rules of ethical decision-making in organizations:

Rule 1   *Consider the well-being of others, including nonparticipants*. This rule emphasizes caring and respect for others.

Rule 2   *Think as a member of the community, not as an isolated individual*. This emphasizes loyalty, integrity, respect for others, and responsible citizenship.

Rule 3   *Obey, but do not depend solely on the law*. This emphasizes integrity and responsible citizenship.

Rule 4   *Ask, What sort of person would do such a thing?* This emphasizes all the values by calling each into question.

Rule 5   *Respect the customs of others, but not at the expense of your own ethics*. This emphasizes accountability, fairness, integrity, and respect for others (Guy, 1990, pp. 18-19).

We will now examine the processes through which the values of an organization, and the rules derived from those values, are applied to the decisions of organizational leaders. It has been noted that moral behavior involves four basic psychological processes:

1. The person must have been able to make some sort of interpretation of the particular situation in terms of what actions were possible, who (including oneself) would be affected by each course of action, and how the interested parties would regard such effects on their welfare.
2. The person must have been able to make a judgment about which course of action was morally right (or fair or just or morally good), thus labeling one

possible line of action as what a person ought (morally ought) to do in that situation.

3. The person must give priority to moral values above other personal values such that a decision is made to intend to do what is morally right.

4. The person must have sufficient perseverance, ego strength, and implementation skills to be able to follow through on his/her intention to behave morally, to withstand fatigue and flagging will, and to overcome obstacles (Rest 1986, pp. 3-4).

These four processes have all been incorporated into a ten-step model for ethical decision-making in organizations. The specific steps in the model are as follows.

I.   Define the problem.
II.   Identify the goal to be achieved.
III. Specify all dimensions of the problem.
IV.   List all possible solutions to each dimension.
V.   Evaluate alternative solutions to each dimension regarding the likelihood of each to maximize the important values at stake.
VI.   Eliminate alternatives which are too costly, not feasible, or maximize the wrong values when combined with solutions to other dimensions.
VII. Rank the alternatives to each dimension according to which are most likely to maximize the most important values.
VIII. Select the alternative to each dimension that is most likely to work in the context of the problem while maximizing the important values at stake.
IX.   Combine the top ranking alternatives for each dimension of the problem in order to develop a solution to the problem as a whole.
X.   Make a commitment to a choice and implement it (Guy, 1990, p. 29).

Let us now consider a hypothetical situation in which this decision-making model could be applied. Suppose the administrators at a community college were to find that students with small children consistently failed to complete their associate degrees within the ten-year time limit established by the institution. Since community colleges are dedicated to increasing accessibility to higher education, we would expect administrators to be concerned if any segment of the population were to be systematically denied the opportunity to successfully complete their degree programs. Therefore, in the first step of the decision-making model, the administrators would probably recognize the pattern of degree completion among parents of small children as a problem.

In the second step, they would probably establish the goal of increasing the percentage of students with small children who complete their degree programs within the time limit established by the institution. The administrators would probably also go one step further, by identifying objectives concerning the exact percentage of these students completing their degree programs within the time limit.

In the third step, the administrators would specify the various aspects of the problem. One obvious factor would be the time allotment itself. Other factors contributing to the low completion rate might be the limited evening course offerings of the institution and the lack of affordable day care in the local community.

During the fourth step of the decision-making process, the administrators would identify alternative solutions targeted at each aspect of the problem. Possible courses of action for dealing with the time limit itself would include:

- Eliminate the time limit.

- Lengthen the amount of time allowed for all students to complete their degrees. This option would in turn raise an infinite number of possibilities concerning the specific time limit to be adopted.

- Allow students to submit requests for extensions on the time limit, and review these requests on an individual basis.

- Allow the current policy to stand, and hope that changes in other areas will solve the overall problem.

The administrators would also have a number of options for dealing with the issue of evening course offerings. Among their possible courses of action would be the following.

- Schedule full-time faculty members to teach their current courses during the evening instead of during the day.

- Hire part-time faculty members to teach evening courses.

- Do nothing to directly address the issue of evening course offerings and hope that initiatives in other areas will solve the general problem.

In dealing with the problem of affordable day care, the administrators would also have a number of options. A brainstorming session might produce the following list of possibilities.

- Establish a day care center on campus staffed entirely by professional child development specialists.

- Open a laboratory preschool staffed primarily by students majoring in Early Childhood Education working under the direct supervision of professional child development specialists.

- Establish a support group for students with preschool children, in order to promote cooperative babysitting arrangements.

- Do nothing to directly address the issue of day care, and rely upon changes in other areas to solve the overall problem.

Once a list of alternatives has been generated, it would become necessary to evaluate each alternative in relation to the values of the organization. In our example, eliminating the time limit might seem like a caring thing to do, at least on the surface, but it would probably be at odds with the values of integrity, accountability, and the pursuit of excellence. Extending the time limit for all students might alleviate some of these concerns, but would not eliminate them completely. On the positive side, this option would probably win points for being fair. Implementing a review process would be a caring approach that could probably be executed fairly and without compromising the values of integrity, accountability, and the pursuit of excellence. On the other hand, it might place a large unexpected burden on the faculty, thus raising issues of loyalty and promise keeping. Such issues would also be raised in the decision concerning staffing of night courses.

Establishing a day care center would be consistent with the values of caring and responsible citizenship. Staffing the center entirely with trained professionals would contribute to excellence in the delivery of services at the center. With adequate supervision, students would probably also be able to provide excellent service. The laboratory preschool would have the added benefit of contributing to excellence in the academic program. The main drawback of either of these options would be the cost. A center staffed entirely by child care professionals would be particularly expensive to operate. It might be possible to obtain a grant to support the implementation of the laboratory preschool. In the meantime, however, the need for day care would remain. Establishing a support group would be a caring response to the problem that could be carried out quickly and easily.

After examining the advantages and disadvantages of the various options, the administrators might decide to eliminate several of them from further consideration. For example, they might decide that eliminating the time limit would undermine the pursuit of excellence far too much for this option to be considered further. They might also decide that a day care center staffed entirely by professionals would be too expensive.

The administrators would then rank the remaining alternatives for dealing with each aspect of the problem according to their likelihood of promoting the most important values. They might, for example, rank the possible courses of action for dealing with the time limit as follows.

1. Allow students to submit requests for extensions on the time limit, and review these requests on an individual basis.
2. Lengthen the amount of time allowed for all students to complete their degrees.
3. Allow the current policy to stand, and hope that changes in other areas will solve the overall problem.

Options for dealing with the issue of evening course offerings might be ranked as follows.

1. Hire part-time faculty members to teach evening courses.
2. Schedule full-time faculty members to teach their current courses during the evening instead of during the day.
3. Do nothing to directly address the issue of evening course offerings and hope that initiatives in other areas will solve the general problem.

In dealing with the problem of affordable day care, the administrators might establish the following priorities.

1. Establish a support group for students with preschool children, in order to promote cooperative babysitting arrangements.
2. Open a laboratory preschool staffed primarily by students majoring in Early Childhood Education working under the direct supervision of professional child development specialists.
3. Do nothing to directly address the issue of day care, and rely upon changes in other areas to solve the overall problem.

Once the various options have been ranked, the preferred alternatives in the different areas must be combined into a single overall plan. At this point, it is necessary to evaluate the various solutions in relation to the overall problem, rather than in relation to any one aspect of it. In our example, the administrators might realize, on further examination, that a support group for parents of small children would potentially increase the likelihood of its members graduating on time, for reasons that have nothing to do with day care. The students might, for example, establish study groups or simply provide one another with moral support. In dealing with the issues of evening instruction and the time limit for degree completion, the administrators might conclude that by hiring part-time instructors to teach evening courses, they could free up the full-time faculty for the additional committee work that might be necessary if program requirements were to become individualized.

In arriving at the final step in the decision-making process, the point at which a commitment is made to a particular course of action, it is a good idea to make sure that all of the implications of the decision have been considered. The following 12 questions were drawn from the management literature. Although they deal primarily with ethical issues in corporations, they can serve as a final check on decisions made in a variety of other organizational contexts as well.

1. Have you defined the problem accurately?
2. How would you define the problem if you stood on the other side of the fence?
3. How did this situation occur in the first place?

4. To whom and to what do you give your loyalty as a person and as a member of the corporation?

5. What is your intention in making this decision?

6. How does this intention compare with the probable results?

7. Whom could your decision or action injure?

8. Can you discuss the problem with the affected parties before you make your decision?

9. Are you confident that your position will be as valid over a long period of time as it seems now?

10. Could you disclose without qualm your decision or action to your boss, your CEO, the board of directors, your family, society as a whole?

11. What is the symbolic potential of your action if understood? if misunderstood?

12. Under what conditions would you allow exceptions to your stand? (Nash, 1981, p. 81)

Developing a Code of Ethics

One of the ways in which leaders can promote high ethical standards within their organizations is through a **code of ethics**. An organization's ethical code is a statement of the basic principles embraced by the organization, and the specific means by which the organization strives to achieve its stated ideals. It has been noted that "a code of ethics should describe a standard of integrity and competence beyond that required by law — which is the bare minimum" (Guy, 1990, pp. 19-20). While it is understood that all citizens have basic responsibilities to society, members of organizations have additional duties to one another and to the various constituencies served by their organizations. A code of ethics provides clarification of these responsibilities, in much the same way that laws specify our duties as citizens.

Ethical codes offer a number of benefits to the organizations that adopt them. Among these benefits are the following.

■ A code of ethics provides a more consistent standard of conduct within an organization than would be achieved through reliance on the value systems of individuals.

■ A code of ethics provides members of an organization with guidance in dealing with moral ambiguity.

■ A code of ethics provides members of an organization with a basis upon which to resist unethical directives from their organizational superiors (Bowie, 1982).

Of course, not all ethical codes are equally well conceived. The following qualities have been cited in the literature as characteristic of an effective code of ethics.

- It is based on a clearly defined moral philosophy.
- It includes general standards which apply to all members of the organization and more detailed standards which apply to those involved in specific functions.
- It responds to the concerns of various constituencies.
- It is written in common terminology.
- It is set forth in a positive spirit (Hitt, 1990).

In developing a code of ethics, there are several considerations that you will need to keep in mind. First, you will need to be clear on the purpose of the code. Are you seeking to establish general guidelines or specific rules? Is the document strictly for internal use, or do you plan to share it with external constituencies in order to improve your organizational image? In addition to general goals, you may also wish to codify specific objectives. These objectives might apply to all members of your organization, or only to those working in certain areas. You will need to determine which members of the organization are to be involved in developing the ethical code. This will, of course, depend upon the specific purposes of the code. Ultimately, those charged with developing the code will need to establish its specific provisions and the mechanisms by which it is to be administered (Behrman, 1988).

It will also be necessary to establish a plan for dissemination of the code. Obviously, the members of an organization cannot reasonably be held to the provisions of an ethical code if these provisions have not been made clear to them. You will want to disseminate your organization's ethical code in such a way that it will reach its intended audience. You will also want to remember that the importance of the code is often conveyed through the manner of dissemination that is chosen. It is common knowledge that high ranking organizational officials do not generally involve themselves in trivial matters. Consequently, their announcements command attention. Acceptance by signature can also convey the message that the provisions of the code are binding (Behrman, 1988).

The following is a step-by-step plan for establishing a code of ethics for a large organization:

1. Appoint a task force to be lead by the chief executive officer of the organization.
2. Articulate the organization's ethical philosophy. Here, you may wish to draw upon the basic principles of utilitarianism, Kantian ethics, natural law, social contract theory, Confucianism, or African traditional ethics.

3. Draft an ethical code.
4. Solicit comments from leaders within the organization.
5. Make revisions in accordance with the feedback received.
6. Distribute the code to all members of the organization (Hitt, 1990).

When developing codes of ethics for smaller units within an organization, you may wish to refer to the following plan:

1. Appoint a task force within each functional area of the organization, under the leadership of the individual charged with overseeing that area.
2. Draft a code of ethics that incorporates the principles set forth in the organizational code and applies them to the unique concerns of the unit.
3. Solicit comments from members of the specific unit.
4. Make revisions in accordance with the feedback received.
5. Submit the code to the chief executive officer, and request that she or he respond.
6. Make any necessary revisions in the code.
7. Disseminate the code to all members of the particular unit (Hitt, 1990).

The following is a "generic" code of ethics, which could apply to nearly any organization:

1. We must conduct our affairs in a manner consistent with the highest legal and ethical standards.
2. We must establish an organizational environment conducive to open discussion of ethical issues.
3. We must be uncompromising in our commitment to ethical conduct.
4. We must strive for decisions that are both "good" from a practical perspective and "right" from a moral perspective.
5. In judging the morality of a decision, consider the consequences for all concerned.
6. In judging the morality of a decision, consider all relevant organizational policies and procedures.
7. In judging the morality of a decision, consider the values of the organization.
8. In judging the morality of a decision, consider your own personal ethical standards (Hitt, 1990).

In actual practice, individual organizations generally adopt more detailed ethical codes, dealing with matters of unique concern to them. The following is an excerpt from an actual code of conduct established by the National Association for Campus

Activities (NACA), a professional association for advisors of student programming boards.[*]

1. Professionals should demonstrate regard for students as individuals who possess dignity, worth and the ability to be self-directed.

2. Professionals should practice active commitment to student development and to the co-curricular educational process.

3. Professionals should facilitate the development of a balanced co-curricular educational process.

4. Professionals should assist students in developing and practicing appropriate balance between curricular, co-curricular and extra-curricular involvements.

5. Professionals should model ethically responsible behavior for students and for staff they supervise.

6. Professionals should practice accountability and should teach students to be accountable.

7. Professionals should adhere to institutional policy and local or federal law as related to campus activities and should teach students to do the same.

8. Professionals should provide student leaders with clear expectations about their role within the institution and feedback on the extent to which the expectations are being met.

9. Professionals should inform students and staff about the consequences of their actions within the same institution, and should inform institutional officials about activities that have a potential for especially positive or negative institutional impact.

10. Professionals should practice ethical industry relationships, and should teach students about NACA's Statement of Business Ethics and Standards.

11. Professionals should help students to present programs and engage in activities that avoid alcohol abuse and encourage responsible use of alcohol.

12. Professionals should encourage students to develop tolerance and respect for, and avoid discrimination toward, persons or groups whose race, religion, age, sex, physical ability, sexual preference or national origin is different from their own.

13. Professionals should respect the limits of confidentiality in their relationships with students, and should refer them to other individuals or agencies when their needs require additional expertise (NACA statement, 1990, p. 57).

---

[*] From CAMPUS ACTIVITIES PROGRAMMING, March 1990, 57, 60. Copyright ©1990 by NACA, Columbia, SC. Reprinted by permission.

As you continue in your leadership activities, you may wish to consider working with the members of your organization to establish a code of ethics, dealing with issues that commonly emerge in your group. Even if you have not encountered matters of ethical concern in your group, it is a good idea to identify potential problems before they occur. In so doing, you might even find that unethical practices have occurred in your organization but have simply gone unnoticed. In any case, you will reduce the likelihood that such activities will occur in the future.

Summary

This chapter provided an introduction to the study of ethics, with special attention to ethical issues that emerge in organizational settings. The term, "group evil," was used to describe the unique characteristics of groups which can give rise to unethical behavior. It was noted that specialization of functions in organizations can lead individual members to lose their sense of responsibility for the behavior of the group. The influence of authority and peer pressure in groups was also examined. The term, "groupthink," was used to describe a pattern of behavior that sometimes occurs in cohesive groups, leading to poor decisions.

This chapter dealt with the organization as both a moral agent and a moral environment. The influence of the leader over both aspects of organizational ethics was examined.

The role of the follower in promoting ethical conduct in groups was also discussed. The term, "whistle blowing," was used in reference to the practice of exposing corruption within one's organization. The motivation behind the practice was examined, along with the social pressures that militate against it. Common psychological reactions to the whistle blowing experience were examined. Recommendations from actual whistle blowers were presented, along with specific criteria for determining whether or not whistle blowing is justified in a particular situation.

This chapter presented a definition of ethics which emphasized the systematic nature of moral inquiry. Ethical decisions were contrasted with impulsive choices in which the implications of various courses of action are never fully contemplated.

The traditional ethical orientation known as utilitarianism was discussed. Because of its emphasis on the outcomes of human behavior, utilitarianism was described as a consequentialist or teleological system. Two types of utilitarianism were described. Act utilitarianism was presented as a system whereby one chooses the course of action that will produce the greatest net good in a particular situation. The other system identified in this chapter, rule utilitarianism, is concerned instead with identifying behavioral standards that will produce the greatest overall good when applied consistently, even if they do not produce the greatest good in every single instance. The work of John Stuart Mill was discussed. Mill was a famous utilitarian, who introduced the "Greatest-happiness principle," which states that one must always act to produce the greatest happiness for all concerned. It was noted that Mill recognized qualitative differences between different forms of pleasure, and favored those which require the use of our higher faculties.

Utilitarianism was contrasted with the nonconsequentialist or deontological theories, which maintain that the morality of a particular act is not determined by its consequences. The deontological theory put forth by Immanuel Kant, which came to be known as Kantian ethics, was discussed. According to Kant, the only human characteristic that is good without qualification is a good will. He described a good will as one that leads an individual to act from duty, as opposed to self interest or direct inclination.

Kant used the term, "imperative," in reference to statements of principles to which one must adhere, even if he or she is not driven to do so by self-interest or direct inclination. Hypothetical imperatives are those which must be obeyed if one desires a particular outcome. Assertorial imperatives form a specific category of hypothetical imperatives, which must be followed if one hopes to be happy. Categorical imperatives are those which must be obeyed, apart from any consideration of consequences.

As noted in this chapter, Kant set forth a categorical imperative which states that one should not act on a principle that one would not wish to see applied universally. It is logically inconceivable for some principles to be applied universally. According to Kant, one has a "perfect duty" to reject such principles. In other instances, a principle can be applied universally, but with results that one would not desire. Under such circumstances, Kant maintained that one has an "imperfect duty" to reject the principle.

Kant's categorical imperative also states that one should always treat others as ends, and not simply as a means toward some other end. According to Kant, one has a "necessary duty" to treat all people with a certain basic level of respect, and a "contingent duty" to help them develop their talents and achieve their goals. According to Kant, we have duties to both ourselves and others.

The final stipulation of Kant's categorical imperative is that all principles from which duties stem must be internally imposed upon the will. A principle that is externally imposed can lead to compliance based on self-interest, but unless it is embraced by the individual, it cannot create a sense of duty.

This chapter also included a discussion of natural law ethics. Those who subscribe to this particular school of thought believe that certain basic principles of right and wrong are fundamental to our nature as human beings, and consequently are binding regardless of whether or not they are supported by human ordinances. The teachings of St. Thomas Aquinas, which form the foundation of a moral philosophy known today as Thomism, served as an example of natural law ethics. According to Aquinas, human beings have a predetermined role to play in the natural order of the universe. However, Aquinas maintained that we arrive at our understanding of this role through reason. He described two types of reason: (1) theoretical reason, which leads us to our understanding of the nature of the universe; and (2) practical reason, which leads us to conclusions concerning proper modes of conduct. He maintained that certain self-evident goods ought to be pursued in action. These goods include: (1) preservation of human life, (2) familial relationships, (3) knowledge, and (4) social order. Aquinas believed, however, that practical reason can lead to many different conclusions concerning how best to achieve these goods. He believed that while we are always bound by natural law, we must submit to human ordinances only if they are just. He asserted that a rule is unjust if: (1) it is not intended to promote the common good, (2) it is enacted by someone who lacks the authority to establish such a rule, or (3) it distributes burdens unfairly.

In this chapter, natural law ethics was contrasted with social contract theory. It was noted that while natural law ethicists believe in a moral law that is higher than any rule established by humanity, social contract theorists view agreements between people as the basis for all ethical duties. According to social contract theorists, a breakdown of the social order, which casts people into a state of nature, leads to a disintegration of all moral obligations. Thomas Hobbes, perhaps the most famous social contract theorist of all time, believed that human beings feel threatened in this natural state, and desire the security of an orderly society. However, he maintained that in order for people to safely abandon their combative practices, it is necessary for them to collectively invest their power in one person who is then charged with enforcing a mutually accepted law. Hobbes referred to societies formed in this manner as commonwealths, and used the term, sovereign, to describe their leaders. It was noted in this chapter that not all social contract theorists share Hobbes's belief in a formal contract that served as the origin of civilization. Some believe that people enter into an implied contract on an ongoing basis. Others believe that morality is based on the terms of a hypothetical contract that would be fair to all concerned.

The fifth traditional ethical orientation discussed in this chapter, Confucianism, is based on the teachings of Confucius. According to the basic tenets of Confucianism, people must always act in compliance with an established natural order known as the "*Tao* of Heaven."

It was noted in this chapter that Confucianism is a distinctly humanistic teaching, which emphasizes social relations. According to Confucian teaching, leadership should be based on moral authority, rather than on physical force. Confucianists use the terms, *tê* and *li*, respectively, in reference to these two distinct power bases.

In this chapter, comparisons were drawn between the teachings of Confucius and those of St. Thomas Aquinas. It was noted that both philosophers emphasized the importance of the individual conscience.

Self-improvement was presented in this chapter as a Confucian ideal. Several Chinese terms were introduced in reference to specific virtues pursued by Confucianists. First among these is *ren*, which refers to "true humanity," an ideally human state that is characterized by empathy. *Yi* refers to "righteousness" or a sense of duty. *Xin* refers to trustworthiness, honesty to oneself, and strength in one's convictions. Finally, the term *cheng* is used by Confucianists to mean integrity and genuineness.

It was noted in this chapter that Confucianists attempt to cultivate within themselves the characteristics of a class of people known as the *chün-tzu*, whose behavior is characterized by moderation. The Confucian emphasis on conciliatory behavior was recognized as a distinctive feature of this particular ethical tradition.

The final ethical tradition discussed in this chapter is known as African traditional ethics. Unlike the ethical orientations discussed previously, African traditional ethics had its origins in the standards of conduct adopted by common people, rather than in the writings of famous philosophers.

Morality, as defined in traditional African thought, was contrasted with the rules of etiquette and taboo, both of which are also elements of African culture. The rules of etiquette are respected simply as a matter of custom, and behaviors prohibited by taboo are avoided for religious reasons. Moral standards, on the other hand, are rationally based standards which promote social welfare and personal development.

African traditional ethicists favor the cultivation of communalism as a foundation for human interaction. Within a communalistic system, individuals share both their burdens and their good fortune with other members of their social units, in a spirit of interdependence.

This chapter presented an overview of contemporary theories of moral development. It was noted that developmental psychologists have typically viewed the process of moral reasoning as one that becomes more complex over the course of a person's life.

The work of William Perry, Jr. was discussed. Perry presented a theory of intellectual and ethical development which incorporated four general stages and nine specific positions. The first stage identified by Perry is characterized by dualism, which is a tendency to trust authority and to seek absolute answers to questions of right and wrong. The second stage is characterized by multiplicity, the tendency to view all opinions as equally valid. Relativism, the defining characteristic of the third stage, involves a recognition that often there is no single best answer to a question, but that some answers are definitely better than others. Commitment in relativism, which emerges in the fourth stage, involves the adoption of certain values and lifestyle preferences as one's own.

This chapter also included a discussion of Lawrence Kohlberg's theory of moral development. Kohlberg's theory incorporates three general levels of development and six specific stages. At the first level, which is described as preconventional, one's moral decisions are driven by self-interest. At the second level, known as the conventional level, attention shifts toward the shared expectations of others as the basis for moral decision-making. At the third level, one's moral decisions are based on principles which are seen as valid aside from any consideration of whether or not they are endorsed by other people. This level of moral reasoning is known as the post-conventional, autonomous, or principled level.

As noted in this chapter, Kohlberg's theory was based entirely on research involving men, thus raising questions concerning its applicability to women. Subsequent research by Carol Gilligan revealed that men and women tend to differ in their moral reasoning. Gilligan described two internal "voices" that drive an individual's decision-making. The female voice raises concern about issues of care, while the male voice calls for attention to matters of justice. Although both voices are present in each person, most people show a preference for one over the other. Most women prefer the female voice and most men prefer the male voice. Gilligan attributed these preferences to differences in men's and women's socialization. While a strong sense of individualism is instilled in men, women's socialization promotes a feeling of interconnectedness with other people.

In this chapter, specific guidelines for ethical decision making were presented. Ten "core values" that relate to organizational decision-making were presented. These values were: (1) caring, (2) honesty, (3) accountability, (4) promise keeping, (5) pursuit of excellence, (6) loyalty, (7) fairness, (8) integrity, (9) respect for others, and (10) responsible citizenship. The value of integrity, in particular, was emphasized. Three components of integrity were identified. These components were: (1) centeredness or self-integration, (2) principled consistency, and (3) self-candor. Five rules derived from the basic values presented here were also included in this chapter. Ethical decision-making was presented as a series of four separate psychological processes: (1) identifying alternative courses of action and their potential consequences, (2) judging one course of action as preferable to the others, (3) placing moral considerations ahead of competing interests in choosing a course of action, and (4) following through on the decision to behave morally. A ten-step model for ethical decision-making, which encompasses the four basic processes, was also presented in this chapter.

The chapter closed with a discussion of ethical codes, their benefits, and their essential characteristics. It was noted that an ethical code provides clarification of the unique responsibilities of members of an organization, just as laws articulate the general duties of all citizens. It was recommended that ethical codes reflect general moral philosophies, that they include standards applicable to the general membership of organizations as well as to specific organizational units, that they address concerns of various constituencies, and that they be written in common terminology with a positive tone. Step-by-step plans were presented for developing ethical codes for both large organizations and smaller organizational units. An example of a "generic" code of ethics was presented, along with an excerpt from an actual code of conduct adopted by a professional association.

References

Adler, N. J. and Bird, F. B. (1988). International dimensions of executive integrity: Who is responsible for the world. In S. Srivastva (Ed.), *Executive Integrity* (pp. 243-267). San Francisco: Jossey-Bass.

Aquinas, T. (1985). Treatises on law and justice. From *Summa Theologica*, trans. M. Velasquez, 1983. In M. Velasquez and C. Rostankowski (Eds.), *Ethics: Theory and Practice* (pp. 41-54). Englewood Cliffs, NJ: Prentice-Hall.

Barry, V. (1983). *Moral Issues in Business*, 2nd ed. Belmont, CA: Wadsworth.

Behrman, J. N. (1988). *Essays on Ethics in Business and the Professions*. Englewood Cliffs, NJ: Prentice Hall.

Bowie, N. (1982). *Business Ethics*. Englewood Cliffs, NJ: Prentice-Hall.

Cleary, J. C. (1991). Introduction. In J. C. Cleary (Ed), *Worldly Wisdom: Confucian Teachings of the Ming Dynasty* (pp. ix-xxv). Boston: Shambhala.

Glazer, M. P. and Glazer, P. M. (1986). Whistle blowing. *Psychology Today, 20* (8), 37-43.

Goodpaster, K. E. (1982). Some avenues for ethical analysis in general management. In K. E. Goodpaster (Ed.), *Ethics in Management* (pp. 3-9). Boston: Division of Research, Harvard Business School.

Guralnik, D. B. (Ed.) (1982). *Webster's New World Dictionary of the American Language*, Second College Edition. New York: Simon & Schuster.

Guy, M. E. (1990) *Ethical Decision Making in Everyday Work Situation*. New York: Quorum.

Hitt, W. D. (1990). *Ethics and Leadership*. Columbus: Battelle.

Hobbes, T. (1839). *The English Works of Thomas Hobbes of Malmesbury*, v. III. W. Molesworth, Ed. London: John Bohn.

Janis, I. J. (1982). *Groupthink: Psychological Studies of Policy Decisions and Fiascoes*. Boston: Houghton Mifflin.

Kant, I. (1985). Foundations of the metaphysics of morals, trans. M. Velasquez, 1983. In M. Velasquez and C. Rostankowski (Eds.), *Ethics: Theory and Practice* (pp. 76-95). Englewood Cliffs, NJ: Prentice-Hall. (Original work published 1785.)

Kohlberg, L. (1971). Stages of moral development as a basis for moral education. In C. M. Beck, B. S. Crittenden, and E. V. Sullivan (Eds.), *Moral Education: Interdisciplinary Approaches* (pp. 23-92). Toronto: University of Toronto Press.

Milgram, S. (1953). Behavioral study of obedience. *Journal of Abnormal and Social Psychology, 67* (4), 371-378.

Milgram, S. (1964). Group pressure and action against a person. *Journal of Abnormal and Social Psychology, 69* (2), 137-143.

Milgram, S. (1965). Liberating effects of group pressure. *Journal of Personality and Social Psychology, 1* (2), 127-134.

Mill, J. S. (1963). *The Six Great Humanistic Essays of John Stuart Mill*. New York: Washington Square Press.

NACA statement of professional ethics (March, 1990). *Campus Activities Programming*, 57, 60.

Nash, L. L. (1981). Ethics without the sermon. *Harvard Business Review, 59* (6), 78-90.

Peck, M. S. (1983). *People of the Lie*. New York: Simon and Schuster.

Omoregbe , J. I. (1989). *Ethics: A Systematic and Historical Study*. Lagos, Nigeria: Cepco.

Perry, W. G., Jr. (1970). *Forms of Intellectual and Ethical Development in the College Years*. New York: Holt, Rinehart and Winston.

Rest, J. R. (1986). *Moral Development*. New York: Praeger.

Soeken, D. R. (1986). J'accuse. *Psychology Today, 20* (8), 44-46.

Stock, G. (1987). *The Book of Questions*. New York: Workman.

Velasquez, M. and Rostankowski, C. (1985). *Ethics: Theory and Practice*. Englewood Cliffs, NJ: Prentice-Hall.

Waley, A. (1989). Introduction to *The Analects of Confucius* (pp. 13-69). New York: Vintage.

Activities

Getting It Straight

Read the following scenario and respond to the items presented by circling the best answer.

The Graduate Student Association at a university sponsored a dance at which alcoholic beverages were sold. On the same weekend, the Residence Hall Council held its annual Siblings Weekend. A number of students attended the dance with their siblings, some of whom were less than ten years old. During the course of the event, supervision of the children became very loose. Many of them were allowed or even encouraged to drink, and ultimately became badly intoxicated.

When questioned about their roles in the incident, individual members of the organization admitted that they saw the children drinking. However, each member of the group maintained that he or she had done nothing wrong in failing to intervene, since none of the group members had been assigned responsibility for monitoring the children's behavior.

In fact, the children's participation in the event was completely unanticipated. Several members of the group indicated that they personally did not think it was a good idea to even admit children to the dance, but they did not feel it was their place to make such a decision.

Others had no objection to children's participation in the event, but felt badly when they saw how the children were being treated. Even so, they were reluctant to confront their peers and felt no obligation to do so.

Students who encouraged the children to drink indicated that they were just having fun. Since nobody objected to their behavior, they assumed that it was acceptable.

Members of the organization who were working at the event were quick to point out that alcohol was not being sold directly to minors. Individual workers further absolved themselves of responsibility for serving students who were purchasing drinks for children, even though these students' intentions were obvious. Several workers stated that they did not actually serve any students at all, but simply sold them tickets which could be exchanged for drinks. The students handling the money argued that it was the responsibility of the bartenders to decide whether or not to serve individual guests. The bartenders argued, however, that such decisions needed to be made at the time the tickets were sold and were not the responsibility of those tending bar.

1. This scenario illustrates the concept of:
    a. Group evil
    b. Groupthink
    c. Both a and b
    d. Neither a nor b
2. In its transaction with the children, the Association functioned as a:
    a. Moral environment
    b. Moral agent
    c. Both a and b
    d. Neither a nor b

Read the following scenario and respond to the item presented by circling the best answer.

> The Campus Women's Association is a cohesive group committed to a clearly articulated feminist agenda. Members feel passionately about their chosen cause. The group has a very strong leader whose judgment is rarely questioned by its members.
>
> Recently, the leader recommended that the organization undertake a new campaign against date rape. The plan would involve posting the names of alleged violators on campus.
>
> Privately, several members of the organization felt uncomfortable with the plan, especially since some of the allegations were based entirely on hearsay. As an alternative, one member of the group mentioned the possibility of establishing a campaign to familiarize women with procedures for reporting violations, and to encourage victims to press charges.
>
> Other members of the group, including the leader, strongly disapproved of the proposed alternative. They raised concern that such an approach could be seen as blaming the victim. They also argued that the university's system for handling allegations of date rape could not be trusted.
>
> Based primarily on a desire for unity and a belief in the legitimacy of the group's goals, those members who harbored doubts about the appropriateness of the leader's original plan decided to keep their concerns to themselves. As a result, the plan to post fliers identifying alleged rapists won unanimous support.

The scenario described above illustrates the concept of:
a. Whistle blowing
b. Groupthink
c. Both a and b
d. Neither a nor b

Read the following scenario and respond to the item presented by circling the best answer.

The Student Government Association at a university maintains background information on students, which is provided by the students themselves at the beginning of each term, as part of the registration process. Students furnish this information with the understanding that it is to be used only for the purposes of the Association.

Not long ago, the President of the Association began selling mailing labels containing students' names and addresses to outside businesses and keeping the money herself. The labels were used for mailings directed toward specific segments of the student population, and were compiled using the information provided at registration.

Eventually, the Vice President and the Secretary of the Association found out about the President's activities and confronted her on the matter. After the President refused to cease the practice of selling labels, the Secretary decided that he would undermine the President's efforts by entering her computer and altering her student records, so that none of the labels would reach the desired student subpopulations. The Vice President decided instead to report the President's activities to the student newspaper, which then ran an expose.

Which of the following could be described as a whistle blower?
   a. The President
   b. The Vice President
   c. The Secretary
   d. All of the above
   e. None of the above
   f. a and b only
   g. b and c only
   h. a and c only

Read the following scenario and respond to the items presented by filling in the blank spaces.

Gloria, Helen, and Grace are students at a university located in a suburban community. The three students also own homes in this particular suburb, and have all decided to attend a public hearing on a proposal to grant a zoning variation to a land developer who hopes to build a shopping mall in an area previously zoned residential.

Gloria is attending the meeting because her home is located directly adjacent to the parcel of land in question, and she believes the value of her property will decrease if the zoning variation is granted. She plans to speak out during the meeting in order to protect the investment that she has made in her home.

Helen and Grace both live on the other side of town, and consequently have much less at stake in the outcome of the meeting. Nevertheless, they have their reasons for attending. Helen chose to attend because she loves controversy. She is a daytime talk show junkie, and is hoping the discussion at the meeting will rival Oprah Winfrey's best efforts. Grace is not interested in the discussion at all, but believes that all people have a civic responsibility to become informed about issues affecting their communities.

1. _____ is motivated by duty to attend the meeting.

2. _____ is motivated by self-interest to attend the meeting.

3. _____ is motivated by direct inclination to attend the meeting.

4. Based on the teachings of Immanuel Kant, it would seem that _____ has exhibited a good will in her decision to attend the meeting.

Respond to the following items by indicating whether the statements are true (T) or false (F.).

1. _____ Stanley Milgram's experiments revealed that very few people remain obedient when their own moral values are directly challenged by authority figures.

2. _____ Milgram's research revealed that people are more likely to stand by their moral convictions, to the point of defying authority, if they experience peer support.

3. _____ Most whistle blowers are motivated by a desire for the material benefits that are invariably bestowed upon them as a result of their whistle blowing activities.

4. _____ Whistle blowers often have a strong sense of individual responsibility.

5. _____ Most ethical decisions are based on the mood of an individual in a particular situation.

6. _____ An assertorial imperative can be either hypothetical or categorical.

7. _____ "Thomism" is the name given to the moral philosophy put forth by Thomas Hobbes.

8. _____ "Kantian ethics" is the name given to the moral philosophy put forth by Immanuel Kant.

9. _____ Necessary duties are sometimes described as "meritorious."

10. _____ Contingent duties are also known as "strict" duties.

11. _____ According to Kant, people have duties to both themselves and others.

12. _____ According to Kant, the only human characteristic that is good without qualification is a "good will."

13. _____ Thomas Hobbes used the term, "sovereign," in reference to a group composed of individuals who establish an orderly society by mutual agreement, and collectively invest their power in an enforcer of the agreement.

14. _____ Hobbes used the term, "commonwealth," in reference to the person charged with upholding the standards of the sovereign.

15. _____ Confucianism is concerned primarily with the supernatural and life in the hereafter.

16. _____ Confucianists favor the use of physical force as the primary tool of leadership.

17. _____ Personal integrity is emphasized in Confucianism.

18. _____ Self-improvement is emphasized in Confucianism.

19. _____ The *chün-tzu* are generally regarded as extremists.

20. _____ African traditional ethics has its foundation in the teachings of a small group of famous philosophers.

21. _____ Adherents to African traditional ethics cultivate "goodness of character" through both the pursuit of virtues and the avoidance of vices.

22. _____ African traditional ethicists subscribe to a philosophy of "rugged individualism."

23. _____ African traditional ethics is a religiously based ethical system.

24. _____ It is generally agreed that the sole purpose of adopting an ethical code is to control the behavior of one's followers.

Place check marks next to all of the statements below that are consistent with the criteria presented in this chapter for determining whether or not whistle blowing is justified.

1. _____ Whistle blowing is justified only if it is done for the reason provided in the definition of whistle blowing.

2. _____ Exposure of organizational corruption is ordinarily justified only if the whistle blower has exhausted all avenues of internal dissent beforehand.

3. _____ Whistle blowing is not justified unless the individual has made certain that his or her beliefs are supported by reasonable evidence.

4. _____ The decision to expose corruption in an organization should not be influenced by considerations of how serious, immediate, or specific the moral violation is.

5. _____ Whistle blowing is justified only if the specific action taken by the individual is commensurate with his or her duty to avoid or expose immoral conduct.

6. _____   Whistle blowers must stand on principle, regardless of whether or not they are likely to bring about change as a result of their efforts.

In the spaces provided, number the stages of whistle blowers' psychological reactions to the experience, according to the sequence in which they typically occur.

_____   Reflection
_____   Discovery
_____   The long haul
_____   Closure
_____   Retaliation
_____   Resolution
_____   Confrontation

In the space provided, identify each of the following as an example of etiquette (E) or taboo (T).

1. _____   A rule which states that, in order to avoid invoking the "wrath of the heavens," one should never speak negatively of the deceased.

2. _____   A custom of removing one's shoes before entering another person's home.

In the space provided, write the letter corresponding to the ethical tradition associated with each philosopher.

1. _____   St. Thomas Aquinas   a. Utilitarianism
2. _____   John Stuart Mill   b. Natural law ethics
3. _____   Thomas Hobbes   c. Social contract theory

In the space provided, write the letter corresponding to the definition of each Chinese term.

1. _____   *Chün-tzu*   a. The will of Heaven
2. _____   *ren*   b. Moral authority, virtue
3. _____   *tê*   c. Physical force
4. _____   *li*   d. "True humanity," empathy
5. _____   *Tao*   e. Righteousness, sense of duty
6. _____   *cheng*   f. Trustworthiness, honesty to oneself, strength in one's convictions.
7. _____   *yi*   g. Integrity, genuineness
8. _____   *xin*   h. Persons of refinement who are emulated by Confucianists

In the space provided, identify each of the following as a necessary (N) or contingent (C) duty.

1. _____ The duty to state the terms of one's agreements without deception.
2. _____ The duty to use one's talents for the betterment of society.
3. _____ The duty to allow freedom of expression.

In the space provided, identify each of the following as a perfect (P) or imperfect (I) duty.

1. _____ The duty to allow others to live.
2. _____ The duty to grant priority to those whose needs are most urgent.
3. _____ The duty to oppose social injustice.

In the space provided, indicate whether each of the following conclusions is a product of theoretical (T) or practical (P) reason.

1. _____ The earth revolves around the sun.
2. _____ Education for all people should be provided by the government.
3. _____ What goes up must come down.
4. _____ For every action there is an equal and opposite reaction.
5. _____ Smoking should not be allowed in public places.

In the space provided, identify each of the following statements as a categorical (C) or hypothetical (H) imperative. Circle the number corresponding to each statement that is also an assertorial imperative.

1. _____ If you want to be happy, you should live a simple life.
2. _____ You should always act in a way in which you would like for other people to act.
3. _____ If you want to be a successful musician, you should practice every day.

Read the following scenario and respond to the items presented by circling the best response.

Betty, Joyce, Marilyn, Hugh, Jim, Audrey, and Stan are all in their fifties and are enrolled as undergraduate students at a university in their community. The seven students usually meet for coffee in the cafeteria on campus before their classes begin.

One morning, Betty mentioned a situation that she had encountered in her job search. She explained that, after sending a resume and cover letter to a major corporation, she received an "applicant information form" that included an item pertaining to her date of birth. The form was accompanied by a letter indicating that any personal information provided would be used only for purposes of record keeping and would not affect the status of a candidate's application for employment. However, Betty had previously learned from a reliable source that the forms were being used to summarily eliminate from further consideration any applicants over 40 years of age. Based on the information available to her, Betty decided to falsify her date of birth on the form.

She explained to the group that her decision came only after weighing the "pros and cons" of responding to the item either truthfully or deceptively. After comparing the alternatives, Betty concluded that it would be to her own advantage to falsify her date of birth, since she would then be considered for the position. She also believed that the company and its clients would benefit from her chosen course of action, since it could result in the hiring of a better qualified candidate. Finally, she believed that society in general would benefit from her decision because equality of opportunity would be advanced.

At hearing of Betty's decision, Joyce was outraged. She argued that Betty should have focused her attention on the general practice of lying to prospective employers, rather than on the specific situation at hand. Had she done so, according to Joyce, she could not possibly have concluded that it would be acceptable to lie, since employers depend upon the information provided by candidates in evaluating their legitimate qualifications for employment. Joyce maintained that if the practice of lying to employers were to become common-place, the result would be greater hardship for all concerned. She concluded, therefore, that lying to employers should be universally rejected, since it would neither promote pleasure nor diminish hardship when practiced consistently.

Marilyn then came to Betty's defense. She stated that it would be wrong to lie to employers who have been honest themselves in their approach to the recruitment process, since there is ordinarily an expectation of honesty that is shared by both parties. However, according to Marilyn, when the employer stated falsely that personal information would not affect the status of the application, the norm prohibiting deception no longer applied, and lying was brought within the bounds of fair play.

Hugh immediately objected to Marilyn's line of argumentation. He stated that lying would be wrong even in the absence of any consensus against it. According to Hugh, there are certain moral principles that are known to all people because they are based on reason. He argued that people cannot ignore these "higher" laws, even by mutual consent. He stated that deceptive practices are morally wrong because they undermine the pursuit of knowledge, which is a fundamental good.

Jim also disagreed with Marilyn and Betty. He argued that an end, no matter how desirable, can never justify the use of an illicit means. He argued that the practice of lying is wrong because it reflects a failure to recognize another person as a rational being. He argued, further, that one who tells the truth when it is not in her or his own interest to do so demonstrates a sense of duty that is inherently good, apart from any consideration of outcomes.

Audrey agreed that it is honorable to tell the truth even when it is not in one's own interest to do so. She explained that such behavior demonstrates the virtues of *xin* and *cheng*, both of which are desirable qualities that people should attempt to develop within themselves.

Stan focused his attention on the social forces that gave rise to the ethical dilemma that Betty faced. He viewed it as a disgrace to our society that individual interests are pitted against one another in the hiring process. He argued that within a healthy civilization, a sense of communalism prevails over the type of ruthless competition between individuals that would lead one to contemplate lying as a means of securing employment.

1. Which of the following could be described as a rule utilitarian?

   a. Betty
   b. Joyce
   c. Jim
   d. All of the above
   e. None of the above
   f. a and b only
   g. a and c only
   h. b and c only

2. Which of the following could be described as an act utilitarian?

   a. Betty
   b. Joyce
   c. Jim
   d. All of the above
   e. None of the above
   f. a and b only
   g. a and c only
   h. b and c only

3. Which of the following could be described as a consequentialist?

   a. Betty
   b. Joyce
   c. Jim
   d. All of the above
   e. None of the above
   f. a and b only
   g. a and c only
   h. b and c only

4. Which of the following appears to embrace teleological ethics?

    a. Betty

    b. Joyce

    c. Jim

    d. All of the above

    e. None of the above

    f. a and b only

    g. a and c only

    h. b and c only

5. Which of the following could be described as a nonconsequentialist?

    a. Betty

    b. Joyce

    c. Jim

    d. All of the above

    e. None of the above

    f. a and b only

    g. a and c only

    h. b and c only

6. Which of the following appears to embrace deontological ethics?

    a. Betty

    b. Joyce

    c. Jim

    d. All of the above

    e. None of the above

    f. a and b only

    g. a and c only

    h. b and c only

7. Which of the following appears to embrace the "Greatest-happiness Principle?"

    a. Joyce

    b. Jim

    c. Hugh

    d. All of the above

    e. None of the above

    f. a and b only

    g. a and c only

    h. b and c only

8. Which of the following appears to embrace social contract theory?

   a. Jim
   b. Marilyn
   c. Hugh
   d. All of the above
   e. None of the above
   f. a and b only
   g. a and c only
   h. b and c only

9. Which of the following appears to embrace Confucianism?

   a. Betty
   b. Audrey
   c. Stan
   d. All of the above
   e. None of the above
   f. a and b only
   g. a and c only
   h. b and c only

10. Which of the following appears to embrace Kantian ethics?

   a. Jim
   b. Marilyn
   c. Hugh
   d. All of the above
   e. None of the above
   f. a and b only
   g. a and c only
   h. b and c only

11. Which of the following appears to embrace African traditional ethics?

   a. Hugh
   b. Audrey
   c. Stan
   d. All of the above
   e. None of the above
   f. a and b only
   g. a and c only
   h. b and c only

12. Which of the following appears to embrace natural law ethics?

    a. Jim
    b. Marilyn
    c. Hugh
    d. All of the above
    e. None of the above
    f. a and b only
    g. a and c only
    h. b and c only

Place a check mark next to each of the following items that describes a psychological process identified in this chapter as an essential component of ethical decision-making.

_____ Identifying alternative courses of action and their potential consequences.
_____ Judging one course of action as preferable to the others.
_____ Placing moral considerations ahead of competing interests in choosing a course of action.
_____ Following through on the decision to behave morally.

In the space provided, identify the developmental stage characterized by each of the behaviors described below. Use Perry's terminology to identify the four general stages of development: relativism (R.), commitment in relativism (C), multiplicity (M), and dualism (D).

1. _____ Julian always keeps his promises, because he believes that it is absolutely wrong to break a promise under any circumstances. Recently, Julian promised to drive to Florida for spring break, with his best friend, Dennis. In accordance with his moral beliefs, Julian fully intends to keep his promise to Dennis.

2. _____ Shortly before spring break, Julian's mother becomes ill and asks Julian to stay with her over the break, in order to care for her. Out of concern for his mother, Julian cancels his plans with Dennis. In the process, Julian begins to question his assumption that it is absolutely wrong to break a promise. Eventually, he concludes that it is morally acceptable to break a promise for any reason. Julian begins to break promises regularly, without explanation or apology.

3. _____ Although Dennis understands Julian's reasons for cancelling the spring break trip, he has been much less tolerant toward Julian's subsequent broken promises. Julian's other friends have also become annoyed with his refusal to consistently keep his word. Perhaps more importantly,

they have grown to distrust him and have become much less inclined to enter into agreements with him. Upon reflection, Julian concludes that promises cannot fulfill their purpose unless they are taken seriously. While continuing to believe that promises can sometimes be broken, Julian now believes that under ordinary circumstances they must be honored. He now believes that promises should be broken only in response to overriding moral considerations.

4. _____ Julian continues to attach importance to the practice of keeping his promises. He now identifies personally with this value, as well as other values which must sometimes be weighed against it. As Julian engages in ongoing reflection, he continues to regard himself as "a man of his word."

Read the following scenario and respond to the items presented by filling in the blanks.

Gina, Clarissa, and Demetria are three sisters who share their parents' belief in the importance of keeping promises. However, they differ from one another in their reasons for honoring their commitments. Gina, the youngest of the three, keeps her promises because she knows that she will "get in trouble" if she does not. Clarissa is less concerned about being punished for breaking promises. However, she makes a practice of keeping her promises because she believes that it is "the right thing to do." "That's just the way I was brought up," she explains. Demetria, the oldest of the three sisters, tries to keep her promises because she sees this practice as a natural outgrowth of her own freely chosen commitment to the "core value" of personal integrity.

1. Of the three sisters, _____ could best be described as operating at an autonomous level of moral reasoning, according to Kohlberg's theory.

2. Of the three sisters, _____ could best be described as operating at a conventional level of moral reasoning, according to Kohlberg's theory.

3. Of the three sisters, _____ could best be described as operating at a principled level of moral reasoning, according to Kohlberg's theory.

4. Of the three sisters, _____ could best be described as operating at a preconventional level of moral reasoning, according to Kohlberg's theory.

5. Of the three sisters, _____ could best be described as operating at a post-conventional level of moral reasoning, according to Kohlberg's theory.

Read the following scenario and respond to the items presented by filling in the blanks.

>   Mary and John are discussing the importance of keeping promises. Mary takes the position that promises should be kept because it is unfair to lead a person to act on false assumptions concerning one's own behavior. She believes that two parties to an agreement must enter into it with the information necessary to make rational decisions. She maintains that by breaking a promise, one party assumes an unfair advantage over the other, and therefore violates the rights of the other. John shares Mary's belief that promises should be kept. However, his primary concern is with the harm that is done to a relationship between two people when one of them breaks a promise to the other. He believes that trust is the backbone of any healthy relationship, and that trust is undermined when promises are broken. He believes that broken promises almost always hurt people, and should therefore be avoided. While acknowledging that individual circumstances must be considered, he maintains that one generally has a responsibility to honor one's commitments.

1. _____ appears to be applying an ethic of care, as described by Gilligan.
2. _____ appears to be applying an ethic of justice, as described by Gilligan.
3. Applying Gilligan's theory, _____ appears to be guided primarily by a male "voice."
4. Applying Gilligan's theory, _____ appears to be guided primarily by a female "voice."

List the ten "core values" that serve as the foundation for the system of organizational decision-making that was presented in this chapter.

1.
2.
3.
4.
5.
6.
7.
8.

9.

10.

List the three components of integrity identified in this chapter.

1.

2.

3.

Place a check mark next to each of the following rules of organizational decision-making that was among those presented in this chapter.

_____   "Consider the well-being of others, including nonparticipants."

_____   "Approach your decision as an isolated individual, rather than as a member of the community."

_____   "Obey, but do not depend solely on the law."

_____   "Ask, What sort of person would do such a thing?"

_____   "Above all else, respect the customs of others."

Place a check mark next to each of the following ethical systems that incorporates the basic principle set forth in the "Golden Rule."

_____   Kantian ethics

_____   Confucian ethics

_____   African traditional ethics

Place a check mark next to each of the following items that illustrates the concept of communalism.

_____   One student lives alone in an apartment. She uses her own earnings to pay all of her living expenses.

_____   Two students live together in an apartment as a couple. They share all of their resources completely. Both partners contribute to the household to the full extent of their ability.

_____   Three students live together in a three bedroom house. The students contribute equally to their rent and utility fees. Each of them assumes sole responsibility for all of his or her other living expenses. The students share none of their belongings and insist that their house mates "pull their own weight."

In the spaces below, number the steps in the process of ethical decision-making, according to the sequence in which they occur.

_____   "List all possible solutions to each dimension."

_____   "Eliminate alternatives which are too costly, not feasible, or maximize the wrong values when combined with solutions to other dimensions."

_____   "Combine the top ranking alternatives for each dimension of the problem in order to develop a solution to the problem as a whole."

_____   "Identify the goal to be achieved."

_____   "Evaluate alternative solutions to each dimension regarding the likelihood of each to maximize the important values at stake."

_____   "Define the problem."

_____   "Make a commitment to a choice and implement it."

_____   "Select the alternative to each dimension that is most likely to work in the context of the problem while maximizing the important values at stake."

_____   "Rank the alternatives to each dimension according to which are most likely to maximize the important values."

_____   "Specify all dimensions of the problem."

Place a check mark next to any of the following statements that were among those used in this chapter to describe an effective code of ethics.

_____   "It is based on a clearly defined moral philosophy."

_____   "It includes only general guidelines, which apply to all members of the organization."

_____   "It responds to the concerns of various constituencies."

_____   "It is written in technical language."

_____   "It is set forth in a positive spirit."

In the spaces provided, number the steps in the process of developing a code of ethics for a large organization, according to the sequence in which they occur.

_____   Distribute the code to all members of the organization.

_____   Draft an ethical code.

_____   Appoint a task force to be lead by the chief executive officer of the organization.

_____   Solicit comments from leaders within the organization.

_____ Make revisions in accordance with the feedback received.

_____ Articulate the organization's ethical philosophy.

In the spaces provided, number the steps in the process of developing a code of ethics for smaller units within an organization, according to the sequence in which they occur.

_____ Submit the code to the chief executive officer, and request that she or he respond.

_____ Appoint a task force within each functional area of the organization, under the leadership of the individual charged with overseeing that area.

_____ Make any necessary revisions in the code.

_____ Solicit comments from members of the specific unit.

_____ Disseminate the code to all members of the particular unit.

_____ Draft a code of ethics that incorporates the principles set forth in the organizational code and applies them to the unique concerns of the unit.

_____ Make revisions in accordance with the feedback received.

Both Sides of the Story

Prepare a defense for both the affirmative and negative positions on the following statements.

1. It is impossible for a group to have a conscience.
2. Members of an organization have a duty to confront ethical violations that occur within the organization.
3. Ethical leadership cannot be taught.

Sorting It Out

Respond to the following questions by taking a position and defending it.

1. In general, should moral decisions be based primarily on considerations of justice or considerations of care?
2. Which of the traditional moral philosophies discussed in this chapter would you be most inclined to endorse?
3. Which of the ten "core values" discussed in this chapter is generally the most important?

It's Your Call

Respond to the following items by providing the information requested.

1. Select a group or organization in which you currently hold membership or in which you held membership at some time in the past. Using the ten-step decision-making model presented in this chapter, develop a plan for dealing with a specific problem confronted by the group. Write an essay describing the decisions made at each step in the process. Include an explanation of your rationale for each of these decisions.

2. Select a group or organization in which you currently hold membership or in which you held membership at some time in the past. Develop a general code of ethics for its members, and prepare an essay explaining your rationale for each provision of the code.

Where Do I Go From Here?

In this chapter, basic principles of organizational planning will be applied to the development of the individual leader. The following concepts will be discussed:

- Goals

- Objectives

- Action plans

The process of change will be discussed, with attention to the following stages and their characteristics:

- Crisis stage

- Hard work stage

- Tough decision stage

- Unexpected pain stage
  - ➤ Fear of success

- Joy and integration stage

A six-step process for effecting personal change will be presented, with an emphasis on the use of reinforcement.

Common barriers to goal attainment will be examined, along with strategies for overcoming these barriers.

The concept of risk will be discussed, and specific guidelines for risk-taking will be presented. Distinctions will be drawn between the following types of risk:

- Dynamic risk

- Static risk

The importance of support systems will be examined, and the following concepts will be introduced:

- Networking
  - ➤ Formal networking
  - ➤ Informal networking
  - ➤ Lateral networking

- ➤ Vertical networking
- ➤ Citywide networking
- ➤ National networking
- ■ Mentoring
  - ➤ Mentors
  - ➤ Proteges
- ■ Peer/mentor partnerships

Guidelines for building and maintaining support systems will be presented.

The chapter will close with an emphasis on the importance of balancing concern for the future with enjoyment of the present and openness to the unexpected.

Chapter 9

Where Do I Go From Here?

There are risks and costs to a program of action. But they are far less than the long-range risks and costs of comfortable inaction.
John F. Kennedy

Why Establish a Leadership Development Plan?

When people read personal development books, they usually have a desire to make changes in certain areas of their lives. They may wish to lose weight, find love, quit smoking, get rich, or overcome insomnia. Whatever the problem, there seems to be a book that presumably contains the solution.

To their credit, "self-help" books usually do have the effect of feeding the reader's desire for change and inspiring confidence in his or her own ability to change. Unfortunately, the motivational power of this type of publication is often momentary. Within weeks or even days after a book is closed, old patterns of thought and behavior often resurface.

Although I would love to believe that somehow this book could be an exception to the rule, deep down inside I know that it is not. No book has the power to change a person's life. Ultimately, the individual must assume responsibility for changing her or his own conditions.

One of the most effective ways for you to ensure your continued development as a leader, even after you have finished reading this book, is by establishing a personal leadership development plan now. A well articulated leadership development plan will stay with you, providing a focus for your continued growth, long after the "feel good" response to the book's message has faded.

Clarifying Your Purpose

In Chapter 7, we discussed the importance of goals and objectives as part of the planning process in organizations. In formulating your own personal leadership development plan, you will also need to begin by clarifying the outcomes that you desire.

Your goals and objectives will be similar in form to those of your organization, but the focus will be on you. For example, you might decide that one of your goals will be to improve your skills as a public speaker. Based on this general goal, you would then establish more specific short-term objectives. Initially, your objectives might relate to the specific activities in which you will engage as a means of developing the necessary skills. For example, one of your initial objectives might state "I will deliver at least two prepared speeches to audiences of ten or more during the current academic term." Eventually, your objectives should relate more directly to demonstrated improvement in the quality of your performance. For example, you might establish an objective stating "within the current academic term, I will speak for at least ten minutes, to an audience of ten or more, and will say 'you know' no more than twice."

A number of benefits have been attributed to personal development goals. Among these benefits are the following.

- Insisting on high self-esteem

- Being in control of negative thoughts

- Feeling independent of others' negative moods

- Choosing to be in control of your own feelings

- Claiming the freedom to make your own decisions

- Accepting and embracing success (O'Grady, 1992, p. 124)

Additionally, several negative consequences of goallessness have been identified. These include: (1) low self-esteem, (2) inwardly directed anger, (3) difficulty in interpersonal relationships, (4) feelings of helplessness, and ultimately (5) failure to succeed (O'Grady, 1992).

It has been noted that the first step in establishing your goals is to determine what you really want. All too often, people's goals are influenced by the expectations of others, rather than by their own desires (Hagan, 1987).

According to Morscher and Jones (1992), you can begin to clarify your goals and objectives by examining your current situation, your anticipated future circumstances, and your desires for the future. Your goals and objectives should reflect the differences between your current conditions and your hopes for the future.

It is important that you establish priorities between various goals and objectives. Failure to accomplish goals is often due to a lack of focus. Important goals can sometimes get lost among other goals which are actually of less significance. In establishing your priorities, you will need to determine which of your goals and objectives are most important to you personally. You will also need to pay attention to those goals which must be accomplished within a particular time frame. External events, over which we have no control, often influence the urgency with which we must attend to certain matters (Hagan, 1987).

For example, if you were interested in applying for both a summer fellowship and admission to the entering fall class of a master's degree program, it would be a good idea for you to pay close attention to the application deadlines for both programs, and to attend to the earlier deadline first, since this would increase the likelihood of your being able to participate in both programs. If you were to disregard the deadlines, you would run the risk of having one of your opportunities slip away while you were attending to the other.

In establishing your goals, you will want to make sure that they are fairly tangible. You should also work to create a clear mental image of their accomplishment. As I mentioned previously, long-term goals must be broken down into short-term objectives. These smaller steps should be written down along with your more general goals (Hagan, 1987).

According to O'Grady (1992), you are more likely to take your goals seriously if you: (1) "take time to think about what you want most" (p. 137), (2) "have the courage to decide on what you want most" (p. 138), and (3) "focus all your energies on one goal at a time" (p. 138). He also offered the following guidelines for goal-setting.

- Make a commitment to your change goals

- Permit yourself to make new choices

- Write down your goals in specific terms

- Place your written goals where you can see them

- Jot down ideas daily to move forward on your goals

- Review your goals when you are feeling frustrated

- Repeat each step as often as needed (p. 121)

Just as organizations must establish action plans for accomplishing their goals and objectives, so too must individuals. Once you have established your personal goals and objectives, your next step will be to identify as many alternative strategies for their accomplishment as possible. You will then examine the "pros and cons" of each approach, and choose the single most effective strategy (Morscher and Jones, 1992). According to Hagan (1987), it is particularly important to identify the most direct way to accomplish each of your goals.

Table 1 provides an example of a written action plan for a personal development objective. Table 2 can be duplicated and used to prepare your own personal development action plans. You will notice many similarities between an individual action plan and an action plan that is established by a group. However, there are some important differences as well. As I mentioned previously, the focus of the personal objective itself is different from that of the organizational objective, in that it relates to the growth of the individual rather than to the functions of the group. Additionally, you will recall that different group members are usually assigned responsibility for the various steps in an action plan that relates to an organizational objective. In contrast, when you establish an action plan for accomplishing a personal objective, complete responsibility for its implementation falls upon you.

You will notice, however, that a personal development action plan does include the names of other people who can provide support in its implementation. The support that you receive from others might take the form of information, advice, words of encouragement, or direct involvement in the various activities described. Later in this chapter, we will talk further about the specific ways in which you can draw support from those around you.

Once you have settled on an action plan, you will be ready to implement it. Remember, however, that action must be accompanied by evaluation of results. If necessary, you must be prepared to modify your plans or even your objectives, based on your appraisal of the outcomes (Morscher and Jones, 1992). For example, suppose you were to successfully purge the phrase, "you know," from your public speaking vocabulary, only to find it replaced with other meaningless utterances, such as "um," "uh," and "like." If your previous objective dealt only with eliminating your use of the phrase "you know," then you would probably want to establish a broader objective. Your new objective might state "within the current academic term, I will speak for at least ten minutes, to an audience of ten or more, and will emit no more than four extraneous sounds in the process."

Table 1. EXAMPLE OF A PERSONAL DEVELOPMENT ACTION PLAN

Objective: <u>I will speak before an audience of ten or more people at least twice during the current term.</u>

	Task	Completion Date	Resources	Support Persons
1.	Sign up to do readings at church	9/20		Rev. James
2.	Read passages silently.	t.b.a.		
3.	Read passages orally in front of a mirror	t.b.a.		
4.	Read passages orally in front of a small group	t.b.a.		Bill, the kids
5.	Do readings at church	t.b.a.		Rev. James, Bill, the kids, the choir
6.	Select a general topic for hospice volunteers in-service training session.	9/25	University library	Hospice volunteers
7.	Identify content of presentation and sources	10/7	University library	Sharon, Deborah, Bob
8.	Schedule presentation	10/10	Master calendar	Sharon
9.	Reserve conference room	10/10		Deborah
10.	Prepare and submit announcement for newsletter	10/15	Computer	Deborah
11.	Prepare detailed outline of presentation	10/20	Computer	
12.	Prepare handouts	10/25	Computer, Photocopies ($10)	
13.	Conduct presentation in front of mirror	10/27		
14.	Conduct presentation in front of family	10/29		Bill, the kids
15.	Conduct presentation in front of staff	11/1		Sharon, Deborah, Bob
16.	Conduct presentation for volunteers	t.b.a.		Sharon, Deborah, Bob

Table 2. PERSONAL DEVELOPMENT ACTION PLAN FORM

Objective: _____

_____

_____

Task	Completion Date	Resources	Support Persons

Understanding the Process of Change

Before you embark upon plans to bring about specific changes in your life, it is important that you develop a general understanding of the nature of change itself. The process of change can be divided into five separate stages: (1) "the **crisis** stage," (2) "the **hard work** stage," (3) "the **tough decision** stage," (4) "the **unexpected pain** stage," and (5) "the **joy and integration** stage" (O'Grady, 1992, pp. 156-157).

During the first stage, a crisis of some sort results in a need for the individual to change. As he or she confronts new circumstances, it becomes evident that previous patterns of behavior are insufficient for coping with the demands of the present (O'Grady, 1992). For example, if you are like many students, you might have discovered during your first term in college that your previous study habits, which might have served you well in high school, simply would not "cut it" at the college level. This realization might have created a crisis for you, which might in turn have prompted behavioral changes on your part.

Unfortunately, people sometimes respond to crises with negativity, and assume that they must accept an undesirable fate rather than making necessary adaptations (O'Grady, 1992). Each year, a number of students conclude that they are not "college material," based on their first term grades, rather than concluding that they simply must alter their study habits.

In contrast, individuals who recognize the need for change and commit themselves to personal development advance to the hard work stage. During this stage, the individual must exercise self-discipline, as she or he begins to develop new skills (O'Grady, 1992). In our example, a necessary first step in developing effective study habits would be to develop skills in reading, writing, analyzing and synthesizing information, and managing time effectively.

During the tough decision stage, the individual must make difficult choices that will affect his or her life. At this stage, it is important to realize that courses of action that are most comfortable for us are not always in our best interests. During the tough decision stage, a person's goal is to choose the most effective course of action, not necessarily the one that is most comfortable (O'Grady, 1992). Again using our example, if you were to find that an inordinate amount of your time was being devoted to cocurricular activities, you might conclude that cutting back on your organizational involvement would enable you to improve your academic performance. This might lead to a series of difficult choices between specific activities. You might ultimately find it necessary to withdraw from your favorite student organization if another activity would make a more substantial contribution to your long-term development.

During the unexpected pain stage, the individual experiences feelings of ambivalence, resulting from a **fear of success**. This particular fear is often characterized by the following symptoms.

1. Feelings of inspiration and giddiness . . . alternating with increased anxiety.
2. Profound levels of trust and closeness . . . alternating with stark lonesomeness.
3. Unconditional self-acceptance . . . alternating with shades of old self-critical anger.
4. Letting go of negative feelings . . . alternating with guilt for feeling so good.
5. Decreased need for approval . . . alternating with hunger for positive strokes.
6. Higher self-esteem and success . . . alternating with self-doubt and fears of failure.
7. Great faith in setting goals . . . alternating with pessimism about progress made.
8. Enjoying the freedom to be who you are . . . alternating with resentment at change-back artists (O'Grady, 1992, p. 181).

In our example, if you were to implement a plan for improving your study skills, you might find yourself experiencing increased anxiety, regardless of whether or not the plan appeared to be working. Even if you had every reason to believe that your academic performance was improving, you might hear a nagging voice inside you saying "this can't possibly last" or "this can't really be happening." This type of self-talk would be characteristic of the fourth stage of the change process.

During the final stage of the process, joy and integration are achieved. The individual feels good about her or his life, and understands why things are going well (O'Grady, 1992). In our example, you might ultimately conclude that you are indeed a good student, and that your academic success is a result of your own planning, hard work, and talent.

Robbins (1992) devised a six-step process through which you can bring about changes within yourself. The system involves applying the basic principles of psychological conditioning.

The first step in the process is to decide what you would like to achieve and to determine why you have not yet achieved it (Robbins, 1992). You might decide, for example, that you would like to be on the Dean's List for this term. You might also conclude that your failure to attend to reading assignments is what prevented you from being on the Dean's List previously. Based on this conclusion, you might choose to focus your attention on improving your reading behavior.

Once you have identified your objective and any obstacles to its achievement, you will need to motivate yourself to change by associating pleasure with change and pain with continuation of the status quo (Robbins, 1992). In our example, you might remind yourself of the pride that you would feel in showing your grades to your parents or in seeing your name posted on a campus bulletin board. You might also remind yourself just how unbearable it would be to see your roommate's name on the Dean's List but not your own. If necessary, you could even create an additional incentive by declaring to all of your friends that you *will* be on the Dean's List.

Once you have established an objective and created a source of motivation through mental associations, you can promote ongoing progress by interrupting counterproductive patterns of thought (Robbins, 1992). In our example, if you were to find yourself thinking that your reading material was of no practical value, you might interrupt the pattern by identifying ways in which the information could be applied to your own life, regardless of how outrageous the particular applications might be. In general, humor can be a very effective tool for interrupting negative self-talk.

The fourth step in the process is to find alternative patterns of thought or behavior to replace old patterns that have proven to be debilitating. It has been noted that even after a person has broken a pattern of addictive behavior, there is a good chance that the addiction will emerge again at some time in the future, unless the individual has found an alternative means by which to experience pleasure and avoid pain (Robbins, 1992). If you were to find that your academic performance was suffering as a result of activities in which you and your friends participated, it might be a good idea for you to distance yourself from the particular group of friends. However, unless you would find another more supportive group of friends, it would probably only be a matter of time before you would again be involved with the group that contributed to your problem.

The fifth step in the process involves repeating a new pattern of behavior or thought until it becomes habitual, and providing **reinforcement** by establishing pleasurable consequences (Robbins, 1992). You could use reinforcement to improve your study habits by providing yourself with some type of reward each time that you are diligent in your studies. Eventually, good study habits would become second nature to you.

The final step in the change process is to test the new behavioral or attitudinal pattern in real or imaginary situations, in order to make sure that it is appropriate and that a permanent change has occurred. If the new pattern is found to be inadequate, the previous steps in the process should be repeated (Robbins, 1992).

Overcoming Barriers to Change

There are several common obstacles to the achievement of goals. Some of these barriers exist within people's environments. In many instances, however, people's own behavior and attitudes obstruct their efforts to bring about changes in their lives. Even when dealing with environmental constraints, people often underestimate the extent to which they can assume control over their futures.

According to Hagan (1987), one of the most common barriers to goal attainment is lack of discipline. Discipline can be established by learning to delay gratification and by building self-control. It is important to recognize your own ability to manage your feelings, rather than allowing your decisions to be driven directly by impulses or emotions. It is also important to analyze the future implications of your decisions, rather than focusing exclusively on the present.

Additionally, Hagan (1987) identified fear and a lack of self-confidence as common barriers to goal attainment. He noted that in order to succeed a person must be willing to move beyond her or his "comfort zone," and learn to take risks. According to Hagan (1987), "confidence comes from acting against our fears and taking charge of our lives."

Morscher and Jones (1992) also emphasized the importance of risk-taking. They identified two distinct categories of risk. The first type, the **dynamic risk**, is one in which "gain and loss are pitted against one another" (p. 30). In contrast, a **static risk** is one in which "the opportunity may simply be to consolidate and protect present gains" (p. 30). When you purchase an insurance policy, you are taking a static risk, because your intent is to reduce your potential loss. In contrast, purchasing a lottery ticket would involve a dynamic risk, since there would be a possibility of gain or loss.

According to Morscher and Jones (1992), risk-taking is a process that consists of four steps: (1) recognizing the necessity of risk, (2) making the decision to take a risk, (3) planning a strategy, and (4) following through on the plan. They offered the following "Dos" and "Don'ts" of risk-taking.

- "Have a clear goal and specific purpose in mind" (p. 30).

- "Consider your options and choose the most viable ones" (p. 30).

- "Get advice from people who have no stake in the outcome except for caring about what happens to you. (Before choosing advice-givers, however, take into consideration their own track records on successful risking.)" (p. 30).

- "Always have alternatives as backup. The more options you have, the more leverage you can use" (p. 30).

- "Be sure to take yourself into account. Do you have the abilities, the courage, and the knowledge to succeed? You as the risk-taker influence the risk and the outcome. There is a difference between taking a chance where you have no control over the odds and risking in a situation where you are a factor with some weight" (p. 30)

- "Do be serious about risking. Playing around when the stakes are high can relieve tension, perhaps, but could also get you into trouble by making you careless. Fooling or kidding around might also give you a reputation for being insincere or flippant" (p. 30).

- "Don't count on always being completely successful or having one risk solve all your problems" (p. 30).

- "Never risk more than you can afford to lose" (p. 30)

- "Don't take risks for someone else or allow someone to take them for you" (p. 31).

- "Don't use other people as an excuse for inaction" (p. 31).

- "Don't risk a lot for a little" (p. 31)

- "Don't risk just to avoid losing face" (p. 31)

- "Don't discount your intuition or your feelings" (p. 31).

Morscher and Jones (1992) developed a six-step process for dealing with barriers to success. The first step in the process is to identify all of the factors preventing you from achieving your goals. Once you have generated a list of obstacles, your next step is to determine whether each obstacle exists within you or within your organization. The third step in the process is to review those barriers attributed to the organization and determine whether or not you are able to do anything about them. The fourth step is to conduct a similar analysis of those obstacles which exist within you. The fifth step is to again examine those barriers over which you are believed to have no control. If you are absolutely certain that you cannot do anything about them, you simply must accept them as factors in your strategy. The final step in the process is to devise a plan, by focusing on those circumstances over which you have some control and asking yourself the question, "What are you going to do to try to remove or lessen those barriers?" (p. 111).

According to Robbins (1992), we cannot make changes in our lives unless we believe in our ability to change and our personal responsibility for doing so. He also noted that we must recognize the need for change in order to feel motivated to bring it about. Clearly one of the keys to overcoming barriers to goal attainment is the development of a positive attitude.

Developing a Support System

While you must ultimately assume responsibility for bringing about changes in your life, it is unreasonable to think that you must "go it alone." Throughout history, successful leaders have drawn support from others. The establishment of a strong support system remains an important factor in the successful implementation of any personal development plan. According to Hagan (1987), we can increase the likelihood of accomplishing our goals by drawing support, encouragement, and insight from those who are closest to us, including friends and relatives. Morscher and Jones (1992) developed a five-step process for establishing a support system. The following is their description of the five-steps.

Step One   Continue (harder, if necessary) getting to know who you are as a person.

Step Two   Trust yourself to know what's best for you. Cast out lingering doubts and mental put-downs.

Step Three Open up to more friendly associations with others. This means getting yourself out and among people. It also means that you initiate contacts and stop sitting back waiting to be chosen.

Step Four   Decide what you want to do and the kinds of help you'll need in order to do it well and quickly.

Step Five   Build a community to support your efforts. Surround yourself with people who validate your existence and make you feel good about yourself and life in general. Make sure they are energy givers, not energy depleters (pp. 154-155).

We will now direct our attention toward two specific types of supportive relationships, which are particularly important to aspiring leaders. The first category includes relationships that are established through a process known as **networking**. The second type of relationship that we will discuss involves a process known as **mentoring**.

Networking

Networking has been described as "a means of making contacts, of linking up with people and ideas, of getting and giving information" (Zuker, 1983, p. 187). Networks bring people together in egalitarian relationships that are mutually beneficial. Although each party may approach a relationship with a particular agenda in mind, in order for networking to successfully occur, all parties must be prepared to give support as well as receive it (Baber and Waymon, 1991).

Consider, for example, the challenges faced by a very competent student of the natural sciences who has only limited aptitude for writing. No matter how good his grades might be in his chemistry and biology courses, unless this student can somehow find a way to overcome his writing deficiency, his overall academic performance will undoubtedly suffer. To his benefit, there are probably other students on campus who have decidedly nonscientific minds but are gifted writers nonetheless. Through networking, our troubled student might be able to find a peer who would be willing to proofread his papers and offer suggestions for improvement. The only catch is that he might be expected to explain one or two laws of nature to this new friend.

Networks can be either **formal** or **informal**. According to Baber and Waymon (1991, p. 165), "formal networks include a wide variety of groups, such as professional associations, Chambers of Commerce, and community or civic organizations." Formal networks are generally driven by clearly articulated agendas, which are shared by all members. These agendas are typically incorporated into the mission statements of the various groups, and serve as the basis for their existence. In contrast, informal networks have been described by Baber and Waymon (1991) as "a web of contacts you put together for your own pleasure and purposes" (p. 166).

A distinction has also been drawn between **lateral** and **vertical** networking. Lateral networking involves relationships with others who are at your level in the hierarchy of your organization, though perhaps in different units. Vertical networking, on the other hand, involves relationships with individuals who rank higher than you in the organization. Both types of networking are recommended. Vertical networking will enable you to draw advocacy from someone whose influence in the organization is greater than yours. Lateral networking will enable you to draw emotional support and broaden your knowledge base (Zuker, 1983).

In addition to developing mutually beneficial relationships with others in your organization, it is recommended that you establish similar linkages with individuals outside your organization who share your interests. Both **citywide** and **national** networking can provide you with access to valuable information that would not necessarily be accessible to you within your own organization (Zuker, 1983).

For example, if you were to plan a major concert on your campus, with hopes of attracting patrons from the local community, it would be to your advantage to know about other events taking place in the community on various dates. By discussing your plans with the managers of various event centers in the community, you could choose a date for the concert and know that it would be "the only show in town." Discussing the matter with other local event planners would also enable them to avoid inadvertently competing with the concert. As a result, their events would probably also be more successful. This example illustrates the mutually advantageous nature of citywide networking.

It can be particularly beneficial to engage in networking with individuals who hold positions similar to your own on other local campuses. You may also wish to engage in networking on a statewide or regional level, particularly if your institution is located in an area where there are few other colleges and universities.

Whereas citywide networking often provides you with access to information pertaining to practical aspects of your organization's activities, the principal benefit of national networking is the opportunity to broaden your understanding of major issues. According to Zuker (1983, p. 185), "by associating yourself with national groups you will be able to see the big picture."

For example, if you were to hold membership in a fraternity or sorority and began to observe racial tension within the Greek system on your campus, it might be to your advantage to share your observations with members of other chapters of your organization. By comparing notes with members on other campuses, you would be more likely to shift your attention away from specific personalities and toward the broader social issues involved. By broadening your perspective, you would probably be able to deal more directly with the causes of the problems on your campus, rather than generating a series of "band-aid" solutions focusing only on the symptoms.

According to Zuker (1983), your first step in building a network is to examine both your own needs and the resources that you would be able to share with others. You will then identify the people you know who might benefit from inclusion in your network while serving your needs as well. There are three categories into which your contacts are likely to fall: (1) "those who give you information," (2) "those you turn to for emotional support," and (3) "those who are resources for social or professional contacts" (Zuker, 1983, p. 189).

It is important to have a record-keeping system that allows you to maintain convenient and up-to-date information on the members of your network. A file card system works particularly well, since it can be easily updated, expanded, or reorganized. It is also a good idea to maintain a datebook or calendar, in order to keep track of events where networking can occur (Zuker, 1983).

Even after you have established a strong network, it is important that you continue to cultivate your relationships with individual contacts. According to Zuker (1983, p. 190), "networking turns exploitive if you do not nurture the relationships behind the expectations." Baber and Waymon (1991) established the following rules for ensuring mutually satisfying relationships with the members of your network.

1. Make your primary contacts with the friends and colleagues who know and respect your accomplishments and really want to help you.

2. Observe common and even uncommon courtesies. When you telephone a contact, ask if the person has time to talk. When you are trying to meet with a person, be flexible about his or her schedule. Don't expect to network only on company time. You must invest your own time also. Determine a meeting place that's equally convenient for both of you. Be ready to pick up the check and leave a tip. If your contact offers to split the check, accept graciously.

3. Don't jump the gun. Allow your contact to determine the timing.

4. Move beyond the superficial. Handing a business card to someone does not constitute a networking relationship.

5. Make contacts based on your achievements, not your needs. That's another way of saying to look at what you can give, as well as what you want to get in the networking exchange.

6. Be specific and honest about what you want.

7. Don't make unreasonable requests.

8. Pay your dues. Remember, effective networking is always reciprocal. It's an exchange. Have something to give and give generously; don't expect just to take.

9. Be helpful to others. Inevitably, you will benefit from contact with someone whom you can't immediately — or perhaps ever — pay back.

10. Learn to praise your own skills and be confident about what you can offer (pp. 177-179).

Mentoring

Both current and aspiring leaders can often benefit greatly from a process known as "**mentoring**." As explained by Zuker (1983, p. 193), "in mentoring, a younger person, a **protege**, and an older, more experienced person, a **mentor**, form a relationship that is beneficial to each." According to Zey (1984), the functions of the mentor include "teaching, counseling, providing psychological support, protecting, and at times promoting or sponsoring" (p. 7). These activities obviously benefit the protege by allowing her or him to learn new skills and to advance in the organization. The benefits to the mentor may be more subtle, but are every bit as real. It has been noted that proteges often provide their mentors with assistance, information, and advice (Zey, 1984).

In addition to benefiting the mentor and the protege, the process of mentoring can contribute to the effectiveness of the entire organization. Among the direct benefits to the organization are the establishment of a natural line of succession, preservation of organizational traditions and values, and a strong leadership team. In turn, the position and power of both the mentor and protege are enhanced as the organization continues to develop further (Zey, 1984).

The benefits that you will draw from the mentoring relationship will depend upon the characteristics of the individual serving as your mentor. An individual who is not respected, knowledgeable, and concerned about your welfare will be a questionable asset to you. When seeking out a mentor, it is recommended that you consider the following questions.

1. Is the mentor good at what he [sic] does?
2. Is the mentor getting support?
3. How does the organization judge the mentor?
4. Is the mentor a good teacher?
5. Is the mentor a good motivator?
6. What are the protege's needs and goals?
7. What are the needs and goals of the prospective mentor??
8. How powerful is the mentor?
9. Is the mentor secure in his [sic] own position? (Zey, 1984, p. 167)

It is important to also remember that a mentoring relationship must be mutually beneficial. While you are pondering the aforementioned questions, prospective mentors will be sizing you up as well. In order to attract a mentor, you should be visible and demonstrate both competence and a desire to learn. You should also take initiative in interacting with the prospective mentor, and establish linkages with other key individuals in the organization. It is also a good idea to become involved in projects that are widely regarded as important. Finally, it is important that you make yourself accessible and demonstrate a willingness to contribute to the accomplishment of the prospective mentor's goals (Zey, 1984).

According to a study by Zey (1984), certain qualities of potential proteges are widely regarded as desirable. Among the most commonly cited characteristics that mentors seek in potential proteges are:

1. Intelligence.
2. Ambition.
3. Desire and ability to accept power and risk.
4. Ability to perform the mentor's job.
5. Loyalty.
6. Similar perceptions of work and organization.
7. Commitment to organization.
8. Organizational savvy.
9. Positive perception of the protege by the organization.
10. Ability to establish alliances (p. 182).

Even after a mentoring relationship has been established, you will need to work at maintaining the relationship. According to Zuker (1983), proteges can strengthen their relationships with their mentors by:

- maintaining high standards of performance

- demonstrating assertiveness

- remaining open to criticism

- remaining loyal to their mentors

Zey (1984) emphasized the importance of evaluating the mentoring relationship periodically. He noted that both parties generally enter into a mentoring relationship with certain shared goals, yet this common vision can deteriorate unless it is reexamined from time to time. It is necessary to regularly evaluate the performance of the protege, with attention to both the quality of his or her work and the manner in which he or she relates to other members of the organization. It is also important to determine whether or not the protege's work is helping him or her to develop, and whether or not the protege is receiving adequate information about the organization.

According to Zey (1984), one area of concern that warrants special attention is the quality of the protege's relationships with her or his peers. Under the best of circumstances, the protege who is singled out as a "rising star" will be admired by her or his peers. Unfortunately, most proteges seem to experience at least some jealousy on the part of their peers, as a result of their mentoring relationships. Zey (1984) recommended that proteges use the following strategies to alleviate peer resentment.

1. Demonstrating competence, establishing credibility
2. Downplaying interaction whenever possible
3. Continuing regular interaction with peers
4. Becoming source of information for peers
5. Serving as upward conduit of peer ideas, plans, and information (p. 194)

Another important consideration, when evaluating the mentoring relationship, is the question of whether or not the relationship should continue further. As explained by Zuker (1983, p. 195), "the pretext for the relationship is the development of the protege, so when that happens, the protege must become independent." Once the mentoring process has run its course, both parties must be willing to let go of the relationship or to continue it in some other form.

The Peer/Mentor Partnership

A "peer/mentor partnership" is a unique relationship that can incorporate elements of both networking and mentoring. According to Zuker (1983, p. 196), "a peer/mentor partnership evolves when two people of similar professional levels but different talents link up in a way that matches the strength of one to the weakness of the other."

You have probably noticed that university professors often engage in collaborative research projects with one another, and publish their findings with joint authorship. One of the reasons why this approach is so common is that research can be quite complicated. While professors are generally smart people, they are not all equally skilled in the full range of activities that a major research project entails. Some faculty members, for example, are very good at developing research questions and explaining the implications of their findings, but have difficulty in analyzing data. Others are very good with numbers but have a difficult time putting their thoughts into words. By forming a peer/mentor partnership, it is possible for two or more researchers to ensure a high level of quality in their overall finished product, and to learn from one another in the process.

As you seek out individuals from whom you wish to draw support, try to identify those with whom you could form effective peer/mentor partnerships. The mutually beneficial nature of support systems is perhaps best exemplified in this particular type of relationship. As you begin to engage more frequently in this type of reciprocal arrangement, you will not only increase the likelihood of achieving your own goals, but will undoubtedly enjoy the satisfaction of knowing that you are helping others to grow as well.

One Final Thought

Throughout this book, I have emphasized the importance of planning for the future. In closing, I would like to also remind you to take pleasure in the present, and to remain open to the unexpected opportunities for growth that you will undoubtedly encounter along the way.

Jennifer James (1983), a cultural anthropologist and noted media personality in the Pacific Northwest, summed up beautifully the importance of treasuring every moment of your life. I will leave you with her words to ponder.

> Success is every minute you live. It's the process of living. It's stopping for the moments of beauty, of pleasure; the moments of peace. Success is not a destination that you ever reach. Success is the quality of the journey (p. 38).

Summary

In this chapter, the importance of planning for your future leadership development was stressed. Personal goals, objectives, and action plans were discussed, and examples were provided.

The process of change was examined, and five distinct stages in the process were identified. It was noted that change is often prompted by a crisis, followed by a period of hard work, which in turn leads to a series of difficult decisions. It was further explained that once the individual has resolved the emerging conflicts, he or she may experience a period of fear, followed by exhilaration and stability.

A six-step model for bringing about personal change was presented. In the first step of this process, objectives are established and obstacles to their achievement are identified. Motivation is then enhanced by associating pain with current conditions and pleasure with change. In the third step, debilitating patterns of thought are interrupted. Counterproductive patterns of thought and behavior are then replaced with alternative patterns. These new patterns are then repeated until they become habitual. Reinforcement is used to strengthen the association of pleasure with the newly adopted thoughts and behaviors. In the final step of the process, new patterns are tested, in order to verify their permanence and appropriateness.

Common barriers to goal attainment were discussed in this chapter, and recommendations for overcoming these barriers were presented. Management of emotions and a willingness to delay gratification were encouraged. The importance of judicious risk-taking was also stressed. Contrasts were drawn between dynamic risks, in which there is a possibility of gain or loss, and static risks, which are taken simply in order to secure gains. It was noted that risk-taking is a four-step process that involves recognizing the necessity of risk, deciding to take a risk, developing a plan, and implementing the plan. Specific guidelines for risk-taking were provided.

A six-step process for overcoming barriers to success was presented. This process consists of: (1) identifying obstacles to achievement, (2) determining whether the obstacles exist within the individual or the environment, (3) determining whether or not environmental barriers can be controlled by the individual, (4) determining whether or not internal barriers can be controlled by the individual, (5) reviewing those obstacles over which control is believed to be lacking, and (6) developing a plan that is focused on those barriers over which control is known to exist.

The importance of support systems was emphasized in this chapter. A five-step process for establishing support systems was presented. The process involves the development of self-knowledge, self-confidence, and openness toward others. It also involves identification of personal goals and needs, and active involvement with supportive people.

The concept of networking was discussed, and the mutually beneficial nature of the process was emphasized. Formal networks, which are officially organized, were contrasted with informal networks, which often consist of numerous individual contacts. Lateral networking was presented as a process whereby an individual establishes relationships with his or her organizational peers. This process was contrasted with vertical networking, which involves relationships with individuals who are at higher levels of the organizational hierarchy. Citywide and national networking were presented as ways of establishing mutually supportive relationships outside one's organization. It was noted that citywide networking frequently helps an individual in dealing with immediate concerns of a practical nature, whereas national networking usually broadens his or her perspective on conceptual matters. Recommendations for building and maintaining a network were presented.

The concept of mentoring was also discussed in this chapter. The process was described as the establishment of a mutually beneficial relationship between a more experienced individual, known as a mentor, and a less experienced individual, known as a protege. Various roles of the mentor were discussed. These roles include teacher, counselor, protector, supporter, promoter, and sponsor. It was noted that proteges frequently provide their mentors with assistance, information, and advice. It was also noted that organizations draw benefits from the mentoring process, including the establishment of a natural line of succession, preservation of organizational traditions and values, and the leadership of a strong team. Recommendations for establishing and maintaining mentoring relationships were provided.

The importance of periodic evaluation of the mentoring relationship was emphasized, and typical areas of concern were identified. Issues related to the protege's development and his or her relationship to others in the organization were raised. The chapter also dealt with the importance of terminating or modifying the mentoring relationship once its purpose has been served.

The concept of a peer/mentor partnership was introduced. This type of relationship was described as one that exists between individuals who are at approximately the same level but differ from one another in their skills. The relationship allows them to benefit from one another's skills and to compensate for one another's weaknesses. In the process, the parties in the relationship learn from one another about equally.

The chapter closed with an emphasis on the importance of enjoying the present while preparing for the future. It was noted that opportunities for growth are often unexpected. Openness to this type of opportunity was encouraged.

References

Baber, A. and Waymon, L. (1991). *Great Connections: Small Talk and Networking for Businesspeople*. Woodbridge, VA: Impact.

Hagan, J. (1987). *How to Reach Any Goal* (audio recording). Shawnee Mission, KS: Sourcecom.

James, J. (1983). *Success is the Quality of Your Journey*, Expanded Edition. New York: Newmarket.

Morscher, B. and Jones, B. S. (1992). *Go For It! Successful Risk-Taking for Women*. New York: Warner.

O'Grady, D. (1992). *Taking the Fear Out of Changing*. Dayton, OH: New Insights.

Robbins, A. (1992). *Awakening the Giant Within*. New York: Fireside.

Zey, M. G. (1984). *The Mentor Connection*. Homewood, IL: Dow Jones-Irwin.

Zuker, E. (1983). *Mastering Assertiveness Skills*. New York: AMACOM.

═══Activities═══

Getting It Straight

Identify each of the following as a goal (G.), objective (O) or action plan (A).

_____   I will complete an introductory seminar in *Lotus 1-2-3*, with a passing grade, before the end of the current academic year.

_____

	Task	Completion Date	Resources	Support Persons
1.	Obtain seminar schedule	10/1		Registrar's staff
2.	Discuss schedule with academic advisor	10/10	Seminar schedule, my course schedule, my work schedule	Dr. Stone
3.	Select seminar section	10/12	Seminar schedule, my course schedule, my work schedule	
4.	Register for seminar	10/15	Seminar fee ($150)	Registrar's staff
5.	Purchase book	10/17	Cost of book ($20)	
6.	Attend seminar	t.b.a.		
7.	Schedule laboratory time	t.b.a.	Seminar schedule, my course schedule, my work schedule	
8.	Review lessons independently	t.b.a.	Computer lab	
9.	Discuss any problems with "computer whiz" friends	t.b.a.	Book, Darnell's computer	Karen, Darnell
10.	Take exam	t.b.a.		

_____   To increase my proficiency in the use of computers for basic managerial functions.

In the spaces provided, number the following stages from 1 to 5, according to the sequence in which they occur within the process of change.

_____   Unexpected pain stage
_____   Tough decision stage
_____   Crisis stage
_____   Joy and integration stage
_____   Hard work stage

Identify each of the following as an example of the hard work (H), crisis (C), unexpected pain (U), tough decision (T), or joy and integration (J) stage of change.

_____   A mother of four, who has not worked outside the home for the past 15 years, is suddenly widowed. She concludes that she must return to school in order to prepare for reentry into the work force.

_____   The woman begins taking classes at her local community college. Initially, she feels overwhelmed by the demands of her studies and feels uncomfortable in the college environment. Nevertheless, she persists.

_____   Once the student becomes acclimated to the college environment, she finds herself faced with difficult choices. Her courses have allowed her to explore several different subject areas which interest her. She is now experiencing difficulty in selecting an area in which to specialize.

_____   As she continues in her course work, the student is pleased to find that she is able to perform well academically. She develops a clearer sense of direction and greater self-confidence, but continues to experience periods of self-doubt.

_____   The student develops a feeling of security and satisfaction with the course her life has taken. She feels a sense of control over her own destiny.

Place a check mark next to each of the following feelings that may accompany the fear of success.

_____   Inspiration and giddiness
_____   Unconditional self-acceptance

_____   Self-critical anger
_____   Guilt
_____   Improved self-esteem
_____   Self-doubt

In the spaces provided, number the following steps from 1 to 6, according to the sequence in which they occur within the change model presented in this chapter.

_____   Counterproductive patterns of thought and behavior are replaced with alternative patterns.

_____   New patterns are repeated until they become habitual. Reinforcement is used to strengthen the association of pleasure with these patterns.

_____   Objectives are established and obstacles to their achievement are identified.

_____   New patterns of thought and behavior are tested, in order to verify their permanence and appropriateness.

_____   Debilitating patterns of thought are interrupted.

_____   Motivation to change is enhanced by associating pain with current conditions and pleasure with change.

Place a check mark next to any of the following recommendations for goal-setting that were presented in this chapter.

_____   "Make a commitment to your change goals."

_____   "Do not allow yourself to make new choices once a decision has been made."

_____   "Write down your goals in specific terms."

_____   "Place your written goals where you can see them."

_____   "Jot down ideas daily to move forward on your goals."

_____   "Take your mind off of your goals when you are feeling frustrated."

Place a check mark next to any of the following recommendations for goal attainment that were presented in this chapter.

_____   Establish priorities between various goals and objectives.

_____   Develop a clear mental image of the accomplishment of your goals.

_____   Try to concentrate on many goals simultaneously.

_____   Be willing to delay gratification.

_____   Allow your emotions to be your guide in decision-making.

_____   Do not move beyond your "comfort zone" in planning your course of action.

_____   Identify obstacles to goal attainment over which you have no control.

_____   Focus your strategies on conditions that you can change.

_____   Focus your strategies only on conditions that exist within you.

_____   Believe in your ability to change.

_____   Recognize the need for change.

Place a check mark next to any of the following recommendations for risk-taking that were presented in this chapter.

_____   "Have a clear goal and specific purpose in mind."

_____   "Consider your options and choose the most viable ones."

_____   "Get advice only from people who have some material interest in the outcome."

_____   "Always have alternatives as backup."

_____   "Don't allow your decisions to be influenced by the amount of control that you have over the situation."

_____   "Don't count on always being completely successful or having one risk solve all your problems."

_____   "Never risk more than you can afford to lose"

_____   "Don't take risks for others, but allow others to take them for you."

_____   "Don't use other people as an excuse for inaction."

_____   "Don't be afraid to risk a lot or a little."

_____   "Don't risk just to avoid losing face."

_____   "When evaluating risks, disregard all feelings and intuition."

Place a check mark next to any of the following recommendations for networking that were presented in this chapter.

_____   "Make your primary contacts with the friends and colleagues who know and respect your accomplishments and really want to help you."

_____   "Observe common and even uncommon courtesies."

_____   "Make sure that you assume responsibility for determining the timing of the networking process."

_____   "Move beyond the superficial."

_____ "Make contacts based on your needs, not your achievements."

_____ "Be specific and honest about what you want."

_____ "Don't make unreasonable requests."

_____ "Pay your dues. Remember, effective networking is always reciprocal."

_____ "Be helpful to others. Inevitably, you will benefit from contact with someone whom you can't immediately — or perhaps ever — pay back."

_____ "Avoid praising your own skills."

Place a check mark next to any of the following behaviors that were recommended in this chapter as ways for proteges to dissipate peer resentment toward them.

_____ Demonstrating competence and establishing credibility.

_____ Downplaying the mentoring relationship.

_____ Discontinuing communication with peers.

List the four steps in the risk-taking process that were identified in this chapter.

1.

2.

3.

4.

In the space provided, identify each of the following as a static (S) or dynamic (D) risk.

_____ A full-time student, with a particularly heavy course load, takes a part-time job. He realizes that his grades might suffer because of the amount of time that his new job will require. Nevertheless, he decides to take the job, because he doubts that he can afford to remain in school without it.

_____ A full-time medical student decides to take out a major loan in order to finance her medical education. She realizes that there is a possibility that she will not be able to pay back the loan without significant hardship. However, she believes that it is much more likely that she will complete medical school and have a very successful career as a physician. Her decision to take out the loan is based on the belief that her potential gain far outweighs any possible loss.

Respond to the following items by circling the letter corresponding to the best response.

1. Which of the following is an example of reinforcement, as the concept has been presented in this chapter?
   a. A student buys a new outfit to reward herself for losing weight.
   b. A student supplements her diet with an exercise program.
   c. A student covers her bulletin board with pictures of models clipped from fashion magazines, in order to create a visual image of the desired outcome of her diet and exercise program.
   d. All of the above
   e. a and b only
   f. a and c only
   g. b and c only

2. The members of a person's network may include:
   a. those who provide information.
   b. those who provide emotional support.
   c. those who are resources for social or professional contacts.
   d. All of the above
   e. a and b only
   f. a and c only
   g. b and c only

In the space provided, identify each of the following as an example of formal networking (F), informal networking (I), mentoring (M), or a peer/mentor partnership (P).

_____ Two students, Corinne and Clare, meet through a mutual friend. In conversation, they learn that Clare is currently attending a community college where Corinne would like to take some summer courses, and that Corinne is attending a university where Clare would like to pursue a bachelor's degree upon completion of her associate's degree program. The two students decide to have lunch together, in order to compare notes on the two institutions.

_____ Ellen is a student teacher who has been assigned to Mr. Fisher's third grade class. Ellen has appreciated the opportunity to learn the "tricks of the trade" from Mr. Fisher, who has benefited from the assistance that Ellen has provided and from the enthusiasm that she has brought to her work.

_____ Two students, Dorothy and Mitch, are interested in establishing an adult literacy program in their local community. They both feel confident in their ability to succeed as a team, because of the skills that each of them possesses. Dorothy has strong managerial skills and is very good at identifying sources of funding. Mitch is creative and has a strong background in education for literacy. He also is very good at working with people in helping relationships.

_____ Kim, Gail, and Kendall are members of their campus chapter of the Public Relations Student Society of America. They have enjoyed their experience in the organization because it has provided them with an opportunity to interact with other students who share their professional interests, and to participate in organized programs which address their concerns.

In the space provided, identify each of the following as an example of lateral (L), vertical (V), citywide (C), or national (N) networking.

_____ Paul, Tim, and Susan are Peer Advisors on their campus. Recently, they attended a meeting of the National Orientation Directors Association, where they got a lot of good ideas from people who work with incoming students at colleges and universities throughout the country. They also had an opportunity to share information with others about their own work.

_____ Joan does volunteer work at a homeless shelter. Whenever she gets a chance, she likes to talk with the caseworkers at the shelter, because she is considering a career in social work and wants to find out more about the rewards and frustrations that are commonly experienced by those in the field.

_____ Mr. Murphy and Ms. Hathaway are Student Life Advisors at two different institutions located in the same community. They decide to meet for lunch one day, to discuss ideas for alcohol education programs on their campuses.

_____ Bennett and Yvonne are Resident Assistants in two different residence halls on their campus. The two R.A.'s regularly talk with each other about their jobs. They have appreciated the opportunity to learn together and to draw moral support from each other.

Read the following paragraph and respond to the items presented by filling in the blank spaces.

Roy is a college senior who is majoring in political science. Currently, he is working as an unpaid intern with Senator Ramsey, who is midway through her first term in the state legislature. Both Roy and Senator Ramsey are pleased with their working relationship. They share a common philosophy and a clear vision of their state's future. Senator Ramsey has appreciated the assistance that Roy has provided, and he has appreciated her willingness to discuss legislative issues with him and to help him "learn the ropes."

1. Senator Ramsey could be described as Roy's _____.
2. Roy could be described as Senator Ramsey's _____.

In the space provided, indicate whether each of the following statements is true (T) or false (F).

_____   Only the protege benefits from a mentoring relationship.

_____   National networking can enable a person to broaden his or her perspective.

_____   A protege who can do the job of his or her mentor is usually seen as a threat to the mentor. Consequently, most mentors prefer proteges who are more dependent.

_____   Mentors generally value loyalty in their proteges.

_____   Proteges rarely experience difficulties in their relationships with their peers.

_____   If a mentoring relationship serves its purpose, the protege will eventually become independent from the mentor.

Both Sides of the Story

Prepare a defense for both the affirmative and negative positions on the following statements.

1. Regardless of environmental conditions, a person who is talented and diligent can achieve success.
2. Adults can sometimes change their behavior or their appearances, but their personality traits cannot be changed.
3. It is not the responsibility of society to protect individuals against the negative consequences of their own risk-taking.

Sorting Out

Respond to the following questions by taking a position and defending it.

1. Of the various types of networking described in this chapter, which is most important for aspiring leaders?
2. In general, is it more important for an aspiring leader to have a mentor or a network?
3. In general, is it more important to prepare for the future or to enjoy the present?

It's Your Call

Respond to the following items by providing the information requested.

1. Write three goals pertaining to areas of your life in which you would like to bring about change. Choose the most important of these goals and explain why it is most important to you.
2. Write three objectives pertaining to the goal that you have chosen as most important. Choose the most urgent of the three objectives and explain why it should take precedence over the other two.
3. Devise two or more strategies for achieving your most urgent objective. Present the strategies in the form of action plans. Select the most appropriate strategy and explain your rationale in choosing it.